# Pauline Theology & Mission Practice

DEAN S. GILLILAND

**Baker Book House**

Grand Rapids, Michigan 49506

ISBN: 0-8010-3788-3

Library of Congress Card Catalog Number: 82-73971

Printed in the United States of America

To Lois, my wife,
who is also the best friend I have

# Contents

# Foreword

It is not a frequent occurrence that solid theology, extensive missionary experience, and imaginative presentation come together, and that quite consistently, in the same book on missionary theory and practice. Equally unusual is the book that will simultaneously challenge the thought of the missiologist, concretely help the grass-roots missionary, and provide understandable and edifying reading for the concerned supporter of missions at the home base. In this book Dr. Gilliland brings all these desiderata together as he leads the reader into and through the thought and the practice of the first and greatest "foreign missionary" in the history of the church.

Dr. Gilliland's qualifications to undertake this rather exacting task are clear. He began his missionary career in 1956 in northern Nigeria as a bush missionary. His success in this work and his early proficiency in the Hausa language pointed to him when a teacher was needed to train vernacular evangelists and pastors in his mission school. It was while he was engaged in this work that mission and church went through the demanding experience of transferring authority from the one to the other, a process in which he played the leading missionary role. When the Theological College of Northern Nigeria, serving seven missions and eight Nigerian churches, was but a few years under way, Dean Gilliland was asked to serve there as teacher. This he did in 1969 after he had largely finished his doctoral study program at Hartford Seminary Foundation. In 1972 he became principal (president) of the college, in which capacity he served until his return to the United States in 1976. Since 1977 he has had the advantage of teaching in the immensely varied church and missionary context of the School of World Mission at Fuller Theological Seminary.

The book Dr. Gilliland has written may not improperly be called a spiritual biography of the Christian movement in a missionary context. The author moves from conversion to an examination of the new life in Christ, and from that to a consideration of the church: its foundations, its diversity, its varied environment, its leadership, and its worship. The nettling problems of discipline and financial stewardship are not skirted. A chapter about the qualifications for a missionary ministry in today's world, relevantly illustrated from Paul's missionary experience and teaching, concludes the book.

The value of this comprehensive survey lies in two basic qualities of the book. Every discussion of its parts and subparts is grounded in careful expository studies of Paul's ministry as revealed in Acts and in the corpus of the Pauline epistles. Again and again Dr. Gilliland illustrates the abiding relevance of Paul's first-century insights for our missionary thought and practice at the end of the second millennium. In doing so he not only draws on Scripture and personal missionary experience, but also enters into significant dialogue with representative missionary literature of the modern period.

The second quality is occasioned by the author's sense of history. All but the first few years of his missionary service in Nigeria were spent in post-colonial and therefore independent Nigeria. In all the countries of the so-called Third World, the freedom that the church has in Christ—so significant a concept in Paul's missionary vision—finds today a context of national independence in which to express itself. It makes almost unreal a great mass of devout missionary counsel and practice that was given and engaged in during the colonial period.

It is a pleasure to welcome this book to the existing body of significant missionary literature, and to recommend it warmly to all friends of the church's missionary enterprise.

Harry R. Boer
*Grand Rapids, Michigan*

# Introduction

The voice was one of the greatest the world has ever heard. His personality dominated the apostolic age and his message formed the church of all time. He obeyed his conscience by fighting to exterminate a heresy, only to find himself an apostle of the same controversial doctrine. In a single turn, as it were, he joined the Way that he had forbidden to others. For thirty years after this transformation, his life was a model of the joy and the pain of the true missionary. He discovered that the gospel must be preached to all, can be understood by all, and changes the lives of all, regardless of history, language, or culture. The man was Paul.

Paul's theology was irresistible because it was energized by a fresh, life-changing experience and supported by a new love for all people. The mold in which the old forms had been cast was not broken. Expressions loved by Jews but often misunderstood and even ridiculed by Gentiles no longer ruled his speech. The theology that Paul carried across the Roman world was, above all, a theology that developed from life-changing events. Nothing said about saving faith was as important as experiencing saving faith.

This miracle of the new mission began at Antioch. A mixed congregation was at prayer when, as Luke records, "The Holy Spirit said to them, 'Set apart for me Barnabas and Saul, to do the work to which I have called them'" (Acts 13:2). Here was the beginning of something new in theology. It was a theology of the active Spirit and of world mission. In a little more than one generation following the death of its Jewish founder, Christianity was to be recognized by Roman authorities as a Gentile religion. Beyond that, this "sect" that arose among Aramaic-speaking peoples in southwest Asia was soon to become a European religion communicated through the Greek language of the common man.[1]

1. See the discussion in F. F. Bruce, *Paul, Apostle of the Heart Set Free* (Grand Rapids: Eerdmans, 1978), p. 17.

How could principally one man, Paul, and a few close friends establish churches in four provinces of the Roman Empire in less than ten years?[2] How could he then speak of having fully proclaimed the Good News (Rom. 15:19) while only basically unlearned and inexperienced converts were left to maintain and multiply the fledgling churches? It is because the theology that supported Paul's ministry was born in mission and produced by mission. Such a theology bears close examination, for at no time since has the church expanded so rapidly and into so many communities, in various cultures, through so few people.

When I first began to teach at a theological seminary in Nigeria, I was uncomfortable, almost resentful, when first-year students who often had only primary education would refer to themselves as "theologians." Somehow I felt this did not do justice to a discipline mastered by only the few and which, I felt, required at least university and seminary training. I asked a young student one day if he really understood what it is to be a theologian. He disarmed me with his simple answer. He said, "I am a theologian because what I say and think about God is just as important as what you think and say about God!" In one stroke he cut through the formalism of academic systems and claimed the right that is his: authority as a Christian to formulate his own ideas about the Christian faith, based on Spirit-enlightened perceptions that arise from his own culture and that can be corroborated by Scripture.

The very origin of the word *theology* reveals that theology is a discipline that leans heavily on a particular methodology for thinking about God. Classic definitions for theology include the word *science.* It is stated by Augustus H. Strong, for example, that "theology is the science of God," and that the aim of theology is "the ascertainment of facts in their rational unity."[3] The emphasis is on logic and orderly structure. J. Orton Wiley says theology aims to "set forth in a systematic manner the doctrines of the Christian faith."[4] W. G. T. Shedd begins his *Dogmatic Theology* with an introduction on "The True Method in Theological Science."[5] This is the legacy of theology, beginning with the early church fathers who constructed theological systems on a philosophical base.

Overall, however, the preaching and teaching ministry of Paul was not in the genre of a scholastic defense of Christian truth. Admittedly, a book such as Galatians is, indeed, a profound theological argument within the context of Judaism. Colossians is an example of the way in which Paul could forcefully argue Christian truth against an early heresy. Probably the most theological book that Paul wrote was Romans. But here again, to say that Romans

2. A.D. 47-57; Galatia, Macedonia, Achaia, and Asia.

3. *Systematic Theology: A Compendium* (London: Pickering and Inglis, 1907 [24th printing, 1965]), pp. 1, 2.

4. *Christian Theology* (Kansas City: Beacon Hill Press, 1940), vol. 1, p. 16.

5. (New York: Charles Scribner's Sons, 1888-1894), vol. 1, p. 16.

was even close to a systematic statement of Christian doctrine misrepresents the content and does not describe the purpose that Paul had in writing. Had he meant the book to be a doctrinal text, he would have been much more explicit, for example, about Christology. In relation to other themes of the book, the references to Christ are few and isolated. The same could be said for his scant treatment of the church. Thus, while Paul's writings do carry a massive impact of theological truth, it must be called to mind constantly that Paul did not write theological treatises.

Further, Paul's writings are not a record of the way in which he communicated the Good News on first contact. Because Paul moved from place to place, the original proclamation of the Pauline kerygma was concrete, experience-oriented, personally applied, and contextually relevant. Unfortunately, the system for theologizing that developed later, and into which Paul's writings are too often forced, tended to scholasticism and abstraction. Theology became an exercise for trained minds only—fighting a battle on ground quite removed from ordinary people. This is often the dilemma of classic theology, but this is not Pauline theology.

Yet there is no question about Paul's place as a theologian. The books that have been written, viewing this amazing man from many angles, would fill shelves. He is held by some to be the consummate thinker and organizer of the Christian faith. Some have regarded him, on the other hand, as the perverter of Christianity who turned the early church away from the religion of Jesus into a "sect" of Christ.[6] Or he is seen as one who forced Jesus' gospel of the kingdom into a doctrinal system, thus creating an ecclesiastical, sacramentarian institution.[7] The true Paul is not to be found in any of these extremes. He was highly educated (if that is what theology calls for). But, more importantly, he was motivated, beyond everything else, by the commission to preach and teach the Good News and to nurture those who enter the new way by saving faith.

So, if by theology we mean a dogmatic construct of concepts presented in an orderly and balanced manner, Paul does not qualify as a theologian.[8] Paul's theology is not a logically consistent or even a complete system of thought.[9] The letters he wrote are the primary record of what he preached

6. M. S. Enslin describes how he once regarded Paul as "an arrogant and muddleheaded theologian" but later discovered him as "one of my dearest friends." *Reapproaching Paul* (Philadelphia: Westminster, 1972), p. 13.

7. For a summary of the varying views of Paul in the history of theology, see H. J. Holtzmann, *Lehrbuch der Neutestamentlichen Theologie* (Frurburg and Leipzig: Mohr, 1897), pp. 9-11.

8. Maurice Goguel overstates the case when he says, "We must not regard [Paul's letters] as a species of encyclical letters, but as incidental writings, hastily improvised between journeys . . . dictated . . . by a man overburdened with fatigue and cares of the churches. . . ." *The Life of Jesus* (New York: Macmillan, 1945), pp. 105-127.

9. "The Pauline theology is not a dogmatic system which exhibits the ideal world of Christian belief or a uniform building. . . ." Paul Fiene, *St. Paul As a Theologian* (New York:

and taught. They reveal that Paul's primary interest was not intellectual, though they show clearly that he could approach his churches with precise thinking and with a thoroughly trained mind. He was not a philosopher in search of truth. The speculative, philosophical spirit does not belong naturally to the Jewish character, and Paul was no exception. Judaism is not a philosophical system but is more directly connected to revelation. The attempt to unite the philosophy of the Greek world with the Jewish religion of revelation was attempted by Philo, in the first century A.D., but the attempt was not very successful and something was lost from both sides in the effort.[10]

Paul was a deeply religious Jew who had been literally turned around by an encounter with the risen Lord and, having discovered life for himself, now saw it as his divinely given task to bring the word of life to others. This fact was the sine qua non of his entire ministry. It means, therefore, that his theology was shaped and energized by the power of the gospel (Rom. 1:16). There are four characteristics about Paul's theology that underlie everything else that can be said about it: it is dynamic, it is evangelical, it is pastoral, and it is holistic.

Paul's theology is dynamic. A dynamic theology is one that relates specifically to the needs of people in a particular place and situation. Paul was convinced of two points and these became the underpinnings of his entire ministry. First, the gospel is absolute in its central message and, second, it must be made vital to every people and place. Paul addressed his teaching and preaching to the moment. He knew that people must be met on their own terms and in the context of their own world.

This dynamism was more than a match for traditional Gentile religion, and it also met, on its own ground, the ingrown Judaism of Paul's day. A young girl in Philippi who possessed the power of divination became the center of a controversy when Paul publicly charged the evil spirit to come out of her (Acts 16:16-18). Following this, the jailer who was to keep Paul and Silas locked up feared for his own life when an earthquake shook the prison that same night. Paul seized on this crisis as an opportunity for witness. He told the jailer that his real need was not physical but spiritual (Acts 16:31), and the man was saved with his entire household. The content of Paul's message to a Gentile audience was always appropriate to the particular situation and the effect was unforgettable. Even if the message did not always bring phenomenal results (e.g., Acts 14:15-18), the Jews had little choice but to believe or to reject what Paul said. It was virtually

---

Eaton-Mains, 1908), pt. 1, p. 7. Cf. G. B. Caird, *The Apostolic Age* (London: Gerald Duckworth, 1955), p. 136.

10. Fiene, *St. Paul As a Theologian*, p. 7.

impossible to ignore him.[11] He was an uncompromising realist and a persuasive debater. His style was to systematically place the argument concerning Christ alongside prophecies that the Jews knew well (Acts 17:3). The effect, though controversial, was consistent, separating those who believed and accepted from those who rejected (Acts 14:4; 18:6).

Throughout his ministry, Paul was involved in a violent struggle with Judaism and, for the most part, this encounter was carried out on theological grounds. He was committed totally to a new way; this meant that through Christ the walls of his own religion must be broken down (Eph. 2). A dynamic theology is addressed to the present as well as the future, whereas a dogmatic theology is oriented to the past.[12] In drawing on the present real world for his message, the truths that grew out of the Jewish past were that much more dramatic. Paul's perception of truth in context opened the way for him to see Christianity as a dynamic supracultural religion; indeed, as a world religion for all peoples.

Paul's theology is evangelical. Before all else, the ministry of Paul was the proclamation of Good News. To say that Paul's theology is evangelical means that what God has accomplished in Christ is the word of the gospel, that the central message of the cross is the very content of the gospel (Eph. 2:16; Col. 1:20), and that all that Paul did, taught, and preached is judged by the gospel (I Cor. 1:17). "We proclaim the crucified Christ" sums up what Paul understood as the power and wisdom of God (I Cor. 1:23-24). There was no other rationale for the ceaseless travel, the self-deprivation, and the tireless preaching and teaching, other than that *"God was in Christ reconciling the world to himself"* and *"entrusting to us the message of reconciliation"* (II Cor. 5:19, RSV; italics added). This ministry was, in fact, Paul's very life (I Cor. 9:16). God has initiated salvation and persons are the instruments in God's hands to accomplish the saving miracle of the gospel.

Paul called his work, flatly and simply, "the ministry of reconciliation," the cross being the means by which this reconciliation is accomplished (Rom. 5:8). The mainspring of this conviction lies in the love of God, reaching out to the concrete human situation in which humankind is alienated from the image and Spirit of God (Eph. 2:12; 4:18). To speak of Paul's theology as evangelical means that he did not indulge in the speculative or the abstract. He was in close touch with real people. The Jews were bound by culture and the law. Gentiles were deluded by the world and naturalistic religion. These he calls to face a living God squarely and honestly. All men everywhere

11. To Caird Paul is "not a man to whom you could remain indifferent; you had either to love him or to hate him." *The Apostolic Age,* p. 127.

12. The aim of dogmatic theology is a "comprehensive, connected and even synthetic structure." The aim of contextual (dynamic) theology is to analyze "particular themes and situations." See the article by A. O. Dyson, "Dogmatic or Contextual Theology," *Study Encounter,* vol. 8, no. 3, 1972, pp. 2-8.

are desperately in need of a new life, and God has provided that new and living way.

Paul's theology is pastoral. A theology that caters to the intellect, is built on theories, and emphasizes the rightness of belief, but fails to nurture the soul and the spirit, was alien to Paul. In the search for a mission theology, it is here, in the area of pastoral responsibility, that much has gone wrong. Paul put the cure and the care of souls before any other issue in his ministry. Right doctrine and correct belief were not so important, at the outset, at least, as whether the Christian had given allegiance to a new Authority. Paul's first concern was that people respond to Jesus' lordship and that young Christians be surrounded by all the strength and the warmth that the fellowship of the Body can give.

Theology, Paul discovered, was to be found not only in a discourse in the synagogue, but also in the meeting of friends in a home for a careful study of new truth and in the company of other young Christians. His concern was always for the new church. He retraced his steps in Galatia before returning to Jerusalem (Acts 14:21), then visited the same churches again as he commenced his second journey (Acts 15:36). When problems in Corinth threatened to split the church, Paul tried again and again to help the Christians see their wrong, not only visiting twice but also sending letters and dispatching Timothy to act on his behalf (I Cor. 4:17; 16:10). The farewell at Ephesus (Acts 20:17-38) leaves us with an unforgettable lesson in pastoral care as Paul admonishes the elders to "be shepherds of the church of God" (Acts 20:28). He was at great pains to instruct the Thessalonians about the ethic of work for Christians and to answer theological problems that arose concerning the parousia and the end of the age. Yet Paul answered these in a way that showed that he truly cared for the welfare of young Christians. His teaching was based on real needs, as a response, for example, to the anguish of the Thessalonians that some Christians had died and therefore could not witness the second coming. Paul would not have agreed that right doctrine produces faith, but that a living, trusting, and active faith, properly understood, will result in the right doctrine.

Third-World Christians today are helping us understand that an adequate theology must include this nurturing, caring dimension. Charles Nyamiti, an African, lists the pastoral responsibility of theology as being of first importance for African Christians.[13] When he speaks of a "spiritual approach" to theology, Nyamiti means that the communicator of the gospel must see the deeply religious character of those to whom he ministers and that theology must meet the needs of the heart and the soul, not simply the intellect.[14]

13. *The Scope of African Theology* (Kampala, Uganda: Gaba Publications, 1973), pp. 29-30.

14. Ibid.

The pastoral dimension of teaching is too often ignored, especially in mission.

I shall never forget my disappointment as a first-term missionary when, with another missionary and an African pastor, I took a day's journey by foot to a small village church. The purpose of the trip was to examine and to baptize supposedly new Christians. One who was brought in for her baptismal examination was an old woman. She had been coming for three successive years and asking for baptism, but had been refused each time because she could not read the Bible or recite the catechism. On this trip, her fourth attempt, she was refused again. As a recent arrival, I had little to say. Sadly, "knowledge" was given a higher value than faith.

Paul's theology is holistic. Paul showed in many ways and in various situations that he was concerned with people in their total life, and with the effect that the gospel could have on the whole of life. He was, before everything else, the evangelist, calling for the heart and the mind to be put right with God. The decision to come under the lordship of Jesus Christ had its immediate effect on the home (Col. 3:18-22), on marriage (Eph. 5:22-25), on social ethics (II Thess. 3:10), on politics (Rom. 13:1-7), on physical health (I Tim. 5:23), and on personal relationships (Col. 3:13; Phil. 4:2). Again, practical application of Christian truth was more important to Paul than apprehension of all the content.

When Paul spoke of the "new creation" (II Cor. 5:17, RSV), he referred to a completely new kind of person. This is a radical concept that describes a whole new being. "Holistic" is a term that theology has profitably borrowed from philosophy. This word emphasizes the opposite of an atomistic philosophy, which is concerned with the specific parts and with the minutiae of detail. Holism sees the various parts in their relatedness to each other and to the whole. One of Paul's most common expressions describes the Christian as being "alive." The assumption is that this living organism will develop normally into the truly whole person—mature, complete, and positive in every way (*teleios*). His emphasis on growth is comprehensive, touching the mind, the spirit, the psyche, and even the body.[15]

Too often our preoccupation is with Paul as the preacher of salvation only, as one who appealed mainly to the intellect of his hearers. However, every part of a person comes into the prayer of Paul for the Thessalonians, when he implores the God of peace to "make you holy in every way" (I Thess. 5:23). Spirit and soul, as well as body, are to be kept sound, complete, and blameless. Every aspect of the person is now under the

15. Howard Tillman Kuist writes that one aim of the teaching of Paul was to emphasize wholeness and maturity, touching the moral, social, intellectual, spiritual, volitional, and emotional aspects of the life. *The Pedagogy of St. Paul* (New York: Doran, 1925), pp. 62-81.

authority of Christ and is not to be ministered to apart from the whole person. Paul's religion was indeed a new way. It was not for the building of a mission or the erecting of institutions or for numbers alone that Paul labored. Rather, it was the expression of loyalty to a Person who gives freedom and completeness to all of life (Rom. 8:2).

# *Part One*

# Paul

## *The Theologian in Mission*

# 1

# Approaching Paul's Theology

In all our studies of Paul—the systematizing of his teachings or the analysis and documentation of his work—we want to see the person, Paul, for the man that he was. What he preached and taught can never be understood apart from the *person.* It is not impossible to reconstruct the humanness of the man Paul from what he wrote. I have said that his ministry developed from real life and from being in touch with real people. These persons, like himself, felt deep needs and emotions; they were creatures of life, overjoyed by success and broken by failure. There is a transparent sincerity about Paul that enabled him to reveal himself honestly and openly. He did not write as though posterity would be judging him. He might have written some things differently, especially about himself, if he had known that his letters were going to be read for all time. While he was taught of the Spirit as he wrote, he did not know he was forming a body of sacred Scripture. He poured out praise, indignation, entreaty, thanksgiving, and argument. He followed his heart as well as his head when he dealt with people.

## Sources for Paul's Theology

When we speak of sources we are enquiring about two issues: What factors accounted for the content of Paul's message and what formed the basis of his methodology in the spreading of the gospel? It would have been one thing to have received new insights as a Jew and to have communicated these truths to the Jews. Paul, however, broke with Jewish thought and with the Jewish community in a way that both amazed and infuriated his own people. The Jews had spread to all parts of the Roman world, giving Paul the opportunity to witness both as a cross-cultural missionary and to his own people. Four major factors combined to produce his theology, and each factor contributes something to an understanding of his character. His theology was influenced by his own history, shaped by his conversion, illuminated by revelation, and motivated by his call to evangelize.

### *Influenced by Paul's Own History*

There is no question about the impact of Paul's early life on the authority of his ministry. That Paul was able to move among people who had different thoughts and customs from his own can be explained as much by his early life as by his special call. Paul was a man of three worlds, Jewish, Roman, and Greek. Each of these cultures influenced his thought and world view. Paul was always the Jew, but his sensitivity to the non-Jewish world was firsthand, since he belonged to that world as well, by both birth and upbringing. It is important to summarize the contribution this unique background had on Paul the missionary.

*Jewish heritage*

For all of his commitment to the Gentile world, Paul never abandoned his Jewish background. He was devoted to the traditions of his ancestors and, as for keeping the law, he was a Pharisee (Gal. 1:14; Phil. 3:5). An active Jew in his early years, he remained devoted to his own people, was proud of their distinction as the elect of God (Rom. 9:3-5), and was deeply moved by their resistance to the gospel. His words to the Galatians revealed his absolute loyalty when he said, "I was ahead of most fellow Jews of my age in my practice of the Jewish religion" (Gal. 1:14). We take him at his word that he was a typical Pharisee. This would mean that Paul embraced with all his heart the belief and the tradition of his peers.

The first factor that conditioned Paul's thinking was his Jewish concept of God. Paul would never allow the Greco-Roman idea of god to overtake him. This Gentile idea of god was at best a philosophical principle, remote and impassive. For the Jew, God is the only, the living and altogether righteous One, working out his purposes in the world, entering into fellowship with people, and creating a family for himself here on earth. God at the center made Paul's religion personal, ethical, historical, and officially monotheistic: "Hear, O Israel: The LORD our God is one LORD" (Deut. 6:4, RSV). This was the first and last word confessed by the true Jew. This conviction brooks no compromise. It was at once the piety, the ethic and binding force of this covenant people. That God is one and totally sovereign carried over into Paul's new life, and remained a fundamental law of his gospel to the very end (I Cor. 8:5-6; Gal. 3:20).

A second factor in the tradition, which becomes a source for Paul, is the Jewish attitude toward the Scriptures.[1] For the Jew, the Torah is the will of God and the absolute and final authority. Pharisaic Judaism represented the highest attempt at achieving loyalty to the divine revelation of God, given first to Moses and passed on to Joshua and to the priests and the elders of

1. H. F. Rall, *According to Paul* (New York: Charles Scribner's Sons, 1945), p. 19.

Israel.[2] The praise of the Torah as Paul would have learned it was often excessive and unreal. The Torah was frequently described as "God's daughter" by the rabbis.[3] Nevertheless, the law caused Paul great anguish because in his gospel of life he could not espouse, at every point, the letter that kills (II Cor. 3:6; Rom. 7:6). Great sections of the beloved Scriptures had to be set aside, in particular those prescriptions of obedience that constituted the largest part of Jewish practice. The new way made rituals and ceremonies anomalous. However, Paul the theologian did appeal to the authority of the Old Testament, which he knew so well. In his writings Paul referred to the law more than 130 times. The phrase "it is written" occurs more than thirty times. Often a positive attitude toward the law shines through.[4] In setting ethics at Corinth for the young Christians, who were mainly Gentiles, Paul admonished that they should "observe the proper rules" (I Cor. 4:6). This sounds very much like the Pharisee that he was.

A third element in Paul's world view as a Jew must be mentioned because of the way it affected his teaching. This is the Jewish view of evil. The dilemma of evil is always a serious problem. In working for a solution, the Jews had arrived at a sort of ethical or practical dualism. They believed in two worlds—not matter against spirit, as in philosophy, but in two worlds of spirit, one controlling good and the other evil. Evil is not just an individual matter. It arises from a real but invisible kingdom that Paul would reckon with in his teaching about the "powers."[5] Paul understood that the world of God's Spirit is also active in influencing the lives of people; and while both these levels of spirit are real they are not equal. The ultimate overthrow of the forces of evil would prove this (Col. 2:15).

The Pharisee also believed in the idea of two ages. This was the distinguishing mark of apocalyptic teaching that Paul carried with new fervor and fresh meaning into his teaching about the gospel. Thus Paul's concept of "this world and . . . the next" (Eph. 1:21) borrowed heavily on the Jewish hope of the coming consummation that would usher in a new age. This was familiar language to Paul, and he used it frequently as the note of the two ages is struck in his teaching.[6]

2. Ralph P. Martin, *Reconciliation: A Study of Paul's Theology* (Atlanta: John Knox, 1981), p. 10.

3. Martin notes that it is recorded in Exodus Rabbah 33:1 that a king could not bear to be separated from his daughter. After she was married, the daughter provided a bedroom in her house for the king. In the same way Jehovah said, "I have given you the law but I cannot be separated from it." *Reconciliation,* pp. 10-11.

4. See, for example, Romans 7:12-19; 15:4; I Corinthians 10:11; I Timothy 1:18.

5. Romans 8:38; II Corinthians 4:4; Ephesians 3:10; 6:12; Colossians 1:16; 2:15.

6. Romans 8:38-39; 13:12; I Corinthians 7:29, 31; 10:11; II Corinthians 4:18; Ephesians 1:21; 2:7; 5:16.

*Greco-Roman influence*

When it developed that Paul was to become the first cross-cultural missionary,[7] it was no small matter that he had been reared in close touch with both Hellenism and the Roman world. His own city of Tarsus was the crossroads of the world. Greek was Paul's mother tongue. Since he spoke and wrote in Greek, he did not need an interpreter when he went beyond the boundaries of Palestine. What was also to prove significant for Paul was that in Tarsus one found both pious Judaism and gross paganism. The high god of Tarsus was Baal Tars (lord of Tarsus) and the secondary deity was called Sandan. Sandan figured heavily in the fertility rites that were climaxed annually by a funeral observance representing the death and the resurrection of this god of vegetation.[8] But Tarsus also had developed as an important center of Greek learning. Ralph P. Martin notes that Paul "owed far more to his immediate background in the world of Graeco-Roman civilization than is popularly thought."[9] The use of the Septuagint, for example, obviously influenced his vocabulary and thinking. At will he could appeal to contemporary literature, such as Greek poetry,[10] as well as to the practices of the arena;[11] and his language is colored with an abundance of Greek terms. This would come to him naturally, because the city of Tarsus swarmed with peripatetic lecturers and students. The ordinary citizen would have come into daily contact with the ideologies of the non-Jewish world as a normal thing. Furthermore, the wealth of the Greek spirit had become allied with the genius of world-conquering Rome. Paul was a Roman citizen and came from a family that could be considered a part of the lesser nobility. As a result Paul had a fascination with Rome, and his rights as a Roman figure heavily in his ministry and ethics.[12]

Thus it is evident that, in addition to all his natural gifts, Paul's ministry was significantly enhanced by this unique background. Much was given by providential design even before he was "called." Paul was to realize with deep reverence that the whole course of his life was a miracle of divine planning (Gal. 1:15-16).

7. By contrast, Peter, who was given special teaching as to the validity of the gospel for the Gentiles (Acts 10:9-15), did not consistently show the openness to and ease of ministry with the Gentiles (Gal. 2:11-14).

8. A picture of the deity was placed high on a decorated float, paraded through the streets of the city, and then burned on the funeral pyre. The funeral service was followed by the feast of the living in which the resurrection of the god was acclaimed triumphantly while the devotees of the god gave themselves over to all kinds of excesses. Joseph Holzner, *St. Paul the Apostle: His Life and Times,* William J. Doheny, CSC, trans. and rev. (Vatican City: Private distribution, 1978), p. 29.

9. *Reconciliation,* p. 12.

10. Acts 17:28; I Corinthians 15:33; Titus 1:12.

11. I Corinthians 9:26-27; Ephesians 6:12; Philippians 3:13.

12. Acts 23:27-28; 25:8-11; Romans 13:1.

### *Shaped by Conversion*

A second source of Paul's theology was even more empirical. This source was the historical facts that were woven into his experience. Above all, Paul's conversion stands in first importance as a source for knowledge. The detailed phenomena of his conversion will be dealt with in chapter 2, but here I must note ways in which his conversion helped to shape his theology. Paul's gospel reflected his conversion in five directions.

*Truth about a living Christ*

First, the gospel is truth about a living Christ.[13] There was no question about the Person who addressed Paul. He identified himself clearly when he said, "I am Jesus of Nazareth, whom you persecute" (Acts 22:8). Further, it was this Jesus himself who said, "I have appeared to you to appoint you as my servant" (Acts 26:16). In speaking of his right to apostleship, Paul believed that this living Jesus had appeared to him just as vividly as he had appeared to any of the other apostles (I Cor. 9:1). Paul was alive in Christ because it was the living Christ who dwelt in him (Gal. 2:20). A vital fact of the gospel is that Christ has been raised and is living *now.* Without that, Paul's preaching and entire ministry would have been useless (I Cor. 15:14). The vibrant connection between himself and the risen Christ amazed and encouraged Paul at every turn. He realized at some point soon after his conversion that he had been set apart before his birth for a reconciling ministry. Paul was to see this life-changing confrontation on the way to Damascus as an expression of God's loving grace. From this, he could go on to say that God decided "to reveal his Son to me, so that I might preach the Good News about him to the Gentiles" (Gal. 1:16). The Christ whom Paul preached is a risen, living Christ. The references to the resurrection are so abundant throughout the letters of Paul that even a casual reading shows that Paul could not think of Christ without remembering him as the Savior who died, but who is, indeed, alive. The overwhelming personal experience of the living Christ at the time of his conversion was proof, beyond any doubt, that the gospel is news of the *living* Christ.[14]

*Salvation as a new way*

In the second place, Paul's conversion influenced his theology because salvation was revealed as the new way. The spontaneous character of his

13. New life and radical changes are the underlying themes of Paul's gospel, according to G. E. Ladd. All that has changed in Judaism depends on the resurrection, proving to Paul that the Christian proclamation is correct; by the resurrection Jesus proves his messiahship and sonship. *A Theology of the New Testament* (Grand Rapids: Eerdmans, 1974), p. 368.

14. According to G. B. Caird, Paul's conversion convinced him of three facts: Christ is alive, the risen Christ is identified with disciples whom Paul had persecuted, and through this

conversion was enough to stop this ardent Jew, turn him around, and totally reorient his life. Salvation results in a completely new life, and a new lifestyle. The strongest, most convincing appeals Paul made were those in which he compared the old order with the new. "Before the time for faith came, the Law kept us all locked up as prisoners . . ." (Gal. 3:23-26; cf. 4:3-5), but this was only until Christ came. "For we ourselves were once foolish, disobedient, and wrong. . . . But when the kindness and love of God our Savior was revealed, he saved us" (Titus 3:3-5). "Now that the time for faith is here, the Law is no longer in charge of us" (Gal. 3:25). Before we were "enemies," but now that he has "made us his friends" we shall "be saved by Christ's life" (Rom. 5:10). In the past we were spiritually dead because of disobedience and sin (Eph. 2:1), but now we are alive in Christ Jesus (Rom. 6:11). The references to this newness of life that has so little resemblance to anything the Jewish world had ever known give a vibrant, victorious ring to Paul's message. One does not need too much imagination to see how the dramatic circumstances of his own conversion provided Paul with the proof of Christ's resurrection, thus grounding his gospel in his own experience.

*God initiates; man responds*

Third, the conversion carried an unforgettable lesson that God takes the initiative and persons respond. This is the God who had acted throughout history, and who now sent a shaft of his grace into the day of one man, Paul. He is caught in an act of rage against the church by the overwhelming initiative of a personal God. Fearfully, Paul asked, "Who are you, Lord?" (Acts 9:5). Paul saw his cruelty against the Christians as meritorious, but God touched him, and in an instant he was weak and blind. From personal experience he wrote to the Romans that "when we were still helpless, Christ died for the wicked at the time that God chose" (Rom. 5:6). God intervened by choosing the weak, the despised, and the lowly to bring down the strong and the proud (I Cor. 1:27-29). Coincident with the conversion of Saul came the visitation by Ananias. His message for Paul was that God had already chosen Paul to bear witness of the new and living way, not only before the descendants of Israel but before Gentiles and kings as well (Acts 9:15). God had spoken his will clearly through acts recorded in the minds of every Jew. Now Paul experienced, beyond any doubt, that God had acted through the man Jesus Christ and mankind must respond in a new way, for the time for faith has come (Gal. 3:25). The gospel is God's power to save. Based on the incontestable data of his own experience, Paul knew that God calls for man's response to his mighty acts in Christ, and this theme runs clearly throughout Paul's theology.

---

revelation of Christ, God was commissioning him to a great new enterprise. *The Apostolic Age* (London: Gerald Duckworth, 1955), p. 120.

*Reconciling grace*

A fourth theme exemplified in Paul's conversion and that gave shape to his theology is that of reconciling grace. We shall see that, overall, no concept so well describes what God did in salvation as does the term *reconciliation* (*katallassō*) (cf. Rom. 5:10; II Cor. 5:19, RSV).[15] The word is typically Pauline and reveals what his own conversion meant in terms of new relationships. Enmity was given over to friendship. Jesus whom he had persecuted and the followers of Jesus whom he hated, he now loved. Obviously this could not have happened if God had not acted out of grace, for Paul's actions had not given the slightest hope of change. The confrontation on the Damascus road was a phenomenal turning about, and the reconciliation that resulted formed the terms of reference for Paul's gospel. God had opened the way for this change in relationship, bringing harmony and peace between a man and his God. Paul made personal relationships between men and God a basic theme in his theology, and this, in turn, was connected to a number of vital subthemes.[16]

It is impossible to imagine the message of Paul without the idea of grace at the center. Reconciliation that comes by the means of grace describes salvation in its simplest terms. Men and women are brought into harmony with God through a voluntary act on God's part that is inexpressibly beautiful and powerfully winsome. This is a gift that is undeserved and requires no merit. Grace that reconciles is like nothing that rabbinical Judaism had ever known. It is true that the Jewish religion claimed to depend upon the mercy of God and his mercy alone, but the massive burden of the law prevailed over mercy. So the Jew was bent on acquiring credits to offset the debts.[17] It was this desire to fulfill all the law that drove Paul to ransack the church. But he was literally turned around by his conversion. The unmerited favor of God became the essence of his salvation message. All that man can do is to accept humbly and in amazement that which God freely and generously does. Every letter that Paul wrote begins and ends with the theme of grace.[18] This is convincing proof that Paul never forgot what grace had done for him and could do for all people everywhere who received it.

15. Martin's recent study on Paul's theology is summed up under the theme of reconciliation (see n. 17). Martin, however, recognizes other scholars, particularly T. W. Manson, who says, "The driving force behind the Gospel is the love of God. The *modus operandi* is reconciliation." Quoted in *Reconciliation*, p. 4, from T. W. Manson, *On Paul and Jesus*, M. Block, ed. (London: SCM, 1963), p. 50.

16. Martin, *Reconciliation*, p. 61.

17. A commentary on the legalism of Jewish orthodoxy as to strict payments and law-keeping is found in William Barclay, *The Mind of St. Paul* (New York: Harper and Row, 1975), p. 156. Barclay quotes from *Sayings of the Fathers* (3:22ff.), "The world is ruled by goodness, yet everything is according to the amount of work."

18. Barclay, *The Mind of St. Paul*, pp. 157-159.

### *Jesus is Lord*

A fifth fact that Paul's conversion taught him in terms of an experiential theology is that Jesus is Lord. Could anything have been more convincing of the power of the risen Christ and his authority over a life than this meeting between Paul and his new Lord? Loyalties changed radically and quickly when at midday he heard a voice asking, "Saul, Saul! Why do you persecute me?" (Acts 9:4). At that moment he was in the overwhelming presence of Jesus. His arrogant spirit melted; the convictions of his soul that had stood against the truth gave way and he literally became a prisoner of his new Lord. The shattering experience demanded that he settle once and for all that Jesus Christ is Lord. Indeed, all those who will follow the risen Christ will be known as people who have given their lives over to his authority. Hereafter, the first requirement of a new Christian will be that he confess with his lips that "Jesus is Lord" (Rom. 10:9). The resurrection was not only a matter of belief, but it also was an experience of new life. Christ died and rose again. By this his lordship is affirmed over all people, both the dead and the living (Rom. 14:9).

This change in lordship is the difference between Christians and non-Christians. Conversion for all people is, as it was for Paul, a transfer in allegiance from what formerly controlled the life to a new Center, even though it may not be clear at first what the implications of this new lordship are. If one were to judge from the standpoint of "right belief" or "right action," it would have appeared to the outsider from, let us say, Jerusalem, that most new Christians in Asia Minor or Europe had completely misunderstood the gospel. But Paul did not confuse growth and discipling with those first steps of faith that turn a person in the direction of Christ. The new loyalty, an attitude of the heart known fully only to God, will have its effect on the totality of life as time passes. But the all-important step at the beginning of the new way is to acknowledge the lordship of Christ. All that follows this crucial, first affirmation arises from the spirit of Paul's second question to Jesus, "What shall I do, Lord?" (Acts 22:10).

### ***Illuminated by Revelation***

When we speak of sources for Paul's theology, it must not be forgotten that God dealt with him in highly personal and subjective ways. God used Paul's openness to visions and dreams to enable him to clarify messages, receive new insights, and find answers to difficult problems. Paul has been characterized by his most severe critics as one who was easily influenced by his emotions and susceptible to all kinds of extrasensory messages (see II Cor. 12:1ff.). But for Paul it was no weakness or liability to be taught by spiritual communication. It was his purest guidance and source of strength.

The references to divinely given information are recorded in such a matter-of-fact way that we can only assume that visions and dreams were accepted as a source of authority in Paul's day. Paul's claims to personal encounter with the Lord through various direct revelations not only added veracity to his teaching but also enhanced his status as a teacher of truth. It was as though God brought him compensatory information to make up for the untimeliness of his calling into the apostolic office. As a later apostle, he said, "I am like someone whose birth was abnormal" (I Cor. 15:8). Paul was not blessed by personal comradeship with Jesus as were the other apostles and, therefore, the intensely personal vision of the risen Jesus verified his right to apostleship (Acts 26:16).

*A valid source of truth*

The references to revelation are abundant and describe various kinds of experiences from quiet inward insights to the dramatic visitations at Troas (Acts 16:9) and on board the doomed ship in the Mediterranean (Acts 27:23-24). Paul spoke in twelve different instances, by inference or with direct statement, of the "mystery" that had been revealed to him.[19] For example, he wrote, "If you will read what I have written, you can learn about my understanding of the secret of Christ. In past times mankind was not told this secret, but God has revealed it now by the Spirit to his holy apostles and prophets" (Eph. 3:4-5). The revelation of the "secret" is the core of Paul's gospel, and its proclamation became the very task that was entrusted to him (Col. 1:25-26; cf. Rom. 16:25-26).

The word *reveal* (*apokaluptō*) means "the transmission of a previously hidden truth," something that God deferred until its precise time. At the right moment this truth, brought through the gospel, was divinely explicated through the ministry given to Paul, and was preached and taught by him to all men and women everywhere.[20] Paul insisted that his knowledge, in contrast to secular teachings and the heresies of other so-called apostles, was transmitted through revelation—he did not receive it from men nor was he even taught it by men (Gal. 1:11-12). This put his truth in a totally different category from the teachings of those who only claimed to be apostles (II Cor. 11:12-15).

True wisdom is the subject of Paul's appeal to the Corinthians. The gospel revealed is the very wisdom of God. A candid statement of the divine source of the gospel is in I Corinthians 2:10-16, where Paul says, "We do

19. See Herman N. Ridderbos, *Paul, an Outline of His Theology,* J. R. DeWitt, trans. (Grand Rapids: Eerdmans, 1975), p. 46. Ridderbos speaks of the theme (that which was "kept secret" [mystery] is now "revealed") as being dominant in all of Paul's writings: Romans 16:25-26; I Corinthians 2:7; Ephesians 1:9-10; 3:4-5; Colossians 1:26; 2:2-3; II Timothy 1:9-10; Titus 1:2-3.

20. Ibid., pp. 46-47.

not speak in words taught by human wisdom, but in words taught by the Spirit" (v. 13). His direct access to truth and direction touched the cognitive dimensions of Paul's life as well as the practical. He was given information about the Lord's Supper that the other disciples knew through experience (I Cor. 11:23). Problems that arose concerning the second coming are dealt with in one of his earliest letters. But Paul is confident of his divine source of instruction (I Thess. 4:15).[21] Intervention by revelation, the speaking presence of the Lord, was a constant reminder of God's call and affirmation of his ministry (Acts 18:9-10). When he was tempted to despair, the Lord, more than once, "stood by him" and provided strength as well as new insights (Acts 23:11; II Tim. 4:17). When fear overtook Paul, it was a visitation by the risen Lord that refreshed him, making it possible for him to take up any task, whether it was a return trip to Jerusalem (Gal. 2:2) or the long journey to Rome (Acts 23:11). This practical guidance given through dreams actually set the course of missions. In a simple statement, Luke recorded that it was the "Spirit of Jesus" who forbade the journey into Bithynia, so redirecting Paul and Silas into the cities of Macedonia and Achaia (Acts 16:6-10).

*Direct revelation today*

The idea of receiving truth from God by dreams, visions, and revelations of various kinds is generally discounted by most Westerners. The person who claims to have received supernatural information is suspect, ignored, or may be advised to seek therapy! It is difficult to relate to a source of knowledge that is outside of the written tradition. But Paul's claims that truth can be communicated through dreams and visions still have powerful implications for people in the greater part of the world. Many societies are in close touch with spiritual forces both good and evil. Extrasensory contacts or spontaneous visitations by spirits believed to represent the ancestors are a very real part of the daily life of millions of people. God speaks, or is interpreted as speaking, to ordinary folk, to prophets and practitioners of all kinds, and with an amazing assortment of messages. The activity of the spirit world is something that missionaries from the West have never taken very seriously, even though they present a gospel that was informed and validated by direct revelation. Paul does not go out of his way to affirm the authority of revelations. It is simply reported as matter of course. By the world view of his day, the strongest proofs for truth were attached to such revelations. While much of the information received through voices and dreams today is

21. Leander Keck sees Paul's reference to "religious experiences" as rare and that he appeals to them only in polemical discussions. Keck feels that I Thessalonians 4:15 only *implies* revelation, but might refer to tradition. *Paul and His Letters,* Proclamation Commentaries, the New Testament Witnesses for Preaching, Gerhard Krodel, ed. (Philadelphia: Fortress, 1979), p. 26.

erroneous, the reality of revelation claimed by Paul cannot be discounted or ignored. God convinced Paul of truth in the supernatural way. Among peoples who had no difficulty in accepting this kind of revelation it was one of the most powerful sources of truth available to Paul.

### *Motivated by a Call to Evangelize*

To speak of Paul's conversion as an experience that shaped basic convictions about his theology leads to the fact that coincident with his conversion he received the call to evangelize. It is impossible to separate the phenomena of his conversion and his call. The sequence of events in Acts 9 brought Ananias, a choice disciple, into the drama. God sent him to Saul with the promise, "I have chosen him to serve me, to make my name known to Gentiles and kings and to the people of Israel" (Acts 9:15). It was this word that quelled Ananias' fears about Saul. Paul himself witnessed to this three years later in Jerusalem when he declared before Agrippa that Jesus had appeared to him and had been revealed to him (Acts 26:16).

This "call" aspect of Paul's conversion has been treated to an extreme by Krister Stendahl, who argues that it is misleading to apply to Paul's experience the terminology of conversion. He feels, rather, that the Damascus encounter marked the beginning of a new function for Paul, as the apostle who had a divine commissioning. While this is in continuity with his life as a Jew, he is now given a distinct message for the Gentiles.[22] Stendahl highlights that Paul was miraculously set apart for a new ministry. This is an important emphasis. But unless the "call" is supported by the reality of his changed life, the commissioning would make little sense. His commissioning brought him a new assessment of the church and of the person of Jesus Christ who called him. For it was the resurrected Jesus who addressed him; it was to a completely new covenant that Paul was called and to which he committed himself.

The amazing sequel to Paul's conversion is recorded in Acts 9:20, where we learn that he immediately began to proclaim in the synagogue "that Jesus was the Son of God." This was the testimony of a man who was both called and changed. It was the beginning of a ministry that always took its message and strength from the reality of a reconciling gospel. This was a new age for the man Paul. The new age had been ushered in by the Messiah, who was indeed the risen Christ. To understand it and accept it was for Paul a true reversal, and the mandate to proclaim it to all now consumed his life.[23]

22. *Paul among Jews and Gentiles* (Philadelphia: Fortress, 1976), pp. 1-77. See the critique of Stendahl's position by Martin, *Reconciliation*, pp. 24-31.

23. See Ladd's discussion on the new way and its contrast to Judaism, *Theology of the New*

References to the impact of the call to evangelize are abundant, and illustrate that any idea of Paul's theology that misses the message of forgiveness and reconciliation for all people is wide of the mark. How clearly and forcefully he spoke of the burden of evangelizing: "I am under orders . . ." (I Cor. 9:16). It was something with which he had been entrusted, a high and holy trust (Gal. 2:7; I Tim. 1:11); it was not tied to any notion of reward (I Cor. 9:17), but simply and always his aim was to please God (I Thess. 2:4).

While his message was uniquely for the Gentiles, Paul never lost the vision for his own people. He could not forget that the Messiah's kingdom was intended primarily for them, and that this Messiah "as to his humanity . . . was born a descendant of David" (Rom. 1:3). Yet his eagerness for the evangelization of all, Jew and Greek alike, is expressed even while he is agonizing about the closed attitude of the Jews. "'Everyone who calls out to the Lord for help will be saved.' But how can they call to him for help if they have not believed? And how can they believe if they have not heard the message?" (Rom. 10:13-14). The ruling impulse of his life was to carry Jesus' Good News of universal grace far and wide.

It has already been noted that it was far from Paul's mind to found a system of theology. Rather, to fill the office of the apostle as an expert builder who lays the foundation (I Cor. 3:10) was his highest and most urgent calling. His understanding of apostleship was built on this conviction. He was predetermined by God to be a witness; he was one set apart, even before he was born. Called by grace, Paul says that God "decided to reveal his Son to me, so that I might preach the Good News about him to the Gentiles" (Gal. 1:15-16).

So Paul's theology was energized by the call to preach and the conviction that this gospel really saves. The boldness with which he preached his gospel of liberty and his fearless defense against the Judaizers sprang from the intensity of his commitment to the central focus of his ministry. "How terrible it would be for me if I did not preach the gospel!" (I Cor. 9:16).[24]

## The Nature of Paul's Theology

When looking for a definition of the kind of theology that motivates and energizes the church to witness, we shall need to set aside, for the time

---

*Testament,* pp. 373-375. "Paul's conversion meant a recovery of the sense of redemptive history that Judaism had lost," p. 375. Closely related is the discussion of the tension between tradition and revelation, also by Ladd, in *Apostolic History and the Gospel,* Ward W. Gasque and Ralph P. Martin, eds. (Grand Rapids: Eerdmans, 1970), chapter 14, pp. 223-230.

24. See also Romans 1:1; I Corinthians 9:1; II Corinthians 4:5-6; Galatians 1:1.

being, the idea that theology is a science, a rational logical construct, a defense for God, or an exercise for the few. Christianity declares one great fact, which Paul sums up when he says, "Christ Jesus came into the world to save sinners" (I Tim. 1:15), and it is the outworking of this that forms a mission theology. This means there must be recognition of the universal needs of men, and of the provision to meet those needs through a remaking of the entire person and his world. Theology, therefore, becomes a reflection upon, and an explanation of, convictions that grow out of real experiences, in which people have encountered a living God. It is presumptive to describe Paul's theology in any summary way. But what concerns us here are the aspects of his theology that have bearing on his missionary ministry, as he carried the Word into regions of unbelief.

### *A Theology of Mission*

Paul's theology could be described as a "theology on the move," which speaks both about what motivated Paul and about the formative quality of the things that he taught.[25] Paul, of course, had no written authority other than the Old Testament to carry along with him. No written Gospel record could have been given to those new Christians, much less a catechism or a book of discipline. Obviously, he was a learner himself on some issues. For example, in the early stages of his ministry he seems to say that he himself expected to see the return of Christ (I Thess. 4:15). Later he did not count himself among those who will witness Christ's second coming (II Tim. 4:6). Paul did not have a final statement of faith to give to every enquirer. His ministry was from a different perspective.

There is no question but that the miracle and the meaning of Pentecost energized Paul's ministry. Pentecost as the basis of missionary life has been convincingly argued by Harry R. Boer.[26] All other things accounted for, including the Great Commission, it is still the irresistible and spontaneous witness of Pentecost that reveals, above all else, what the new dispensation of the Spirit means (Acts 4:33). Jesus' own command to preach the gospel to all nations does not directly provide the motivation for Paul's mission to the Gentiles. Rather we may say that it was the Spirit's powerful coming at Pentecost that gave sense and purpose to all that Jesus said,[27] and it was the urging of this selfsame Spirit that was confirmed to Saul by Ananias (Acts

25. Rall observes, "One might call his the theology of the missionary because it was his work as a missionary which gave content to his thought." *According to Paul,* p. 17. By contrast, see Gunther Bornkamm, *Paul,* M. G. Stalker, trans. (New York: Harper and Row, 1971), p. 118, nn. 8, 9.

27. *Pentecost and Missions* (Grand Rapids: Eerdmans, 1961).

27. Ibid., pp. 98-134.

22:12-15). The speaking, active Holy Spirit so motivated the ministry of Paul that he could not resist the call to preach (I Cor. 9:16). Even though the Jerusalem Council ordered a breakthrough for cross-cultural mission by lifting the regulation about circumcision from the Gentiles, we do not know, from the record, if Paul carried the council's letter any further than the Antioch church (Acts 15:30). Paul was acting under primary orders. The Pentecostal Spirit who revealed the wisdom of the council's decision (Acts 15:28) had already claimed Paul. Mission to all nations was the natural, unquestioned outcome for him.

A mission theology is marked by two characteristics: it underscores that which is essential to the gospel, and it communicates in a manner relevant to each situation. The term *essentials* means that no truth, no fact of the gospel that is absolute to salvation can be ignored or changed (Gal. 1:6-8). This would mean that Paul declared the basic kerygma of the apostles; that the life, death, and resurrection of Jesus constitute a call upon men everywhere to repent (Acts 17:30), and that the community of those who believe is the true church of Christ. However, Paul communicated these absolutes through a variety of metaphors and symbols. Very early, arguments had to be found that could counter his enemies' attacks and local heresies of many kinds. He entered cities and towns where the message about the cross was considered nonsense (I Cor. 1:18). Yet, every effort had to be made to be understood, and this meant presenting the gospel in ways that were as appropriate as possible, without altering the core of truth that all must believe and accept. The balance between essentials and relevance is what Paul had in mind when he said, "I become all things to all men, that I may save some of them by whatever means are possible" (I Cor. 9:22).

In speaking of a mission theology, then, the first commitment is to the Word—the Word that saves. Thus, Paul explains, "I have an obligation to all peoples . . . to the educated and to the ignorant" (Rom. 1:14). Further, in the Epistle to the Romans, we find that the purpose of his visit was not simply to "win converts" or to "share a spiritual blessing" (Rom. 1:11-13). It was, rather, to impress the church with its part in his plans for extended ministry. Since it was his ambition to preach the gospel where Christ's name was not already known (Rom. 15:20), he would, after a short visit to Rome, move on to Spain. The epistle prepares these believers in every way possible, especially in the area of right belief, to rise to the challenge and become a missionary center (Rom. 15:24, 28).

The content of what Paul taught was amazingly simple (I Cor. 15:1-8). The teaching was stated and restated, and the implications of what this meant for one people or for one group as against another people or group were carefully formed. Thus, in his writing the beginnings of a theology were formed. However, these letters always bring us back to my earlier statement that they do not, in fact, reveal much about how Paul spoke or taught for the first time in any given situation.

What I mean by a theology of mission for our own day is that, while it builds on the Bible, such a theology must be in touch with real needs and find ways to meet them. The holistic quality of Paul's teaching stands in judgment on any theology that elevates the cognitive and the reflective above the pastoral and the practical. The task of theology, says H. F. Rall, is to "serve the fellowship of faith by inquiring what convictions mean" for the contemporary world and by "testing its validity as it faces the life and thought of its age."[28] The appeal here is for an outgoing, untiring commitment to a gospel that uplifts and redeems, because it is oriented to ministry rather than to the reproduction of a creed taken from one people or one place and insisted upon among another people and in another place. An assumption for any good theology is that the symbols and terms used must connect authentically with the common life and the real needs of the day.[29] For Paul, this kind of theology did not come from the ingrown, traditional texts of Judaism as practiced in Jerusalem, but sprang with freshness from the liberating, active Spirit who testifies to Jesus Christ. This is the "serving" theology of Paul, validating the authority of the gospel in ways that are appropriate to each people and place. A mission theology not only is recognized by the fact that it enables its bearer to penetrate into areas of unbelief and ignorance with the gospel message; but it also demands that the messenger, as well as those who accept the message, think through the meaning and the application of the Good News in that particular situation.

One of the exciting things about Paul's approach to missions lies just here. For while he was successful, above all others, in planting churches and in nurturing new Christians, he accomplished this, for the most part, by leaving neophyte Christians to seek out the answers to the questions posed by their new life. The traditional mission pattern has been for the missionary to stay, often for years, in one place, in a culture not his own, and to form the church by his own theological convictions, rather than showing the church how to think for itself. Paul would have been criticized by knowledgeable Jews for not providing a guidebook for recent converts.[30] Instead, as we

28. *According to Paul,* p. 1.

29. David Tracy, in a helpful analysis of various models for theology, sees a weakness in orthodoxy in that it tends not to come to terms with the existential modernity; while on the other hand secularist theology is so oriented to the contemporary that it has no meaningful way to affirm the reality of God. See *Blessed Rage for Order: The New Pluralism in Theology,* Library of Contemporary Theology series (New York: Seabury, 1979), chapter 2, pp. 22-42.

30. It was common for converts to Judaism to be provided with a written catechism. Adolf von Harnack makes the point that "the Jewish synagogues had already drawn up a catechism for proselytes and . . . it had already instituted a training for Religion." *The Mission and Expansion of Christianity in the First Three Centuries,* John Moffatt, ed. and trans. (London: Williams, Norgate, 1908), vol. 1, pp. 391-392.

shall see further, he insisted that each and every believer become an authentic Christian, able to think through the new faith and act upon it.

### *A Theology of Experience*

It is virtually impossible to be disinterested in or casual about this man who broke out of Antioch to take the word of life to cities and towns of Asia. What Paul carried was not academic or theoretical. The word of Paul was not the deadness of the law or the repetition of worn-out traditions. The news that his missionary team brought was fresh and moving because it was the product of concrete and life-changing events. Paul's theology had an empirical ring to it. It was rational and connected to history. But it was not this aspect that turned the cities upside down, moving people to accept willingly or, on the other hand, to turn against him. It was the uncompromising insistence that God had done something for humankind, and that something will happen to people when they believe and accept what God had done.

The facts concerning Jesus were uncontestable and formed a body of empirical data. The message was based on Jesus' life, his deeds, his death, his resurrection, and his continuing presence through the Spirit. These facts were translated into a personal, life-directing encounter with God. When Paul's entire life and ministry are taken into account, one cannot help but feel that his own conversion was the one experience that shaped his thought and his missionary vision.

The experiential nature of Paul's theology, its living, moving quality, constantly takes us back to the day when he, Paul, personally encountered the resurrected Christ. His conversion was not simply a redirection of his life; even less was it a "call" within the context of Judaism.[31] For the man Saul, this meeting with the living Christ was the great reversal. Paul spoke about the experience in a direct way on two occasions,[32] showing that, indeed, it had all happened by the power of God, that it was a revelation of the living Christ, and that there, on the Damascus road, this Jesus appeared to him in person. This divine encounter clearly formed convictions about Christian truth in Paul's mind. We shall study what conversion is in the next chapter, but I note here that the attractiveness and the power of Paul's gospel find their wellspring in his own conversion.

What God does for people and what people experience (how people respond to the divine initiative) is a dual theme that can be traced through all the major letters of Paul. Salvation carries these two foci, and such

31. See note 22.
32. Acts 22:6-16; 26:12-18.

teaching by Paul became the ground upon which the gospel went forwa
Table 1 illustrates how Paul stresses both of these aspects.

**Table 1**

**Two Aspects of Salvation**

| What God does for people | What persons experience as a result |
|---|---|
| **Romans 1:3-4** | **Romans 1:5** |
| He was born a descendant of David; as to his divine holiness, he was shown with great power to be the Son of God by being raised from death. | Through him God gave [one] the privilege of being an apostle. |
| **5:8** | **5:9, 11** |
| Christ died for us. | We are now put right with God. . . . who has now made us God's friends. |
| **6:4** | **6:4** |
| Christ was raised from death . . . | so also we might live a new life. |
| **8:3** | **8:2** |
| What the law could not do . . . God did. He condemned sin in human nature by sending his own Son, who came with a nature like man's sinful nature. | The law of the Spirit, which brings us life in union with Christ Jesus, has set me free from the law of sin and death. |
| **8:11** | **8:11** |
| If the Spirit of God, who raised Jesus from death, | lives in you, |
| then he who raised Christ from death | will also give life to your mortal bodies by the presence of his Spirit in you. |
| **II Cor. 5:15** | **II Cor. 5:15** |
| He died for all, | so that those who live should no longer live for themselves. . . . |
| **Eph. 1:7** | **Eph. 1:7** |
| By the sacrificial death of Christ | we are set free, that is, our sins are forgiven. |
| **1:19-20** | **1:19-20** |
| This power working in us is the same as the mighty strength which he used when he raised Christ from death. | How very great is his power at work in us who believe. |
| **4:8** | **4:11** |
| When he went up to the very heights . . . he gave gifts to mankind. | He appointed some to be apostles, others, to be prophets. . . . |
| It was he who gave gifts to mankind. | |

**Table 1,** *Continued*

| What God does for people | What persons experience as a result |
|---|---|
| **Col. 2:9** | **Col. 2:10** |
| For the full content of divine nature lives in Christ, in his humanity, | and you have been given full life in union with him. |
| **2:15** | **2:20** |
| On that cross Christ freed himself from the power of the spiritual rulers and authorities . . . leading them as captives in his victory procession. | You have died with Christ and are set free from the ruling spirit of the universe. Why, then, do you live as though you belonged to this world? |

This gospel centers, therefore, on God's giving and man's receiving. God's gift of salvation was precisely what was needed for the new way, in contrast to both Jewish law and Gentile paganism. Through what God did, Paul experienced freedom: legal freedom, personal freedom, and social freedom.[33] Paul understood this freedom not through reason but by a new law that he experienced in Christ Jesus, the Spirit of life who set him free from the law of sin and death (Rom. 8:2). God gave and Paul experienced love, the essence of true freedom. This love is a gift, nothing less, given through the Holy Spirit and confirmed by the presence of the Holy Spirit. There is no basis other than love in Paul's ministry. Christians are taught to love one another (I Thess. 4:9). This is because God has acted out of the great love with which he loved us (Eph. 2:4). So the Christian, being ruled by Christ's love (II Cor. 5:14), is expected to walk in love. This is just as important as experiencing God's love in the first place (Eph. 5:2). Again, what God did brought fellowship that Paul calls "fellowship with his son, Jesus Christ, our Lord" (I Cor. 1:9). This fellowship would have its fullest expression in the new covenant community, the church. "The church is Christ's body, the completion of him who himself completes all things everywhere" (Eph. 1:23). Therefore, as we examine Paul's practice in mission we shall see that what individuals experienced and demonstrated as the outcome of their faith was more important, initially at least, than what they believed in terms of doctrine.

We would be wrong if a phrase such as "theology of experience" leads us to think that personal experience results automatically in correct ideas and concepts. The empirical, rather, always requires interpretation. This was a continuing exercise for Paul, as it must be for anyone who thinks through his faith. Paul had experiential knowledge that was highly personal and distinctive. Paul's thinking took a radical new turn with his conversion, so that the character of his ministry became one that was truly existential. His message was one in which the whole man became involved and that

33. See the discussion in Richard N. Longenecker, *Paul, Apostle of Liberty* (Grand Rapids: Baker, 1976), pp. 170-174.

demanded action for its completion. Hence, his theology would, in one sense, always be a theology in the making, coextensive with his whole life, involving a squaring of absolute facts with the various situations in which these facts must be communicated and understood.

### *A Theology of Faith*

Christ was, indeed, the Messiah. A new age had begun with the coming of Jesus and his resurrection became the seal upon his claim to be the Son of God. This was a new concept, which made Paul's gospel experiential and transforming. But a second conviction dawned on Paul. This was a principle he summed up in one word. With this word he would offer God's gift to all people, because all, Jew and Gentile, were able to comprehend and apply it. It is the principle of faith. From Damascus onward Paul began to live in a new world. Faith, saving faith, as he would teach it, reaches under the old life to uproot it and extends around the new life to embrace it and prove it at every point. Faith as the salvation principle was far different from the dialectic he had learned in Gamaliel's school. This was not the cold, calculating analysis of the divine will, nor was it an intellectual acceptance of dogma. Even though the facts came through revelation, this faith was not philosophizing about the contents of those revelations, it was not intuition, nor was it searching out the hidden riches of a mystery. How, then, are we to understand Paul's theology of simple faith?

This faith, while hidden from the unbeliever, is something that is within the capabilities of the unlearned and the poor (Matt. 11:25). Properly understood, by this faith, invisible things become real and tangible; they take on substance; they are drawn in from metaphysical distance and brought into immediate and concrete reality (Heb. 11:1). No wonder Paul used the Greek word *pistis* (which we translate "faith") at least 109 times in his epistles.

#### *Faith in a Person*

This faith is, above all else, personal faith. It is the reaching out in acceptance on the part of a person and is rewarded and met by a Person. It is this personal dimension of faith that sets Christianity apart from other religions. I have already said that Paul did not insist on a statement of faith or a long creedal confession that would divert the attention of his hearers from the person of Christ. His reference was always to the historical Jesus, whether in synagogues or among pagan Gentiles. Faith was presented as inseparable from Christ.[34] Paul's own life-change was based on a single, emotional

34. Faith and the concept of "in Christ" can never be separated. Adolf Deissmann stresses this. Faith is accomplished in union of life with the spiritual Christ; it is faith alive in fellowship with the spiritual Christ. (See the discussion on Paul's use of the genitive to make the point.) *Paul,* W. E. Wilson, trans. (New York: Doran, 1926), pp. 161-164.

commitment to a Person. So, remembering his own conversion, he told the Philippians that they not only were called to believe in Jesus, but also to suffer for his sake (Phil. 1:29). This new life was plainly life by faith in the Son of God (Gal. 2:20). Paul's own rightness, in the eyes of God, did not come by any merit from his family background or his personal zeal, but came by what he calls faith in Christ Jesus (Rom. 3:26; Gal. 2:16). Faith, then, is not allegiance to a creed and is not a system; it is living contact, person to Person. It is as dramatically simple as are Jesus' own words when he says, "Follow me" (Matt. 9:9, etc.). Obviously, the whys and wherefores would have to be thought out and the truth examined and defended against detractors, but the moving force of Paul's primary message is this fact of personal faith in Jesus Christ.[35]

*Faith in living facts*

We have cited the person of Jesus as the source of faith because his story is supported by incontrovertible data that became the essence of Paul's gospel. Before we talk of theology we need to establish the irreducible truths that are themselves the gospel. These facts are best gathered together from the kerygma of Peter and Paul, with special attention to Paul's preaching, since his target audience was Gentile as well as Jew. We cannot really speak of any organized creed until much later. There is, possibly, the beginning of a creed as some kind of set formula by the time of the Pastorals. It takes quite a lot of rearranging of Pauline material to arrive at an orderly compilation of the teaching that might have been given to the early Christians.[36] But the important thing was the acceptance of the basic facts—life-changing truths that carried power when understood through faith. The Book of Acts does not provide us with much if we wish to study the content of Paul's preaching. His longest sermon, at Antioch of Pisidia (Acts 13: 16-41), does, however, show that the facts concerning the life and death of Jesus overshadowed any other emphasis. While this sermon was in a Jewish frame of reference, with a strong appeal to the past and the baptism of John the Baptist, Paul declared the facts of Jesus clearly: he was killed as a result of false accusations; God raised him up and he "appeared to his disciples"; Jesus is God's Son and through him come forgiveness of sin and freedom from the law.

The nearest thing to any kind of required creedal statement in the early

35. Barclay says, about personal faith, "When [Jesus] came to men, he did not say to them, 'I have a system that I would like you to examine; I have a philosophy I would like you to discuss; I have a theory I would like to lay before you'. . . . The moving force of Christianity is in fact this act of personal faith in Jesus Christ." *The Mind of St. Paul,* p. 139.

36. Roland Allen sees I Thessalonians as a compendium of the early teaching of Paul and has arranged the content under nine topics. *Missionary Methods: St. Paul's or Ours?* (1912; reprint ed. London: World Dominion Press, 1960), p. 68.

church is recorded in Romans 10:9, where two things are expected: the believer must confess the Lord Jesus by mouth, and, beyond that, there must be belief from the heart that God raised him from the dead. Belief in the resurrection was very important because it presupposed all other facts about Jesus, including his death, and held out real and welcome hope for all who were dead in their disobedience and sins (Eph. 2:1). Christ indeed had come, had died, and was now raised again. These are the facts that Paul preached, and that people of both Jewish and Gentile worlds believed (I Cor. 15:11).

One way of looking at faith might be to say that it is an acceptance of a proposition that cannot be proved, or cannot be completely proved. To have faith at this level is the first step to salvation, since the facts of Jesus were known to comparatively few people, and to Paul by special revelation.[37] It is this giving of one's self beyond one's own experience, when all the facts are not fully understood, that is of the very essence of faith. Faith is trust in God in the face of doubt or when things do not happen in expected ways.

The term *faith* became the word that actually described and summarized the new religion. "The faith" was, in effect, a name for Paul's religion of Jesus, and early became an expression that was synonymous with Christianity.[38] As the ideal of the lordship of Christ took on the meaning of the rule of Jesus over persons of faith, so faith became renunciation of self and abandonment to God. For Paul, then, this faith is an acceptance of the gospel at the mental level at first, but goes on to be a kind of faith that leads the believer to stand and prove himself.[39] Faith is the way to express a person's total response to the love of God.

### *A Theology of Practice*

I have already made several references to the fact that Paul was so driven by the call to evangelize that he must be seen primarily as a planter of churches, and only secondarily as a teacher of doctrine. He was always on the move, and his theology, while not formless, was on the move with him. His letters were written as part of the dynamic interaction he had with his churches. Practically all we know about what Paul taught has to be reconstructed from what he wrote in his epistles. They are letters that are very close in time to the original gospel of Jesus and the explosive effects of

37. There is some conjecture that Paul was present at the crucifixion with the Jewish priests and that he carried away the unforgettable impression of Christ's death, hence Paul's personal reference to Christ's death in Galatians 3:1. Holzner, *St. Paul the Apostle,* p. 78.

38. Acts 14:22; 16:15, RSV; I Corinthians 16:13; II Corinthians 13:5; I Timothy 1:2; 3:9; 4:1; II Timothy 4:7; Titus 3:15.

39. See the helpful discussion on the meaning of the faith in light of the Abrahamic faith in Bornkamm, *Paul,* pp. 144-146.

Pentecost. The content, therefore, is never abstract. The interrelatedness of Paul's life and letters is a most important point to remember in understanding him. What he felt within himself as a person, as he reflected on his work, and his response to that work, runs unmistakably through all his writings.

The result is that in Paul's epistles so many topics are intermingled or only partially dealt with—discussed partly here and partly there—that it is impossible to deal exhaustively with any single subject without making cross-references and paying careful attention to symbolic words and key phrases. As Gunther Bornkamm says, "His theology is as little a system of universal timeless truths and religious experiences as his life was simply a series of favorable or adverse events."[40] This may be an overstatement of the situation, for Paul does not treat Christian truth in a whimsical way, by any means. He brought his classical training as a rabbi into his thinking at every point where it was called for, and showed perception of the historical and cultural issues in each situation. Always, he pondered very deeply, in dependence upon the Holy Spirit, what would be the right thinking and the right action in each situation.

Glenn Barker prefers to designate Paul as a "task theologian," that is, "one who has worked out his theological insights within the frame of reference provided by his task as an apostle to the Gentiles."[41] Further, says Barker, "it was in the context of human relationships, of conflict and anguish, of deep concern for the truth of the gospel and the freedom to which it called men, that Paul found the stimuli for theological reflection." Paul was, therefore, a praxis theologian. He could not work in a vacuum. He did not theologize about God, sin, salvation through Christ, the church, or the last things except, and unless, these issues arose from the living situation.

Because new Christians in the region of Galatia, for example, had been harassed and confused by Judaizers, Paul wrote not only to defend his own authority, but also to make the strongest kind of appeal for the principle of faith and liberty in the gospel. The teachings on personal ethics and political responsibilities for new Christians in Corinth were no classroom exercise. They came from the pen of a man who suffered intensely because Christians in Corinth tended to disregard the implications of their actions. He was shocked by their secularity and pride so soon after his ministry (I Cor. 5:1-2, 6) and by the naïveté they showed concerning Christian truth (e.g., I Cor. 3:1-4). Concrete questions that had never been raised before about marriage in a permissive society (I Cor. 7) or the need for specific directions on worship (I Cor. 11:17-33) gave the occasion to state principles that are axiomatic to the Christian faith in any age. Theology was formed through the resolution of controversy, the answering of detractors, or the scolding of

40. Ibid., p. xxciii.
41. Glenn Barker et al., *The New Testament Speaks* (New York: Harper, 1967), p. 198.

a defector, while reassuring the weak and admonishing the strong. He was committed to building up the churches that had been so recently planted. The unity of what he taught is not self-evident, and the understanding of the body of ideas that constitutes Paul's theology has been the work of scholars through the hundreds of years since his time.

The missionary, obviously, is not going to find himself or herself operating in Paul's world, yet the reasons why Paul was a practical theologian rather than a systematic theologian are as valid for the modern missionary as they were for Paul.

### *The nature of Paul's ministry*

First, Paul held to a theology of practice because of the nature of his ministry. Consumed with his call, he was always the mobile evangelist. He described himself as a foundation builder (I Cor. 3:10), and as a seed planter (I Cor. 9:11). This meant he would not stay in one place long enough to erect or administer an institute of learning or become a resident expert in theology. No one has treated Paul as the preacher-teacher on the move as memorably as Roland Allen. Allen showed that Paul ministered from a totally different paradigm than do most missionaries today. Paul's method was to preach, pressing the claims of Christ at every point, then to move on. Allen takes note of the summary kind of teaching Paul would give a new Christian, including him in the fellowship of new Christians and commending him to the Spirit:

> Saint Paul baptized the jailer at Philippi, for instance, upon his bare confession on his belief in Jesus as Saviour, after an instruction which lasted an hour or two in the night. Under such circumstances he certainly could not have taught the man very much of the life and doctrine of Christ. He was satisfied that a spiritual change had taken place; there was some sign of repentance, some profession of faith and that sufficed.[42]

It was not that Paul deliberately ignored the need for sustained instruction, for his letters show the patience he had in repeating and explaining in detail the fundamentals of the teaching. But Paul's ministry was marked by mobility. He moved on to Thessalonica from Philippi, and then on to Berea and Athens, so that the pace of his work precluded any extended periods of indoctrination or theologizing as we know it today.[43]

### *The format of Paul's ministry*

A second reason for Paul's theology of practice is that he was the first to communicate Christian truth in a non-Jewish context. The format of Paul's

42. *Missionary Methods,* p. 95.
43. With the exceptions of Ephesus (Acts 19:10) and Corinth (Acts 18:11).

ministry was different from anything known to the Jews. It demanded that the old concepts be modified for Gentile ears or, in some cases, be set aside. To communicate Christian truth so that it is understood means that the receptor must be taken into account. The terminology, the symbols, the references to history and culture employed by the messenger must correspond to the hearers' frame of reference. Even though the institutions of Judaism would have had little meaning for the Gentiles, yet Jesus, the apostles, and the new way of Christianity were all firmly tied to the Jewish traditions. Paul had to search for the kind of language and symbolism that would break the hold of Aramaic Judaism on the gospel. The right questions had to be asked of the particular culture, and the data that came out of this inquiry then had to be used to determine the best methods to convey the gospel's meaning.

I have referred to the Jerusalem Council, recorded in Acts 15, as the most important event that opened the door to the Gentile world.[44] Here the apostles at Jerusalem faced openly what had taken place in Galatia among the Gentiles, and accorded major concessions to the so-called pagan world. When the assembly gathered, Paul was obviously the main speaker, recounting the Galatian mission and how God had performed signs and wonders through him and Barnabas. The Gentiles had been dramatically converted by the selfsame gospel that had changed Paul. Peter himself was the first to see that the yoke of Jewish practice would be even more intolerable for the Gentiles than it had been for the Jews (Acts 15:10). The church at Jerusalem must not require cultural forms that misrepresent the liberty and the universality of the gospel. That circumcision was set aside was a breakthrough that had no precedent in Judaism. This was a radical move toward what, today, we would call contextualization. It does not mean that Jewish churches rallied in wholehearted support of the decree. Obviously, the status quo would have ruled among the majority of Jewish Christians. Still, the action taken by the council did free the hands of Paul and effectively signaled to Gentiles, as well as to Jews, that salvation no longer belonged only to the Jews.

Even though Paul's references to the assembly's action are scant in his writings, there is no reason to think that the council acted reluctantly or out of expediency. Paul told the Galatians, for example, that this lifting of the Jewish restriction was done because the apostles realized that he, Paul, was ordained by God to preach among the Gentiles (Gal. 2:7). The Jerusalem apostles had come to see that the cross-cultural impact of the gospel required new approaches, new forms, and a careful restatement of what the essential gospel was. The approaches that Paul used as he addressed his ministry to Jewish, Roman, and Greek audiences constitute a hermeneutical

44. Bornkamm, *Paul,* p. 31.

question of highest importance. The careful way he made use of various concepts and expressions shows him to be a practical communicator of truth.[45] He did not export the clichés of his own background or force the ideas and the views of his own training on those who had a totally different perspective. This God, who had never left himself without a witness (Acts 14:17), can be understood and expressed in fresh, dynamic ways, depending on the situation, and it is the task of the communicator to find and use these insights.

### *The character of the churches*

A third reason why Paul's theology may be called a theology of practice arises out of his conviction that authentic churches should develop in each place. This meant that each covenant community that came into being through saving faith should understand and express the gospel in ways appropriate to that particular place. Much more will be said about this as we move on, but it needs to be understood from the beginning that Paul did not plant copies of the Jerusalem church, or even the Antioch church, as he traveled. As Allen insists, unity among the churches had nothing to do with whether the churches he established conformed to the sending church or mission. Unity, rather, centered on Christ, while each local church was free to develop its authentic life and witness. Allen was not popular in his day for criticizing the way in which sending mission agencies controlled the mission church. This concern led him to write,

> He [Paul] refused to transplant the law and customs of the churches in Judea into the Four Provinces. He refused to set up any central administrative authority from which the whole church was to receive directions in the conduct of local affairs. He declined to set up apriori tests of orthodoxy which should be applicable for all time under all circumstances everywhere. He refused to allow the universal application of particular precedents.[46]

Allen's insights were those of more than seventy years ago and carried a deep concern for truly indigenous churches, which we often speak of today as contextualized churches. The churches of Paul were authentic because they were allowed, even encouraged, to adopt local forms, adapting them as necessary, and to use them for God's glory and for the upbuilding of the fellowship in each place. Charles H. Kraft has popularized the expression *dynamic equivalence churches* as a description of what Paul aimed for. In an article published in 1973, Kraft summarizes this kind of church as one

45. See chapter 10, pp. 265-266.
46. *Missionary Methods*, p. 131.

"that produces the same kind of impact on the people of the society of which it is a part as the original church produced upon the hearers."[47]

Allen had comparatively little to say about this cultural aspect of Paul's theology; yet his concern for the spiritual freedom and the political autonomy of mission churches shows his concepts to be very close to the concept of dynamic equivalence. Writing about Corinthian worship, Allen made it clear that Paul had no problem with allowing appropriate local forms to shape the life and practice of the church. His description is memorable:

> The Jewish Christian in Corinth must have thought the church there given over to unbridled license. Uncircumcised Christians attended the feasts of their pagan friends in heathen temples. Every letter of the ceremonial law was apparently broken every day without rebuke. Even in the meetings of the church, preachings and prayers were built on a strange system of thought which could hardly be called Christian, and there was a most undignified freedom of conduct.[48]

Allen was not condoning a form of Christianity that watered down or compromised the gospel when he called for mission leaders to go back to Paul's methods. He saw in Paul what most miss, namely, that if people are to be changed by God's grace, if they are to embrace the Good News as something special for *them,* then the messenger must allow the gospel to become incarnate in each place, to take on the qualities of each locale. What this required from Paul was a sensitivity to the culture of each place within the provinces, and a willingness to seek for communication devices that would best convey Christian truth in that situation. These principles of authentic church-planting will be dealt with in more detail later.

*Reliance on the Spirit*

A fourth reason why Paul's theology is a theology of practice is found in his reliance on the Holy Spirit. This was, for Paul, a fundamental conviction. He refused to lay down rules that might contradict the voice of the Spirit to the churches or lead young Christians astray through following prescribed ideas. The reliance of Paul on the Holy Spirit and the dynamic ways in which he taught this same reliance to the young Christians of Asia and Europe was the first principle of his ministry. It is not my intention to deal with this comprehensively here, as it is a theme that will recur frequently in the material to follow. This issue is raised here, however, because of the tendency of theologians to portray Paul as one who taught a prescribed system of theology. This is an impossible way to deal with Paul and the reason lies

47. See "Dynamic Equivalence Churches: An Ethnotheological Approach to Indigeneity," *Missiology,* vol. 1, no. 1 (January 1973), pp. 39-57.

48. *Missionary Methods,* p. 129.

just at this point. The Spirit will not be contained in creeds, terminologies, or formulas, however precious these may be to the missionary. Paul had boundless confidence in the Holy Spirit. This is the Spirit who has energized the church to enlarge its borders by ceaseless evangelism (Acts 1:8), the Spirit who graces the church in each place with the gifts to sustain and multiply its own life (I Cor. 12:4-11), and the Spirit who teaches and empowers each believer and covenant community (I Cor. 2:12). This is the witnessing Spirit, the Spirit of liberty, and the Spirit who leads believing people into a continued and maturing dependency on Christ. Boer entitled the final chapter of his book "Quench Not the Spirit." Since much of what follows is a development of the principle of openness to the Holy Spirit, a quote from Boer will put the principle of the "whole Spirit for the whole church" into perspective.

> If we transmit to others the life of the Spirit we must not hinder them in fully expressing the freedom and joy of life. If we are eager to see them gather knowledge in the Spirit, we should also be eager to see them express the knowledge they have gathered. If we exert ourselves to give them the Spirit of holiness and of life, we should be eager to give them the Spirit of liberty through which that life comes to expression. Life means spontaneity and freedom, liberty to be one's self, independence from others. That individuality, that particularity, that distinctiveness of personality and character that God has given each man, is in the Spirit hallowed and given divine right of existence.[49]

This is the Spirit of the churches that Paul founded. It meant he would spend himself without reserve to defend the faith against all who would dilute the truth with "another gospel," but *he* would not order the thinking and the acting of new Christians who have been liberated. This flexibility of Paul was no accident or compromise. He gave the right to his churches to think for themselves. The requirement this placed on Paul is something the modern missionary has too often missed. We are not to impose a theology on young churches or do all the thinking for them. That the "Spirit will guide into all truth" is the promise of the Lord himself. "Where Christians and churches are allowed to be what the unfettered Spirit makes them, where they are set free from men and placed in full dependence on Christ, there we may expect her witness to flourish and her numbers to grow."[50]

49. *Pentecost and Missions,* p. 222.
50. Ibid., p. 224.

# 2

# Paul's Theological Assumptions for Mission

The Jews were not as philosophical as the Greeks. The Jews tended to look at the world in a much more practical way. They believed strongly in divine revelation, of course, but the manner in which Yahweh had revealed himself was through mighty acts and ethical demands, rather than through ideas or a speculative mysticism. A living, moving history and a special, select people were central to all that the Jew understood and taught about God. Theology was not thought out so much as it was lived out. Paul had to build on the situation created by Jesus' last days with his own disciples. Paul had not been part of that intimate group, but his teaching began with the facts of that very recent history during which the disciples lived with Jesus.

It would be accurate to say that Jesus' disciples had a faith but not a theology, and, in the same way, that they were a fellowship but not a church.[1] The disciples not only had the dynamic tradition of their God and their nation Israel but also had, beyond other Jews, the precious memory of Jesus, his word, and his work. Their faith had survived the shock of his death. Their fellowship no longer rested simply on a past relationship with Jesus but on a future hope, based on his living presence through the gift of the Holy Spirit, and on mutual ties of love.[2] Organized thought and systematic teaching were scant, but there was developing, nevertheless, the beginning of a Christian theology within this amazing group. Theology has always been the attempt on the part of the church to interpret the meaning of faith in life, and to answer the questions raised by that faith by using the thought current in that particular time and place. Quite soon after Pentecost, questions touching various issues clearly had arisen.

1. Judaism was the basic theology. The disciples thought of themselves as Israelites in every respect. Olaf Moe states that "they did not as yet have any idea of expanding their missionary message beyond the limits of God's chosen people." *The Apostle Paul: His Life and Work,* L. A. Vigness, trans. (Minneapolis: Augsburg, 1950), p. 93.

2. H. F. Rall, *According to Paul* (New York: Charles Scribner's Sons, 1945), p. 3.

> These questions concerned their leader. Why did Christ need to die? What was the significance of the resurrection? What of His relation to God and their relation to Him and His work in the future? There were questions that were pressed upon them as Jews. What was the relation of the new and the old, of the Christian fellowship to the old Israel, of the new way to the laws and practices of the old?[3]

A true search for Christian theology was launched in the interchange between Paul the man and the group of early believers that had been touched by his ministry. In one way or another, nearly all the issues relevant to a theology for Paul's day were dealt with as his letters were written. In that first generation of the church, he saw, perhaps more clearly than any other, the distinctive meaning of the new faith and how the fundamental structures of the universal Christian religion would be formulated. His writing touches on widespread categories such as God, man, the nature of sin, salvation, the Christian walk, the church, the sacraments, and the last things. Paul can be seen from many sides, and the way in which one focuses upon Paul's overall approach will greatly influence the way in which one views the *theologian* Paul.[4] My aim here is to highlight the themes that are basic to his thought, and that underlie both the missionary purpose of his teaching and the entire mission enterprise.

Paul's mission theology cannot be understood properly unless it is seen as the earliest extension of Judeo-Christian teaching on a large scale outside of Palestine. The legacy of Jesus' teaching is very much the theology of Paul. But the spiritual closeness of Paul to Jesus, through the revitalizing touch of Jesus on Paul's life, influences above all else his thinking about the gospel. This "Christ experience" is preached and taught in a variety of ways and with rich expressions suitable to varied audiences. Adolf Deissmann builds on the relationship of Paul with Jesus in a memorable way when he says that "communion with Christ" best describes how Paul worked out his doctrine of salvation. It is the great assurance of the experience on the Damascus road that becomes the key to truth: "Christ in me," with its corollary, "I in Christ." In fact, faith, in the thinking of Paul, is rooted not so much in events related to the historical Jesus as it is in an experiential relationship. It is a kind of faith that reverberates in him through the spiritual fellowship that he has with Christ.[5]

3. Ibid., pp. 4-5.

4. See the valuable discussion of the main lines of history in Pauline interpretation in Herman N. Ridderbos, *Paul, an Outline of His Theology,* J. R. DeWitt, trans. (Grand Rapids: Eerdmans, 1975), chapter 1, pp. 13-43, and in Ralph P. Martin, *Reconciliation: A Study of Paul's Theology* (Atlanta: John Knox, 1981), pp. 9-31.

5. Deissmann emphasized the Christ-experience or Christ-intimacy (*Christ-Innigkeit*) as the most important aspect of Paul's theology. *Paul,* trans. W. E. Wilson (New York: Doran, 1926), pp. 138-142; 162ff.

In our approach to Paul as the missionary-theologian, the heart of the gospel will always be found to derive from the action of God, through grace, in Paul's life. Salvation is God's "new creation" (II Cor. 5:17, RSV), and Paul's theology is the explanation of this concept expressed through a great variety of similes and metaphors. Most prominent are the terms "justification" (Rom. 4:25; 5:16, RSV), "reconciliation" (II Cor. 5:18; Col. 1:20, RSV), "forgiveness" (Eph. 1:7; Col. 1:14), "redemption" (Rom. 3:24; Eph. 1:7, RSV), and "adoption" (Rom. 8:23; Gal. 4:5, RSV). Each of these must be understood in its context, bearing in mind that Paul always addressed the particular background of the receptors, whether Jew, Greek, or Roman. Much has been made of these metaphors, and they are, indeed, rich in theological substance.[6] But all arise from an experience, subjective yet observable and real, in which everything centers on the reality of the life in Christ. It is from this quite simple testimony of the renewed life in Christ that all other confessions radiate.

The truths that form the very underpinnings of mission are as absolute in our own day as they were in Paul's, and they will be found to be central in the apostle's theology. Paul advanced his teachings principally on five assumptions: God is self-revealing, the gospel is universal, the church is the new people of God, there is freedom in Christ, and salvation is wholeness for all of life.

## The Self-revelation of God

Paul, the gospel messenger, saw no need to begin his discourse with philosophical proofs for God. First of all, that would have been unthinkable for a Jew who loved the history of God's dealings with his nation Israel. Paul was one of the "natural branches" to whom belonged "the sonship, the glory, the covenants, the giving of the law, the worship, and the promises" (Rom. 9:4, RSV). What Paul already knew about God fitted perfectly into the message of Christ, for God always had taken the initiative and always revealed himself by his direct intervention into history, as well as through the sacred Scriptures. On the first missionary journey Luke records an incident at Lystra, where Paul and Barnabas were mistaken for Zeus and Hermes (Acts 14:12). What could have been more "pagan" than that motley gathering?

> A confusion of shrieking voices rises above the crowd. Perhaps a cripple is standing, swinging his crutches high in the air. The priests of Zeus were

6. For example, justification, reconciliation, and liberation—all metaphorical terms to Paul, depending on the context—have become filled with specific theological meaning.

> already being told about the divine appearance and a procession with flute players and two sacrificial steers was on the way to the shrine of Zeus at the city gate.[7]

Barnabas and Paul, sensing the misunderstanding, rushed out into the crowd. What followed in their speech to the Lystrans not only clarified their identify, but also gave a sure word concerning the Christian God, the living God who has never left himself without a witness (Acts 14:17). Is anything more basic to the mission of God in the world than this?

I shall never forget the surprise and the embarrassment I felt in Nigeria when teaching in a lay training school. I had worked out all the rational proofs for the existence of God, struggled with the language in translating them, and was feeling the burden of trying to get these African men to understand. One of the men interrupted me in the middle of a lecture and asked, disarmingly, "Why have you worked so hard to convince us about something we already believe? We would be more interested as to why your people should even think that God does not exist." God's revelation of himself through nature and in the consciences of persons is axiomatic to missions (Rom. 1:19-20). For it is through this self-disclosure that we understand God to be one, a God who is Lord, and a God who takes the initiative.

### *God Reveals Himself As One*

To Paul, mission was founded on a fact that is the bedrock of Jewish belief: the self-revealing God is Yahweh, and he is one. There is no other God beside him. All other gods are false gods. It was this intolerant monotheism that set the Jewish religion apart from all other religions.[8] In this matter of the oneness of God, Paul's faith was intensely Judaistic. Paul could not even imagine another God; "even if there are so-called 'gods,' whether in heaven or on earth . . . [,]" in fact "there is for us only one God, the Father, who is the Creator of all things and for whom we live" (I Cor. 8:5-6). This was the message for all peoples and cultures, for if there is but one God, then he is the God of all peoples. The unity of God is no speculative, academic issue. The rhetorical question is the true mission question, "Is God the God of the Jews only? Is he not the God of the Gentiles also? Of course he is. God is one" (Rom. 3:29-30; cf. 10:12). Indeed, God, this God,

7. Joseph Holzner, *St. Paul the Apostle: His Life and Times,* William J. Doheny, CSC, trans. and rev. (Vatican City: Private distribution, 1978), p. 142.

8. "In that Israel's faith not only commanded the exclusion of the gods from Israel, but also deprived them of all function and powers in the universe as non-entities, it certainly deserves to be called a monotheism." John Bright, *The Kingdom of God* (Nashville: Abingdon, 1953), p. 25. See also the discussion by H. H. Rowley, *The Faith of Israel* (London: SCM, 1965), pp. 71ff.

is the one God and Father of us all who is above all and through all and in all (Rom. 11:36; Eph. 4:6). Paul rediscovered the true universalism that God had planted into the history of Judaism. The patriarchal story of Abraham has a sharp missionary perspective: "Through you I will bless all the nations" (Gen. 12:3).

To insist on God's revelation of himself as one was pure Judaism. But, beyond that, Paul's dedication to the whole world was also rooted in this conviction. "Were there no other motivation, belief in one God, who is thereby the God of all men, lays on the church an inescapable obligation to mission," says Donald G. Miller.[9] Our message to those who worship the gods of traditional religions is that this *is* the God whom they are seeking and who is the real and only God. Even though they do not comprehend it, this is the true object of their worship.

### *God Reveals Himself As Lord*

This oneness of God carries a second aspect of his self-revelation. Because there is but one true God, by that fact alone he has the right to rule in men's lives. Paul made this clear in writing to the Corinthians when he said that because God is the one Father who is the source of all things, so Jesus Christ, whom he sent, has the right to lordship, for it is he "through whom all things were created and through whom we live" (I Cor. 8:6).

The theme of God's lordship, beginning with creation and continuing through redemption in Christ, provides a solid theological basis for mission.[10] The very force of his name, Yahweh, "the one who is and who causes to be what comes into existence,"[11] brings men everywhere under his right to rule. All that is belongs to him. "Nature exists to serve his purposes. Man is a creature made to live under the loving rule of his creator."[12]

The matter of lordship is settled, it would appear, by creation; yet this theme is further developed in Paul's insistence on the right of God's Son to rule. Jesus' claim to lordship extends over both the lives of people and the world in which they live (Rom. 14:9, 11; I Cor. 8:6). Jesus Christ is given a place in Paul's teaching that incontestably raises him above all other loyalties. Conversion, Paul shows, is to "confess that Jesus is Lord" (Rom. 10:9). This is what it means to follow in the new way. How could it be otherwise? "For

9. "Pauline Motives for the Christian Mission," in *The Theology of the Christian Mission,* G. H. Anderson, ed. (New York: McGraw-Hill, 1961), p. 74.

10. Yahweh reveals himself as the God of grace and mercy (Exod. 3:7-8; Isa. 43:1), yet at the same time reserves the right to be Lord and rule over all peoples, both the elect nation of Israel and those outside (Exod. 12:12).

11. W. F. Albright makes this observation in *From the Stone Age to Christianity* (Baltimore: Johns Hopkins, 1940), pp. 197-198. See also Bright, *The Kingdom of God,* p. 25.

12. Miller, "Pauline Motives," p. 75.

through him [Jesus] God created everything in heaven and on earth, the seen and the unseen things, including spiritual powers, lords, rulers, and authorities. God created the whole universe through him and for him" (Col. 1:16). All rebellion against God's will, therefore, and all indifference to the claims of his love made known in Christ constitute a challenge to his rightful lordship. There can be no truce between the kingdom of Christ and alien forces. It is Christ's purpose to subdue all enmity against God, to "overcome all spiritual rulers, authorities, and powers," including death, so that "God will rule completely over all" (I Cor. 15:24, 28).

Accepting Jesus' lordship does not mean imitating Western churches or making superficial changes. This acceptance is not conformity to the ways of Western missionaries or to the lifestyle of any preacher of the gospel. It is not imitation of a foreign mission board or denomination, or the outward appearance of some kind of model church. Turning from darkness to light (Acts 26:18; I Thess. 1:9), in whatever human situation, is accepting the right of the one true God to rule one's life. The inner truths of a culture, including values and world view, must progressively be brought into conformity with the highest and the best that God has intended for a given people. Allegiance to God through his Son Jesus Christ is the ground of the new life for every individual, and the means by which the demonic and the sinful in culture are exposed and judged. Mission is witness to that right of God to rule supreme until "all beings in heaven, on earth, and in the world below will fall on their knees, and all will openly proclaim that Jesus Christ is Lord" (Phil. 2:10-11; see also I Cor. 15:24-25; Eph. 1:21).

## The Church As a New People of God

A new way demands a new people who will walk that way. Paul's understanding of this new community of believers is a departure from anything the Jews had ever known. The passing of the old age of Israel and the formation of a "new Israel" are what Paul believed and taught. This teaching was a thorn in the side of orthodoxy and became the leading theme of Paul's message to the Gentile world. Paul could not have carried on his ministry without this conviction. His theology of the church declared that the true Israel of God is now a spiritual fellowship of all those who have faith in Jesus Christ (Gal. 3:26-29). Only one condition of entry is required of all, whether circumcised or not, and that is stated simply in Galatians 3:29: "If you belong to Christ, then you are the descendents of Abraham and will receive what God has promised."[13]

13. This represents a break with classical Judaism that put Paul at odds with the tradition of his own people, that is, only the Jews belonged to God. See Lucien Cerfaux's treatment of

There is no other way to understand the idea of the election of Israel by Jehovah God than to see it as a call to serve the nations. That the election of Israel is for service is a strong theme in the writings of my colleague Arthur F. Glasser. It was to bless the nations that "God chose a particular people . . . and commenced to prepare them for this task." The biblical sequence is always "election, redemption, revelation, and discipleship."[14] When God established the covenant with Abraham —"through you I will bless all nations" (Gen. 12:3)—he pointed far ahead in time to the redemptive purpose of God that would one day culminate in the coming of Jesus Christ, the son of David and of Abraham (Matt. 1:1). The "election" was not to glorify the line of Abraham after the "flesh," nor was it to honor the people of natural descent. Rather, election was a holy, divine work built upon a sacred promise that included all nations and that would be fulfilled by the power of God's Spirit.[15] Therefore, the call and the response of Abraham form a basic missionary mandate in biblical history, and the role of the Jews in fulfillment of that call is a basic biblical principle.[16] The true mission of Israel is best seen in the work of Christ, who came to bring all people together as one new family in himself. "If you belong to Christ, then you are the descendants of Abraham and will receive what God has promised" (Gal. 3:29). The promise, Paul declares, is "also to those who believe as Abraham did. For Abraham is the spiritual father of us all" (Rom. 4:16). Hence, the new definition of the church as the people of God is not based on natural, national, or ceremonial prerequisites, but includes all who are of Christ and share in the gifts of the Spirit.

> He is not a Jew who is one outwardly, and that may not be called circumcision which takes place in the flesh; but he is a Jew who is one in secret and circumcision is that which takes place in the heart by the Spirit, not by the letter.[17]

The new people are, in fact, the true Israel of God, but "it does not matter at all whether or not one is circumcised; what does matter is being a new creature" (Gal. 6:15). The new people, created as a new thing out of the old (Eph. 2:12-15), are described as the *ekklesia* ("church"). This is a term that reaches back in history, carrying the double import of a purpose that

---

"God's People in the Old Testament," in *The Church in the Theology of St. Paul* (New York: Herder and Herder, 1959), pp. 9-48.

14. Arthur F. Glasser, "Mission and Cultural Environment," in *Toward a Theology for the Future,* C. Pinnock and D. Wells, eds. (Carol Stream, IL: Creation House, 1971), pp. 301-302.

15. Ridderbos, *Paul,* pp. 341ff.

16. Ferdinand Hahn, *Mission in the New Testament,* Studies in Biblical Theology, no. 47 (London: SCM, 1963), pp. 89-90.

17. Ridderbos, *Paul,* p. 334.

began with the nation Israel and continues in the fact that God is creating for himself a new people upon the earth, a people fitted for fellowship with Him. The richest metaphor used by Paul to describe the character of the church is that of the body of Christ (Eph. 1:22-23; Col. 1:24). The most important aspect taught by the use of this term *body of Christ* is that of organic wholeness (Rom. 12:5; I Cor. 12:13, 27). The church, as Paul saw it, is not like anything else known before. It is a fellowship, a community that shares a common life. "It is not a mere sum of individuals, each separately joined by faith to God. There is a unified life which no individual by himself can fully express."[18]

Mission, as far as the church is concerned, is built on the fact that all peoples are potentially one in Christ. This body is not divided by history, language, or culture but exists, as no community ever has before, to express the will of its Head in concrete terms, and to give continuous incarnate expression to the will of God in Jesus Christ.

## The Gospel Is Universal

This church, as a new people of God who respond from every culture, is predicated on the fact that the gospel is for all, and reaches into every place. It could not be stated more clearly than in Paul's own words, when he said that the gospel is "God's power to save *all who believe,* first the Jews and also the Gentiles" (Rom. 1:16; italics added). In his great missionary appeal to the Roman church he reminded the believers that "everyone who calls out to the Lord for help will be saved" (Rom. 10:13), and this is because "God has revealed his grace for the salvation of all mankind" (Titus 2:11). The grace that is the very heart of the gospel "has been preached to everybody in the world" (Col. 1:23). It simply never occurred to Paul that the gospel is not for everyone. Christ died for everyone in every place.[19]

This conviction is inseparable from Paul's theology and affects his thinking in a variety of ways. It enables him to counter the mistaken idea that the Jews had: that the doorway to salvation for Gentiles was circumcision. I have already shown that it was the mission of Israel to make the Lord known among the nations. But even among those Jews who accepted this mission, keeping the whole law was essential. Here is the radical difference between Jewish ideas of universalism and the understanding of Paul.[20] This spiritual fellowship of believers in Christ had no racial or religious limitations.

18. Rall, *According to Paul,* p. 155. The Holy Spirit cements this fellowship together and energizes its life (I Cor. 12:12; II Cor. 13:14; Eph. 2:22).

19. See also Romans 5:18; I Timothy 2:4; Titus 2:11.

20. A broad universalism in Judaism was not uncommon in the prophets (especially

### *Grace and Apostleship*

It is difficult to separate the grace of God given to Paul at his conversion from the "call" into service. The conversion and the call are so much a part of each other, so nearly a single event, that they must be taken together to be properly understood. The risen Christ wanted this "chosen vessel" to carry his name before Gentiles, kings, and the sons of Israel (Acts 9:15). It was by God's sovereign will that Paul was called into the apostolic group just as Christ called the twelve disciples. This was an absolute and immovable conviction with Paul. Quite simply, Paul accepted that the vision of the risen Lord made him the full equal of the twelve.[21] At Corinth, when doubt was thrown against Paul's rights as an apostle, he delivered a heated defense of his authority. It is no accident that the very essence of the gospel is linked with his right to apostleship. In I Corinthians 15:3-9 (italics added) he summarized his defense:

> I passed on to you what I received, which is of the greatest importance: that Christ died for our sins, as written in the Scriptures; that he was buried and that he was raised to life three days later, as written in the Scriptures; that he appeared to Peter and then to all twelve apostles. . . . Then he appeared to James, and afterward to all apostles. Last of all *he appeared also to me*—even though I am like someone whose birth was abnormal. For I am the least of all the apostles.

The grace given to Paul and the mandate to testify of this grace go together. He speaks in Romans 1:5 (RSV) of special "grace and apostleship" to bring about obedience to the faith. Paul's concept of apostleship was characterized by the fact that his conversion carried the irreversible responsibility to witness. For Paul it was a special gift that he was commissioned for a special ministry (to the Gentiles).[22]

But the point for mission theology is this: just as God has shown his reconciling grace through Christ and has taken the initiative in man's

---

Isaiah) and in the psalms. Jewish proselytism attempted to Judaize the Gentiles in this spirit, but this would not result in "full privilege of the chosen people." See James McKinnon, *The Gospel in the Early Church* (New York: Longmans, Green, 1933), pp. 124-132; also Kaufmann Kohler, *Jewish Theology* (New York: Macmillan, 1918), pp. 332ff.

21. The resurrection appearance of Christ to the apostles reviewed the first call he made to them in Galilee. This second postresurrection call is more decisive than the first and Paul had full rights in this call from the risen Lord. See the discussion by Cerfaux in *The Spiritual Journey of St. Paul*, J. C. Guinness, trans. (New York: Sheed and Ward, 1968), pp. 23ff.

22. Hahn notes that Paul is conscious that however much equality there may be among apostles, "his apostolic office is different from that of the people who were apostles before him." *Mission in the New Testament*, pp. 82-83. On the use of the word *gift*, see Romans 15:15; I Corinthians 3:10; Galatians 2:9.

redemption, so those who experience reconciliation through this grace must, in turn, become messengers of grace to the unredeemed. "God, . . . through Christ reconciled us to himself and gave us the ministry of reconciliation . . . God was in Christ reconciling the world to himself. . . . *So we* are ambassadors for Christ, God making his appeal through us" (II Cor. 5:18-20, RSV; italics added). The importance of the transitional words "so we" is that the same ministry, the same mandate that God entrusted to Christ is given to the people who have been reconciled. Grace is the message and apostleship is the means. In mission, these are inseparable. Through Jesus Christ, our Lord, Paul says, "God gave me the privilege of being an apostle . . . in order to lead *people of all nations* to believe and obey" (Rom. 1:5; italics added; cf. 15:15-16). The apostolic office meant a commissioning for service from which it proved impossible for Paul to withdraw.[23] The preaching of the gospel was an absolute necessity (I Cor. 9:16); this is the natural, immediate response to grace.

### *Paul's Mission to the Gentiles*

To break the chains of ethnocentrism, to cross cultural barriers, and to live openly and creatively with people who are "different" is a serious, risky task for anyone, even in our own day. For Paul, the Jew, it was a defiant, almost traitorous act that he should identify himself as "an apostle to the Gentiles" (Rom. 11:13).[24] He spoke of the Jews as having been "broken off" the tree that had grown from Abraham's roots, and the Gentiles as those who had been "grafted in" as wild shoots (Rom. 11:17). But this, Paul's special ministry, was in the mind of God from the beginning, for as Paul said, "God . . . chose me even before I was born, and called me to serve him. . . . he decided to reveal his Son to me, so that I might preach the Good News about him to the Gentiles" (Gal. 1:15-16). The distinctive mark of Paul's apostleship was that the gospel was for the Gentiles, and while he claimed equality with the other disciples, he was convinced of the uniqueness of his own calling. It was something different from that of any apostle before him. His commission was to serve among the Gentiles. This was his first and highest credential, so that he could state without equivocation to the Romans, "I am an apostle to the Gentiles" (11:13). The grace already referred to was the "privilege of taking to the Gentiles the Good News about the infinite riches of Christ" (Eph. 3:8).[25]

23. Ibid., pp. 83-84. See Paul Minear, "Gratitude and Mission in the Epistle to the Romans," in *Basileia*, Jan Hermelink and Hans Jochen Margull, eds. (Stuttgart: Evangelische Missionsverlag, 1959), pp. 42-48. "To the extent that Paul was indebted to God for his call, to that very extent he was indebted to those Gentiles for whose sake God had called him," p. 44.

24. See also Acts 18:6; 22:21; 26:17; Romans 1:13-14; Galatians 2:2, 8.

25. See also Acts 9:15; Romans 15:15-21; Galatians 1:16.

This was not the easy way. The attitude of the Jews toward Paul in his own day ranged from suspicion to outright rejection and militant action. Reading about Paul in the writings of the late Rabbi Joseph Klausner gives a general impression of what might have been the attitude of the Jews in Paul's day. He points out that there is nothing easier than preaching to the Jews when one is a Jew and that Paul always found the Jewish community first. But since Paul was not successful with the Jews he turned to the pagans, "because his message was more acceptable to them." Klausner sums up Paul's "pagan-oriented message":

> The Messiah who was crucified and arose from the dead is the sinless Son of God who died of His own good-will in order to atone, by His blood, for the sins of the world. By this means, the world was redeemed from sin so that there is no longer any need to observe the ceremonial laws for the purpose of making one's self worthy for earthly life. It is sufficient only to believe in the Messiah who will shortly appear at the right hand of God to judge all people, and to gain the privileges of eternal life and the kingdom of heaven for those believing in Him.[26]

This, we might say, is an accurate summary of Paul's gospel, but, speaking again as a Jew, Klausner notes that these teachings represent a world view that would be completely foreign to a Palestinian Jew. At the most, some of the Hellenized Jews would be receptive to this message, because this group had allowed the mixing-in of "half-pagan ideas from their gentile neighbors. The effect was one of weakening fundamental Judaism." Paul understood that his ministry to the Gentiles would mean an open break with Judaism. He did not purposely antagonize his own people, but his gospel with its universal content and appeal was not to be compromised or watered down. His most serious charges were leveled against his own people who wanted to change the message of a free salvation and return it to bondage.

The people outside of Judaism long had been considered by Jews as having only an indirect relationship with God. Paul came to understand, perhaps during his years in Arabia (Gal. 1:17), that this notion was incompatible with his call to proclaim the gospel to the Gentiles. He resisted the institutional demands of Judaism and opened himself to a new concept. It was basic to his ministry that the Gentiles be seen as living in direct contact with God's actions. They *could* understand him, know him, and enter into relationship with him. In the same way, their guilt and rebellion brought them to common ground with the Jews. They were equally under God's judgment.[27]

26. *From Jesus to Paul,* W. F. Stinespring, trans. (New York: Macmillan, 1944), p. 354.

27. The *ethnē* concept in primitive Christianity was first clearly thought out and precisely defined by Paul. Early Christians, in the main, took over from Judaism the traditional concept

Paul's courage and consistent confrontation with the Jerusalem "system" is something that needs to be remembered today. To live and minister among peoples who perceive reality differently and who follow an ethic based on their own culture demands a very different kind of sensitivity and style from that required of the home missionary. The shackles of ethnocentrism and the myopia of monocultural values have to be confronted squarely and with determination. That there was a gospel for the Gentile world must mean that God communicates with people precisely where they are, and can transform individual lives and, in time, culture itself. The missionary will have to break away from the idea that God has revealed himself in a unique or an absolute way through the Western church or, even more narrowly, through a particular denomination or tradition. That the gospel is for the Gentiles means any church or institution that plans for mission must remember this: Mission is not the extension of the church as an institution or the reproduction of visible structures. It is the receiving of the Word by the people as they are, where they are, for the redemption of unfulfilled lives and the transformation of demonic systems.

### *Paul's Mission to the World*

In Mark's version of the Great Commission, Jesus is recorded as saying: "Go into all the world and preach the gospel to the whole creation."[28] It is this term "creation" (*cosmos*) that opens up the widest meaning to the mission of grace. Not only the people and the nations (*ethnē*), but also all of creation, are subject to the power of the gospel. The spirits, good and bad, and powers that are at work in the world are likewise subject to transformation. In Paul's sermon to the Athenians, he spoke of "God, who made the world (*cosmos*) and everything in it" (Acts 17:24). And Paul went on to say that "he will judge the whole world with justice" (v. 31). This world, the whole of the *cosmos,* is the object of God's saving work. Not only did Jesus come into the world to save sinful men and women (I Tim. 1:15), but also the world itself is the object of God's reconciling grace (II Cor. 5:19).

It is important to understand the comprehensive way in which Paul uses the word *cosmos.* He views it from at least five perspectives in his writings, and each helps us to grasp the completeness of mission.[29] G. E. Ladd gives a helpful summary of the varied dimensions of the use of the term. It refers to

---

that the people outside Israel are only indirectly in contact with God's actions. See Hahn, *Mission in the New Testament,* pp. 86-87, n. 1.

28. Mark 16:15 (RSV). Some ancient texts do not include this verse, as they end with Mark 16:8.

29. G. E. Ladd, *A Theology of the New Testament* (Grand Rapids: Eerdmans, 1974), pp. 397-399.

the universe—the totality of all that exists.[30] Paul also uses *cosmos* to refer to the inhabited earth, the dwelling place of man, the scene of history. The references are numerous and illuminating on this point.[31] Further, *cosmos* is used of mankind, of people, and of the totality of human society that inhabits the earth. Here are all levels of humanity, and one reference to the "world" (I Cor. 4:9) includes both men and angels.[32] Again, mankind is seen as having fallen into a hostile and rebellious state so that the "world" is sinful and evil. When it is stated that the Gentiles "followed the world's evil way" (Eph. 2:2), it is the profane and secular "age" that is basically against God that Paul has in mind.[33] Finally, the broadest use of *cosmos* includes man, earthly relationships, and the totality of human activity. "It is not merely the world of men but the worldly system and the complex of relationships that have been created by men."[34] This would refer to social and economic structures that control mankind.

"The world" is not sinful in and of itself. It is of an order, however, that does not naturally cause man to seek or to worship the Creator. "Worldliness," therefore, is entanglement with things that draw mankind away from God and that foster pride on the human level, rather than acknowledgment and exaltation of the Creator.[35]

It is difficult to separate culture, as we understand it in modern anthropology, from Paul's concept of "the world." Paul's use of the term *world* is so all-encompassing that it may be said to include culture, yet at the same time the meaning extends beyond culture and surrounds it. More than a century ago, E. B. Tylor spoke of culture as "the total non-biologically transmitted heritage of man."[36] This would mean, then, that the institutions of society, the characteristics of behavior, the artifacts, the supportive myths and symbols that are the heritage of any people, all have to do with "culture." When Paul spoke of the "world" as the systems and the structures created by men, and the interaction between peoples who inhabit the earth, there is a near identity of "culture" with the "world." However, there is also a very real sense in which the *cosmos* goes beyond this technical, limited idea of culture to include the existence of what Paul variously calls "principalities," "authorities," and "dominions." These realities, while difficult to translate meaningfully into the language of our day, are forces that are common to all

30. Romans 1:20; I Corinthians 3:22; 8:4-5; Ephesians 1:4.

31. Romans 1:8; 4:13; I Corinthians 5:10; Ephesians 2:2; Colossians 1:16; I Timothy 6:7.

32. Romans 3:6, 19; 11:5; I Corinthians 4:9; II Corinthians 1:12; 5:19.

33. I Corinthians 1:20ff.; 2:12; 3:19; Galatians 4:3; Ephesians 2:2; Colossians 2:8.

34. Ladd, *Theology of the New Testament,* p. 399. See I Corinthians 7:29-31.

35. Ibid., p. 400.

36. See Clyde Kluckhohn and Alfred L. Kroeber, *Culture: A Critical Review of Concepts and Definition* (New York: Vintage, 1952), for a full discussion of the various uses of the term *culture.*

cultures. "Powers," as they are generally referred to, are usually seen as demonic, because they establish their rule over human life outside of Christ.[37] For example, the "rulers of this age" (*archontōn;* I Cor. 2:8, RSV) are not men as such, but are those powers that lie behind men and can cause them to rebel against God. The totality of life is what Paul has in mind when he speaks of "the world." This designation cannot be understood apart from culture, yet it includes those entities that transcend culture and that are common to men everywhere.

We cannot really speak of the transformation of persons without speaking also of the potential transformation of their world, including their cultures. Charles H. Kraft, in *Christianity in Culture,* draws heavily on the thesis that God not only is above culture,[38] but also that he is using culture (and we may say "the world") to interact with mankind and to convey His message.[39] But it was also the conviction of Paul that God is working to change, however slowly, this raw and unredeemed "world." Transformation will not be completed until that day of days when the "angelic rulers and powers in the heavenly world . . . learn of his wisdom" (Eph. 3:10). Yet when Paul declared that the work of reconciliation encompasses "the world" (II Cor. 5:19), he was saying that God through Christ can change cultures where they are wrong and transform evil systems here, in the present. We believe with Paul that when human beings are touched by God's grace, the concerted power generated by transformed lives will affect the world for good. Kraft speaks of this from the cultural point of view:

> When individual transformations take place, they lead to changes both in the individual's use of the culture and the structuring itself in terms of which the person lives. When groups of people undergo such transformation, more pervasive changes may be made both in use and in structuring. When such tranformation takes place as a result of a relationship with God, we may speak of the influence of God on culture change.[40]

The history of missions is filled with miracles of redeemed people who, in time, have actually seen their own systems change.[41] There are well-known

37. The "powers" as a Pauline theme are best handled by Hendrikus Berkhof in *Christ and the Powers,* J. H. Yoder, trans. (Scottdale, PA: Herald Press, 1966), p. 62. See Romans 8:38; I Corinthians 15:24-26; Galatians 4:3, 9; Ephesians 1:21; 2:1-2; 3:10; 6:12.

38. As in H. R. Neibuhr, *Christ and Culture* (New York: Harper, 1956).

39. Kraft works with the concept of "Christian transformational change." He sees this as a biblical and historical principle that takes place over a period of time, developing from the center (world view) to the whole of the culture. See "Transforming Culture with God" in *Christianity and Culture* (Maryknoll, NY: Orbis Books, 1979), pp. 345-359.

40. Ibid., p. 114.

41. The excellent book by Alan R. Tippett, *Solomon Island Christianity: A Study in Growth and Obstruction,* Applied Cultural Anthropology series (1967; reprint ed. Pasadena, CA: William Carey Library, 1975), is unique as a study of growth and transformation.

records of people who have been transformed by the gospel, and have been led into new practices that conform to Christian truth and the Christian ethic and whose institutions of society, politics, and family have been altered in one or two generations. Is there anything more exciting, for example, than the story of a whole nation on the island of Fiji, which in less than one hundred years turned from primitive cannibalism to a life of quietude and respectful Christian living? On the other hand, evils have persisted even in the name of Christianity. Oppression of peoples, racism, authoritarianism, and poverty all are well known in nations that are officially "Christian."

But all of this is no reflection on the power and the adequacy of the gospel to redeem the world. The problem is found, rather, in the pride and the sinfulness of humankind. Odious systemic evils will be dealt with, and change will come, even here. The struggle is severe and real, but the issue is at no time in doubt. John Bright concludes *The Kingdom of God* with these sure words: "The battle has already been won at Calvary by him who in his sacrifice had taken men out of every nation and made them into the true people of God . . . the powers of evil simply cannot win, they have already been broken."[42] Paul's victorious words to the Colossians are that Christ has "freed himself from the power of the spiritual rulers and authorities; he made a public spectacle of them by leading them as captives in his victory procession" (2:15).

## There Is Freedom in Christ

Paul fought for freedom. It is the very spirit of his own life and the main text of his message. The universality of the gospel can never be taught or demonstrated in mission without the concept of freedom. Freedom is the Good Word that peoples of the world everywhere must hear—people who are bound by ties of archaic cultures, held in fear by authoritarian systems, hemmed in by social and economic structures, living in prisons of guilt and in the grip of condemning memories. Here is the universal Good News that sends people from one land and nation into another. Men and women who are free will declare the right to freedom to any and all.

Freedom for Paul was not a spiritualized or a symbolic idea. It was comprehensive and concrete. It meant freedom from sin and death (Rom. 8:2), freedom from idols (I Thess. 1:9), freedom from the law (Rom. 10:4), freedom in the Spirit of Christ (II Cor. 3:18), freedom, even, for freedom's sake (Gal. 5:1).

That this freedom for new converts should be compromised in any way was utterly repugnant to Paul. No clearer picture of this is given than in

42. P. 241.

Galatians. It was appalling to him that in such a short time the Judaizers could have brought such contention into the young churches that had begun in peace and in the Spirit, so that now they were "like wild animals, hurting and harming each other" (Gal. 5:15). If these enemies had attacked Paul personally, that would have been one thing, but to have robbed recent believers of their greatest possession—freedom—was a heinous act. The converts had prayed and sung spontaneously, had offered prayers and fasting to Christ, and had, no doubt, spoken in various tongues, healed the sick, and worked miracles. Was this exaltant rhythm of the new life to be replaced by the somber chill of the old law? On the question of liberty, the whole substance of Christianity was at stake. It was this freedom that had become the hallmark of the gospel. Without the "freedom we have through our union with Christ Jesus" (Gal. 2:4), Christianity would have become mere external observances like those of the old pagan religions, and little different from Judaism itself.

F. F. Bruce entitled his 1977 volume on Paul *The Apostle of the Free Spirit.*[43] It is a thorough study of Paul that is written in Bruce's exemplary style. The victorious wording of the title is intentional, for by it he has caught the spirit of the man and his teaching. Bruce speaks of Paul's attractive warmth, his intellectual stature, and the "exhilarating release effected by his gospel of redeeming grace and the dynamism with which he propagated that gospel throughout the world."[44] The "exhilarating release" experienced by Paul is the hope he offered to all. Richard N. Longenecker's major study bears the title *Paul, Apostle of Liberty.* This careful work looks at the issue of liberty from its background in Jewish history, contrasting this with the teaching of Paul and the ways in which he practiced liberty among the Christians and in the context of Judaism. "In Christ" is a term that provides the context for so much of Paul's theological and ethical teaching. It is from this experience of being "in Christ" that Longenecker develops his analysis of what Christian freedom means to the individual believer.[45]

Our new relationship to God is that we are made legally free. Above all else it is declared by God that there is freedom from condemnation for those who are in Christ Jesus (Rom. 8:1). So, in a very straightforward way, Paul can declare, "Who will accuse God's chosen people? God himself declares them not guilty! Who then will condemn them?" (Rom. 8:33-34). This freedom has been declared by God, since the Christian has been "redeemed . . . from the curse that the Law brings" (Gal. 3:13), and, what is

43. This was Bruce's original title. He speaks of the American title, *Paul, Apostle of the Heart Set Free,* as a corruption. This is also the book that was most satisfying to him personally. See "A Man of Unchanging Faith," an interview with Bruce, in *Christianity Today,* vol. 24, no. 17 (October 1980), pp. 16-18.

44. *Paul, Apostle of the Heart Set Free* (Grand Rapids: Eerdmans, 1978), p. 15.

45. *Paul, Apostle of Liberty* (Grand Rapids: Baker, 1976), pp. 156-180.

more, the Father has delivered both Gentiles and Jews from the "power of darkness and brought us safe into the kingdom of his dear Son" (Col. 1:13). "This realization of forensic freedom was the cornerstone for Paul's doctrine of liberty."[46]

Second, the new Christian who is "in Christ" has personal liberty. Paul speaks at great length of the liberty that is expressed as freedom from personal sin, freedom from the power and the compulsion of sin (Rom. 3:9). This is the heart of Paul's message and he sounds this note of personal release in many ways. The Christian has died to sin (Rom. 6:2), and the Christian is "set free from sin" (Rom. 6:18, 22; 8:2). For the first time, the person who has chosen to live by the new law of Christ Jesus finds that "to live a new life" (Rom. 6:4) is to be "set . . . free from the law of sin and death" (Rom. 8:2). To be set free from sin is to experience the beginning of a life that leads to sanctification and continues on into eternity (Rom. 6:22). What a contrast to the tyranny of the former life, when the person did not know God and was in bondage to beings that by nature are not gods at all (Gal. 4:8). This personal freedom is experienced as freedom from self, from the law, and from the unseen spiritual forces of evil.[47]

There are also references to social freedom, though these references are less direct and less frequent. The argument in Galatians, although primarily doctrinal and for Jews, nevertheless points to a much wider kind of freedom than simply that of the individual and that which is inward. When Paul says, "My brothers, you were called to be free" (Gal. 5:13), the implications for social liberties are included. Deissmann says that Paul's phrase indicated that the Christian is completely free and is now able to "do the things that he will," since the limitations of the old world have been removed.[48] While this does not mean that all restraints have been thrown aside or that there is no more customary law, still the actions and the relationships of the new person will never be the same. It is wrong to "spiritualize" this liberty by restricting it to the inner man. Freedom touches the body and the mind as well as the spirit. For "if the Son sets you free, then you will be really free" (John 8:36).

## Salvation Is for the Whole Person

Too often the picture we have of Paul is a distortion of one kind or another. We have already mentioned that it is wrong to portray him as the

46. Ibid., p. 171.

47. Ibid., pp. 172-173.

48. Longenecker observes this from Deissmann, *Light from the Ancient East* (Grand Rapids: Baker, 1980), pp. 324-334, in *Paul, Apostle of Liberty,* p. 174, n. 100.

academic theoretician. We are equally wrong when we assume that he is interested simply in the converting of the soul, caring, as it were, only about the spiritual side of people. Looking at Paul carefully, and trying to see him as a person—following him into the complex human situations, catching the nuances of his words—will enable us to discover how pervasive his ministry really was. While motivated by his apostolic call to evangelize, he was never unmindful of the comprehensive make-up of man and the need for a salvation that touches and heals at every level.

### *The New Creation*

The total remaking of people is the way the gospel works. In two places Paul speaks of the new creation. To the Galatians (6:15) he makes it clear that the decisive nature of the new life is not manifested in intensified observance of rites, such as circumcision, but in nothing less than "being a new creature." No expression describes better than II Corinthians 5:17 what salvation really is. Paul says, "When anyone is joined to Christ, he is a new being; the old is gone, the new has come." The Greek words that Paul uses in both instances to describe the new creation (***kainē ktisis***) convey that something dramatic has happened. The meaning is comprehensive and radical. The word *creation* leads us to reflect upon what God had in mind when he created man. Man was a living soul and body; he had a world to relate to, a work to do, an ethic to follow, a partner to live with, and God to glorify. This time the new creation is not only by omnipotence but also, primarily, by grace.[41] It is an all-encompassing renewal, touching every area of the personal life. For, as the old is cast aside, something new takes its place. Paul's conception of the remaking of persons is this massive spiritual change that touches the ethical, the moral, the aesthetic, the physical, and the social.

Paul suggests this wholeness when, in his very early letter to the Thessalonians, he prays that the God who gives us peace will himself "make you holy in every way." He then goes on to ask that "spirit, soul, and body" be kept free from every fault (I Thess. 5:23). The term *body* has wide usage in Paul's letters. It is sometimes used for the whole organism (II Cor. 4:10; Gal. 6:17); in other places it refers to the sexual aspect of life (Rom. 1:24; 4:19; I Cor. 7:4). It can also mean the physical presence of a person (II Cor. 10:10). The words *soul* and *spirit* are used interchangeably, denoting, generally, the human spirit, not as something distinct from the body, but for the more general, natural life of man. Expressions, therefore, such as "soul" and

49. R. C. H. Lenski, *Interpretation of I and II Corinthians* (Columbus: Wartburg, 1946), pp. 1039-1040.

"spirit" are used by Paul to refer to the inner life of man as a way of distinguishing this from the outer, physical aspect.[50]

### *Wholeness in Paul's Ministry*

Unquestionably, the call to work for spiritual conversion had prior claim on Paul's life. But we also have evidence of his sensitivity to physical needs, and of the care he gave to social concerns. He was concerned in natural, almost casual ways, and the record is so matter-of-fact that it would be easy to miss this feature of mission in Paul.

*Physical concerns*

The unforgettable days at Ephesus were some of the most productive of Paul's entire ministry. From the Bible school held in the hall of Tyrannus a concentrated program of witness was launched so that "*all* the people who lived in the province of Asia, . . . heard the word of the Lord" (Acts 19:10; italics added). But along with this, extraordinary miracles were being performed "at the hands of Paul," so that "handkerchiefs and aprons he had used were taken to the sick, and their diseases were driven away, and the evil spirits would go out of them" (Acts 19:12). He personally healed in several other instances, such as the lame man at Lystra (Acts 14:8-10). On his way to Rome he amazed the pagans on Malta by healing the father of the headman of the island of his fever and dysentery. After this, many others on the island were cured by him (Acts 28:8-9). A slave girl at Philippi was controlled by a spirit of divination, and Paul exorcised the demon with obvious good results (Acts 16:16ff.). While Paul preached a long sermon at Troas, Eutychus fell from a high window and lost consciousness or even, as it would appear, died (Acts 20:9).[51] Paul ministered to Eutychus and assured the congregation that he would recover, then returned to the service and continued preaching until daybreak. The reporter of these incidents was one of Paul's closest companions, Luke, who, we can imagine, brought his talents for healing alongside the teaching and the preaching of Paul. Paul taught people to regard their bodies with reverence as the temple of God and the dwelling place of God's Spirit (I Cor. 3:17). The body must be kept pure. It is "not to be used for sexual immorality, but to serve the Lord; and the Lord provides for the body" (I Cor. 6:13). "You do not belong to

50. For a more helpful discussion on "body," "mind," "heart," "soul," and "spirit," and their meaning to both the "outward" and "inward" man, see Ridderbos, *Paul,* pp. 115-121.

51. William Ramsey feels that Luke, as the writer of Acts and a physician, had satisfied himself that Eutychus was, in fact, dead. *St. Paul the Traveller and the Roman Citizen* (1897; reprint ed. Grand Rapids: Baker, 1982), pp. 290-291. F. F. Bruce's comment is that Paul's treatment suggests artificial respiration. *The Book of the Acts,* New International Commentary on the New Testament (Grand Rapids: Eerdmans, 1954), p. 408.

yourselves but to God; he bought you for a price. So use your bodies for God's glory" (I Cor. 6:19-20).

*Psychological and intellectual concerns*

In cultivating the spiritual nature of man, the volitional and emotional aspects of Paul's teaching become apparent. Howard Tillman Kuist takes note of these when he deals with Paul as the model Christian teacher.[52] Kuist shows how Paul speaks of joy throughout the Epistle to the Philippians, and in other places such as I Thessalonians 5:16. Peace is a notable theme,[53] as are love (classically described in I Corinthians 13), sympathy (Rom. 12:15), courage (Acts 27:22, 25, 36), thankfulness (I Thess. 5:18), hopefulness (Rom. 15:13), and confidence (Phil. 1:6). Paul appreciated the aesthetic and emotional response that comes from music: "Teach and instruct one another with all wisdom. Sing psalms, hymns, and sacred songs" (Col. 3:16), and "sing hymns and psalms to the Lord with praise in your hearts" (Eph. 5:19).[54]

The intellectual side was not disregarded. Paul himself gave the model of using his own mind in every way possible, to awaken understanding and to encourage sound judgment and a reasoned response. Strong words in Acts show this side of Paul as he variously "expounded" (28:23, RSV), "exhorted" (20:1, RSV), "disputed" (9:29), "argu[ed]" (19:8-9, RSV), "testifi[ed]" (28:23, RSV), "declar[ed]" (20:20, RSV), "related" (21:19, RSV), and "commend[ed]" (20:32). He directed the minds of young believers toward ennobling and exalted thoughts (Phil. 4:8-9), yet warned against speculation and controversy over what some people wrongly called "knowledge" (I Tim. 6:20; see also 4:7) and called for independent thinking and carefully constructed arguments (see Eph. 5:6; Col. 4:6).

*Social and community concerns*

If Paul is to be faulted for not taking up, directly, the social issues of his day, it must be remembered that Christians in Paul's day were living in a hostile environment. There was no precedent for the convictions held by this new sect. Jesus himself had known the dangers of the new kingdom teaching and the danger of his followers being charged with revolution. He taught them to carry the baggage of the Roman army beyond the compulsory mile (Matt. 5:41) and to pay taxes in a peaceful way (Mark 12:17). So it was with Paul. G. B. Caird observes, "The Christian leaders were aware, also, that they might appear to an outsider to be revolutionaries bent on overturning

52. *The Pedagogy of St. Paul* (New York: Doran, 1925).

53. See Romans 5:1; 8:6; 14:17; 15:13; I Corinthians 7:15; II Corinthians 13:11; Galatians 5:22; Ephesians 2:14-15; Philippians 4:7; I Thessalonians 5:13.

54. Kuist, *The Pedagogy of St. Paul*, p. 73.

the accepted order of society."[55] Yet, in truth, Paul's gospel demanded conformity to a fellowship in which all are one (Gal. 3:28) and that would be known by its tolerance and mutual love (Gal. 5:13-14). How, for example, could slavery long endure if the master, Philemon, is to hear the plea of Paul? He asked that the runaway slave, Onesimus, be received as his, Paul's, "own son" (Philem. 10). Rather than taking action against him in the legal manner, Philemon should now receive Onesimus as a fellow Christian. He is "not just a slave . . . he is a dear brother in Christ" (Philem. 16).[56] This is the true foundation on which society will be put right; without this basis of forgiving, respectful, God-fearing love, all attempts to correct social evils can only fail.

In summary, when Paul uses the term *new creation* he speaks of a radical change in the spiritual life of the individual, and this also means that the church now represents a new era, a new order of things.[57]

When the Spirit begins the transforming work, there is a "putting off" of the former things together with the old self and a "putting on" of the new self. "This is the new being which God, its Creator, is constantly renewing in his own image" (Col. 3:10). This renewed person is to become fully developed, wholesome, and well balanced. Such a person is what Paul describes when he uses the word *mature* (*teleios;* Eph. 4:13).

The soul is not recreated in some separate way from the body and the mind. Nor is the wholeness of a person described by the spiritual aspect of life, as though there are no physical, psychological, cultural, and social needs. The new creation touches all of life and integrates the various components under the lordship of Christ.

In turning to a study of conversion, it is this holism—the redemption and enrichment of every part of life—that we must preach and teach.

55. *The Apostolic Age* (London: Gerald Duckworth, 1955), p. 159.

56. Yet, as Caird states, "Christians had to avoid the charge of tampering with other men's slaves . . . he [Paul] did not dare to lay himself or the church open to the accusations of harbouring a fugitive from justice." Ibid., p. 160.

57. See Ridderbos, *Paul,* p. 224.

*Part Two*

# Conversion

## *Entering the New Life*

# 3

# Conversion and the Experience of Paul

The word *conversion* is much-debated and controversial. The term has been as useful to science as it has been to religion. But the religious connotation of the Latin word *convertere* ("to turn around") is the most well known. The idea of "turning to God" or "turning from one ethnic religion to another" has been with us from the very beginning of the church.

As early as A.D. 600, the term *conversio* already referred not only to the revolution of celestial bodies but also to the "turning of sinful men to God."[1] It is interesting that for all its importance in the New Testament, the word *conversion* is used as a noun only once. This is in Acts 15:3 (RSV), where Luke refers to the "conversion of the Gentiles." Yet the entire ministry of Paul turns on the fact that lives are changed by the living Christ, creating communities of converted people who have broken through the barriers of race, class, and cultural prejudices to form the body of Christ. In a study of conversion we are dealing with what is at once the most important, the most personal, and the most spiritual phenomenon of mission. However, doctrine about conversion is too often misunderstood, misrepresented, or improperly taught.

## What Is Conversion?

To be converted is to manifest an inward yet objective spiritual awakening by which a person comes to terms with God in a radically new way. Conversion refers to an abrupt or a gradual change in which a person's life is redirected, loyalties are revised, and values are reappraised. It does not imply

1. A book that views conversion in a broad way is *Conversion: Perspectives on Personal and Social Transformation,* Walter Conn, ed. (New York: Alba House, 1978). This quote is from John E. Smith, "Concept of Conversion," pp. 51-52.

a complete understanding of the new faith, but marks a beginning. This beginning, which may have resulted from conditioning over a long period of time, initiates a process of transforming, spiritual growth. Conversion is, fundamentally, a decision with regard to God, a basic choice to turn the life in the direction of God. Because conversion is so highly personal and occurs in the particular context of life, it may be impossible for some to identify it with a definite point in their lifetime. On the other hand, conversion may be, as Wayne Oates describes it, "an abrupt change toward an enthusiastic, religious attitude with highly emotional features being conspicuously evident."[2]

In approaching this chapter, we need to be aware of the wide range of ways in which conversion is evidenced in the lives of persons. The people with whom I worked for twenty years in West Africa were, in most cases, turning to Christ from animism. For them conversion was a memorable, emotional, and objective experience of a personal meeting with God. Very few of these people had Christian parents or any previous knowledge of Christian teaching. To hear the account of conversion experiences and to see and feel the excitement of people responding to the powerful call of God upon their lives is still the most fulfilling memory of my mission work. Although I would not have wanted to admit it at the time, I went to Nigeria in 1955 with a false notion of my own importance. I imagined that, given enough teaching, and enough of the presence of a Western missionary like myself, these people would, in time, turn to Christ simply because of us. I was wrong, of course. God dealt with them directly and dynamically. How enriching it was to live among people who openly and emotionally recounted their conversion stories and who counted the day they "repented and became a follower" as the greatest event since their physical birth.

Conversion is normative for mission. It is the self-evident, a priori event, however experienced or understood, that both initiates and afterward nurtures the Christian life. In simplest terms, the non-Christian cannot *be* a Christian without *becoming* a Christian. Conversion is *becoming* a Christian. Conversion is entering into the new life. There is no way to describe mission to the non-Christian world without being very candid about this greatest of miracles.

Conversion, as the highest goal of Christian missions, must free itself from the habit of making people over into American or European Christian types. Conversion is not the cloning of the Western missionary. In 1970 a diplomat from Nigeria told me in Washington that he felt mission work was "the last stand of colonialism," and he saw it as his duty to "put it down." He was referring to the way in which becoming a Christian appeared to him to mean membership in a Western-type church and economic and cultural

2. "Conversion," in *Conversion,* p. 150.

dependence on a few missionaries who represented the massive power blocs of Europe and America.

Conversion, as we understand it from Paul, affects people at the deepest level of their personal lives so that it touches, and ultimately redeems, the very essence of culture; it shifts allegiances, forms new loyalties, awakens desire for the highest values in the society, and promotes the gathering of spiritual communities that serve and glorify God. It is this kind of conversion that we seek to rediscover from Paul.

## Conversion and the Jews

Leaving one religion and joining another certainly did not begin with Paul, or even with Jesus and the apostles. What is often overlooked in biblical history is that God intended that his people, Israel, be a community made up not only of the descendants of Abraham but also of any and all others who desired to convert to Judaism. It was a regrettable and, in the end, a fatal shortcoming of the Jews that as a nation they failed to keep their doors open to the outside world. Paul's recovery of a universal gospel put him at odds with his own people. For he saw the ingrownness and the exclusiveness of Jewish history more clearly than any other apostle, including Peter. No wonder he posed the rhetorical question to the Romans, "Is God the God of the Jews only? Is he not the God of the Gentiles also? Of course he is. God is one" (Rom. 3:29-30). That God had to provide a special vision for Peter (Acts 10:9-16) shows how hard it was for him to break through the hardened shell of an exclusive Judaism. With the conversion of Cornelius, Peter could say, "I now realize that it is true that God treats everyone on the same basis" (Acts 10:34). Even so, it was not long before Paul had to rebuke Peter at Antioch for his failure to keep the lines of communication open to the Gentiles (Gal. 2:14).

After the death of Stephen, Philip preached in Samaria, where Simon the magician was converted (Acts 8:13). The Spirit then sent Philip to Gaza, and there the Ethiopian was converted. Like Simon, he was immediately baptized (Acts 8:38). It was as though something completely new had taken place. Yet, since the days of Abraham, it had been explicit that Israel would be the means by which blessing was to come upon all peoples. It was never God's intention that the people of God should be made up exclusively of those born of Abraham. After all, Abraham himself was a "convert" who left his own land, people, and culture to follow a new way. He became the first Jew—a proselyte. Today Jews recite Deuteronomy 26:5 twice each year in synagogue worship to recall that Abraham was not born an Israelite: "And you shall make response before the LORD your God, 'A wandering Aramean was my father; and he went down to Egypt and sojourned there, few in number; and there he became a nation, great, mighty, and populous.'" D. M. Eichhorn, commenting on Jewish ethnic plurality, says, "From the inception of this folk and faith, the religion of Israel was born with and born by converts."[3]

Indeed, Israel did have a mission to the foreign nations and her history was always intermingled with those who were not Jewish born. At the time of the exodus, it is recorded that, in addition to the children of Abraham, a "mixed multitude also went up with them" (Exod. 12:38, RSV). It is well known that, hundreds of years and generations later, among those leaving the captivity of Babylon under Ezra was a great number who had been converted to Judaism during the captivity.[4] There are references to people in the Old Testament who were not born Israelites, but who found a home within Israel and even gained positions of responsibility.[5] The list of the mighty men of David's army contains a number from a variety of non-Israelite tribes (I Chron. 11:46-47). Jacob Salmon Raisin points out that David's entourage included Cretans, Philistines, Itureans, Arameans, and Hittites.[6] When Solomon took a census of all the resident aliens, they were found to number 153,600 (II Chron. 2:17). Many of these were servants, but even they came under the provisions laid down at Sinai that gave strangers the rights and the privileges of true Jews should they be desired. When "all Israel" is referred to in Joshua 8:33 (RSV), further mention is made of "sojourner[s] as well as homeborn." This reference shows, obviously, that those who were not "homeborn" also enjoyed covenant privileges and obligations. "Strangers" and "sojourners" were free to associate very closely with the house of Israel. Even though these varying degrees of affiliation cannot be clearly distinguished, yet we know that, in De Ridder's words, "when the *ger* [stranger] assumed all the group obligations—ethnic, social and religious—he became a full-fledged member of the congregation of Israel and his descendants were legally indistinguishable from other Israelites."[7]

Conversion to Judaism would have entailed at least three assumptions, each important to the meaning of conversion in any age. It would have meant disenchantment or unhappiness with the status quo, willingness to

3. *Conversion to Judaism: History and Analysis* (New York: Ktav, 1966), p. 113.

4. Richard R. De Ridder notes that the term *proselyte* did not really become a religious word until the Babylonian exile, when the Jews became convinced it was their duty to make converts of the strangers (*gerim*) in Babylon. *Discipling the Nations* (1971; reprint ed. Grand Rapids: Baker, 1979), pp. 45, 67.

5. II Samuel 11:3; 24:23; I Chronicles 11:46.

6. *Gentile Reactions to Jewish Ideals* (New York: Philosophical Library, 1953), p. 119; quoted in De Ridder, *Discipling the Nations,* p. 42.

7. *Discipling the Nations,* p. 44. A full treatment of this subject is found in Eichhorn, *Conversion to Judaism,* pp. 33ff.

identify with the new community, and personal acceptance of a new code. This change of religion became very common, especially during the period of the exile. It is the Septuagint of the third century B.C. that gives currency to the term *proselyte.*[8] Conversion to the Jewish religion was validated, in the case of men, by both circumcision and baptism and, for women, by baptism. Images and phrases that were commonly used by Judaism to express such religious change appear also in the New Testament, especially in Paul's writings. Joachim Jeremias has brought these together in a helpful paragraph:

> The Gentile who changes his religion, who previously was far from God, has now come near to Him (Ephesians 2:13; Acts 2:39). He was dead (Ephesians 2:1), lay, in a manner of speaking, in the grave (I Clem. 38:3), and has been raised from the dead (Colossians 3:1). A new creation has taken place (Galatians 6:15; II Corinthians 5:17). Thereby his past is blotted out, he has entered a completely new existence, is like a newborn child (I Peter 2:2), is a νεόφυτος (I Timothy 3:6). All this happened through forgiveness of all his sins being granted to the Gentile on his change of religion (Colossians 2:2). Henceforth he is in holiness (I Thessalonians 3:13).[9]

The terminology of Jewish conversion theology is reflected in references to early Christian baptism and, Jeremias adds, "How powerfully the thought that conversion signified the beginning of a completely new life had penetrated the consciousness of the great mass of the people is proved by the numerous . . . changes of names of proselytes."[10]

The terminology and the concept of conversion go back much further than the beginning of proselyte baptism. The right of the foreigner to turn to the house of Israel for citizenship and privilege was an Old Testament picture of salvation. Such a convert, said the rabbis, was "as a child newly born."[11] He must be treated tenderly because he has "forsaken his family, and his father, and has left behind his people and all the people of the world, and has chosen to come to us [Israel]."[12]

How could Israel have forgotten her mission to the stranger and the sojourner? She had been commanded from the beginning to treat the stranger as a native and to allow him to live under the same law (Lev.

8. De Ridder, *Discipling the Nations,* pp. 45, 67. There are a number of references in the New Testament to Jewish proselytes who afterward became Christians. See Acts 6:15; 13:43.

9. *Infant Baptism in the First Four Centuries,* David Cairns, trans. (Philadelphia: Westminster, 1961), p. 36; quoted in De Ridder, *Discipling the Nations,* p. 100.

10. Quoted in De Ridder, *Discipling the Nations,* p. 100.

11. Joachim Jeremias, *Jerusalem in the Time of Jesus* (London: SCM, 1969), p. 263, commenting on Exodus 12:49. In this volume Jeremias gives careful treatment of the legal rights of the proselytes. See also De Ridder, *Discipling the Nations,* p. 45.

12. Jeremias, *Jerusalem in the Time of Jesus,* p. 263.

24:22). Israel was never to forget that *she* was, at one time, the "stranger," and this fact was to underlie her dealings with others: "Show love for those foreigners, because you were once foreigners in Egypt" (Deut. 10:19). It was Israel's mission to draw the nations to her. Isaiah the prophet saw the temple itself as a symbol of the attraction of the gospel and said, "The mountain where the Temple stands will be the highest one of all. . . . Many nations will come streaming to it, and their people will say, 'Let us go up to the hill of the LORD, to the Temple of Israel's God'" (Isa. 2:2-3).

Jesus was angered because the Jews had turned against the nations, closed the door on the Gentiles, and actually shut them out from their right of access to the precincts of the temple. He therefore began his ministry with strong action against the temple merchants (John 2:13-16) and in so doing dramatically opened the court of the Gentiles, which had been closed to them for so long (John 2:15). At the end of his ministry, once again Jesus cleansed the temple (Mark 11:15-17), reminding the self-centered people of Jerusalem that God had meant the temple to be a "house of prayer for the people of *all nations*" (v. 15; italics added). How prophetic, therefore, his words were when, upon healing the centurion's son, he said, "I assure you that many will come from the east and the west and sit down with Abraham, Isaac, and Jacob at the feast in the Kingdom of heaven" (Matt. 8:11).

While conversion was not a new phenomenon for the Jews, they had disregarded and corrupted it. Now Jesus' own body became the new symbol of the temple—that mountain to which the nations shall flow (Isa. 2:2; John 12:32-33). It is around this new center of faith that the nations will gather.

## Pauline Conversion in the Book of Acts

Earlier the point was made that Paul's conversion greatly influenced his theology. He must have remembered the experience on the Damascus road until his death. One can only imagine how often he retold this story as he journeyed from place to place. We shall look at this miraculous conversion of Paul at close range to see the elements that will be helpful for an understanding of conversion, especially in the mission context.

I do not mean that Paul's conversion should become the model for all others. The situations within which God works to bring about conversion are endless. We must be aware not only of the great variety of places where the gospel word is heard, but also of the important differences among the people who live in those places. Conversion for an upper-class educated woman in the city of Brasilia, for example, will be very different from that for an illiterate woman living in an African village. Because God respects us as persons, conversion is unique to every individual. Even so, there is a striking similarity between Paul's own conversion and the experience of those whose lives were changed by his ministry. We want to look carefully at this in the Book of Acts, with Paul receiving our primary attention, because the dynamic quality of change evidenced in these early converts has very much to do with the success of Paul's churches.[13]

We are asking questions such as: When does conversion take place? Is there a true and a false conversion? How can we know the difference? What is the relative importance of so-called outward signs as compared with the inward manifestations of conversion? What factors do we expect to see in all conversion regardless of culture? Is Paul's experience and that of his converts relevant to mission situations today? These kinds of considerations will be in the background as we consider the accounts given in the Book of Acts. The conversion of Saul will be discussed under three headings, each of which has its special importance for a mission theology of conversion: the prologue to conversion; the encounter (or crisis) in conversion; and the validation of conversion. The chapter will conclude with a summary of the accounts of conversion resulting from the ministry of Paul.

## *The Prologue to Conversion*

No conversion can take place apart from the conditioning influences that bear upon the personal life of the individual. Saul's personal background figures heavily in the conversion event itself as well as in the aftermath of that encounter as it is recorded in Acts 9. In his defense before his own people, as well as before King Agrippa, years after the actual experience, Paul carefully calls attention to the circumstances that led up to his conversion (Acts 22:3-6; 26:9-11). In his autobiographical narrative certain features stand out in the account of his pre-Christian days in particular: his training under Gamaliel, his standing as a Pharisee, and his persecution of the Christians. All of these factors illustrate that there is a preconditioning aspect of conversion that is intensely personal and that becomes crucial as God works to bring about the "turning" of a life.

### *The influence of Gamaliel*

Speaking in Hebrew before a Jewish assembly, Paul identified himself with the people of the city of Jerusalem. He said he was "brought up . . . as a student of Gamaliel. . . . [and] received strict instruction in the Law of our

13. The Book of Acts, though written *after* many of the epistles of Paul, seems to have been written quite independently of the Epistles. Even so, we affirm that Acts is a reliable source for Pauline history. See the discussion by G. R. C. Macgregor, who says in summary, "When Luke gives the facts which we cannot check by reference to the Epistles, we may have a corresponding confidence in them." *The Interpreters Bible: The Acts of the Apostles* (New York: Abingdon, 1954), vol. 9, p. 10.

ancestors" (Acts 22:3). In Philippians 3:5-6 he spoke of himself as a Pharisee and said, "As far as a person can be righteous by obeying the commands of the Law, I was without fault." As a pupil of Gamaliel he had been greatly affected by Gamaliel's teachings, while as a Pharisee he had stood out as a powerful upholder of the Jewish law. For example, he could not believe that anyone who negated the law at any point could even be considered as the Messiah.[14]

Gamaliel's reputation carried great weight in the frenzy of events recorded in Acts 5. Peter and the other apostles were standing trial before the Jewish council, which wished to have them killed. At the strategic moment Gamaliel asked to speak. Luke described him as a "teacher of the Law . . . highly respected by all the people" (Acts 5:34). Although a deeply committed Hebrew, Gamaliel was, nevertheless, a broad-minded and wise person. He advised the council, "Do not take any action against these men. Leave them alone! If what they have planned and done is of human origin, it will disappear, but if it comes from God, you cannot possibly defeat them" (Acts 5:38-39). Gamaliel's advice was heeded and the apostles were set free. One who almost certainly would have heard of Gamaliel's action was Saul, his former pupil.[15]

*The relationship of Saul the Pharisee to the Sadducees*

Gamaliel's attitude toward Jesus' followers would not have been so important but for a second factor. As it happened, Saul had to get written authority from the high priest, who was a Sadducee, in order to harass the church. Acts 9:1-2 states that it was to the high priest that he went to ask "for letters of introduction to the synagogues in Damascus, so that if he should find there any followers of the Way of the Lord, he would be able to arrest them, both men and women, and bring them back." The resentment of the Pharisees against the Sadducees is well known. The Sadducees were descendents of the priestly party in Jerusalem that, toward the close of the Greek period of Israel's history, tried very hard to Hellenize the Palestinian Jews. D. Eaton traces the suppression of this attempt during the period of the Maccabees, showing how the Sadducees had developed into a political party that worked for an independent Jewish state that would follow Hellenistic lines.[16] The Pharisees opposed this bitterly, seeing the state as a purely Jewish community. Furthermore, there was a sociological breach between the Pharisees and the Sadducees, in that the Pharisees came mainly from the

14. R. R. Williams, *The Acts of the Apostles* (London: SCM, 1912), pp. 21-22.

15. See W. Gordon Robinson, *The Gospel and the Church in a Pagan World* (London: Independent Press, 1958), p. 31.

16. "Sadducees," *Dictionary of the Bible*, James Hastings, ed. (New York: Scribner, 1963), vol. 4, p. 349.

common people while the Sadducees were of the nobility. Their differences also involved the law and how it was to be administered, as well as doctrinal questions such as the resurrection of the body and punishments.[17]

The Jews had obtained a number of privileges from the Romans, among them the right to manage their own judicial affairs. This jurisdiction was exercised through the synagogue.[18] As already noted, it was from the Sadducean high priest that Saul obtained permission to enter Damascus in order to bring Christians to stand trial before the Sanhedrin. Submission to the Sadducees in this way was for Saul a violation of the principles that he felt deeply as a Pharisee, so he would have been heavy with resentment. Not only had his own respected teacher pointedly stated that "followers of the Way" should be left alone, but also, as a Pharisee, Saul had to fight back his personal dislike for the Sadducees when he sought to obtain the right to persecute the Christians.

### *Hellenism and the death of Stephen*

I have already mentioned that the Sadducees had a historical connection with Hellenism and that the Pharisees, by contrast, found little to commend in the rational temperament of the Sadducees. The first reference to Hellenists in the Book of Acts (chap. 6) introduces us to the story of Stephen, in which a distinction is clearly made between the Hellenists (*tōn Hellēnistōn*) and the Hebrews (*tous Hebraious*). The designations mean Greek-speaking Jews as opposed to Aramaic-speaking Jews. The setting, of course, is Jerusalem, and both the parties include Christian and non-Christian Jews.[19] Acts 6:5 shows Stephen to be one of the seven Hellenists appointed to care for the special interests of Hellenistic Jews. As it turns out, however, the false charges made against Stephen, as well as the style of Stephen's defense, reflect Judeo-Pharisaical thought much more than Hellenistic thought.[20] Stephen vehemently denies speaking against the law, and in so doing he places himself against the Sanhedrin and the rational mode of the Hellenists. B. S. Easton observes,

> Stephen stresses that Palestine is God's Holy Land. Moses is glorified; so marvelous a 'ruler and judge' is he that 'like unto Moses' is a title reserved for Jesus alone, while Moses' law is no less than 'living oracles,' delivered by angels (7:53). Moses was the type of Jesus, for the Jews had continually

17. Ibid., p. 350.

18. R. B. Rackham, *The Acts of the Apostles,* third edition (London: Methuen, 1906), p. 129.

19. H. J. Cadbury, *Beginnings of Christianity,* F. Jackson and K. Lake, eds. (London: Macmillan, 1933), vol. 4, p. 60.

20. C. S. C. Williams, *A Commentary on the Acts of the Apostles* (London: Adam and Charles Black, 1957), p. 100.

> rejected Moses; in 7:51-53 Stephen unmasks his batteries; the Jews of old rejected Moses, those of Stephen's day rejected Moses' successor. If Moses' law was broken, not Stephen but members of the Sanhedrin had broken it![21]

Thus Saul who "approved of his murder" (Acts 8:1) was in a dilemma. As a fierce Hebrew he had rejected all attempts by the Hellenists and the Sanhedrin to downgrade the law. Stephen was counted among the Hellenists, and yet in his defense he took a position that was between that of the Hellenists and Pharisees with regard to the law. Stephen became a victim of the fabrications of traditional Judaism. He built his apologetic on a Judaistic base and members of the Sanhedrin themselves were caught in the charge. To the extent that Saul as a Pharisee realized this, so to this extent his support would have been with Stephen. While the impact of this and of the particular role of Gamaliel may not have been consciously manifest to Paul at the time, such factors cannot be disregarded in considering the kinds of forces that work on a man's conscience.

*On the Damascus road*

It was after the death of Stephen that Saul "tried to destroy the church; going from house to house, he dragged out the believers, both men and women, and threw them into jail" (Acts 8:3). The frenzy with which Saul hunted down the Christians is expressed in Acts 9:1, which speaks of "his violent threats of murder." Tension and guilt had been built up, though perhaps subconsciously. He would not have admitted it, or perhaps even recognized it. For all Paul knew he was the zealous Pharisee simply doing what his convictions commanded. The King James Version has it that Saul was "breathing out threatenings and slaughter against the disciples." H. J. Cadbury noted that the term for breathing (*empneō*) is a special word that is used in Semitic poetry. In Semitic physiology the emotion of anger was connected with breath.[22] Saul was in a highly emotional and angry frame of mind. The journey itself would have further contributed to the crisis that followed.[23]

Paul had come very close to Damascus. He had journeyed across the desert and in his white-hot passion he soon would enter Damascus, all the while violating a growing and disturbing conviction.

The point of the discussion thus far has been to say that Paul was in a vulnerable state of mind and conscience when the living Christ stopped him on the Damascus road. The idea that there were no conditioning factors, that nothing of the events that I have cited figured in his conversion is

21. *The Purpose of Acts* (London: SPCK, 1936), p. 47.
22. *Beginnings of Christianity,* p. 99.
23. R. R. Williams, *The Acts of the Apostles,* p. 85.

unacceptable. F. F. Bruce suggests that when Jesus said, "It hurts you to kick against the goads" (Acts 26:14, RSV), the reference was solely to the compelling presence of the Lord Jesus himself on the Damascus road.[24] But there is more here than that. The "goads" symbolized the prodding and chastening of Paul's own heart that he had been stubbornly resisting. A. T. Robertson comments on "the goads," noting that

> they suggest a struggle in Saul's soul that had been going on for some time. Our ignorance of such a struggle does not controvert the words of Christ on the subject. Saul does not contradict the indictment of Jesus. Saul had failed in the moment of his triumph. Persecution was futile. Saul's state of mind may have been more ready for the capture by Jesus than we know.[25]

Johannes Weiss is convinced that Saul's ideas about Jesus had begun to change even before the experience on the Damascus road. "He must already have been half persuaded," says Weiss, "and plunged into the task of persecution with forced zeal and an uneasy conscience."[26]

A. B. Bruce also defends the view that Saul had much more of a fascination with Jesus than he was ready to admit. Saul, therefore, had secret misgivings as to whether, after all, Stephen might have been right. How else could Paul have written in such vivid detail in Romans 7 concerning the struggle in his own soul and body if he had not experienced it?[27] The description of his preconversion state is ideal biography. It is, as Arthur Holmes says, "neither entirely individual nor wholly universal, but rather his own experience universalized."[28] His bitter reaction against the church is at least a part of what Paul remembered when he wrote,

> My inner being delights in the law of God. But I see a different law at work in my body—a law that fights against the law which my mind approves of. It makes me a prisoner to the law of sin which is at work in my body. What an unhappy man I am! Who will rescue me from this body that is taking me to death? [Rom. 7:22-24]

Robertson agrees that the "very vehemence of Saul's persecution was partly due to the lurking doubt that Jesus might be in truth the Messiah."

24. *Paul, Apostle of the Heart Set Free* (Grand Rapids: Eerdmans, 1978), p. 75.

25. *Epochs in the Life of Paul* (New York: Charles Scribner and Sons, 1916), p. 99. Robertson also notes that the "goad" might also be seen as Saul's struggle with the law from the awakened curse of sin (Rom. 7:9).

26. *Paul and Jesus*, J. J. Chaytor, trans. (London and New York: Harper, 1909), p. 35.

27. "Before Christ appeared *to* him on the way to Damascus he had been revealed *in* him, not yet as an object of faith, but as an object of earnest thought." *St. Paul's Conception of Christianity* (New York: Charles Scribner's, 1894). See pp. 31-37.

28. *The Mind of St. Paul: A Psychological Study* (New York: Macmillan, 1929), p. 39.

Often the man who shouts the loudest his own orthodoxy is a heretic at heart. All that may be needed for crystallization is a jar of the glass. It is one of the causes for gratitude that it was not psychologically impossible for Saul of Tarsus to turn his face in full surrender to Jesus of Nazareth.[29]

*The preparation factor in mission conversion*

I have taken time to deal with this part of Paul's own conversion because it is extremely important in understanding how God works in the process of conversion of individuals and groups. It is this sensitive period when the ground of the heart is being broken for acceptance of Christ that we understand the least. Conversion begins with those first, perhaps almost imperceptible, nuances of change, when even the individual may not realize what God is doing. No one is converted in a vacuum. To move out of "darkness" into "light," to confess Christ as Lord without any factors that condition such a decision is highly unlikely and does not happen in Scripture. Each person within each culture represents a specific situation that God deals with in a unique way. The early stages of change, just as much as the "decision" itself, are mysteriously the work of God's Spirit. The length of time will vary. It may be a matter of hours; in the case of some, it may be years. But the series of events, the circumstances that bring the life, or lives, to a point of decision are crucial. To understand this as the way God works should give confidence to the missionary when, for example, it seems there is little evidence of lives being changed even over a long period of time.

The United Methodist branch of the Sudan United Mission began its evangelistic work among the Wurkum people of northern Nigeria in 1922. The first results were not visible until 1933 when three men, Kura, Kasala, and Ndule, were baptized. Those eleven years of patient labor and witness by a few missionaries were what might be called pre-evangelism.[30] Even the preparation period of those three men would have been seen as conversion by the animistic world in which they lived, because their thinking and their values were slowly being changed. Preparation for conversion, therefore, is very much a part of the conversion process—preceding it yet merging with it—and its importance must be recognized.

Religious change has been the subject of much study by anthropologists. Alan R. Tippett sees the process of conversion following closely the paradigm of any religious change and, as a missiologist, uses the concept to make a valuable application. He sees the process as involving three states: awareness,

29. *Epochs,* p. 50.

30. Pre-evangelization, as Joseph A. Grassi calls it, is the attention given to ideas already held in the culture that best demonstrate the need for the gospel and effectively communicate its truth. See *A World to Win* (New York: Maryknoll Publications, 1965), chapter 10, pp. 107-114. Compare the concepts of "dynamic equivalence" in Charles H. Kraft's *Christianity in Culture* (Maryknoll, NY: Orbis Books, 1979) and "redemptive analogy" in Don Richardson's *Peace Child* (Glendale, CA: Regal, 1974).

decision, and incorporation.[31] This parallels the sequence that in the case of Paul I am calling preparation, encounter, and validation. Since Tippett deals with group conversion, some of the factors that bring about awareness have particular relevance to people who make a group decision to become Christians. The factors that bring pressure on a group, moving its members to religious change, do not have to be strictly "spiritual." They may be natural developments such as education or economic changes. There may be pressures from the outside, such as imposed leaders or military action. There may be internal pressures as well: personal or community crises. I recall how a terrible epidemic of smallpox figured prominently in the turning of one African tribe to Christianity. Christianity presents a new option to the person or the group facing problems and needing solutions. An additional catalyst for change is the Christian advocate, often called the evangelist. The Word of God proclaimed at the right time may quickly move people into decisive conversion. Tippett says,

> Although . . . a situation has to be ripe for change, an agent is frequently involved in bringing about that change. . . . In secular life he may be a salesman or an applied anthropologist. In our context, he may be a preacher, a prophet, a teacher, an evangelist or a witness. . . . What matters is that we have here a convergence of two factors. A situation is ripe for change and here is a man with something specific to say about it. When the situation and the man converge then things are likely to happen."[32]

Paul saw that the role he often had was to be an advocate for change—the preparer of hearts. He said, "I [Paul] planted the seed, Apollos watered the plant, but it was God who made the plant grow" (I Cor. 3:6). And who can speak of the mystery of the preparation for conversion without remembering that in it all is the activity of the Holy Spirit? Conversion at every stage is the work of God. Our work is to see how he moves people toward "a clear-cut encounter, a definite verdict for Christ," as Tippett calls it.[33]

Some will say, especially in mission evangelism, that it is quite possible for a person to turn immediately to Christ without any pre-evangelism, stepping, as it were, out of darkness into light in a decisive, spontaneous way. One of my friends in the Church of Christ describes how he has held services of preaching in public places, such as the village market, where people who responded were led immediately to baptism even though they had never heard the gospel before. I too have participated in evangelistic

31. There is a connecting factor between each stage: realization and encounter. *Verdict Theology in Missionary Theory,* revised edition (Pasadena, CA: William Carey Library, 1973), pp. 122-128. Tippett has since added a fourth stage in change, that of maturation.

32. Ibid., p. 122.

33. Ibid., p. 124.

meetings, large and small, where it seemed that people made a public confession of Christ without any previous contact with the gospel. During the 1960s the New Life for All movement in West Africa was greatly blessed of God in bringing scores of people to accept Jesus Christ.[34] Appearances, at least, would lead one to say that in a number of instances decisions to accept Christ were made immediately. And no one would say that God cannot work in this way if he chooses to do so. Yet in such meetings there was much that the evangelist or the teacher could not see or know. There are always those in any group who are not ready, and there are those whose time has come. Lives and hearts are prepared over longer or shorter periods by personal needs, by direct or indirect teaching, by observation, or by a tender conscience that has become sensitive to God.

The prologue to conversion is the mysterious work of the Holy Spirit, and I contend that this is of first importance for missiology. As good stewards in kingdom work, we must be careful observers of the early signs of the "turning" in individual lives and groups of people and press for that decisive act of faith that saves.

### *The Encounter in Conversion*

What we might speak of as the second stage in Saul's conversion brings him directly into the presence of the living Christ and demands a decision. It is impossible to know precisely when the decision takes place, though this is known to God. Preparation converges with the decision as the human personality and God's grace meet in saving faith. For purposes of study we might say that the encounter in Saul's conversion is described beginning in Acts 9:3b. This might seem to be an arbitrary choice, yet there is a definite change in the mood of the narrative when Luke records that "suddenly a light from the sky flashed around him." Then follow the details of the encounter. Versions of what happened are recorded in Acts 9:3-9 and again in chapters 22 and 26 when Paul makes his defense, first before the council and then before Agrippa. It will be best to study these accounts together, since there is a significant unity among them.

#### *The personal nature of the encounter*

There are no mass movements to Christ in the final sense. Even the more careful term *people movements*[35] has to be qualified to point out that

34. New Life for All, originally organized by the Sudan Interior Mission, soon included nearly every mission and church of northern Nigeria, and is now spread widely throughout Africa. For an assessment of the movement see George W. Peter, *Saturation Evangelism* (Grand Rapids: Zondervan, 1970), pp. 87-126.

35. The term *people movements* was popularized by Donald A. McGavran in *Bridges of*

persons, not groups, come to Christ. Groups that have made decisions to become Christian are well known in mission history, but groups are always made up of individuals who stand before God one by one and who must intelligently confront the meaning of the gospel for their own lives.[36] It is remarkable that in the conversion accounts recorded in Acts each one has a distinctly personal aspect about it that highlights the interaction of a personal God with every person. In the conversion encounter of Saul, three features stand out: the light, the voice, and the dialogue.

*The light* Note that a "light from the sky flashed around him." The word for "flashed around" (*periastraptō*) is not found in classical Greek, and in Scripture it is used exclusively in Acts 9:3 and by Paul himself in recounting this experience (Acts 22:6; 26:13). In Acts 22:6 Paul recalls that the event took place "about midday," when the sun would be at its brightest. Yet the light that flashed around him exceeded the natural light of the sun. The personal nature of this event is further heightened by the fact that the preposition *around* (*peri*), included in the verb, governs the pronoun *me* (referring to Saul). Acts 9:7 tells us that there were other men traveling with Saul, but they were outside of the intention of this miracle.

*The voice* It is next recorded (Acts 9:4) that "he fell to the ground and heard a voice saying to him, 'Saul, Saul! Why do you persecute me?'" The intensely personal factors are again present in the form of the address (cf. 22:7, 13; 26:14). Saul is called twice by the Hebrew form of his name, *Sha'ul,* the form used whenever the Hebrew or Aramaic language was being spoken. Repetition of a name is common whenever God called people in some special way (Gen. 22:11; Exod. 3:4; I Sam. 3:10); it shows that God meant the message to be highly personal.[37] Did the men who were accompanying him hear the voice? There is a variation in the word *heard* in Acts 9:4 and Acts 9:7 that indicates there was a difference between the nature of the hearing on the part of the men and of Saul. It can be said that while the men heard a "sound," Saul heard the "voice" and distinguished the words.[38] As the light was intended for one man, so the message was addressed to the one man, Saul. Both the "light" and the "voice" were specifically Saul's experience.

---

*God* (New York: Friendship Press, 1955) and has always emphasized that groups of related families, rather than simply individuals, ought to be Christianized.

36. The multi-individual aspect of people movements is insisted upon by Tippett, *Verdict Theology in Missionary Theory,* p. 124.

37. F. F. Bruce, *The Acts of the Apostles* (London: Tyndale Press, 1951), p. 198.

38. R. R. Williams suggests that it was Paul's voice that his companions heard (Acts 9:7), but J. Rawson Lumby says Luke is right that they heard a *sound* (Acts 9:7), even though they did not hear the voice that Paul heard (Acts 27:9). *Cambridge Bible,* vol. 1, pp. 110-111.

*The dialogue* It is striking that the voice of Jesus should say, "Why do you persecute me?" (Acts 9:4). The expression transfers Saul's hate for the Christians to the One addressing him. Saul then asks what seems to be a redundant question: "Who are you, Lord?" But the term *Lord* as Saul uses it carries more than the idea of respect. Saul is overwhelmed and instinctively he senses the authority of the One addressing him. Saul's use of the word *Lord* already includes a purpose, a will to follow the voice whether it was that of an angel or of God himself.[39] Saul then hears the simple response, "I am Jesus," the same Jesus whom Saul is persecuting. No major source disputes that this was, indeed, his personal meeting with Christ. Paul's own testimony in Acts 22:8 and 26:15 bears this out. A few scholars, such as Weiss[40] and Albert Schweitzer,[41] contend that this was an internal vision given by God and manifest only to Saul's inner consciousness. But the centrality of the spoken name, "Jesus," in all three accounts in Acts, as well as Paul's own reference to having seen Christ after his resurrection (e.g., I Cor. 15:8), stand against this. "Last of all he appeared also to me—even though I am like someone whose birth was abnormal." God singled out one man and riveted him to the ground with the overwhelming power of this personal encounter. His only response was to follow, even though he was blinded and confused.

*The social nature of the encounter*

In speaking about the corporate aspect of conversion, there comes to mind something that happened twenty years ago in Africa. It was the usual procedure that at the end of each month the lay evangelists living in various villages around the mother church would report on their work. The church concerned had been organized for only six years but had supervision of twelve outstations. The lay preachers in these villages kept record of attendances at services, the number of services held, and finances. Besides giving information to the supervising pastor, they also would report on how many had "repented" and become Christians during the month. One evangelist, I recall, had visited a nearby village where there were no Christians. He had preached at the chief's house before quite a large crowd. He reported that following the message one young man had come to him and said that he had "heard the voice in his spirit and wanted to repent and follow Jesus." The supervising pastor (also an African) asked the evangelist, "Did he really mean that? Did he really want to become a Christian?" Then the pastor enquired, "Is he there at Balasa now, by himself? Did you leave him there in

39. R. J. Knowling, *The Acts of the Apostles, The Expositor's Greek New Testament,* W. R. Nicoll, ed. (London: Hodder and Stoughton, n.d.), vol. 2, pt. 1, p. 233.

40. See the summary of the discussion by Weiss in *Paul and Jesus,* p. 37.

41. *The Mysticism of Paul the Apostle,* William Montgomery, trans. (New York: Henry Holt, 1931).

that village as the only Christian among all those unbelievers?" The evangelist answered, "Yes. I could not refuse his request to follow Jesus. What else could I have done?" To my surprise, the pastor replied, "It is impossible for someone to become a Christian all by himself. He can't really know what being a Christian means unless he has someone to share it with. You should have stayed long enough to gain another convert, or else taken him along with you."

I was amazed at the insight of this pastor who had had very little formal training. It was hard for me to agree with him, and yet the truth of what he said was compelling, even though it sounded very close to saying that it would have been better for the young man never to have been converted than to leave him there as a solitary believer. In the context of an African culture where community is everything, an individual understands his own identity only as he lives with others.

Conversion must have its social dimension, because entering into the new life is entering into the Body. How important this is. The new convert, by his confession of Jesus as Lord, is a member of his body—and this must be felt and experienced immediately.

In Paul's case, the visit by Ananias played an important social role in confirming his conversion. Ananias is identified by Paul in Acts 22:12 as a devout man, highly respected by all the Jews living in Damascus.[42] The first function of his ministry to Paul was to represent the fellowship of the Body. How beautifully Ananias addressed Saul. Knowing full well the treachery with which Saul had persecuted the church, Ananias laid his hand on him and called him "brother." This hater and persecutor of the Christians was, in the moment of his acceptance of Jesus as Lord, a "brother," not only to Ananias, but also to all who are "in Christ." This greeting was given not as an expression of national solidarity, but in the distinctly new sense of identifying a brother in Christ (see 2:29; 22:1; 28:17).

### *The decision factor in mission conversion*

When does conversion take place? We shall need to be very careful about the answer we give. Saul's experience was highly emotional, and the crisis covered a comparatively short period of time. Even so, we still ask, "When did saving faith actually take place?" Was it with Paul's question, "Who are you, Lord?" Was it at the moment he was struck blind, or was it after Ananias baptized him? Just as is true of preparation, so the decision may encompass a long or a short period of time. Signs of change in the life will witness that

42. Paul's conversion narrative of Acts 26:12-18 does not mention Ananias. Some scholars doubt the historicity of the meeting, but Paul's statement before a crowd of Jewish pilgrims (22:12) would lead us to say that 26:12-18 is a condensed version, omitting the segment about Ananias. See *The Expositor's Greek New Testament,* vol. 2, p. 234.

conversion has taken place, yet it is important to see that the decision factor can also be a process, sometimes one of extended time. This is especially true in group conversion. A group, of course, does not have a mind to do this or that apart from the individuals who make up the group. In the context of group conversion, one can easily see the importance of both the time factor and the personal and social aspects of the conversion encounter. "The decision of the group must be its own multi-individual decision."[43] God deals with each and every person in the context of his own life, but, at the same time, the decision finally made by a person affects him socially on at least two levels. By deciding to accept the new way in Christ there is a new body to which the convert is joined, that is, the church; there is also a new set of relationships with the traditional community. For many people in the world, there is no meaningful way to make a decision except as members of a group.[44]

One of the most exciting illustrations of the way in which preparation and encounter are blended in a group decision comes from northern Nigeria where, over a period of years, a community of Muslims has been seriously considering what it would mean to become "followers of Jesus." For a long time, before missionaries or the African church leaders had known anything about them, these Muslims had decided to call themselves "Isawa," which in the Hausa language means, roughly, "Jesus people." This was not a large group, perhaps 150 people, and they had come to their convictions about Jesus primarily through what is written about him in the Koran. The Koran alone led them to feel that Jesus is a preeminently worthy prophet to follow, and they began to regard him even more highly than the prophet Mohammed. For a number of years, visits by national pastors were made to the leaders of the Isawa in the area of Ningi, a predominently Muslim rural town that lies southeast of Kano. The discussions held were clandestine and infrequent because social pressure from the rest of the Muslim community was so strong that the leaders of the Isawa feared they would be ostracized for capitulating to Christians. This amazing work of the Spirit continued from 1975 to 1978, and gradually the Isawa became more open, less fearful of reprisals, and more willing to consult the Bible. By 1979 they actually met openly with Christians, and permitted their children to come under Christian teaching.

Some things about the conversion of the Isawa may not seem so clear-cut as most Western Christians might like them to be. For example, it is not easy for a Muslim to accept the Bible as a book that has authority above the

43. Tippett, *Verdict Theology in Missionary Theory,* p. 124.

44. Tippett sets out four possible responses in a group decision: the group may reject, totally accept, accept with modifications, or fuse. Fusion is splitting into groups with various kinds of responses. Ibid., pp. 124-128.

Koran. Equally problematic is that the death of Jesus, the central truth of the gospel, is looked upon as an insult to Jesus. Muslims believe that no prophet as great as Jesus could have been put to death, not even by the Jews. These areas of belief that create difficulty for Muslims show how closely linked culture and religious change often are. What is beyond man's judgment is the faith of the heart that is known only to God.

The miracle of group conversion is a process through which individuals make their own decisions in response to various stimuli coming from the work of God's Spirit.[45] At the same time, the persons in their decisions are joined to the entire group, thus giving veracity and corporateness to the decision. Over the years, the movement among the Isawa has been slow but steady in the direction of God's truth and in progressive acceptance of the new way. All the while adjustments were being made in belief and behavior patterns, centering on what it means to be a Muslim who now accepts Jesus as Lord. The Isawa show how years of preparation apart from the direct witness of the African church or missionaries led to a period of decision-making that also covered many months. The movement from one stage of belief and acceptance to another is something we cannot dictate or hurry. It is the work of the risen Christ, and of God's Spirit, in the hearts and minds of people.

Driven as he was to near-madness, struck by the blinding light, and arrested by a voice from heaven, Saul asked for the identity of the power behind it all. And the Lord said, "I am Jesus, whom you persecute." The preparation and the encounter merged at that moment.

### *The Validation of Conversion*

A third stage in Saul's conversion had to do with the bringing of assurance to Saul, to the secular world, and to the church that his conversion was real. We may call this the validation of the conversion experience. It is very important that confirmation of saving faith be given to the new believer. In studies of conversion in the Book of Acts this is a consistent feature of the new life. Again, it would be wrong for us to lay down a set of rules or tests, for conversion is the work of the Spirit. Validation, as I am calling it, will be evidenced in various ways according to personal circumstances and cultural situations. I am being careful here because too often mission practice has adopted the attitude: "Show the church that you are a truly converted person and then we will baptize you and accept you." Of course, it is true

45. Kraft speaks of "a large number of discrete decisions: both preceding the actual 'conversion point' as well as following it. These decisions, some vivid in memory, and others, scarcely remembered, combine to become the conversion process." *Christianity in Culture,* p. 337.

that confirming signs will follow the encounter of believing faith, and we must look for and encourage these. But there is a danger lest we put too much emphasis on these outward signs. While we should look for evidence that the convert has indeed been touched by God, we must not allow that which should uplift and confirm to be turned into a negative, sterile experience for the new Christian. This can happen, for example, if the church leadership insists that a probation period must be covered or certain ideals achieved before the convert is to be fully accepted into the church.

In what ways did immediate events in Saul's experience confirm his conversion?

*Saul's baptism*

The baptism of Saul, we believe, was administered by Ananias and is a pivotal event in the whole narrative. Whatever our views as to the theological significance of baptism, the account of Saul's conversion clearly shows it to be a sign of repentance and faith. Two things happen just before Saul is baptized, and both amplify that great change has taken place. For one thing, Saul regains his sight. How symbolic it was that he could now see a new world, for, spiritually, new sight had come to his mind and conscience. Ananias' commission was for the express purpose of restoring Saul's sight (Acts 9:12, 17). Second, Ananias welcomes him warmly as a "brother," and Luke records that it was on this note of fellowship that "he [Saul] stood up and was baptized" (Acts 9:18).

Ananias' words seem to stress the urgency of baptism. It was something that could not be delayed, for he said, "And now, why wait any longer? Get up and be baptized by having your sins washed away by praying to him" (Acts 22:16). This call to Saul to be baptized was evidently an essential part of the message with which Ananias had been charged. In baptizing him Ananias not only validated Saul's faith and changed life, but then and there welcomed him into the fellowship as a brother.

The way in which baptism took place, as almost part of the experience of saving faith, gives the sacrament greater significance than much current practice would indicate. In looking at the detailed accounts we have of persons such as Lydia, the Philippian jailer, and Crispus, who were converted under Paul's ministry, it would seem that Paul practiced what he himself had experienced; that is, baptism is given to confirm and witness to saving faith. It is not something that follows after weeks or months, but is the sacrament that unites the individual, through faith that reaches up from the heart, with the grace of God, which in turn reaches down in validation of the conversion experience.

This is something Roland Allen saw more than seventy years ago, and he stated his case with conviction. In *Missionary Methods: St. Paul's or*

*Ours?*,[46] Allen saw the need for baptism as a validation of conversion with or without a full course of instruction. Baptism celebrates what God has done and what God alone may judge, as he looks at the human heart. Later I shall explain why withholding baptism from new believers is an unbiblical practice, but the point here is that baptism is central to our understanding of conversion. Years ago Allen reminded his Anglican colleagues that by insisting on a very long period of probation

> we have run a great risk of confusing the minds of the converts as to the true meaning and nature of baptism. . . . We have taught them that the one need of men is Christ and that without Christ men cannot attain to righteousness, and then [by delaying baptism] that they must attain to righteousness by themselves in order to receive Christ.[47]

Baptism not only is meant to validate saving faith and the union between the new believer and God, but also stands for the new fellowship into which the believer has entered. Tippett and Charles H. Kraft both emphasize this third stage of conversion with the term *incorporation* because, as Tippett says, "people like to know who they are and where they belong." It is tragic if, when individuals have turned "away from idols" and turned to the "living God," the church does not work for their incorporation.[48]

> The Bible is quite definite on this point. The demon-possessed house, you will remember, was swept and garnished and then left empty. The fears that have dominated the people concerned all their lives have suddenly been overcome in the power of Christ. The exodus from the old way is a traumatic experience. Their houses are swept and garnished, they should not be left empty.[49]

Baptism must not be a reward for study, literacy, class attendance, or any other similar good things. It is true that Saul would have been highly trained in the Scripture and, by contrast, the Philippian jailer would have known little or nothing at all about "the faith." But in both cases their lives changed direction. They had been turned about by God's power. This turning must be sealed early with the testimony of baptism, the sign of believing faith and assurance that one has found a place in the fellowship.

46. (1912; reprint ed. London: World Dominion Press, 1960). Allen wrote in a prophetic way about the methodology of Paul. His insights were unrecognized, even repudiated, when he wrote, but they have greatly influenced mission and church practice in the last twenty-five years.

47. Ibid., p. 97.

48. Tippett, *Verdict Theology in Missionary Theory,* pp. 128-129.

49. Ibid., p. 129.

*Saul's witnessing and the people's response*

After Saul's baptism and a very brief time at Damascus an amazing thing happened. In Acts 9:20 we read, "He went straight to the synagogues and began to preach that Jesus was the Son of God." Saul began to proclaim aloud what only days before he would have denounced. There is no question but that this man had begun to see from a completely new vantage point. This is the only occasion in the entire Book of Acts where the expression *Son of God* is used as a title for Jesus.[50] C. S. C. Williams, noting that the Greek text here quotes Saul as using this particular title, says, "It is significant that it occurs on Paul's lips, for in New Testament times it is a striking phrase for a monotheistic Jew to use."[51] Saul had already begun to build the *kerygma* that he would carry into cities and synagogues throughout the Roman world. Speaking to the Jews, he pointed to Jesus as the true representative of the Israel of God. The use of such a term was no accident and must be seen as an emphatic validation of his conversion.

This preaching was a natural consequence of the truly changed life of Saul and was a most powerful way for him to demonstrate his salvation to his own people. The Greek emphasizes the effect his preaching had on the people. Those who heard him were greatly moved. For example, the word for "amazed" (*existanto*) is related to the classical word *existemi,* which originally meant "to be driven out of one's senses." The weakened form is used in Acts 9:21, but this would, nevertheless, imply that the people experienced a feeling of astonishment, mingled with fear, such as would be caused by events that are miraculous or hard to understand. It is this word that describes, unforgettably, the people's reaction to Saul's proclamation of Christ.

We read that "Saul's preaching became even more powerful" as he continued his witnessing. Luke uses two words in Acts 9:22 (RSV) to underline the fervor and conviction of Saul's testimony. Saul "confounded" (*sunechunnen*) the Jews by "proving" (*sumbibazōn*) that Jesus was the Christ. The first word, "confound," means literally "to pour and mingle together," and one may picture Saul raising issues in such abundance and variety that he mixed up his detractors. The word "proving" means literally "putting together." The related verb, *sumbibazō,* describes the uniting of parts, as the body is held together by sinews, ligaments, and joints.[52] It was as if Saul had already known all these arguments that he used, but he brought them forward in such a way as to build a completely different case. The very

50. Bruce, *The Acts of the Apostles,* p. 203.

51. *A Commentary on the Acts of the Apostles,* p. 125.

52. W. F. Arndt and F. W. Gingrich, eds. *A Greek-English Lexicon of the New Testament,* (Chicago: University of Chicago Press, 1957), p. 276.

arguments that he had fought so bitterly against he now used to prove convincingly that "Jesus was the Messiah" (Acts 9:22).

*The validation factor in mission conversion*

The conversion experience always makes a difference, and we must expect there will be little doubt left in the minds of those who are close to the convert that change has taken place. However, few who turn to Christ will be as able as Paul to astound the public by immediately preaching Christ. This was special for Paul and must be seen in the light of his background and the commission he had been given. Yet the validation phase of conversion does mean that, however faltering or unsure, the new convert will give evidence of his or her salvation. For one thing, as we have seen, there will be a new relationship to the group that is already "in Christ." The church, the members of Christ's body, will extend the right hand of fellowship to the convert and he or she will reach out for this new identity and experience of belonging. Baptism, as we have seen, is to be both a deeply moving expression of God's acceptance of the person and a way of including the convert in the warm, supportive fellowship of the Body. The reaching out of the young Christian for a new identity and the openness of the older Christians to receive him are essential for the validation of conversion.

### *Conversion in the Ministry of Paul*

One of the interesting things about the record of Paul's ministry is the small number of conversion accounts in which Paul himself is directly involved.[53] We do not have a complete record, by any means, of all the contacts made by Paul. Generally, we find reference to groups, both large and small, that turned to Christ during the journeys of Paul. We read simply that in Antioch "those who had been chosen for eternal life became believers" (Acts 13:48). At Derbe, Paul "won many disciples" (Acts 14:21). That churches were planted and elders appointed in each place indicates that there were many converts. The impact of Paul's ministry may be seen in that both Jews and Gentiles were so changed that it was said of Paul and Silas in Thessalonica that they "have turned the world upside down" (Acts 17:6, KJV). This is not hard to believe when we consider the dramatic events that later took place at Ephesus. When, for example, miracles and an exorcism cause both fear and the praise of Jesus' name, it is recorded that "many of the believers came, publicly admitting and revealing what they had done" (Acts 19:18). These were mighty movements, obviously involving large numbers of people.

53. Paul said, "I thank God that I did not baptize any of you except Crispus and Gaius," and, "Christ did not send me to baptize. He sent me to tell the Good News . . ." (I Cor. 1:14, 17).

**Table 2**

**Conversion in the Ministry of Paul**

| Person | Life Context | Preparation | Encounter | Validation |
|---|---|---|---|---|
| Lydia<br>(Acts 16:12-15) | Met Paul in Philippi<br>Businesswoman<br>Went to the place of prayer<br>In charge of a household | Convert to Judaism (indicates openness)<br>Faithfully attended prayer services<br>God-fearer (showed religious sensitivity)<br>Positive leader<br>"One . . . who heard us" (v. 14) | ". . . the Lord opened her mind" (v. 14)<br>Paid attention, acted on what she heard, and experienced full belief<br>Was baptized | Received instruction<br>Household was baptized<br>Offered hospitality "if you have judged me to be faithful to the Lord" (v. 15, RSV) |
| The Philippian Jailer<br>(Acts 16:25-34) | Lived in Philippi<br>Head of a household<br>Emotional<br>In charge of the city jail<br>Lived in a context of pagan religion<br>Exorcism of slave girl threatened her owners' profits | Gentile<br>Slave girl recognized Paul and Silas as servants of God (v. 17)<br>Owners of slave girl were threatened by Paul's power (vv. 18-20)<br>Earthquake confirmed his fears<br>Asked how he could be saved | Accepted Paul's answer<br>Listened to the Word of the Lord<br>Was baptized at once, with his whole house (v. 33) | Bathed prisoners' wounds<br>Brought Paul and Silas into his house<br>Fed Paul and Silas<br>Rejoiced, along with his household |
| Crispus<br>(Acts 18:1-8) | Lived in Corinth<br>Head of the synagogue<br>Head of a household<br>Aware of Paul's break with the Jews (v. 6; implied)<br>Theologically knowledgeable (assumed) | Paul argued and persuaded in the synagogue (v. 4)<br>Paul left the Jews for the Gentiles (v. 6)<br>Paul lived next to Crispus (v. 7; implied)<br>Witnessed all events (assumed) | Believed (v. 8)<br>Household believed<br>All were baptized<br>First Israelite (cf. I Cor. 1:14) | After Crispus was baptized, many heard Paul and were baptized<br>Example had a positive effect |

But there are the rare instances when, in a few verses, we are introduced to a particular person who is so moved by God's Spirit as to accept forgiving grace and become converted to Christ. These passages are personal vignettes of saving faith. Paul is the messenger, the missionary, who brings the person to a confirmation of his or her faith, just as Ananias once ministered to him. For this reason these accounts are very special to our study. They reveal the way in which Paul approached the person who was on the verge of belief and how he integrated his teaching with baptism itself. The accounts show how the need to accept the gospel was variously perceived, and how the particular life-context of each individual gave a uniqueness to every experience.

The most complete narratives come from Philippi and Corinth. At Philippi both Lydia and the jailer are converted, and at Corinth Crispus, the head of the synagogue, becomes a believer. In each case, sufficient information is given so that no doubt remains concerning their genuine conversion.

Although the accounts are much shorter than that of Paul's conversion, we are able to see the similarity between the experiences of these persons as they opened their hearts to the truth and that of Paul himself. The summary (Table 2) only suggests, but shows how closely the leadership Paul gave in the conversion of others conforms to his own experience, especially in the three areas of preparation, encounter, and validation. Together these accounts underline the important factors about conversion that will be found to hold true in any culture.

# 4

# The Dimensions of Mission Conversion

I have mentioned that in West Africa, where I served as a missionary, the conversion experience is usually the most memorable event in the life of a Christian, especially for someone who is converted as an adult. This is because conversion takes place at the level of deeply felt needs and goes on to touch every part of the life. It is much more a matter of feelings and emotion than of reason or creedal belief.

## Conversion As Reality

In 1963 I was involved in teaching sixteen men who were preparing to become pastors. None of these men had Christian parents; most of them had decided to follow Christ in their early twenties. I recall a particular day when a class in evangelism developed naturally into a sharing period, as one by one the men told of their conversion. They spoke of the circumstances that brought them to a decision, of providential events, of personal and social pressures that revealed God as Judge as well as merciful Savior and Lord. The testimonies were fervent and were fully documented, describing the seasons, the places, and the people who were involved. The session continued for more than two hours, as we listened to stories that told of the mingling of the natural and the supernatural, of the human and the divine, of culture and revelation, of the voice of tradition blended with the voice of the Spirit. In some cases Scripture was a factor; in other cases not. Sometimes an evangelist, whether missionary or national, was a catalyst in conversion. But it was amazing how often God spoke directly, in the heart, through a voice, through dreams, or through a crisis of one kind or another. I was impressed by the reality of conversion as a gracious gift of God to people whose cultures were very different from my own, and who had little, if any, "doctrinal" background. These men showed conversion to be a highly personal and intensely spiritual matter, transcending our ability to adequately theorize about it.

Technical theological data defining conversion are, quite obviously, not given to us in Scripture. As William Barclay notes, it may come as a surprise to find that the words *convert* and *conversion* occur only eight times in the New Testament.[1] Four of the relevent passages are quotations from Isaiah 6:9-10.[2] The verb occurs twice in James 5:19-20; the remaining three references are Matthew 18:3, Luke 22:32, and Acts 15:3. This last verse speaks of the conversion of the Gentiles, and is the only reference involving Paul. In one other place (I Tim. 3:6) Paul writes that if one aspires to the office of bishop, he should not be a *neophyte,* usually translated as "recent convert." At most, there are only fifteen words in the Greek New Testament that could possibly be translated as "conversion" or "convert," and, in fact, in not a single place are these particular words used in every translation.[3]

## *Conversion Expressed Theologically*

### *Restoring relationships*

Although when we look at the Pauline material, the English word *conversion* does not appear to take us very far, yet we do find an abundance of metaphors to describe the rich theological implications of what happens or what God does when a person is converted. It is important that we confess our inability to explain fully the miracle of conversion. We do have ways of expressing it theologically, but the use Paul makes of metaphors and similes enables us to come much closer to understanding what conversion really is. These expressions focus our attention primarily on the action of God.

*Forgiveness, cleansing, and redemption* For Paul, conversion involves the God who forgives. This was paramount in Paul's mind, since this fact formed a part of his own commissioning to apostleship at the time of his conversion. Paul was sent to the Gentiles so that "they will have their sins forgiven" (Acts 26:18). The forgiveness offered by Christ is always of highest importance in Paul's preaching. It was on this theme that he concluded his sermon at Antioch in Pisidia (Acts 13:38), showing that the way to enter into fellowship with God is through the forgiveness of sins announced in his message about Jesus. This was the door, so to speak, to a changed life.[4]

A helpful metaphor is to say that God cleanses. Both the word *cleansing* and the closely allied term *washing* refer to the removal of the stains left by

1. *Turning to God* (Philadelphia: Westminster, 1964), p. 14.
2. Matthew 13:15; Mark 4:12; John 12:40; Acts 28:27.
3. Barclay, *Turning to God,* p. 15.
4. See Ephesians 4:32; Colossians 1:14; 2:13.

old habits and sins that have been committed.[5] The momentous Council of Jerusalem heard from none other than Peter himself that God makes no distinction between Jews and Gentiles, since he "cleansed their [the Gentiles'] hearts by faith" (Acts 15:9, RSV). The references to "washing" and "cleansing" would have immediate significance in Paul's day, since both Jews and Gentiles had rituals of cleansing. But the difference here lies in both the object and the method: it is a cleansing of the heart and a washing by faith. Nothing like this had been announced before.

The word *redeem* also describes what takes place at conversion. As my students in Nigeria were telling of their conversion experiences, they used the vernacular (Hausa) equivalents of these words I am discussing. They spoke of conversion as both *gafara* ("forgiveness") and *wankan zunubi* ("washing from sin"). But when one of them, Faruku, used the word *pansa* ("redeem") I stopped him, for I was curious to know if this word *pansa* belonged in the "Christian vocabulary" he had learned since becoming a Christian. He said he had first used the word when trying to tell a group of people what had happened at his conversion. This is how he explained his reason for using the term. His father had been born a servant to a Muslim royal family. However, his father did not want his son, Faruku, to grow up as a slave, so he determined to purchase his freedom. A sum was named by the master and Faruku remembered how his father saved carefully for five years until he had enough money to "redeem" him. Now, as he was trying to find some way to express what conversion meant, it had come to him clearly: God had found a way to set him free from the guilt of sin and the fear that dominated his life. *Pansa* was the best word to express this, since God had done for him in the spiritual dimension what his earthly father had done for him in a legal context. Faruku knew, without having heard it from anyone else, that "Christ has redeemed us from the curse that the Law brings" (Gal. 3:13), and that he "gave himself for us to *redeem* us from all iniquity" (Titus 2:14, RSV; italics added).

*Justification, liberation, and reconciliation* The metaphors that Paul used powerfully communicated what God does in conversion because they suited so well the context of the hearers' experience. When Paul spoke of justification, or of reconciliation, he usually meant the same thing. For example, in Romans 5:9-10 he says that we are "now justified by his blood" and "we were reconciled to God by the death of his Son" (KJV). Both speak of the assurance of being admitted to a new relationship. Ralph P. Martin feels this relational aspect is the underlying idea that Paul had in mind

5. "The expression 'washing of regeneration' denotes . . . what is elsewhere called the new life affected by the Holy Spirit and appropriated to believers by baptism . . . a total renewal wrought by the power of the Holy Spirit." Herman N. Ridderbos, *Paul, an Outline of His Theology*, J. R. DeWitt, trans. (Grand Rapids: Eerdmans, 1975), p. 226.

because it indicates interpersonal relationships that have been put right. Therefore the word *justification*

> carries for Paul a dynamic nuance of new attitude of God to man. . . . It leads to a change of events on God's part. He takes steps to carry through the enterprise of human recovery and renewal while on the human side the initial act of 'right-wising'—to use an old English term—begins a process of moral transformation associated with union with Christ. . . .[6]

This relational aspect of justification leads to the use of the almost interchangeable term *reconciliation.* However, the readers who would best understand the concept of reconciliation were not the Jews but the Greeks. It was characteristic of the Greek mind to search for the resolution of tension, or even alienation, between men and their gods. The gospel is a message of restored relations, and it is this that Paul deals with in Romans 5:6-11 and in II Corinthians 5:18-21. For the Greeks reconciliation was all-encompassing. The whole world of the convert is indeed changed as a result of the deeply personal nature of the harmony that has been restored between a sinful man or woman and his or her God. Those who were once outright "enemies" of God and had every right to fear the consequences of the wrath of God are now at peace and are saved by the initiative that God took through Jesus Christ (Rom. 5:6-11).[7]

If conversion for the Jew is meaningfully summed up in the word *justification,* and for the Greek is expressed best as reconciliation, there is yet a third term that may have had a special message for the Roman world, as well as for the Jew and the Greek. This is the word *liberation.* I have already discussed liberation and freedom in Christ as one of the basic assumptions of Paul's missionary theology. The meaning of freedom in connection with Jewish enslavement to the law is one thing. But Roman rule was a fierce kind of colonialism. Imprisonment was common even for minor offenses. Slaves and masters, captives and victors were very much a part of everyday life. G. B. Caird notes that the number of slaves in the empire was a constant threat to the peace of Rome because of the danger of revolt and rebellion.[8]

In the same sharing session to which I referred earlier, Bulus, who was in his middle thirties and the father of six children, spoke of the bondage of his own life before becoming a Christian. His tribe had a strong belief in the pervasive influence of the dead. His father had been buried very close to the door of his house and Bulus always left a small token of food in his porridge bowl in order to feed the spirits of the "living dead." This term *living dead* was for him an accurate way of describing those who had recently left this

6. *Reconciliation: A Study of Paul's Theology* (Atlanta: John Knox, 1981), p. 37.
7. See also II Corinthians 5:15-16; Ephesians 2:14-16; Colossians 1:21-22.
8. *The Apostolic Age* (London: Gerald Duckworth, 1955), p. 160.

life, because they had power to influence almost everything for good or bad. Hunting and harvest, conception and health, death and fortune all were believed to be under the management of the dead. The dead seemed to have more power as free spirits than they ever had when they were alive and in the body. Hence, a great variety of rituals was performed. Talismans of every description were worn or hung about the house to keep the ancestors happy. Bulus had no words to describe his imprisonment in worry and fear except to say that he was "tied by ropes." So when he came to speak of his conversion he used the Hausa word *yanta,* which means "to give freedom to a slave." He said, "I was not a slave to a foreign government or to another family, but I was a slave to the power of beliefs that had bound me since I was a child. My own beloved ancestors controlled my life but I knew that I had found salvation when I felt the ropes fall away and I could run and laugh as a free man."

*Jesus is Lord*

Conversion has a certain ambiguity about it if we attempt to confine the experience to a particular point in time. Conversion is both a completed and a continuous act. Charles H. Kraft speaks of conversion as a "faith-allegiance decision." In its narrowest definition, conversion takes place at the time when the decision is made to realign one's loyalties through faith in Jesus Christ.[9] There are factors before this specific decision that are crucial to conversion, and there is likewise a series of choices and critical events that follows the decision. This entire cycle is best understood as conversion. Unless we recognize the "process" aspect of conversion, it is impossible to understand conversion as "turning" to Jesus Christ and making him, progressively, the new center for faith allegiance.

Paul's own words about a change in lordship best serve to describe conversion: "Even though there are many of these 'gods' and 'lords,' yet there is for us only one God . . . and there is only one Lord, Jesus Christ, through whom all things were created and through whom we live" (I Cor. 8:5-6). When the human will has found new direction, traditional gods and lords are set aside for the one God who reveals himself through Christ, and when this new Authority is given the right to rule over the life, a person is converted. This act of submission and pledge of complete loyalty to Christ cannot be completed in the short range, much less in a given day or moment. And yet when the heart of the believer first reaches out in faith to a new Lord, we can speak of conversion occurring at a point in time. The earliest Christian confession of the new faith proclaimed that Jesus is Lord (Rom. 10:9). In one sense, all that can be said about the Christian life and all that is

9. See Kraft's discussion of "Christian Conversion as a Dynamic Process" in *Christianity in Culture* (Maryknoll, NY: Orbis Books, 1979), pp. 328-344; also see page 98 and note 43.

written in these pages derives from the promise that to be converted is to put one's self under the lordship of Christ.[10]

Paul speaks of the lordship of Jesus in several ways. One important dimension of this lordship is that by it the convert is incorporated into a new community. Paul speaks of "our Lord Jesus Christ" more than twenty-eight times and of "our Lord Jesus" nine times. Those who confess Jesus as Lord do not do this in isolation. Christians form a fellowship together with those who have already confessed this same Jesus as their Lord (I Cor. 1:9).[11]

Again, the lordship of Jesus provides the means by which people are redeemed from the false gods of traditional religions. Paul does not say that the gods of animistic religions are totally powerless to excite people or that they hold out no promises of hope. But he does make it clear that these are counterfeit gods that stand in total opposition to Jesus Christ. It is therefore no small thing to affirm the lordship of Christ in the face of these dark powers that have such a hold upon the unbeliever. To be able to testify that "Jesus is Lord" is proof that one has the Spirit within (I Cor. 12:3). The phrase *Jesus is Lord* means that life has a new center of loyalty, a fixed point to which everything must now conform. Jesus is the new Head and he will have his preeminence in everything (Phil. 2:10-11; Col. 1:18).

### *Conversion Expressed Existentially*

In using the metaphors that I have discussed thus far, Paul would have spoken eloquently and effectively about conversion to his congregations. But these metaphors deal primarily with what God does on the spiritual level, and in order to fully understand them a certain amount of abstract thinking is demanded of us. For, unfortunately, these terms that Paul used spontaneously have now become heavily freighted with theological meanings. They are now primarily the technical expressions of theology that have their place in a formal statement of doctrine. A newly converted person would likely not say that he or she has been justified. This calls for quite sophisticated study, familiarity with ecclesiastical language, or a knowledge of certain translations of the Scriptures. A missiological definition of conversion will have to do with the concrete evidences of change. What is the new lifestyle? What new set of values can be expected? What differences in thinking and behavior does conversion make? Although we do not have one precise term for conversion in the New Testament, we do have two expressions that are used by Paul to describe what happens and why a life is

10. See I Corinthians 8:5-6; 12:2-3.

11. G. E. Ladd discussed "Jesus the Lord," in *A Theology of the New Testament* (Grand Rapids: Eerdmans, 1974), pp. 415-416.

different after conversion. These words are *epistrephō* ("to turn") and *metanoia* ("change" and "repentance").

*Conversion is "turning"*

The helpful expression *epistrephō,* meaning "to turn," is used more than thirty-five times in the New Testament. Nine times it is used by Paul himself or in connection with events in which Paul was involved. It is a very common Greek word that originally had no special religious connotations. In Greek literature it was used to describe everyday things such as turning one's back on another, turning a ship to set it off on a new course, or making horses wheel around.[12] But it could also mean a "turning of the mind," in the sense of paying attention to something, or refusing to pay attention, as the case may be. In this way the word came to be used for Christian conversion. A person's attention is turned to the message that, by warning or by correcting, leads him to repentance; this brings about a series of adjustments to the old life that can also be spoken of as "turnings." Thus conversion may be said to involve both mental and spiritual activity, as well as a redirection of the external life.

Even though the term *epistrephō* is used in very ordinary ways in the New Testament,[13] it occurs most frequently in connection with this kind of mental or spiritual turn. Peter's call to repentance on the day of Pentecost was a call to "turn to God, so that he will forgive your sins" (Acts 3:19). When Peter healed Aeneas, all the residents of Lydda and Sharon saw Aeneas and "turned to the Lord" (Acts 9:35). During the preaching at Antioch, "a great number of people believed and turned to the Lord" (Acts 11:21).

Luke records four incidents that involved Paul. The first is Paul's sermon at Lystra, among people who were mainly pagan. Paul tells them he has come "to turn you away from these worthless things to the living God" (Acts 14:15). It is important to note that the call is to change direction from that which is unreal and impotent to a dynamic living God. Jewish and Gentile believers have a new common Center. Gentiles who made the turn were not to be given second-class status. This was the important decision of the Council of Jerusalem (Acts 15:19). An important use of the word by Paul occurs as part of his testimony before King Agrippa. He says that his commission from God was to go to the Gentiles "to open their eyes and *turn* them from the darkness to the light and from the power of Satan to God" (Acts 26:18; italics added). Paul writes in II Corinthians 3:16 that it is when a person turns to the Lord that "the veil" is removed; and he rejoices that the Thessalonians have turned to God from idols (I Thess. 1:9).

It is important to accept that there has been simply a turning that indicates

12. For use of the word *epistrephō,* see Barclay, *Turning to God,* pp. 18-23.
13. Ibid.

conversion. For Paul it was enough that a beginning had been made. Conversion is change of heart, and while this change may not be fully understood by the convert at the moment of faith, it does, nevertheless, constitute conversion in the eyes of God. Conversion, in other words, is not the ability to explain in formal theological terms what has taken place in one's life, nor is it the making of a great number of moral and ethical adjustments, although those will follow. The central focus of *epistrephō* is that of changing or reversing direction, so that movement is now toward God rather than away from him.[14]

*Conversion is "change by repentance"*

We have not thus far considered that conversion in Scripture is based on a powerful prerequisite—true sorrow for willful acts against God. This dimension of repentance is expressed by the second New Testament word for conversion: *metanoia.* This word is most frequently used by Paul to express the means of conversion. Beginning with Peter's Pentecost sermon, no apostolic preaching was complete without the uncompromising call to repentance.[15] Luke recalls that Paul used the word *metanoia* on three different occasions. In Acts 17:30 Paul concluded his sermon from the Areopagus by saying, "Now he commands all [men] . . . everywhere to turn away from their evil ways." The unforgettable words of Paul to the Ephesian elders included the testimony of his own ministry. "To Jews and Gentiles alike," he says, "I gave solemn warning that they should turn from their sins to God and believe in our Lord Jesus" (Acts 20:21). Before Agrippa, Paul said that his heavenly vision brought a call to preach to the Gentiles "that they must repent of their sins and turn to God and do the things that would show they had repented" (Acts 26:20). In Paul's own writings he uses the word *metanoia* four times in various contexts. In each case the idea of repentance is the best way to express the message of *metanoia.* In Romans 2:4, for example, he says, "Surely you know that God is kind, because he is trying to lead you to repent."[16]

The literal meaning of *metanoia,* "afterthought," would seem to fall far short of the deep issues included in the Christian concept of repentance. However, the word is used with such force in the New Testament that it came to express far more than its etymology would suggest. *Metanoia* originally stood as the precise opposite of *pronoia,* which meant "forethought." For example, if a person had no forethought or if his forethought

14. The simple fact of *turning* is conversion. It is enough for Paul that a change in the direction of the risen Christ has been made. While it is not a *completed* act, the change of heart and attitudes constitutes conversion. (See Kraft, "Dynamic Response to an Invitation by God," *Christianity in Culture,* p. 333.)

15. See Acts 2:38; 3:19; 5:31; 8:22.

16. See also II Corinthians 7:10; 12:21; II Timothy 2:25.

was faulty, there arose a need to think things through again in order to make corrections. Thus *metanoia* became closely linked with the idea of repentance. As Barclay states, "*metanoia* comes to involve not only a new judgement on some previous action, but also regret and sorrow for it. Here then is the meaning of repentance. Repentance is the awakened awareness and regret of past sins."[17] Obviously the "turning" (*epistrephō*) and the "change of mind" or "repentance" (*metanoia*) are so closely related that both aspects are needed to express what actually takes place in conversion.

## Conversion As Experience

The way in which Paul totally accepted new people into the fellowship of Christ in place after place, even addressing them as "saints" while they were still immature in their understanding of the faith, has to be one of the most important aspects of his ministry. This is because he was convinced that the understanding of conversion must come through experiences that are authentic to each and every situation. Kraft has dealt with this in *Christianity in Culture.* The concept of "dynamic equivalence" grows out of the principle in translation theory that "a translator must be able to describe the world in which the language being translated applies."[18] Kraft explains what this implies:

> Jesus needs to walk their paths and eat in their homes. The receptor needs to live and learn, as the original disciples did, in Jesus' presence today. For this they need dynamic witnesses, living and speaking dynamically equivalent messages.[19]

God's Spirit deals with people in culturally relevant ways. This is what is meant by the term *dynamic conversion.* It does not have to be a phenomenal or cataclysmic event, but it must be one that is intensely personal and that results in a life changed in ways that are completely relevant to the culture. We cannot ignore the vitality of Paul's letters to each of his groups of converts, whether in Greece, Galatia, or Asia. There is the ring of acceptance for each of these new communities of faith, each within its particular situation and culture. He shows a tolerance of the differences, and resists pressure that would make them conform to Jerusalem's, or even to Antioch's, idea of

17. *Turning to God,* p. 48.

18. Thomas S. Kuhn, *The Structure of Scientific Revolutions: International Encyclopedia of Unified Science,* Foundations of the Unity of Science series, vol. 2, no. 2 (Chicago: University of Chicago Press, 1970), p. 202, n. 17, quoted by Kraft in *Christianity in Culture.*

19. *Christianity in Culture,* p. 276.

how a convert should look or act. God through Christ must become *real,* a living dynamic Presence that turns men away from the false in each place and turns them toward the true and living God.

### *Conversion Is a Dynamic Act of God*

Rather than approaching conversion as a dogmatist on the one hand or as a "lifestylist" on the other, Paul, as I have said, saw that conversion is best described in terms of what God does in the life of a person. There is, therefore, no set of rules to accept. Rather, there must be the vital witness of God within the spirit of the convert that he or she indeed has been touched at the very essence of life itself. Outward changes will follow as the consequence of new teaching and the indwelling of the Spirit of Jesus. But too often the tendency is to emphasize "how a Christian ought to act" and to confuse that with what God does in conversion. With all respect for my African brothers who ministered with me in Africa, I confess that I was unhappy when, once people publicly decided to follow Christ, certain restrictions were immediately imposed as evidence of conversion. For example, after a morning worship service, when a call was made for those who wished to "accept Jesus," very often the pastor would ask those who came forward, "Do you promise not to work on Sunday? Do you promise not to drink any alcohol and to be faithful in attendance at church?" While these questions reveal the ethical code that the church expected of converted people, giving the "proper" answer to these questions did not constitute conversion.

### *The Dynamic Language of Paul*

Paul saw the saving work of God in Christ as the remaking of a person. But this visible reshaping begins with an inner work by God's Spirit, and is a spiritual remaking. Paul expressed this truth many times, using a variety of pictures and symbols, showing how committed he was to putting the emphasis on the work of God and making this understood as precisely as possible in every place. He spoke of conversion as re-creation, as dying and being made alive, as becoming one with Christ, and as that which puts God's Spirit within a person.

#### *Conversion is re-creation*

Paul expresses this truth best in II Corinthians 5:17: "When anyone is joined to Christ, he is a new being; the old has gone, the new has come." He clearly builds this statement on the fact that merely human appreciation of

Jesus can never be enough. Faith is more than knowledge of facts. What is described here is a changed relationship with God, with the world, and with self, which Paul describes as being joined to Christ (literally, "in Christ") as a "new being." The result can be described as someone who resembles what the person was before, but who is now a new creation in Christ Jesus (Eph. 2:10). This is not a matter of omitting a rite formerly practiced or performing a new ritual. It is being a new person. Yet this new person is still a member of the same world in which the turning took place; the re-creation still belongs in that world, is adapted to it, and will be transformed in the context of *that* world, not a different world.[20]

*Conversion is dying and being made alive*

To be converted is not an innocuous, take-it-or-leave-it experience. If for some reason the metaphor about being re-created as a new being should not be well understood, Paul says also, in an even more striking way, that "the old is dead" and there is resurrected life. "You were spiritually dead because of your disobedience and sins. . . . [But] he brought us to life" (Eph. 2:1, 5). To the Romans Paul says, "We have died . . . so far as sin is concerned" (Rom. 6:8, 11). In baptism, the believer, as it were, makes the death of Christ the ground for his faith, and the excitement of the Christian life is that now the believer is alive to God, just as through the resurrection Jesus became alive to God (Rom. 6:1-11). Paul spoke of having died as far as the law was concerned in order that he might live for God; that he had been put to death with Christ so that Christ may now live in him (Gal. 2:19-20).

*Conversion is becoming one with Christ*

Becoming a Christian does not mean putting another layer of teaching over one's traditional religion. It is not enough to mix Christ with other things, even things that may be good and right in what the person already believes. Paul speaks of truly converted persons as those who not only have been raised to life with Christ, but also whose lives are "hidden with Christ in God" (Col. 3:1-4). No other religion has this message—that by faith a person may enter into a living, intimate relationship with God. Nothing is more irrefutable than the testimony of a new Christian who tells how he or she really feels joined to Christ. Paul speaks of this in one way or another in all his letters. In Galatians 3:27 Paul speaks of being "baptized into union with Christ," adding, "and now you are clothed, so to speak, with the life of Christ himself."[21] The frequency with which Paul makes reference to the

20. See Galatians 6:15; Ephesians 3:24; Colossians 3:10.

21. Ridderbos, commenting on I Corinthians 12:13, says that "the one baptized is brought into relation with an already existing person or unity . . . this means incorporation into an already existing body (I Cor. 10:2; Gal. 3:27)." *Paul,* p. 372.

closeness of the convert to his new Lord shows the importance of this new relationship. Something *really* happens. The living God is pleased to translate faith into a living experience, the joining of the human and the divine Spirit.[22]

*Conversion puts the Spirit of God within a person*

A person who has died, so to speak, and has been raised up again as one person with Christ is, in very truth, a new person. This is how Paul again and again describes the recent convert.[23] And the best way to understand what is meant by the term *a new person* is to realize that the mighty re-creating Spirit enters into, and lives with, the believer in a personal and individual way. A person is converted when there is in him or her a new mind, a new Spirit. Romans 8:1-7 presents this in a striking way, but the passage's meaning can be seen only against the background of the preceding chapters. The earlier chapters show man as a sinful, guilty, and helpless creature. God's own grace, to be received in faith, provides the only way out. With the beginning of the eighth chapter, Paul considers the new life made possible through the indwelling Spirit. Here is more than forgiveness for the past; more than God's gracious acceptance. Here is a man who has a totally new linkage with the true and living God through the Holy Spirit. It is this new dynamic interaction with the Spirit that Herman N. Ridderbos helpfully sums up:

> God "sends" the Spirit of His Son into their hearts, (Gal. 4:6) as the earnest and seal of this complete redemption. (II Cor. 1:22) He "pours" his love into their hearts through the Holy Spirit (Rom. 5:5, cf. Titus 3:5), he "writes" his will in their hearts by the Spirit (II Cor. 3:3), he "illumines" their hearts with the knowledge of Christ (II Cor. 4:6), he "enlightens" the "eyes of their hearts," through the Spirit of wisdom and of revelation (Eph. 1:18) . . . indeed the Spirit is sometimes represented as himself in the hearts of believers praying to God. (Rom. 8:26, 27; Gal. 4:6)[24]

Clearly, the entering into the new life is no bland intellectual exercise. God himself is interacting with the person at the spiritual level, touching the very essence of being. Paul's language strains to communicate that new life can reach people in any culture or in any situation. We do not want to produce a list of abstract terms that must be studied before we can understand what conversion means.[25] Paul in his day conceived of the remaking of

22. See Romans 6:11; 12:5; Galatians 3:28; Ephesians 2:6.

23. II Corinthians 5:17; Galatians 6:15; Ephesians 2:10, 15; 3:9; 4:24; Colossians 3:10.

24. *Paul,* p. 229.

25. For example, the terms *dying, rising,* and *in Christ* as descriptive of conversion have been interpreted by some scholars as revealing the extreme mysticism of Paul. See Johannes

people in realistic and understandable terms. For many people today, theological statements and ancient creeds need to be set aside in order for us to see conversion as a truly life-altering experience in which God through Christ comes to us in power.

## Conversion As Process

It might seem from the few accounts in Paul's ministry that the ideal conversion would be one in which there is a definite "before" and "after" situation. Lydia, for example, knew when "the Lord opened her mind" (Acts 16:14) and she could have said, "I was not a Christian before, but I am now." Or, in the case of the jailer, conversion is even more clear-cut. Before his crucial experience with Paul and Silas he was not a Christian, but after that unforgettable night he was, and he would never be the same again. But conversion is not a simple matter of nonbelief one moment and belief the next. I have shown already in a number of ways that the conversion experience is a complex interaction of events and decisions that leads up to a definite encounter, and that things that happen still further on will clarify and confirm that saving faith is real. It is very important that we see God's work in conversion as a continuing process. It is too easy to think of salvation as a single event, a crisis, so to speak, when at one moment a person is unsaved and at another moment he is saved. Or some may insist even further that to be able to recall the precise time of salvation is the essential thing, that this is the only way God deals with people, and therefore is accepted as the norm for everyone. But rarely does conversion take place so simply, and this is especially true among people who have to reckon with complex cultural problems as a part of their turning to Christ.

### *The Continuum*

Paul did not treat a person as though he expected him to take one radical, all-important step of faith that would pick him up from his former life and set him down in a new life. It is remarkable how he could accept as Christians people who had simply manifested a change in their lives and confessed Jesus as Lord. His letters show how he agonized over the problems of immorality, schism, immaturity, syncretism, and other practices that were not "up to standard," yet his favorite way of addressing members of these

---

Weiss, *The History of Primitive Christianity* (New York: Wilson-Erickson, 1937), vol. 2, pp. 405, 464; and Albert Schweitzer, *The Mysticism of St. Paul* (London: Adam and Charles Black, 1931).

young churches was to call them saints. By contrast, so often we who have been missionaries tend to judge who is a Christian and who is not by standards that are cultural rather than spiritual, emphasizing outward evidences that must square with our own opinions about who is converted. We need to look at the process aspect of conversion very carefully.

Orlando Costas feels Paul is speaking about the continuous aspects of conversion when in II Corinthians 3:16-18 he says,

> As the Scripture says about Moses: "His veil was removed when he turned to the Lord." Now, "the Lord" in this passage is the Spirit; and where the Spirit of the Lord is present, there is freedom. All of us, then, reflect the glory of the Lord with uncovered faces; and that same glory, coming from the Lord, who is the Spirit, transforms us into his likeness in an ever greater degree of glory.[26]

Here, says Costas, "Paul is referring to an incapacity to understand the old covenant because of spiritual blindness. Only 'through Christ' can this blindness be removed and Israel come to see the truth of the covenant."[27] This is the case with people everywhere, not only with Israel. Personal sins, very often culture itself, hides us from a clear vision of God. To truly experience the removal of the veil is something God does when we turn to him. It need not be assumed that this is quickly accomplished. The verse says of Moses, "His veil was removed when he turned to the Lord." For some the turning itself may take minutes, for others months, as we finite creatures view time. This time factor is not important to God, since he sees the chronology of faith from his timeless perspective. Beyond the removal of the veil is the second point made by Paul, that of continuous change to "an ever-greater degree of glory." One might say that it is by a series of situations, small or large, that calls for a decision, by this crisis or that, that the meaning of the initial turning becomes increasingly clear and the Spirit of Christ thus transforms us more and more unto his likeness. "Conversion is then both a distinct moment and the first in a series of transforming experiences. It appears as a unique turn and as a continuing transforming movement made possible by the enabling power of the Spirit of freedom."[28]

We really ought to question the notion that conversion, especially in mission, is not legitimate unless all the outward life becomes like that of all other Christians. To say that conversion is, as it were, a one-way street to a quickly changed life takes something away from the reality of the experience. Here again, we need to understand the progressive nature of the kingdom as the rule of God in our lives. It is certainly true that the kingdom is something

26. "Conversion as a Complex Experience," in *Gospel and Culture,* J. R. Stott, ed., Applied Cultural Anthropology series (Pasadena, CA: William Carey Library, 1979), p. 252.

27. Ibid.

28. Ibid., pp. 252-253.

that will fully come in the future, and yet it is being lived out and experienced here and now. The kingdom means Jesus' followers are called to obedience, and in obedience our rights and privileges in the kingdom are granted by God. To see conversion as the entryway into the kingdom puts things into perspective (Mark 1:15). It is not going to surprise us that there is joy in the new faith even while the struggle with the old life continues. The very beginning of the movement toward Christ can best be seen as conversion, as well as the many subsequent adjustments and changes that are a part of the kingdom journey.[29]

### *"Bounded Sets" and "Centered Sets"*

In his article "When is a Christian?," Charles Taber discusses the problem of religious change and the encounter with cultural forms and habits that this will entail.[30] The change in a person from what was to something different always takes time, and involves the process of which I have been writing. Taber says, "It is not an absolute degree of attainment that proves one is a child of God, but discernable progress in the right direction."[31] "Discernable progress in the right direction" is a key phrase and is absolutely Pauline.

Missiologist Paul Heibert has applied a concept from epistemology to illuminate how people become Christians.[32] In discussing what he calls "bounded sets" and "centered sets," he describes two ways in which we may think of people in deciding whether they are Christians or not. The term *bounded sets* refers to the tendency to form fixed ideas or structured pictures of things that belong in a certain category. Once this is done, any unit that is not in accordance with the predetermined pattern does not belong. These bounded sets are formal and uniform. Uniformity is, in fact, the main feature of the bounded set and settles the question as to whether something qualifies (by nature and appearance) for membership in the set. An apple is either an apple or it is not. "If it is an apple it is 100% an apple and it remains an apple whether green, ripe or rotten."[33] For determining

29. Attention is called to Harvie Conn, "Conversion and Culture: A Theological Perspective with Reference to Korea," in *Gospel and Culture.* "Since the Christian lives in two worlds, the world of 'this age and that which is to come' (Eph. 1:21), his dynamic continuous task becomes daily reappraisal of his lifestyle, his worldview, his culture, to bring all more and more into conformity to the new truth of the Kingdom come and coming Christ," p. 204.

30. *Milligan Missiogram,* vol. 3, no. 3, 1976, pp. 1-4.

31. Ibid., p. 3.

32. "Conversion, Culture and Cognitive Categories," *Gospel in Context,* vol. 1, no. 3 (July 1978), pp. 24-29.

33. Ibid., p. 26. See also "Sets and Structures: A Study of Church Patterns," in *New Horizons in World Mission,* D. J. Hesselgrave, ed. (Grand Rapids: Baker, 1980), pp. 217-227.

bounded sets, "the big question, therefore, is whether an object is inside or outside the category."[34]

If we think of conversion in terms of bounded sets, the emphasis will be on the externals that testify to "orthodoxy," that is, certain things that are believed and confessed by others must also be confessed by the convert. Practice that characterizes the group must immediately apply to him also. One is either in or not in; there is no ambiguity. The important factor is conformity to the category and the crossing of the line from outside to inside.

> The crossing of the boundary is a decision event. Once a person is a Christian he is 100 percent Christian. There is essentially nothing more for him to acquire. He might grow spiritually, but this is not an essential part of what it means to be a Christian.[35]

In my missionary experience there has been a tendency to adopt the bounded-set approach to conversion. This means that when someone makes it known that he or she has decided to turn from the old way to follow Christ, the church, instead of offering acceptance and immediate privileges with all other Christians, raises a benevolent barrier. Certain characteristics common to all other Christians must first be seen to apply to this new Christian in order to test the validity of his or her faith. The new Christian is not considered to be "inside" because of the grace of Christ in the life, but is accepted only when behavior and speech and, in some cases, even dress conform to that of the "insiders." This tendency toward bounded sets is seen in the case of those who seek baptism but are turned away from the church, sometimes for months or years, because of this reason or that reason.

In 1964 a young missionary recounted the following incident that illuminates the point. He had preached in a small African village with a population of approximately 150 people. A senior missionary was in charge of the trek (as these excursions for evangelism were called) and even though an African pastor was in the group, the missionary looked after all the details. At the public preaching an elderly man stepped out of the audience. A large hoe was over his shoulder; his hair was unkempt; a monkey skin was all he had ever worn, and it covered only what was necessary. His teeth were deep red, showing that he had chewed betel nut for most of his life. The old man forced his way to the front where the young preacher stood, and said simply, "Here I am. I want salvation." What should have followed was a shout of joy, or a hymn and some dancing, in true African expression of praise. But

34. "Sets and Structures," p. 221.
35. Ibid., p. 222.

instead, a somber benediction ended the meeting, and the old man was taken aside by the senior missionary. He told the old man that in time he would understand the seriousness of the decision, and that Christian people would be able to tell him what it really meant to become a Christian. I don't know if that man was ever received into the church. Unfortunately, church membership was held to be a more significant evidence of conversion than any public confession of faith.

I was interrupted by a schoolteacher while I was preaching a sermon one Sunday morning. The theme of the sermon was "New Life for All," and it was the time of a great movement of evangelism organized under that name among the churches in northern Nigeria. The teacher stood in the congregation and signaled for my attention. He objected to my claim that the gospel is for all. "We know," he said, "that it is not for the polygamist, because after he accepts he will not be allowed communion; and we also know it is not for Muslims, since they do not even feel comfortable in our churches. So why don't you change your sermon and say that this is "New Life for Some, But Not for All?"

The bounded-set Christians in Paul's time were the Judaizers. They insisted on forms that made all alike. They expected loyalty to the tradition of Moses and to the format of the Jerusalem church, even though the converts might be from among the Gentiles.

The Pauline understanding of conversion is much closer to what Hiebert describes in terms of centered sets. Here the emphasis is not on conformity so much as it is on movement toward a center. The boundary is not as important as the turning. There is a fluidity about the centered set, quite distinct from the rigidity characteristic of many institutional churches. The clue to the identity of the membership of a centered set depends much more on that they are all moving toward the same center rather than on how much they resemble one another. Because each member of the set is important, individuality is allowed for, and each is considered in his or her own context. The centered set is a dynamic set, since the individual members are always in motion, either slow or rapid. They may be turning, or they may be moving toward the center, some from a point closer to the center and some from a point further away.

If the same standards had been expected of the Philippian jailer as would be expected of Crispus, the ruler of the synagogue, it would have been impossible to accept the idea that the jailer was converted. His background was "pagan" and secular, and he came from a class of people that would have little time for Christianity. The jailer would have had to make many adjustments before he could ever behave and speak like Crispus and his family. But the conversion of the jailer was authentic, nevertheless, because it was a joyous and dynamic acceptance of the message of Christ. Some in the safer, more structured bounded sets know a lot about the Bible and theology but are, in fact, moving away from the Center. A good example, Hiebert points out, would have been the Pharisees. Conversion, therefore, can be truly judged only by God. If man is to attempt to decide who is Christian and who is not, this must be done carefully on the basis of one question alone. Is the person who has turned from the old way—regardless of who or where he was—now moving toward the Center? It is this question that Paul asked constantly of his converts in many different ways, and of which we shall be reminded frequently as we go on to look at the spiritual expectations Paul had for the young churches.

## Conversion and the Real World

### *The "Deep Structure" of Reality*

If we could portray reality for a given culture, it might be envisaged as a series of concentric circles, each ring representing a category of that reality. At the very center is what phenomenology would describe as the essence of reality. It is here that the "soul" of a culture is to be found, that which is perceived by the culture as the irreducible core of truth, and from which all other values arise. World view begins here and is expressed outwardly as it interacts with all other levels of reality. A second ring would be the symbols and the myths that reveal the "truth" around which a culture moves. Beyond this are customs and habits that arise directly from the center and the symbolic levels of reality. Here we find customs concerning marriage and views of the family and death. Customs tend to be a little more open to change and do change with time, even though the levels of myth and symbol remain constant. Beyond the circle of basic customs are what might be called the more superficial features of a culture. Here is where change takes place most readily, for example, in clothing styles, food habits, architecture; all these are influenced by technical progress, education, and modernity. As the force of change takes hold, these outer, more superficial areas are modified, while the inner circles of the culture remain much more constant. Different kinds of dress, or variety in musical tastes, or how a house is built, or how a government is formed all may be undergoing change while the deep structure remains, altered very little if at all. This view of culture in terms of levels of reality can be diagrammed as in Figure 1.

Two things are important in considering how the new Christian relates to his or her world. We are to remember that the religious nature of a person is not a separate entity in the structure of his world, but it penetrates and interacts with every area of reality. Religion is not a part among parts but is the way through which the spiritual being, man, expresses his true nature. Man still retains God's image, and mankind struggles to communicate its

Figure 1

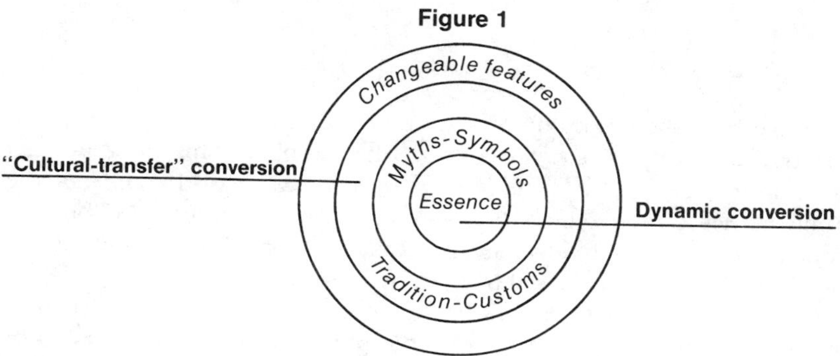


needs to God and to worship him. The way in which people apprehend their culture is fundamentally religious, that is, in terms of their understanding of the Creator. As J. H. Bavinck says,

> There is not a single element in the cultural structure that can be called absolutely neutral. All elements have their secret ties with the religious faith of the people as a whole. Nothing is to be found anywhere that can be called a "no man's" land. Culture is religion made visible; it is religion actualized in the innumerable relations of daily life.[36]

It is wrong, therefore, to speak of religion as world view or of world view as religion. Religion is that basic component, very much of the essence of culture, that forms world view. The convert, then, has turned to a new loyalty that will interact and challenge every institution, custom, and habit of culture. The new Lord cannot be relegated to this or that area of reality. This lordship is lordship over all.

We should expect, therefore, in mission that change will affect the deep structure of the life and not just the superficial edges. Paul's use of the term *new creation* is germane to this point. The transformation process that we have discussed has not really begun until the "heart" of the world of the convert has been brought under the demands of the new Lord. But this will take time. To immediately demand surface changes, such as modifications in lifestyle, vocabulary, dress, or any other aspect of life, usually has very little

36. *The Impact of Christianity on the Non-Christian World* (Grand Rapids: Eerdmans, 1949), p. 57. Compare Conn, "Conversion and Culture," pp. 218ff.

to do with the gospel reaching into the center of the life. Transformation is first a conviction at the center; it then radiates outward, touching the whole life.

### *The Universal Gospel in a Particular World*

Conversion, then, not only will transform the convert, but also will in time transform the world of the convert. Changes must come, but they need to be introduced in the light of the convert's real world. Paul met the problems raised by specific world views and dealt with them in concrete ways. His converts were always called to face the truth of the gospel and square it with the issues raised by their own situations.

At Corinth the new Christians had to apply a changed life to a dynamic, immoral society in which there was little precedent for either worship or ethics. Ephesus was known far and wide for its pagan shrines, rituals, and charms connected with the goddess Diana. Little wonder, with all the magic and divining common in Ephesus, that Paul was to bring healing through the power of the Holy Spirit. From Paul's body, healing was transmitted through handkerchiefs and body cloths. He also performed amazing exorcisms so that even the local practitioners attempted to imitate him (Acts 19:11-20). Only in Ephesus did these kinds of phenomena occur. The local beliefs were right for it. The world view of the people of the city gave Paul the opening to demonstrate God's power in these seemingly magical acts. The people were in touch with this kind of world and Paul built on that fact. Furthermore, their response resulted, in the end, in a great purification of Christianity from hidden paganism, as the believers burned occult books worth 50,000 pieces of silver! When Paul touched the center of their world view and communicated the gospel through this belief system, "the word of the Lord kept spreading and growing stronger" (Acts 19:29).

Nowhere did Paul better confront the issues raised by a culture than at Colossae. The Colossian church was threatened by a warped kind of theosophy derived from both Jewish and Hellenistic speculation. The false teachers were teaching what they supposed was a kind of advanced course for the spiritual elite. The Christians of Colossae, says F. F. Bruce, "were urged to go in for this progressive wisdom and knowledge (*gnosis*) to explore the deeper mysteries by a series of successive initiations until they attained perfection."[37] The way into this was through Christian baptism, but no one would stop there. The idea was to move as far as possible up the ladder of "truth" until, as a highly enlightened person, one could step off into the realm of light! Gnosticism was saying that Christ had "relinquished successive portions of his authority to the planetary powers as he passed

37. *Paul, Apostle of the Heart Set Free* (Grand Rapids: Eerdmans, 1978), p. 414.

through their sphere on his way to the earth . . . and it was these powers that made him suffer on the cross." Paul goes straight to this error and demands uncompromising preeminence for Christ (see Col. 1:15-29).

> Christ, he says, is the image of God, the one who incorporates the plenitude of given essence so that the elemental spirits have no share in it at all. And those who are members of Christ realize their plenitude in Him; they need not seek, for they cannot find perfection anywhere else.[38]

This strong emphasis on Christ is aimed at the heart of the Colossian "religion." It is absolutely essential that the convert see Jesus Christ in cosmic dimensions as an all-encompassing presence, wisdom, and power that replaces and supersedes everything in the old system.

I have shown, although much too quickly, how Paul expected the gospel to interact with the real world of the convert and how the new Christian must grapple with the meaning of the turning to Christ in the particular. No argument from Jerusalem, Philippi, or Thessalonica would have solved the specific problems faced by the Colossian Christians. The missionary has to fit the message to the world of the convert, not simply at the edges of custom and behavior but rather at the center of truth.[39] The convert must be brought to a saving faith that reaches into the very center of his life, the essence from which beliefs and values emerge. It is there that the redeeming impact of the gospel must be felt. The process aspect of conversion addresses this need. It does not take long to alter certain forms of behavior, speech, and external habits. But to know what it is to "turn from idols" and turn "to the living God" calls for deep penetration of God's truth into the very soul of the individual and to the truth-center of his life. The world of persons, as well as persons themselves, must be changed.

38. Ibid.

39. Paul resisted what is called "cultural conversion." Cultural conversion, says Kraft, is the "error of imposing upon one subculture the forms of Christianity appropriate to another, but not to that of the group in question." *Christianity in Culture,* p. 339.

*Part Three*

# The Convert and the New Life

# 5

# The Spiritual Basis of the New Life

The convert has begun a spiritual journey in a complex world. In a real sense, this convert is alone before God, because the decision made is so personal. We want to look at the individual Christian and try to understand the complexities of this new beginning. Whoever has turned from the old way to place himself or herself under Christ's lordship may have done so as part of a group or as a member of a family. People movements and group decisions are well-known phenomena of missions.[1] Yet even in this type of multi-individual decision it is the individual act of faith of each person that really counts. On the other hand, in many societies of the world, conversion can be a very lonely, private act of faith. Individuals who one by one accept this new Lord must join together and become the church in a given place. It is this individual aspect and the nurture and the care of each and every Christian to which we now turn.

## The Importance of the Individual

Of course, the new Christian is a vital part of the body that we call the church. Paul was careful to connect the personal faith of one believer with the faith of others. He referred to the body when speaking about the corporate nature of the church; yet it is his emphasis on each and every member that stands out. "Christ is like a single body which has many parts. . . . There would not *be* a body if it were all only one part! As it is, there are many parts but one body" (I Cor. 12:12, 19-20; italics added).

It is wrong to think of the church as a mere sum of individuals, an aggregate, as it were, of various persons, each joined to the other by separate acts of faith. Even so, the body as a whole would have no meaning apart from

1. See page 148 and note 58.

the participation of each and every member. The unmistakable emphasis that Paul places on every converted person bears out the primary importance of the individual.[2] Under the control of Christ, who himself is the one, the individual, the whole body is held together by every joint (Eph. 4:16; Col. 2:19). The person of Christ symbolized the distinctly personal nature of the new fellowship. The church, for Paul, is a living, organic whole; but it is such because each and every individual member has a particular obligation and function for the good of the whole organism. Karl Barth takes note of the importance of the individual highlighted in Paul's words in Romans 12:6-8 (cf. I Cor. 12:27-31). The emphasis arises out of a discussion of gifts and the way in which each gifted person functions personally, in and for the community. Everyone is an active "sharpshooting" individual who, according to Barth, is a parson. "Parson," the old term for "pastor," is directly built on the idea of *person.*

> But what parsons they are! Not a word about human requirements. Everything revolves around the demand of God to which all must submit. Each man moves like a shell, shot from the mouth of a gun. Indeed they must and can so move, because *each one* has a purpose. None is engaged in piece work. Nothing is arranged by disciplined administration. In performing his own work each one does One thing which is the whole.[3]

The convert lives in two very real worlds. First is the world of his natural birth, the flesh-and-blood world of his parents and of family near and distant. With these attachments, keeping the laws of traditional life comes as naturally as breathing itself. But the converted person is now a changed person in this intimate world; a world that, he will often discover, has not changed at all. How the new convert ought to relate to his biological and cultural environment is a serious problem.

The second world with which the converted individual must interact is the church, the body of Christ. This is the world of spiritual birth. It is a world of new relationships. The convert's new identity carries responsibilities and loyalties that are often at odds with those of the world of natural birth.

In the 1930s, when the church was new in Nigeria's Gongala State, Wadira and his wife, Binta, were the first couple to become Christians in their village. The missionaries taught them that married couples should eat together. Unfortunately, the habit of eating together is something that the missionaries had misinterpreted as being important to African Christians just because it was important to them. It is considered strange, even today,

2. Romans 2:6; 8:9; 12:3; 14:5.

3. *The Epistle to the Romans,* sixth edition, E. C. Hoskyne, trans. (Oxford: At the University Press, 1933), p. 82.

in most West African societies for the husband and the wife to eat together, or even at the same time. A wife prepares the food and gives it first to her husband or to any group of men that may be in the house. After they have finished, the wife or wives and the children eat. Because certain families act in certain ways in the West, the missionaries felt this should be imitated by Christians in Africa. Beyond this, the assumption was wrong, since eating habits have little to do with whether a person is Christian or not. Even so, Wadira and Binta dutifully complied with the teaching and began to eat their evening meal together in view of the whole village. Before long, ridicule from their family and friends was so great that they moved outside the village and began to live quite separately from the rest of their kin. Not only did Christianity appear to be an alien religion, but also it was assumed by all who turned to Christ that part of the price the Christians pay is separation from traditional society and learning foreign habits.

The consequence of this move by Wadira and Binta was that a small "Christian village" grew up apart from the rest of the people. This was the worst kind of solution to problems raised by conversion, and it carried a message that was precisely the opposite of what the gospel really is. Being a Christian meant dislocation instead of reconciliation. Instead of being a force for transformation, Christianity fostered separation. The traditional world of the convert is intensely real, and the community of Christians also brings a powerful set of new relationships. Issues raised by this identity crisis that comes as a result of belonging in two worlds are very difficult for the convert anywhere, but they are especially hard where the church is a newly emerging community and where there is little precedent for Christianity or where there are few Christians. How is the convert to live under new lordship while the authority of the natural, earthly ties is so pervasive?

First in Paul's pedagogy is his desire to train converts so that each and every one will see his individual worth and acceptance by God. Roland Allen, writing more than seventy years ago, saw the urgency that Paul attached to the right training of individual converts. Here is one of the keys to Paul's amazing success. The converts are to use their own spiritual resources to understand the commitment they have made, and to determine what Christian behavior is.

> With us today there is great difficulty. We can gather in converts, we often gather in large numbers; but we cannot train them to maintain their own spiritual life. Our converts often display great virtues but they remain, too often for generations, dependent on us [the missionaries]. . . . This difficulty unquestionably arises from our early training of our converts and it is of supreme importance that we should endeavor to discover, as far as we can, the method of Paul in training his. For he succeeded exactly where we fail.[4]

4. *Missionary Methods: St. Paul's or Ours?* (1912; reprint ed. London: World Dominion Press, 1960), p. 82.

## The Convert's New World and the Holy Spirit

Unless we begin where Paul did, we can never imagine people being formed together into a church. This concept is the simplest statement to make and the hardest to believe or practice. When a person is converted, the Spirit of Jesus, God's Holy Spirit, comes into the life. What this means is all-encompassing. The Spirit in the life of the believer is so dynamic and transforming that missionaries ought to be able to rest from many of their worries about doctrine, morality, church growth, leadership, finances, standards, and a long list of other things that we feel must be carefully managed. To emphasize the truth, that the Holy Spirit is the leading principle of mission, is nothing new. This conviction inspired the prophetic work of Allen and has been emphasized by others as well. Still, vagueness on the subject of the Holy Spirit has, without question, led to nonproductive, even counterproductive, mission practices. The failure to rely upon the Holy Spirit to minister to the total needs of Christians has been one factor in the formation of hundreds of so-called independent churches in Africa and other countries. These churches claim spiritual power, especially for healing and exorcism. That members of these churches are numbered in the thousands shows that there has been inadequate emphasis on a theology of the Holy Spirit in the "orthodox" churches.

### *Life for All Begins in the Spirit*

In Paul's day the chasm between the Gentiles and the Jews was unbridgeable. The idea of converts joining together as a worshiping community of faith would have been seen as preposterous. Questions raised by the gospel appeared insoluble. For example, if uncircumcised Gentiles were admitted into the church, what would be their relation to faithful Jews? How could a keeper of the law associate on equal terms with one who did not keep that law? How could the church ever survive as one body when those who knew nothing of the covenant could ask for and receive salvation just as could those who were of the covenant people? Would not Jewish Christians begin to live as the pagan Gentiles, since no requirements were made of the Gentiles to become Jews? Would a non-Jew who had been baptized ever have the same right to positions of prestige and honor as the Jew? Once we understand the implications such questions carried for new Christians, we might say there are no problems in mission practice today as devastating as these that Paul faced.

Allen's work constantly returns to the question stressed so often in his mission theology. How were these controversial arguments to be answered?

His reply is, "By one fact: God gave them [the Gentiles] the Holy Spirit."[5] The outworking of this conviction is developed most fully with Paul, but we see its beginning in the post-Pentecostal events surrounding the ministry of Peter. "The Jewish believers who had come from Joppa with Peter were amazed that God had poured out his gift of the Holy Spirit on the Gentiles also. They had heard them speaking in strange tongues and praising God. Peter spoke up: 'These people have received the Holy Spirit, just as we also did. Can anyone, then, stop them from being baptized with water?' " (Acts 10:47). When Peter's action was criticized by the leaders at Jerusalem, his answers centered on the Holy Spirit. "The Spirit told me to go with them without hesitation" (Acts 11:12). "The Holy Spirit came down on them just as on us at the beginning" (Acts 11:15). And, "it is clear that God gave those Gentiles the same gift that he gave us when we believed in the Lord Jesus Christ; who was I, then, to try to stop God!" (Acts 11:17).

There is no other way to describe who the Christian is but to say that he or she is a person who has the living Spirit of Jesus within. Allen speaks of the illusory way in which the Holy Spirit is perceived by new converts and claims that this is a direct result of the lack of teaching by the missionary. Since the personal, living presence of the Spirit in the lives of new Christians is a truth of first importance, how can this truth be communicated and understood by the new Christian?

> There is a way of thinking and speaking of the Holy Spirit which banishes the vagueness and makes it perfectly clear why the apostles spoke of the gift of the Holy Spirit as being given only to Christians. If we think of this gift as the gift of the Spirit which dwelt in Jesus Christ, in the man Jesus Christ of whom the gospels speak, instantly the title becomes clear and definite.[6]

Allen was calling for directness and simplicity—a recovery of the primary fact of the Christian life: that the new life means the end of a self-centeredness and the beginning of a life in the Spirit (Rom. 8:9). Herman N. Ridderbos notes that it is the Spirit who sets the believer off on a new course and it is "on the ground of this new principle of life, the sharing in and living under the government of the Spirit," that one can speak of himself as a Christian.[7]

The Christian life of each and every believer is prepared for by the Spirit, is begun in the Spirit, and is nurtured by the Spirit. The Holy Spirit is the agent who brings God's truth to men. The Holy Spirit is also the one who

5. Roland Allen, *The Ministry of the Spirit,* Selected writings of Roland Allen, David M. Paton, ed. (London: World Dominion Press, 1960), p. 56.

6. Ibid., pp. 10-11.

7. *Paul, an Outline of His Theology,* J. R. DeWitt, trans. (Grand Rapids: Eerdmans, 1975), pp. 215-217.

prepares men's hearts to receive the truth, and who enlightens their minds to comprehend and appropriate it. In short, "God's Spirit joins himself to our spirits to declare that we are God's children" (Rom. 8:16).

Regardless of culture or background, it is only the gracious presence of the Spirit in a person that gives the certainty of the new life. William Barclay understands the verse just quoted in the context of the verse immediately preceding (Rom. 8:15). Because we are now God's children, his Spirit within makes it possible to cry out, "Father! my Father!" ("Abba, father"). What gives us the certainty that we are the children of God, and can now call on God for our deepest needs?

> Paul's answer is that the impulse which moves us in the first place to desire these things is the impulse of the Spirit, and the certainty in our hearts that we will not be disappointed is also the work of the Spirit. It is the Spirit who tells us of our need of God, it is the Spirit who starts us on our way to God, it is the Spirit who makes us sure that God is waiting to welcome us, and that he is the Father whom our hearts desire.[8]

That God has knowledge of each and every believer is mentioned in nearly every epistle of Paul. "The Lord knows those who are his" (II Tim. 2:19), and "the person who loves God is known by him" (I Cor. 8:3). God's ownership and knowledge of every believer rests on the fact that the Spirit of God is given to the believer. "Whoever does not have the Spirit of Christ does not belong to him" (Rom. 8:9). "We have received the Spirit sent by God" (I Cor. 2:12). The Spirit's presence will be revealed in some particular way in each person and this will be for the good of all (I Cor. 12:7). No one, regardless of parentage, former religion, race, literacy, or social status, becomes a Christian except by the Spirit. The children of God have the Spirit of his Son in their hearts (Gal. 3:5; 4:6).

We must understand that the Spirit is present, actively present, in every believer, regardless of how recent the conversion, or how "unchristian" the background, or how improbable conversion may seem. All that the convert will now decide and all the progress he will make in his Christian life depends upon this truth.

### *The Spirit Must Be Trusted in Each Convert*

It is, therefore, a fact of the new life that the Holy Spirit is God's special gift (Rom. 5:5), a reality in each person who has turned in faith to Christ. This is not something that man has done; it is the way God meant salvation to be. Paul had to remind the Jews many times that they had the Spirit of

8. William Barclay, *The Mind of St. Paul* (New York: Harper and Row, 1975), p. 178.

Christ within them and that it had nothing to do with the law. "Tell me this one thing: did you receive God's Spirit by doing what the Law requires or by hearing the gospel and believing it? How can you be so foolish! You began by God's Spirit; do you now want to finish by your own power?" (Gal. 3:2-3). If we, as God's servants, cannot trust young Christians to be taught by God's Spirit, then these words of Paul are important. For the Galatians, the law, rules, and regulations could no longer suffice. As Christians they had no other beginning but in the Spirit, and by that Spirit alone they had to understand what the Christian life is.

In 1960 I was a student of Otto Piper at Princeton Theological Seminary. When he heard that I was a missionary his first question was, "Tell me, what substitutes do you and your mission colleagues have for the Holy Spirit?" He was saying that missionaries rarely give the Holy Spirit the right to lead or instruct the church. Rather, they feel their teaching and regulations can better produce the standards required. We do not trust the Spirit to teach the newly converted because we are not deeply convinced that the Spirit is really present in the life. Because we doubt that the new Christian can sense the Spirit's presence, the missionaries become the presence. We trust our own selves and systems more than we trust the Holy Spirit of Christ.

We do want people to know the Spirit of regeneration. We rejoice when we see the change when someone from a very "different" kind of non-Christian background confesses that the resurrected Christ is now his or her Lord. But then comes the danger that we will insist on supervising everything from that point onward. We feel it our duty to describe what a Christian is and it is usually we who begin to interpret Scripture for that person. Rarely do we ask anything of the Christian, such as, "What has the Spirit been telling you about your new Lord and your new life?" Again, if persons cannot read, we rush to get them into a literacy class. While we agree that reading what the Spirit says to us in the Bible is important, may we not trust the Spirit and the new convert to communicate together in deeply personal dialogue even without the Scripture?

The written text of the Bible is certainly the supreme source of the truth. Yet, the Holy Spirit is an active and true guide in the life of every believer and we must trust him to speak directly to the regenerated human spirit. This is one of the hardest lessons for the missionary to learn. At Pentecost God's own Spirit—nothing less—was given, and it is a dependency on this totally adequate Spirit in the life of every believer that Paul models for us. Harry R. Boer says,

> This we have not fully appreciated. For it means that if we transmit to others the life of the Spirit we must not hinder them in fully expressing the freedom and joy of life. If we are eager to see them gather knowledge in the Spirit we should also be eager to see them express that knowledge they have

gathered. If we exert ourselves to give them the Spirit of holiness and of life, we should be eager to give them the spirit of liberty through which that life comes to expression.[9]

*Early responsibility for new Christians*

It is evident that we have not learned to trust the Holy Spirit to communicate to new Christians. All too often pastors, elders, and older Christians, including the missionary, think they must do all the thinking for them. We cripple young Christians by doing everything for them. We fear that they will "go wrong," "backslide," or "live substandard Christian lives," and do not give them room to breathe in the Spirit.

We shall see that Paul trusted his churches to elders who were appointed very soon after conversion. He believed that the only way to show a new Christian what the seriousness of the Christian life really is is to give him responsibility. When someone receives Christ as Lord, that person is expected to live as though Christ is Lord (Col. 2:6). It was not carelessness or compromise that led Paul to commend his new converts to the Spirit. He was convinced that sonship carried heavy responsibility for witness and, equally, that the Holy Spirit would instruct and guide. He wrote simply, "Do not grieve the Holy Spirit of God" (Eph. 4:30, RSV). This meant that the converts were to live "a life which measures up to the standard God set when he called you" (Eph. 4:1). These were recent converts, but Paul handed them the responsibility of "liv[ing] like people who belong to the light" (Eph. 5:8). The key command of the entire letter to the Colossians was based on the fact that Christians of only a few months were expected to live in Christ Jesus the Lord in the same manner in which they received him (2:6).[10]

Jesus promised that the Holy Spirit would be in touch with the human spirit if given the freedom to do so, and would teach what is right. We must be convinced about this. The Spirit both teaches all things and guides into all truth (John 14:26; 16:13). I, for one, should have recognized that the mission of the Spirit is to teach truth to all Christians regardless of how much or how little background they may have had. This means that they should be given responsibility to make decisions. I recall not one or two but many instances where new Christians with little or no previous teaching, who often could not read the Bible, found the answers to their own questions within themselves, or showed amazing insight without any outside help.

Saraya, for example, was one of three wives in a traditional African family. She lived in the village of Salla where there were only three or four other

9. *Pentecost and Missions* (Grand Rapids: Eerdmans, 1961), p. 222.
10. See also Romans 8:11-12; Galatians 5:16; I Thessalonians 2:12.

Christians. When she told her husband that she had left her old life to follow Jesus the Lord, he treated her very badly. He withheld the privileges of marriage from her even though she was the senior wife, yet forced her to carry water and cook. When I visited Salla with an African pastor, Saraya came to the Sunday service. We could tell she had been beaten around the face and the shoulders. Saraya explained her predicament and did not even ask us what she should do. She had already decided to stay with her husband and try to get along with the other wives. She said she would cook his food, even though she had to carry it to him from another house to which she had been banished. She would not return the abuse she was receiving from the other women. I asked her why she was sure this was the right way, and whether she ever felt she had the right to leave her husband. Her answer surprised me, but seemingly not the Africans who were listening. She said, "I will not leave him, but I will serve him and try to respect him. The reason for this is that a voice tells me in my heart that if I am careful and try to love him, he will be overcome by God's power. After some time he will see that God wants him to be different!" (See I Cor. 7:13-14.)

I could recount a number of instances where no Christian answer to a personal problem could have been given but by the Spirit, communicating directly to a new Christian. It amazes me that I and my colleagues, and even pastors and evangelists whom I have trained, have not really grasped that God is in the believer by his Spirit and he *will* teach, if we allow it.

*Young Christians should "think through" their faith*

Paul insisted that his converts begin to exercise their responsibility to find the answers to their questions within themselves. Right thinking is possible with the help of the ever-present Spirit. It is clear that Paul never left his new converts without teaching. He reminded them in numerous places of his faithfulness in teaching while he was with them. Nevertheless, he expected these Christians to think through the meaning of their new faith *on their own,* knowing full well that the Lord would not abandon them. Paul was disappointed when new Christians, even those with little background, would not think for themselves. This led to their being carried away by false teachers (Eph. 4:14) and sidetracked through lack of spiritual reasoning (Gal. 4:9-11).

Paul was not able to make everyday decisions for these young Christians because he was not permanently identified with any one group. As they faced problems raised by the new way, Christians were to find the right answers themselves. He expected their reflection on important issues to show that growth was taking place. He wrote, "Do not be like children in your thinking, my brothers" (I Cor. 14:20; cf. Eph. 4:14). In writing to various groups of Christians around Ephesus he said, "[I] ask . . . God . . . to give you the Spirit, who will make you wise and reveal God to you, so that you will know him." He added, "I ask that your minds may be opened to see his light" (Eph. 1:17-18). Anything less than finding out what the will of the Lord is would be foolishness (Eph. 5:17). Paul could not have made it clearer than he did when he said that believers have all received the Spirit sent by God and this is for the purpose of knowing all that God has given us (I Cor. 2:12). Responsibility for this kind of thinking is possible and right for new Christians because they "have the mind of Christ" (I Cor. 2:16).

### *The Spirit As Love*

There is one way above all others to describe the life of the convert to whom the Spirit of Christ has been given; this is by using the word *love.* Any understanding of what God has done through Christ or of how a person is to relate to others is impossible except in terms of love. Love is the principal characteristic of the new heart. This foundation of Paul's teaching provided a solid basis for dealing with unbelievably diverse and fallible communities of people. Nothing is more fundamental to the individual's experience in Christ than to know his love. Love as *agapē* is the simplest and truest expression of the distinctive nature of the Christian religion. Jesus showed how all-inclusive this love is in its scope, how free in its mercy, how searching in its demand, and how strong in its transforming power. Paul faithfully taught and preached the gospel of love.

To have one's roots in Christ is to say that one is rooted and grounded in love (Eph. 3:17; Col. 2:7). Being a new creature (Gal. 6:15) can also be expressed as the faith that works itself out in love (Gal. 5:6). Love together with faith is the heart and the content of the Christian life;[11] there is simply no other way to imagine the fellowship of Christians except as a fellowship of love.[12] "It is love, then, that you should strive for" (I Cor. 14:1). "Do all your work in love" (I Cor. 16:14). "Your life must be controlled by love" (Eph. 5:2). "Above all these put on love" (Col. 3:14, RSV). "The only obligation you have is to love one another" (Rom. 13:8). How Paul's injunctions to love stand out! They cover all attitudes, judge all motives, and guard every action. The individual Christian is to learn love because he has been changed by love. Love is characteristic of the Spirit and the Spirit is the source of love (Rom. 15:30; Gal. 5:22). How casual yet how insistent Paul is about this love. "There is no need to write to you about love. . . . You yourselves have been taught by God how you should love one another" (I Thess. 4:9).

Love through the Spirit brings the individual believer in touch with the other members of the body. The basic principle of mutual care and concern

11. See the discussion by Ridderbos in *Paul,* pp. 293ff.

12. I Corinthians 13:13; Galatians 5:5ff.; Colossians 1:4; I Thessalonians 1:3; I Timothy 6:11; II Timothy 3:10; Titus 2:2.

is found in Paul's earliest letter. He appeals to the Thessalonians to make it their aim to "do good to one another and to all people" (I Thess. 5:15). It is not a light thing that Christians should be concerned for each other. Paul could say that whoever had fulfilled the commandment of love stood as one who had fulfilled the whole law (Gal. 5:14; cf. Rom. 13:8-10). So Paul is speaking here of a new law. There were no other laws that could be lifted above this law. M. S. Enslin comments, "Just as faith takes the place of law between man and God, so love took the place of definite legal enactments between man and man."[13]

It is interesting that Paul writes only twice about the more earthly, friendly love (*philadelphia*) that the "brethren" are to have for one another (Rom. 12:10; I Thess. 4:9). It is *agapē* love with which Paul is most concerned. When he writes in so many places about *agapē* love he is referring to a mutual nurturing love between believers. Each Christian is to be a servant of the other in love (Gal. 5:13). They are to owe no one anything except love (Rom. 13:8). Carefully, therefore, "the apostle time and again takes the field against every form of spiritual individualism."[14] Ridderbos shows how easily the individual can get out of touch with the body and how quickly, without love, the spirit of humility and service can be set aside. For example, the liberty into which each believer has been called can divide the weak from the strong. Some may say they may eat this or drink that even though others are offended or misled. This is not acting out of love. For obviously "if you hurt your brother because of something you eat, then you are no longer acting from love" (Rom. 14:15). On the subject of spiritual gifts, there is a danger of the *charismata* separating people. One believer may tend to see his ministry as more valuable than that of someone else (I Cor. 12). "No where does love emerge more clearly than here in its character as binding together and involving the entire church."[15] These ethical problems will be taken up in some detail later, but we must see that the principle of love is more important than knowledge—more basic to a right beginning for the Christian than right doctrine or "keeping the rules." The Spirit is given to every believer and it is by the Holy Spirit that God has poured out his love into our hearts. This is God's gift (Rom. 5:5).

That every Christian has been given the Holy Spirit has been one of the least-shared truths of missionary theology. The traditional world from which the convert turns is very likely dominated by a belief in many spirits and rituals of power to accomplish all kinds of things and meet an array of needs. Typically this convert is expected to attend an inquirers' class in which the

13. *The Ethics of Paul* (Nashville: Abingdon, 1957), p. 241. Enslin notes that *agapē* was for Paul the "queen of virtues," and that the word never occurs outside of biblical usage. See Enslin, p. 241, n. 40, for related secular usage.

14. Ridderbos, *Paul*, p. 295.

15. Ibid.

questions and the answers have usually been handed down in rote fashion, perhaps from a pastor or an elder, for the new Christian to learn. Consequently, these instruction classes probably will not deal with the deep needs of those who attend them or confront the problems that an encounter with the old religion raises. As a result, Christians are forced to live their lives on two levels. There is the level of Christian faith in which the person believes and memorizes the facts of the religion called Christianity. On another level he or she is left to live with the traditional world, familiar from birth. The Holy Spirit must become real in belief and experience from the very commencement of life in Christ. Unless the Spirit is known as an active reality, there will not be the motivation, the strength, or the understanding to cope with the many temptations and questions that will arise. To know this Spirit as the Spirit of love means that, above all, Christ and the believer are joined in unbreakable ties of faith. It will mean for the church that there will be great patience shown to the new convert as he makes progress in understanding what is required of him as a Christian. We need more love and less law, more of the Spirit and less of the human leaders when persons are taking their first steps in the Christian walk.

### *The Spirit As Liberty*

Another characteristic of the Spirit that the convert must understand in living is that which Paul speaks of as being "free in Christ." Chapter 1 showed that freedom is of the very nature of Paul's theology. That freedom can be translated into the experience of the individual believer and must be carefully taught and joyfully practiced. When Paul wrote to the Galatians about liberty he showed what the Master meant when he said, "If the Son sets you free, then you will be really free" (John 8:36). The entire Epistle to the Galatians is summed up fittingly with the words, "Freedom is what we have—Christ has set us free! Stand, then, as free people, and do not allow yourselves to become slaves again" (Gal. 5:1).

Through conversion has come a new sense of well-being, and the individual Christian has achieved a new status that is both exhilarating and truly liberating.[16] By this new freedom "the spiritual man has seen the heart of the Eternal, the meaning of life and of all being, of his own true nature and of the highest good; and he has made the supreme choice, the great surrender."[17] Although his final authority now belongs to Another, yet there is

16. An insightful description of conversion with an African independent movement is by Bennette Jules-Rosette, "The Conversion Experience: The Apostle of John Maranke." Conversion is seen as a "new experience of self" and as "new status." *Journal of Religion in Africa* (Leiden: Brill, 1975), vol. 7, pp. 132-164.

17. H. F. Rall, *According to Paul* (New York: Charles Scribner's Sons, 1945), p. 198.

real freedom for the outward life as the expression of the inward spirit that has been set free. The freedom is real but always carries with it serious responsibilities and certain limitations.

*Release from tradition*

Paul's audiences were made up of people who felt that certain rites had to be observed in order to keep favor with the gods. Among the Romans, it was believed that the empire was kept from disaster through the careful performance of sacrifices and the rigid practice of various religious duties. "This attitude bred fear and a spirit of compulsion; there was always the possibility that something was left undone in the service of the gods."[18] Paul reminded his converts about this bondage when he wrote, "In the past you did not know God, so you were slaves of beings who are not gods" (Gal. 4:8). What a sense of release must have overtaken the Gentile Christians as they experienced being set free from these "weak and pitiful ruling spirits." It was incredible that anyone would ever, for a moment, slip back into their control (Gal. 4:9-11). What a changed world also for the Jews, as they felt the shackles of the law drop away! By this forgiveness God, through Christ, "canceled the unfavorable record of our debts [to the law] with its binding rules and did away with it completely by nailing it to the cross" (Col. 2:14; cf. Gal. 5:1).

We who have the advantage of being reared in Christian families and being surrounded by God's people of faith all our lives can scarcely know what release there can be when the Spirit's power sets a person free. Guilt and the burden of sin carry their own enslavement from which the soul of every man must be liberated. In our own society we know that men and women are being released from the stranglehold of drugs and the occult. For many these things have become a way of life, and the hold of habits can almost be spoken of as tradition. It is unforgettable to see persons liberated from the bondage of certain aspects of a traditional culture where the gospel had not been known.

In 1962 I was a part of a group of pastors conducting an evangelistic conference in the Nigerian village of Didango. An average of six hundred people attended the evening services and rarely did a service close without between ten and twenty people hearing the call of God and seeking personal salvation. One night as the African pastors, another missionary, and I were praying with each of those who had made his decision, an unusual thing happened. One of those who had repented stood and said, "I thank God." With that, he picked up his stick and literally ran from the thatched prayer house. He circled the entire village and continued running into the woods.

18. Joseph A. Grassi, *The Secret of Paul the Apostle* (Maryknoll, NY: Orbis Books, 1978), p. 90.

No one went after him, nor did anyone think his actions irrational. When he returned, he called those of us who remained and said simply, "For nearly two years I have been the victim of a curse put upon me by a witch who lives in another town. I have tried many ways to get release from this, but it is no use because none of the 'doctors' can identify who my accuser is. This curse has made me sick in my thinking as well as in my body. No one told me that if I repented I would find the secret I have been looking for. But tonight, as I was forgiven, my whole body was released from terror. It was a surprise, and I could not find anything to say. So I tried out this freedom by running in the night. It is wonderful. I have not been free to do anything at night for many months. Tonight God ran along with me and no ghost came near. I have been set free. Thank God."

*Limitations of liberty*

Paul recognized that redemption meant liberty for each new convert—a liberty ministered through the Spirit. This is why he refused to lay down a new set of rules. The Christian is now to be governed by the first law of the Spirit, the law of love under the lordship of Christ. "Living in fellowship with God through Christ Jesus" (Rom. 6:11) means giving oneself to God; "surrender[ing] your whole being to him to be used for righteous purposes" (Rom. 6:13). To be "set free" also means to become "slaves of God" (Rom. 6:22). So for Paul this freedom is not detachment from commitments or disengagement from responsibility. Young Christians will find there is a check on their attitudes and actions as they are sensitive to the Spirit of liberty whom they have received. We shall see there are limitations set upon personal behavior as well as on social ethics, because the indwelling Spirit establishes a new basis for judging right and wrong and lays upon the believer personal responsibility for thinking and acting according to these convictions.

Why did Paul lay such emphasis on freedom, and why was he so concerned that each new Christian understand it? As a Jew, he would not have had a great deal of background in the subject. Even though the story of the exodus was the most precious memory that the Jews had, there is comparatively little in Jewish literature on the subject of freedom. Freedom for the Jews was always theocentric—something that God brought to his people. The implications of freedom at the personal and social levels never became a major theme of rabbinical thought.[19] Paul's convictions about freedom for the individual seem much closer to Greek thought, particularly Stoicism.

19. See the discussion by Richard N. Longenecker in *Paul, Apostle of Liberty* (Grand Rapids: Baker, 1976). Longenecker feels the idea of liberty is always in a nomistic context (e.g., Ps. 119:44-45, "I will keep thy law continually, for ever and ever; and I shall walk at liberty, for I have sought thy precepts"), p. 157.

Richard N. Longenecker, in his careful study on Christian liberty, notes that Epictetus used the word *liberty* four times more frequently than Paul, but comes to the conclusion that the similarities are only superficial.[20] Paul did use the concept of personal liberty in Christ in ways that would appeal to the Greek mind, but, as Enslin says, "freedom meant something quite different to Paul from what it did to the Stoic." For Paul, "freedom was to be tempered with love and mutual forbearance."[21] For the Greek, freedom was self-centered and unrestrained: "That man is free who lives as he wishes; who is proof against compulsion, hinderance and violence; whose impulses are untrammeled, who gets what he wills to get and avoids what he wills to avoid."[22]

The presence of the active Spirit in the life of the new Christian means that love and liberty are joined, as it were, into a single spiritual law. Augustine's thought came very close to that of Paul when he said, "Love, and do as thou wilt." How decisively the parameters of liberty and love govern the church! "Be careful . . . not to let your freedom of action make those who are weak in the faith fall into sin" (I Cor. 8:9). "As for you, my brothers, you were called to be free. But do not let this freedom become an excuse for letting your physical desires control you. Instead, let love make you serve one another" (Gal. 5:13).[23]

One of the Christians at Corinth was apparently so carried away by his claim to be free in Christ that he didn't even respect the moral codes of the traditional community. This man had been sleeping with his own stepmother, an act "so terrible that not even the heathen would be guilty of it" (I Cor. 5:1). Paul was even more shocked by the attitude of the church in allowing this perverse behavior to go on. To be free from the bondage of sin (Rom. 6:7, 18, 22) certainly does not mean continuing in sin (Rom. 6:1). On the contrary, this freedom can be understood only as the new Christian is taught that he is now "a slave to righteousness" (Rom. 6:18) and a "slave of God" (Rom. 6:22). Freedom controlled by love is given through the Holy Spirit, and this freedom can be expressed only through obedience to Christ himself and respect for his body, the church.

## The Convert and Spiritual Gifts

After some fifteen years as a missionary I began to see how deficient my own understanding of the Holy Spirit was. I had come from a Wesleyan

20. Ibid., p. 158. For further comments, see W. A. Oldfather, *Epictetus*, Loeb Classical Library (London: Heinemann, 1925), vol. 1, p. 218.

21. Enslin, *The Ethics of Paul*, p. 39.

22. Epictetus, quoted by Enslin, ibid., note 78 for reference.

23. See also Romans 14:13, 20; 15:1; I Corinthians 9:12, 19.

background that emphasized sanctification and the activity of the Holy Spirit in the life of the Christian. However, there seemed to be little perception of the truth that God's personal Spirit can work through the lives of new believers in a first-generation Christian church. The idea that even illiterate and untrained African Christians have the gifts of the Spirit and should be putting them to work not only was hard to believe, but also seemed irrelevant. In part, this was due to a failure to appreciate the important Pauline teaching,[24] but other factors contributed as well. The missionary, for example, was assumed to be the truly gifted leader. Trained, called, ordained, equipped—the missionary accepted the role of the expert. This role carried the tacit assumption that only specialists, such as missionaries and a few carefully chosen nationals, had the right to exercise spiritual gifts. The underlying idea was that recent converts have a long way to go in Christian nurture before they can be trusted to lead and serve.

### *Gifts and Renewal*

The colonial mentality in missions may have been more devastating than we generally admit. It was assumed that those who came from the outside had the knowledge and authority, while those who were "served" by the expatriate should be followers and learners. As the Christians in the Muri Church of Christ (Nigeria)[25] were allowed to take over tasks that the missionaries had been doing, more and more people filled the churches and more African Christians began to preach, pray, and sing. It was obvious that participation was widespread and that gifts were everywhere. However, the Apostolic and Pentecostal groups were generally looked down upon. Their "prophets" and pastors conducted emotional worship services and gave special attention to healing. This was a dimension that our churches had rarely seen. The so-called independent churches, considered sects by some, were resisted by the missionaries and by most African church leaders, and yet demonstrated an unusual concern for meeting human need. These churches accepted the simple truth that Jesus' religion is the Good News, and that he does excite the spirit, heal the body, and empower the soul.

Until ten or fifteen years ago few historic denominations took seriously the scriptural teaching on spiritual gifts. To be charismatic was to be identified with various Pentecostal churches. Little was said in the major semi-

24. The term *charisma,* meaning "gift given out of good will," is peculiarly Pauline. With the exception of I Peter, the word occurs only in Paul's writings. For a discussion, see the *Dictionary of New Testament Theology,* Colin Brown, ed. (Grand Rapids: Zondervan, 1980), pp. 115-124.

25. Muri Church refers to a district (Muri) in Nigeria that was opened to church planting by the Evangelical Church (now United Methodist) in 1922 and is an affiliate of the Churches of Christ in Nigeria and the Sudan United Mission.

naries about gifts. *Charismata* were mentioned only in connection with the first-century church. Spiritual gifts were seen as a provision for rapid mission expansion in the time of Paul and the apostle John, but of little importance today. Obviously, therefore, the churches planted by most "orthodox" boards received little or no teaching concerning gifts. The missionaries in the non-Pentecostal churches saw so little evidence of gifts in themselves and reacted so negatively to Pentecostal stereotypes that they regarded this teaching as poor theology and its results as pure emotionalism.

However, the situation is changing. In the past ten years an impressive body of literature has been written about the role of spiritual gifts.[26] C. Peter Wagner states that

> rarely, if ever, in the history of the Church has such a widespread interest in moving beyond creeds and theologies to a personal experience of the Holy Spirit in everyday life swept over the people of God to the degree we are now witnessing. The most prominent facet of this new experience of the Holy Spirit is spiritual gifts.[27]

This wave of charismatic renewal in the church as a whole is having its effect for good on mission theology and practice. We are realizing slowly that to understand and put into use the gift or gifts given by the Holy Spirit is the responsibility of each convert. Considering the variety of gifts, some spectacular and others modest,[28] it is not unreasonable to say that each convert has a gift that must be recognized and cultivated.[29] These gifts not only are demonstrated in great displays of healing power, effective preaching, and marvelous administrative abilities, but also include many gifts that appear to be of lesser value (I Cor. 14:1, 5). Humble gifts, such as being a helper or showing mercy (Rom. 12:8), when used completely, can be more useful than speaking in tongues—which, in fact, Paul sees as a lesser gift, even though it reveals itself as more spectacular than others (I Cor. 14). I shall say more about this later. The essential point is that each one is to see himself as a minister and each one is equipped in some way to serve.

Paul states simply, *"The Spirit's presence is shown in some way in each person for the good of all"* (I Cor. 12:7; italics added). This emphasis on the responsibility of each member—each convert—within the body is a hallmark

26. For a summary of current writing on spiritual gifts, see C. Peter Wagner, *Your Spiritual Gifts Can Help Your Church Grow* (Glendale, CA: Regal, 1979), pp. 27-29.

27. Ibid., p. 19.

28. A practical treatment of spiritual gifts, covering the variety and the purposes, is found in David Watson, *I Believe in the Church* (Grand Rapids: Eerdmans, 1978), pp. 104-110.

29. Ridderbos states, "Each has his own *charisma* from God. . . . and everyone has to live and act therein according to the nature of his *charisma,* and not according to another (Rom. 12:3ff.)." *Paul,* pp. 442-443.

of Paul's teaching (I Cor. 12:27). "Every one of the members is placed in the Body according to God's design," says Wagner. "No Christian needs to feel left out when it comes to possessing a spiritual gift."[30] (See I Cor. 12:18.) What lies behind every emphasis on gifts is the function that they have within and for the church. Paul's all-important first lesson is that each and every member has a share in the responsibility for ministry (*diakonia*), and that spiritual gifts (*charismata*) provide the means by which this ministry is to be accomplished.

### *The Responsibility to Serve*

The idea of serving as a mark of being a disciple was a revolutionary teaching of Jesus. He taught that greatness is achieved through service and made ministry to others a requirement for those who would follow him. The difference between empty profession and true discipleship was whether a person served others. In the judgment, those who claim to know him but who have learned only the creed and observed only the ritual will be rejected. "Away from me, you that are under God's curse! . . . I was hungry but you would not feed me, thirsty but you would not give me drink; I was a stranger but you would not welcome me in your homes, naked but you would not clothe me; I was sick and in prison but you would not take care of me" (Matt. 25:41-43). The key thought here is expressed by the phrase "you did not serve me" (*ou diēkonēsate*).

Association with Jesus is possible only as his disciples serve one another in love. When James and John asked for the prominent places in the kingdom, Jesus made it abundantly clear that "if one of you wants to be great, he must be the servant of the rest. . . . For even the Son of Man did not come to be served; he came to serve and to give his life to redeem many people" (Mark 10:43, 45). Jesus did not claim his lordship without first exercising his servanthood. The community that Jesus founded is made up of individuals who serve one another.

Paul builds on the teachings of Jesus and develops more fully the concept of service (*diakonia;* Phil. 2:5-11). This is a distinctly New Testament concept. Obedience to God under the lordship of Christ is now much more than sterile rituals or ceremonial offices.[31] Service is to be by means of spiritual gifts (*charismata*). Having understood that the church is to be a serving community, Paul leads us directly to the provision for service. Each member exists for every other member. The serving, ministering function is

30. *Your Spiritual Gifts,* p. 40.

31. G. W. Bromiley emphasizes that ministry is concerned more with humble obedience to God than with the prerogatives of office. *Christian Ministry* (Grand Rapids: Eerdmans, 1960), p. 46.

based on the variety of gifts,[32] so that the members of the church are enabled to effectively serve one another by means of their special God-given abilities.

> As each one in the Body of Christ serves God by using his gift in the service of others, he is clearly stamped with the characteristics of a servant. Even the gifts he uses need not be his own natural abilities. The convert has nothing of which he/she may boast (Romans 12:3-6), but is completely at the service of the Church.[33]

Each one is to consider himself to be as much in ministry as anyone else. There are many different ways of serving and many different abilities, but there is no Christian who is not enabled in some way to perform a service (I Cor. 12:7). Each one is necessary for the others. No one is less important or more important than another, for "God himself has put the body together in such a way as to give greater honor to those that need it. And so there is no division in the body, but all its different parts have the same concern for one another" (I Cor. 12:24-25).

It will always be difficult for missionaries to understand how Paul could plant true churches[34] and not stay longer than he did. It was unusual if he stayed more than a few weeks at one place, Corinth and Ephesus being the notable exceptions.[35] This mobility was supported by two equally important convictions. One was that he was called to be an apostle on the move. Evangelizing rather than administering was his first task. Almost as important was his conviction that the burden for growth and nurture should be carried by each new congregation. This was to be shared equally by all members of the body, regardless of how recently they had become Christians, or how unlikely their background.

In contrast to Paul, today's missionary (who has usually come from the West) finds it hard to allow recent converts to minister. New believers are not taught that the responsibility to serve is normative for each and for all, or that there are gifts and abilities to be sought and put to use. Because of this, young Christians assume that they have no responsibility and that everything will be given to them or taught to them by the "expert," whether expatriate missionary or national pastor and elders.[36] The dependency on

32. See Hans Küng, *The Church,* R. and R. Ockenden, trans. (New York: Sheed and Ward, 1968), p. 39.

33. Paul Watney, "Ministry Gifts: God's Provision for Effective Mission," unpublished dissertation (Pasadena, CA: Fuller Theological Seminary, 1979), p. 13.

34. True churches are those that are self-administering, self-financing, and self-propagating, but also have a theology that is unique to their own interaction and encourage the members of the body to minister to each other and to the world.

35. Acts 18:11; 19:10.

36. Allen did some of his most convincing writing on this point. It is found throughout his

the Holy Spirit that I have been describing does not develop among our mission churches. Leaders, including missionaries, work on the assumption that people have to be mature, seasoned Christians before they can be given tasks to do. No call to service is made. No demand of the young Christians is heard. They may be told to witness orally about their newfound faith, but they will not be pressed into responsibility in the sense of *diakonia.* Because this expectation is not made clear at the beginning of the Christian life, it may never be discussed, with the result that the church's growth is hindered and its power diminished.

### *Enablement to Serve*

The renewal of interest in spiritual gifts is something we must claim for missions today. In so doing we come back to Paul to discover how insistent he was on the *charismata* for all Christians. This is an emphasis that was accepted during the apostolic period and continued without question for at least four centuries. It is very hard to know why an emphasis on gifts gradually disappeared. But as the church became identified with the state and the clergy tragically divided from the laity, gifts all but disappeared from the church.

In the second-century *Didache* the gift of prophecy was taken for granted.[37] Justin Martyr (100-165), who lived in the same period, claimed that the gifts, especially the gift of prophecy, of the Spirit were not unknown even to Jewish prophets and were self-evident in the church.[38] Irenaeus (130-200) taught that "speaking in all languages came with the Holy Spirit."[39] Tertullian (160-220) said that "we acknowledge spiritual gifts" and went on to list revelation and visions as examples, concluding that "the apostle most assuredly foretold that there were to be spiritual gifts in the church."[40] However, after Augustine (A.D. 430) there was not the same consistent emphasis on gifts. Augustine himself first disputed the existence of gifts, then later recounted his own experiences as a witness to a number of miracles, including exorcism and healing.[41] We could go on to show

---

works; see, for example, "The Training of Candidates for Baptism and Ordination" in *Missionary Methods,* pp. 95-107.

37. See J. B. Lightfoot, *The Apostolic Fathers* (London: McMillan, 1917), p. 233 (*Didache*), p. 405 (Hermas), p. 138 (Ignatius).

38. Refer to "A Dialogue with Trypho," in T. B. Falls, *The Fathers of the Church* (New York: Heritage, 1949), vol. 6, p. 278.

39. "Against Heresies" 1.6.1, in *Ante-Nicene Fathers,* A. Roberts and J. Donaldson, trans. (New York: Charles Scribner's Sons, 1925), vol. 1, p. 531.

40. "A Treatise on the Soul," pt. 1; ibid., 4, vol. 3, p. 188.

41. *City of God,* vol. 2, bk. 22, in *The Ancient and Modern Library of Theological Literature,* John Healey, trans. (Edinburgh: John Grant, 1909), pp. 337ff.

scattered references to spiritual gifts in much of the subsequent history of the church. However, with the Pentecostals and more recently with the charismatic groups, we have seen a renewed and consistent emphasis on spiritual gifts. It is an emphasis that is needed, for in it we recognize the wave of new power available to mission churches at a time when it is needed most. National churches everywhere are seeking resources that are spiritual in order to evangelize and nurture the young believers. Carefully taught, the subject of spiritual gifts for service puts us in touch with an empowerment that Paul accepted as normative.[42]

*Gifts build and nurture the churches*

In 1972 the churches located on the Jos Plateau of Nigeria learned firsthand about spiritual gifts. The parent mission[43] and the churches that developed from the mission had considerable Anglican and Brethren influence. Amazing things began to take place in the local church in the village of Gindiri. It so happens that Gindiri is also the location of the oldest, and perhaps the most prestigious, teacher training college and secondary school in the northern states of Nigeria. The local church attached to this great school of more than two thousand students had never been a strong church, nor had it given much leadership over the years. Yet one Sunday morning a woman who had no education and apparently little natural talent began to speak publicly of what God had been telling her. The pastor was wise enough to allow her to continue until she had finished. Her speech was in the form of true biblical prophecy—speaking to spiritual needs, calling for repentance and confession of sins that were hidden in the congregation. She told how God had spoken to her concerning particular wrongs on the part of certain members of the congregation, and with great conviction she called for prayer. It was a complete surprise to all who were present. A fearful hush came over the entire assembly, and in the grip of God's Spirit, there was confession and prayer on the part of many in that Sunday morning worship service. The spirit of repentance, restitution, and prophecy continued throughout the week. Then it spread to the students in the Gindiri schools. Classrooms became meeting places for prayer services, and the normal routine was interrupted as students sought each other out and put things right between themselves. This was followed by public witnessing in the nearby market, in the town, and then in surrounding villages. The account of this quickening movement has been written into the history of the Church of Christ in Nigeria. It will be remembered as a liberating and

42. Wagner says the charismatic movement today "crosses the boundaries of more ecclesiastical traditions, and is more cordially accepted today than any other time this side of the first century, as a legitimate part of Christianity by more Christians who themselves choose not to participate." *Your Spiritual Gifts,* p. 27.

43. Sudan United Mission (British branch).

redeeming force that began with simple and ordinary lay people, especially one woman who ministered to others in the power of the Spirit through the gift of prophecy at a time when the church was in need of renewal.

In 1974 twenty-five students and three faculty members of the Theological College of Northern Nigeria attended a week-long retreat, focusing on spiritual gifts, that was held at the Augustinian Seminary in Jos. The guest leader was the well-known Roman Catholic, Father Francis McNutt, accompanied by a sister and a Methodist pastor. I was principal of the college at this time and had some fears as to how I could explain to church leaders of five denominations why their students had attended this controversial gathering. I need not have worried. Students from Lutheran, Reformed, Anglican, Brethren, and Methodist backgrounds returned, telling of newly found spiritual strength and witnessing to miracles. The conference had centered on the gifts of healing—holistic healing of the mind, spirit, and body. A number of our students experienced the touch of God's Spirit in a new way. One of the expatriate faculty who had taught for years in a seminary of the Church of the Brethren, and had been a missionary for a long time, remembered the week as one that opened up a new life for himself and his wife.

All of us at the college were impressed with the simplicity of the way in which many were enabled to trust in the Holy Spirit, and we felt the strength of Christian commitment that bound the students to each other, without regard for denomination or tribe. Our family had been living in Africa for eighteen years at that time. What came home to me, and to many others, so forcefully was that the New Testament truth concerning gifts, had it been carefully and sincerely taught, would have endowed African Christians with abilities to serve and love each other in ways they had never experienced. Finally I had discovered that mission opens the door to ministry on the part of the whole church and that gifts are given to each to make this possible.

*Many gifts for many needs*

Often too much weight has been laid on the more spectacular gifts such as healing and speaking in tongues. However, this is not necessarily where we should begin when we speak of each convert entering into service within the church. If the church can be taught that gifts refer to whatever is the means by which she is edified, how much easier it would be to find a way for recent Christians to begin to serve immediately. Obviously there are special gifts for special offices—apostles, prophets, and teachers, for example (I Cor. 12:28). Ephesians 4:11 adds evangelists and pastors to this special list. But significantly we find that there are general and commonplace gifts as well, which are as important and as much to be desired as the official gifts (Rom. 12:3; I Cor 12:11; Eph. 4:7). Recognizing only the special gifts tends to produce a special clerical class whose job it is to serve all others. Until the lesser, humbler gifts are honored, any teaching about gifts may divide the body rather than serve to unify and strengthen it (I Cor. 12:22-23).

It is required of every gift that it glorify Jesus Christ solely and absolutely. Whatever one does must have this testimony, for "no one can confess 'Jesus is Lord,' unless he is guided by the Holy Spirit" (I Cor. 12:3). The real test of the gift is that it edify the church, the community in Christ. Our most recent converts need to know that they can immediately perform some service, show some kindness, give witness to some grace, give help in so many tangible ways to serve the body. Whether a spectacular or humble gift, it is "a gratuitous manifestation of the Holy Spirit working in and through but going beyond the believer's natural ability for the common good of the people of God."[44] Always the emphasis Paul makes is that each and all must serve, and that the good of the body, never self, is the aim (Rom. 14:7-19; I Cor. 14:3, 5, 12, 26).

I wish to emphasize clearly the need for an attitude to be generated by the church—the pastors and the elders or the deacons—that will recognize that the Holy Spirit's presence is shown in some way in each person for the good of all (I Cor. 12:7). When this spirit of responsibility, service, and trust is shared by all, and it is understood that God desires to be seen in the life of each new believer, both individual Christians and the whole church will be empowered for growth. Paul mentions three times that young Christians should "set their hearts" on spiritual gifts (I Cor. 12:31; 14:1, 39). He does not permit inactivity, dependency on strong leaders, or preoccupation with being served to paralyze the convert. The Holy Spirit who convicts is also the Holy Spirit who gives the desire and the power to serve. Each convert must be pressed into loving ministry at once and seek the special capacity God will give to serve.

## The Convert and Christian Values

I have said that the convert is a member of two very real worlds: that of his natural origin, with all its traditions and customs, and the new world of Christian fellowship. It is very difficult to reconcile these two worlds. Anyone who has turned to Christ in any culture knows of the new choices that have to be made. That the "old" has passed away and the "new" has come (II Cor. 5:17) never meant straightforward yes-or-no answers to the problems that arise. Attitudes and habits that are the product of centuries of deep-seated beliefs held by a society or the feelings that lie deep in the personality of a people are not easily changed. The basic question that arises at almost every

44. Arnold Bittinger, quoted by Watson in *I Believe in the Church,* p. 105.

level for a new Christian is, How should I think and act *now?* or, What will my peers say, and *what is right before God?*

Chalmer Faw, a missionary colleague and a former professor at Bethany Theological Seminary, has written a little book, *When the Way Is New.*[45] Issues arising from the often contradictory standards of these two worlds are raised in the book. Faw shows how the true Jew must have been thrown into confusion concerning many of the basic tenets of Judaism. On the matter of the law it might have been said by some, "God gave the law to Moses and it was meant to be followed. Until God releases us from it, we are bound to go on following it. A liberal like Paul will destroy the whole people of God!"[46] The debate was most heated on the very sensitive issue of whether the Gentiles should be circumcised. Jewish Christians took very strong positions on both sides. The argument of one side would have sounded like this:

> Not only was Jesus circumcised and we are supposed to be like him, but so were all the early disciples and apostles of our Lord. In fact, up until these modern trends [accepting Gentiles] set in all Christians have been good Jews. Even Paul himself who advocates these dangerous practices is a circumcised Jew.[47]

The Jerusalem Council was the first attempt to confront the dilemma that the liberating gospel carried for the Jews. In the debate over what is often called "the Gentile problem" we have a dramatic account of how differently the gospel affected the Gentile world compared with the world of the Jews. The church as Paul understood it must be one. Yet the Gentile and the Jewish worlds were far apart. The Greek mind had its own peculiarities and these were as important to the Gentile as the law was to the Jew. The Jews would insist that Jesus taught that his disciples must exceed the scribes and the Pharisees in righteousness (Matt. 5:20). F. F. Bruce observes, "Gentiles would have a hard task to bring their practices, especially in relations between the sexes, up to the ordinary Jewish level, let alone that of the scribes and Pharisees. What could be done to protect Christian standards?"[48]

Differences with respect to moral behavior were especially offensive to the Jews. Reading between the lines of Paul's early letters to the Thessalonians, we see that two problems in particular are apparent. There are signs of widespread laxity in sexual practices and marriage (see I Thess. 4:3-5). "Promiscuity across marital lines was common in the culture about them

45. (Elgin, IL: Brethren, 1974).
46. Ibid., p. 69.
47. Ibid.
48. *Paul, Apostle of the Heart Set Free* (Grand Rapids: Eerdmans, 1978), p. 17.

and was even invading the church."[49] The second problem was that the Greeks tended too much toward individualism and divisiveness. It was part of the Greek culture for one to do as he pleased. The provincialism and exaggerated independence this created were problems for Paul. The Greek was proud. Even in the decadent Greek civilization of Paul's day the people still considered themselves to be true citizens of the world and saw all others, including the Jews, as barbarians. It was more than any human could ever do to bring a church out of this entanglement. Who would decide what was right? Who was to say how the gospel judges both Jews and Gentiles? Could these new converts survive as one fellowship?

The Council of Jerusalem (Acts 15) was the first ray of light. Even so, at Jerusalem there was evidence that the same mistake in attitude was made that has plagued cross-cultural church planting through the years: the notion that the one who takes the message can formulate the ethics for those who receive the message and decide what the rules of conduct shall be for Christians in another culture.

The questions that arose among the Christians of one people among whom I ministered (Mumuye) touched on the nerve centers of life, and affected self-worth, status, the meaning of history, and the future. These questions were unsettled for a number of years: Should the young men engage in puberty rites at the end of the great seven-year cycle? Should ancestor rituals be set aside? Is beer drinking, especially at harvest time, wrong? Can a Christian also be a member of the men's secret society? Will Christians keep sacred the festival days that commemorate tribal gods? Do Christian children refuse to work for their non-Christian parents on Sunday? What attitudes should a Christian wife adopt toward her husband and the other wives in a polygamous marriage? The list of questions goes on and on. All center on the problem facing Christians in any culture: what is right thinking and right acting for a particular people and how is the convert to know what to do?

As a missionary, Paul had to work within his own personal view of the law (Rom. 7:12; 14:8-9; I Cor. 9:8). All who minister cross-culturally, from whatever culture they come, will have their own bias. But the law did not govern Paul's teaching on conduct and attitudes. Rather it was the basic spiritual principles that transcend all cultures that Paul emphasized. Expressions such as "in Christ," "in the Spirit," "dead to sin," "alive with Christ," "mind of Christ," and "will of God" are not just catch phrases or magical formulas.[50] To really understand these Pauline principles of the new life is to discover the basis for determining right thinking and action. The presence of God's personal Spirit in each life means a new obedience, guidance for

49. Faw, *When the Way Is New,* p. 80.

50. See G. E. Ladd for a summary of the theological meanings of these metaphors. *A Theology of the New Testament* (Grand Rapids: Eerdmans, 1974), pp. 479-494.

which comes by the laws of the Spirit. The burden of decisions for right and wrong is primarily the responsibility of each and every convert.[51]

### *In Christ*

The truth that lies behind Paul's use of the expression *in Christ* is so foundational to his theology that it might be said to be a fair summation of his faith. Paul uses this phrase and various cognates of it at least seventy-two times in his writings. II Corinthians 5:17 (RSV) catches the meaning in a beautiful way: "Therefore, if any one is in Christ, he is a new creation." The references are many-faceted and all-encompassing, touching personal fellowship with Christ and fellowship with other Christians. Of all his letters, only II Thessalonians does not include some form of the expression. The idea of the phrase *in Christ* has been discussed from all sides in an effort to understand Paul.

> It does not describe or express physical relationship which can be found and lost as presence and absence alternate. It describes a spiritual relationship which is independent of space and time, a relationship of the everywhere present risen Lord and ever living Christ.[52]

The meaning of the phrase *in Christ* is as much in danger of too little development as it is of too much. If it is treated as simply a metaphor (for example, when two people speak of being wrapped up in each other) there is little implied but a sentiment of rather superficial love that falls far short of what Paul has in mind. For years the thinking centered around Adolf Deissmann's position that we are dealing here with Paul's mysticism. He asserted that Paul viewed the Spirit as an ethereal entity, and by equating the personal resurrected Christ with the ethereal Spirit, one could quite easily think of Christ as permeating the Christian.[53] Almost synonymous with this is the explanation that Christ and the believer are in constant communion, so that the phrase describes the "supremely intimate relation of union with Christ."[54] This idea, while helpful in one way, tends toward belief in a kind of

51. Carl von Weizsacker states, "There was no need of a systematic presentation or setting up of definite central commandments. The fairest treatment was possible in an ever varying framework, at the same time the central rules of the ethic appear clearly enough." *The Apostolic Age of the Christian Church,* John Miller, trans. (New York: G. P. Putnam's Sons, 1895), p. 359.

52. Barclay, *The Mind of St. Paul,* p. 122. Barclay also notes that Paul never speaks of being "in Jesus," but in the ever-present resurrected Christ.

53. According to Deissmann, the analogy is that of air, of which it can truly be said that it is in us and we are in it. See the discussion in Longenecker, *Paul, Apostle of Liberty,* p. 164. Johannes Weiss tried to understand the mystery in terms of fluid, which both surrounds and penetrates. See Ladd, *Theology of the New Testament,* p. 481.

54. Eric Wahlstrom, *The New Life in Christ* (Philadelphia: Muhlenberg, 1950), p. 152.

absorption into the divine Spirit that is so congenial to the Eastern mind, and could result in little more than a Buddhist notion of nirvana. Neither do we discover the context for Paul's thinking in the mystery religions of his day. These called for almost hysterical experiences to be achieved through an emotional ritual, but left almost no effect beyond the moment.

What then does the meaning of the phrase *in Christ,* rightfully understood, have to do with the decisions that a convert makes from day to day? Paul is saying that the intimacy of the new relationship between the believer and the personal Christ-Spirit governs the whole of life—action, attitudes, and ideals. The indwelling Christ becomes the standard and the guide. The discussion of immorality in I Corinthians is an example of the way in which this new relationship changes the rationale for behavior (6:12-20). Paul's argument is built on the fact of the indwelling Christ. He leads Christians to see that their bodies not only are God's temple, but also are in the body of Christ. "The very nature of their new status makes it incongruous for them to practice fornication."[55] New converts must be taught that their own relationship to the indwelling Christ shapes their lives and that questions of right and wrong must be answered from within. The ability to judge what is right in each particular situation is the result of a proper understanding of the "in-Christ" relationship. Eric Wahlstrom gives a fitting application of the "in-Christ" principle for all Christians, but the application is especially appropriate for mission practice.

> If we ask how this indwelling Christ operates in the Christian's moral fiber, we would have to answer simply that the Christian, by virtue of the indwelling Christ, knows of himself what is right and proper, even when he comes into situations which never arose in the life of Jesus on earth or in the life of his disciples, and in regard to which, therefore, no word or example of the Master can be found. The Christian is able to decide *what to do* because he is "in Christ." He does not need others to tell him. He needs no code of morals. He can decide for himself what his course of action should be. He is "Christ-autonomous" or in a phrase more familiar to us, he is "the man in Christ."[56]

## *The Mind of Christ and the Will of God*

Supporting the teaching that the convert is "in Christ" are two expressions that are used less frequently but that further help us to understand the way in which a new Christian may face the test of what is right and wrong.

### *The Mind of Christ*

The "spiritual" man, says Paul, has the ability "to judge the value of everything," for, simply stated, "we . . . have the mind of Christ" (I Cor.

55. Ibid., p. 151.
56. Ibid., p. 152.

2:15-16). Paul speaks of the mind often and in various ways (e.g., I Cor. 14:15; Phil. 2:5; 4:7; II Thess. 2:2). The special point about the word *mind* (*nous*) is that it does not mean speculative reason but is anchored to the idea of moral judgment.[57] Christian guidance is not a matter of chance words of human wisdom, but is in very truth the guidance of the mind of Christ given "in words taught by the Spirit" (I Cor. 2:13). The convert has the inner direction of his thinking constantly brought in line with what is right in God's mind (Rom. 11:34). The mind (designating moral consciousness) also concretely determines will and action. The one who has surrendered to the lordship of Christ knows the right and desires to perform it. Paul spoke of having the mind that desires to obey the law (Rom. 7:23), although the flesh overcame him so that he could not perform the good that his mind told him to do (Rom. 7:23-25).

In the West, individuality, even privacy, is given higher honor than the idea of the group. This would not be true of many societies of the world. There is a proverb among peoples of northern Nigeria that says, "*I* am because *we* are." One must be very intimately joined to the community in order to know oneself. In a very real sense, therefore, the mind of the individual is disclosed through the mind of the group. It is from the group that the individual takes his direction and this new community of believers is, in a real way, a group that is directed by the mind of the common Lord.

Alan R. Tippett treats the idea of a group mind quite extensively in *Verdict Theology in Mission Theory.* The ultimate responsibility for decisions, he feels, is with the individual.[58] Tippett's study is addressed primarily to the role of the group in conversion when he says, "Although we agree that groups make decisions as groups and act on these decisions as groups, these are multi-individual acts."[59] Granted, there is the danger of ignoring the personal aspect of the group; but there is now the reality of the church, a corporate fellowship that has responsibility for the individual convert. In verses such as I Corinthians 2:16 ("We, however, have the mind of Christ") and Philippians 2:5 ("Let this mind be in you, which was also in Christ Jesus," KJV), the dimension of the group, the church, is unmistakable.

Scholars do not seem to emphasize the corporate aspect of the mind in verses such as these. John Calvin comes the nearest when he says that this mind refers to Paul himself and other faithful ministers, "after which the gift spreads to the whole church by degrees."[60] The reference to "the mind of

57. Ladd, *Theology of the New Testament,* p. 476.

58. *Verdict Theology in Mission Theory,* revised edition (Pasadena, CA: William Carey Library, 1973), pp. 139-140. Tippett refers to Homer G. Barnett, *Innovation: The Basis of Cultural Change* (New York: McGraw-Hill, 1953), p. 62.

59. *Verdict Theology in Mission Theory,* p. 139.

60. *Calvin's Commentaries,* David W. and Thomas F. Torrance, eds., J. W. Fraser, trans. (Grand Rapids: Eerdmans, 1960), vol. 9, p. 64.

Christ" in Philippians 2:5 is especially complex, but however translated it suggests that this mind belongs to all those who are Christ's by virtue of their vital union with him (Gal. 2:20-21; 3:27; Phil. 1:8).

Whether it can be said finally if there is a group mind is not the point so much as that Paul does speak to the church when referring to the mind of Christ. From this unique relationship of people to each other, a bond will be forged. It is in the communion of saints that the individual now finds his reality. What members of the group experience together will be embraced by the individual as something distinctly his or her own, shaping the thought and the life.

### *The will of God*

The actual doing of what is right—that which the mind of Christ reveals—is taken up in the references to the will of God. This is the term that takes a Christian beyond knowledge to performance. Right conduct always confirms right understanding. Repeatedly Paul expects the young Christians to be serious enough about what is right to have the will to do what is right. It is impossible to think about God's will in the ultimate sense without action. "Don't be fools then, but try to find out what the Lord wants you to do" ("understand what the will of the Lord is," RSV; Eph. 5:17). "With all your heart do what God wants as slaves of Christ." Paul reminds the Colossians that Epaphras' prayer for them is that God will "make you stand firm, as mature and fully convinced Christians, in complete obedience to God's will" (4:12).[61]

All of this discussion—the primary role of the Holy Spirit, the gifts of the Spirit, and the meaning of the believer being in Christ—has one overriding purpose in mission practice. The young Christian is expected to claim fully the rights that are his or hers in becoming a responsible, autonomous, right-thinking, right-acting, spiritual person from the time of turning to Christ. The convictions that the individual Christian holds must be his or her own, as we shall see. The possible choices, the various answers to deep questions of personal morality and right social conduct must be tested by these principles that Paul taught. The problems raised by the culture, the perplexities of the contention between traditional life and the new life in Christ are to be filtered through a series of spiritual screens, if you will, that determines for the convert what is right under the new lordship of Christ (see Figure 2).

61. For a discussion on the will of God, see Victor P. Furnish, *Theology and Ethics in Paul* (Nashville: Abingdon, 1968), pp. 227-241; and Wahlstrom, *The New Life in Christ*, pp. 161-162.

Figure 2

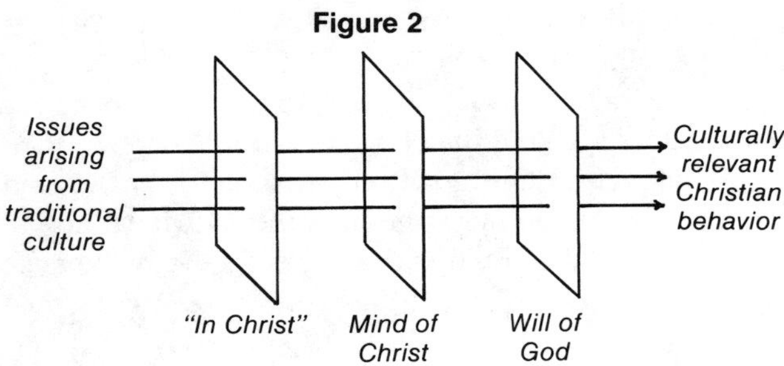


Allen set his thinking firmly in the truth held by the apostle. Paul was persuaded that

> Christians are not only what they are by nature. They are a Spirit-bearing body. It is not a question merely of our faith in them; it is still more a question of faith in the Holy Ghost. We [missionaries] look too much at our converts as they are by nature. St. Paul looked at his converts as they were by grace.[62]

62. *Missionary Methods,* p. 125.

# 6

# How to Live the New Life

We have much more help from Paul than simply theory. He was constantly involved in problems that tested basic principles. Much of what he wrote, as well as large sections of the Book of Acts, describes the conflict between traditional life and the newfound faith.

## Traditional Habits and Christian Living

Among the most indelible memories of my years in Africa are those of the numerous meetings where we discussed the difficulties in which Christians found themselves over ethics of behavior. Often it was the question of what kind of action would be right to take under this circumstance or that. More often, though, these meetings were called because of wrongs that Christians had already committed. As was true with Paul's experience, these situations were often related to marriage and arose from the differences between Christian ideals and traditional sexual customs. But we also spent long and often tedious hours on a wide range of other issues as well. Questions of right and wrong were raised as we dealt with politics or the so-called pagan rites, or discussed "native medicine," bride price, selection of leaders, or family relationships.

### *The New Life Is Different*

There is no question but that the convert is to be different from those who are outside of Christ. The discussion in the last chapter centered on the fact that God's personal Spirit is in the convert's life. There can be no other justification for the way Paul addresses these new Christians as "saints." They were obviously not saints in the sense of having been canonized or being pious by reason of old age. They certainly were not perfect. The convert is a saint because he or she is different. Converts do not continue doing what they have always done. Conversion is not just an improvement on traditional life. When Paul writes to the saints in Rome, Greece, Philippi, and Colossae (Rom. 1:7; II Cor. 1:1; Phil. 1:1; Col. 1:2) he is saying that these people are in Christ, and therefore they speak, act, and think differently from their peers who are unconverted. The difference lies in a quality of life, which is obvious to all those who knew the person before and after. It is a difference that has to be understood in the context of the convert's involvement with others.

*Christian behavior is expected*

We shall see that Paul expected each Christian to take a position on what was right and wrong. But this does not mean that Paul had no standard of ethical behavior or norms for correct Christian thinking.[1] Moral uprightness and personal purity were not to be compromised. He realized the danger of his emphasis on freedom from the law, and made it abundantly clear that the Christian is not to continue to live in sin (Rom. 6:1ff.; Gal. 5:13-25). The heritage of Paul's background would allow him to do nothing other than to demand high moral standards. Jehovah was the God of unblemished holiness and it was a fundamental requirement of the Jewish people that their lives reflect the character of this God who had said, "Be holy, for I am holy" (Lev. 11:44, RSV). When Paul came to an understanding of the mystical union between the believers and Christ it was only natural that strict moral requirements should be made (Rom. 6:1-2; I Cor. 1:2; I Thess. 4:3, 7). This Christ was of the same spotless purity as was Jehovah. M. S. Enslin regards the sinless nature of Christ and the fact that the Christian is ultimately joined to him as the concept that lies at the root of all Paul's thinking:

> As a result, requirements of character which were neglected or unnoticed by the ministrants of the Oriental mystery cults, were of prime importance to Paul. Such was the Lord to whom Christians were most intimately united, who dwelt in them. Anything that would tend to sully Christ, to join him to a harlot, to defile the body which is His holy temple, was an abomination and to be shunned resolutely.[2]

So, in addition to Paul's own background, which called for austere holiness, the person of Jesus Christ is also an absolute standard for Christian behavior. How often Paul leads his young Christians back to Jesus as their example of righteous living. The entire sixth chapter of Romans contrasts the old life with the new. The convert is to think of himself as "dead, so far

1. M. S. Enslin places heavy emphasis on the "light within" (the Holy Spirit) that directed Paul. Hence, "the standards he set were his own standards of conduct," guided by "what was worthy of Christ." *The Ethics of Paul* (Nashville: Abingdon, 1957), p. 130.

2. Ibid., pp. 69-70.

as sin is concerned, but living in fellowship with God through Christ Jesus" (Rom. 6:11). This new Lord is to be "put on" as a garment of warfare, as it were, and thus outfitted, the Christian is to "stop paying attention to [the] sinful nature and satisfying its desires" (Rom. 13:14). It is the new Lord who makes the difference. Those who have put on Christ can no longer live like the "heathen" who give themselves over to vice and "do all sorts of indecent things without restraint" (Eph. 4:17-20). Such living is no longer possible because that is not what these new converts learned about Christ from Paul.

*No formal system of rules exists*

Yet it is just as obvious that Paul did not turn to a list of regulations to teach this new kind of life. Paul was a practical man and realized this is a practical world. Though Christians are united with their Lord, they are also in very close contact with other believers. Paul's converts had similar experiences. They were joined in the same vital union, or should be, with their risen Lord. It would have been a reversal of all that Jesus did to turn again to rules for converts. In contrasting the Jewish converts' lives with their former lives, Paul wrote, "No longer do we serve in the old way of a written law, but in the new way of the Spirit" (Rom. 7:6). As matter of fact, there is really only one place in Acts where the obligations of the convert are laid down in black and white. This comes in the decision of the Council of Jerusalem regarding Gentile converts who enter the church. They are told clearly that they should "not eat any food that is ritually unclean because it has been offered to idols," and they are to "keep themselves from sexual immorality; and not to eat any animal that has been strangled, or any blood" (Acts 15:20).

With such a dramatic rearrangement of relations between Jews and Gentiles taking place in this period, we might have expected that the obligations for new Gentile converts would have been spelled out in great detail. The settlement of the council, therefore, is generous and shows much good will. These were not just rules for rules' sake. They laid down solid Christian principles. An uncompromising personal purity is called for, and an absolute loyalty to Jesus Christ is demanded, as well as a great respect for everyone in the church. Even so, perhaps the terms were too legalistic for Paul. There is no evidence that he referred to the council's letter again, once he had shared it with the church in Antioch (Acts 15:30-31). Paul's implicit trust in the Holy Spirit to guide and teach believers was so strong that he saw no need to lay down such rules. With those who had recently turned to Christ he was extremely patient, even though he held high standards of morality as the norm for behavior for all Christians. His counsel as to what was right was not based on expediency. As Enslin notes, his exhortations were not the "impromptu words of an opportunist, but were the expression of deep-seated principles governing his own life."[3]

The flexibility with which Paul administered the churches gave each convert the freedom and the responsibility to work out in his own daily life the standards that were in accord with the presence of Christ within him. Paul expected that there would be some differences and he welcomed that. The rule that he gave to all the churches is that *each one must follow the leading of the Lord* and live "according to the Lord's gift to him" (I Cor. 7:17). This seeking for the right way to live, with the help of God, comes into his Corinthian letter at a critical juncture. He had been discussing the problem of continence in marriage and he followed the statement of his "rule" (I Cor. 7:17) with a reference to the problem of circumcision. No one can tell another to marry or to be circumcised against his conscience. The emphasis is on the fact that each Christian is to use the wisdom and knowledge that God has given. With this discipline will come Christian growth as well as the development of personal convictions about what is right.

Paul did take stern measures at Corinth, where an unusually chaotic situation called for his intervention. I shall speak about this when I discuss the problems of discipline in chapter 9. But the special case in Corinth underlines Paul's policy in a remarkable way. His prayer and instruction to the churches were that they should decide what is right for themselves and then act. Considering the problems he faced, the relentless attacks from the Judaizers, and the immaturity of the Christians, it is amazing that he did not claim his rights as an apostle more often than he did. Roland Allen notes that Paul preferred "doubt and strife" to an enforced rule that was laid down from the outside.[4] A conviction for what is right must come from within the believer himself and must be the teaching of God's Spirit, not the regulation of authority.

My own life has been enriched in many ways by companionship with an African pastor whose name is Jonah. In the early days of our missionary work, I was extremely judgmental about certain habits of African Christians that appeared to me to represent substandard Christianity. For the most part, I expected the Christians with whom I worked to quickly learn from *me*, and to appropriate *my* convictions. But living close to Pastor Jonah gave me some of the best training I ever had. Pastor Jonah had a natural openness about the way in which God's Spirit would teach new converts. I was much more legalistic and culturally shortsighted. On one of our visits to a village, Salla, I was surprised to see the daughter of the local evangelist wearing

3. Ibid., pp. 77-78.

4. *Missionary Methods: St. Paul's or Ours?* (1912; reprint ed. London: World Dominion Press, 1960), p. 112.

what I considered to be a pagan charm. The *buru,* as it is called, is a leather-covered rope, usually worn around the waist, with a small pouch of "medicine" tied to it. The *buru* is worn by nearly all children as a "protection" against snakebite. It seemed inappropriate to me that a Christian preacher should allow his daughter to wear a *buru.* I followed my first impulse and called the evangelist (his name was Ishaku), and began to tell him that we could not allow this sort of thing! I'm not sure why I felt I was so right or why I had to control. After all, a well-trained and highly committed African pastor was standing right there beside me. To try to enforce what I felt was a biblical standard meant that I did not fully respect Ishaku as a Christian and a brother; besides which, insisting on my own notions about Christian standards gave no room for God's Spirit to work in a culture that was so different from my own. As I began to speak to Ishaku with quite a bit of authority, I felt Pastor Jonah's hand on my shoulder. He was asking me to have patience. Then he reproved me kindly in words that were very close to those of Paul in I Corinthians 7:17. "Perhaps," he said, "it is not yet the time for Ishaku to ask his daughter to take off her *buru.* God has given him the new life. So let's be patient. God will teach him the changes that the new life requires. You, missionary, will not need to tell him once God tells him."

This African pastor instructed me about things that Paul knew by spiritual instinct. Paul expected the convert to make progress without his aid. "He gave freely and then he retired from them that they might learn to exercise the powers which they possessed in Christ. He administered a Gospel, not a law."[5]

### *First Principles for Daily Living*

Day-to-day living requires that certain underlying principles be respected and applied. The point has already been made that the new life must be lived according to a different standard, but that set rules for this new life must not be imposed from the outside if the convert is to readily understand the change that has taken place within. It is, however, important for Paul that he lay down what might be called first principles that will guide both attitudes and conduct. Paul insisted on these basics so that each Christian might become a strong and independent person in his or her own faith. These first principles were taught in the context of everyday problems. We should always look at the purpose that underlies Paul's instruction. It is not the obvious counsel that Paul gave, called forth by particular incidents, that instructs us so much as does the underlying meaning that has relevance for Christians of all times and all cultures. If we were to rigorously follow Paul's advice only on the small number of particular problems he addressed, then

5. Ibid., pp. 118, 148.

the value of his teaching for cross-cultural churches in our own day would be severely limited. Many specific questions for which there are no answers arise every day in mission situations, because Paul lived in another era, among a different set of contemporaries.

We need to be as specific as possible about what Paul's thinking was as he urged young Christians to face their own world and find answers that best fitted their own lives. We find that his teaching provides three basic guidelines by which the convert is made to reflect deeply on his own faith and, in turn, test his decisions in the company of others.

*Each one must have personal convictions*

Paul expected every convert to become a thinking, discerning person who does not have to depend on the missionary, or anyone else, for what he believes is right. Weak compliance with the habits, attitudes, and prejudices of others will never lead to maturity. Most of what Paul said about responsibility for making personal decisions arose out of differences of opinion in the community as to whether it was right or wrong to continue certain former practices. There was quite a bit of leeway in the approach Paul took. Personal preferences were respected. No one was commanded to do this or that in matters of secondary importance. At Rome, for example, there were some who felt it was acceptable to celebrate special days that they had always kept. This kind of problem took on special importance in Rome, because within the Christian community there were two sides, which Paul refers to as "the weak" and "the strong" (Rom. 14:1). In this issue Paul says, quite simply, "Each one should firmly make up *his own mind*" (Rom. 14:5; italics added). The emphasis is not only on the fact that each one must take responsibility for himself or herself, but also that this decision is to be more than a whim or a fancy. Each one should begin to form convictions. These must be reasoned convictions, carefully worked out through guidance from the indwelling Spirit and the mind of Christ, as we have discussed. How important the personal struggle is to find what is right.

This need for personal conviction is expressed further in Romans 14:23, where Paul says that eating questionable food "with doubts" can lead to sin. This is a strong statement. It means that the person who has thought through his action and believes he is right before God is one whom Paul sees as the truly happy person, because he "does not feel guilty when he does something he judges is right" (Rom. 14:22). "But if he has doubts about what he eats, God condemns him when he eats it, because his action is not based on faith" (Rom. 14:23). The dilemma such persons find themselves in is that, by not having a sense of what God wants them to do, they eat because they have been influenced by others, and have no conviction of their own.[6] Any

6. See the helpful discussion in R. C. H. Lenski, *St. Paul's Epistle to the Romans* (Columbus,

action that is not based on faith is, obviously, one about which there is no sure conviction. The convert must have that faith and that assurance.

But Paul did not demand that others follow his personal convictions in either of these controversial matters. It was expected of them that, with prayer and the counsel of the community, they use their own minds to reach their own conclusions. Why do missionaries feel they must regulate the lives of national Christians? If each new Christian, right from the beginning of the new life, were to seek God's answers to ethical questions, the guidance would be given. Mistakes and failures would occur, but the convert may experience forgiveness, and the conscience, made sensitive, will teach a better way. Let the missionary be very careful about imposing his convictions on others. A conviction is a very personal thing.

> We attempt to administer a code which is alien to the thoughts of the people with whom we have to deal, we appeal to precedents which are not precedents to them, and we quote decisions of which our peers do not understand either the history or the reason. Without satisfying their minds or winning the consent of their consciences, we settle all questions with a word.[7]

*No one can be bound to any habit*

Deciding what is right is an exercise of the freedom that we have in Christ, but this freedom must always be checked by the lordship of Jesus. To follow one's conscience and to have convictions does not mean that one can indulge in something to the point where it becomes a habit (I Cor. 6:12). This not only is offensive to other members of the body but also violates the supremacy of Christ. Paul took the position that what he felt quite free to do had to remain for him a *matter of choice,* and not become his master.[8] "I could say that I am allowed to do anything" ("All things are lawful for me," RSV). So Paul used that expression. He was saying that he could speak of freedom in a new and meaningful way because he had the choice of doing something or not doing it. The Corinthians were known for their excesses, especially in sexual matters. In contrast, the Christian is free to do only those things that his convictions will allow him to do; but any indulgence or excess will lead to enslavement, and this is not compatible with Christ's lordship (Rom. 6:16).

---

OH: Wartburg, 1945), pp. 852-855; and G. Cragg, *The Interpreter's Bible: The Epistle to the Romans* (New York: Abingdon, 1954), vol. 9, pp. 613-614.

7. Allen, *Missionary Methods,* p. 118.

8. See G. E. Ladd, *A Theology of the New Testament* (Grand Rapids: Eerdmans, 1974), pp. 516-540.

*Each one must respect the convictions of others*

Rules that are laid down in such a way that every Christian is required to follow them without question cause distortion in the convert's spiritual growth in two ways. First, such rules do not allow the convert to seek his or her own personal convictions. Second, the imposition of rules fails to respect the right of the individual to be different within the community. The local church is a community that we must take very seriously. Conversion is not only conversion to a certain pattern of life, but also conversion into a fellowship. The convert becomes not only a child of God, but also a member of the family of God, which is the church. "The measure of the reality of man's conversion is the extent to which it unites him to his fellowmen as well as to God."[9] The convert who decides what is right for himself does not have the luxury of going his own way without any concern for what others feel is right for them. This society, the church (of which I shall speak more in the next chapter), is not something vague, nor is it an optional fellowship.

The presence of love, and respect for fellow believers who are also searching to find what is right for them are basic to everything else we can say about the church. "We are ruled by the love of Christ," said Paul (II Cor. 5:14). "So then, let us stop judging one another. Instead, you should decide never to do anything that would make your brother stumble or fall into sin" (Rom. 14:13). The problem was that now and then questions arose about certain practices that were not intrinsically bad. Some converts felt they could indulge in these practices, while others questioned the same practices. Those who belonged to "the strong" really believed that this was right for them, but the "weaker" brothers had a different point of view. The situation in which the Christians in both Rome and Corinth found themselves was especially difficult. In these cities there existed almost every conceivable form of idolatry and the Christians found it very hard to extricate themselves from the situation. Purity by avoidance was almost impossible. Even the meat one might eat in a friend's house could have been offered to an idol or could have been purchased in a temple of iniquity. Obviously, for some this was no serious problem; for others it was most serious (I Cor. 10:27-28).

True Christian love is the fundamental rule in an attitude of tolerance. God accepts all, equally, even though personal judgments on ethical details may differ. "If you hurt your brother because of something you eat, then you are no longer acting from love" (Rom. 14:15). It is a very serious matter to insist on doing something that offends another, because then "you will be sinning against Christ by sinning against your Christian brothers and wounding their weak conscience" (I Cor. 8:12).[10]

9. William Barclay, *Turning to God* (Philadelphia: Westminster, 1964), p. 71.

10. See also Romans 14:19; I Corinthians 14:26; Ephesians 4:25, 29.

When the Fellowship of the Churches of Christ in Nigeria[11] was young, divisive issues arose out of a number of aspects of traditional life. One area had been highly influenced by Islam, even though relatively few were practicing Muslims. When a few families became Christian, one of the first things that some of them did was to begin to raise pigs for meat. Soon the pigs became a new source of income, and the problem grew. About half of the Christians ate pork. The others were adamant against it. This created a breach in the fellowship, but to complicate things even further, the pigs had begun to run loose in the village, rooting up farms, causing all kinds of problems, and becoming a general nuisance. Those who kept pigs and ate pork claimed their rights as free people in Christ. One man said, "If God had not intended us to eat pork, he would not have made it taste so sweet!" The community divided into two parties and in the place of love came suspicion and mistrust. Realizing the danger of schism in the church, one pastor and three elders called for a suspension of all activities to give time for discussion and prayer. Nearly two years of trouble was finally resolved as both sides came to a renewal of their oneness in Christ. Prominent in the discussions leading to reconciliation was the injunction of Romans 14:13: "Never do anything that would make your brother stumble or fall into sin." Those who ate pork and those who abstained from pork both applied the principle to themselves. The fault lay not only with those who saw no sin in eating. Those who abstained saw that their anger, judgment, and pride were equally offensive. Given time, the whole issue had been resolved without the intervention of anyone outside the group. No missionary stated the terms of reconciliation.

God's Spirit had enabled this group of young Christians to apply their "in-Christ" relationship to the resolution of their own problem. They saw that Paul's firmness regarding purity was matched by his resolve that converts should understand their own faith and find their own solutions. The convert must find out what "the will of the Lord is" within the context of his obligations to the entire fellowship.

## Basic Principles from Special Cases

The church at Corinth presents a picture of the many difficulties as well as the joys of church planting among a new people. So many factors that would be found in various other places were all present in this almost unbelievable situation. Corinth was a curious melting pot, full of contradictions and antagonisms. Here were both the Hellenic craze for freedom and

11. Seven autonomous African churches (fellowship) that developed from the work of the Sudan United Mission beginning in 1954. For a critique, see Wilber C. Harr in *Frontiers of the Christian World Mission Since 1938* (New York: Harper, 1962), pp. 107-111.

the narrowness of the Jewish ghetto. In one church could be found the sublime spirit of *agapē* love alongside petty partisan jealousy, rich charismatic endowments, and quite shameless immorality. Paul's own words in describing the church at Corinth were that not many there were "wise or powerful or of high social standing" (I Cor. 1:26). We know that there was poverty among some of these groups (II Cor. 8:2). The church evidently included numerous slaves (I Cor. 7:21) and also many slave owners (Eph. 6:9).

Corinth could not have been an easy place to plant the church. It did not have the settled population of, for example, the towns of Galatia, and it lacked an honorable class of citizens such as was found in Philippi. Politically and socially it was in a class by itself. It was the habit of the people to divide into cliques and engage in heated discussions about all sorts of trivia. These Greeks had long since lost their political autonomy, so they were not able to decide anything of importance. "They argued for this dancer, for that singer, for this gladiator in the arena."[12]

The Christians were caught in the Corinthian predicament. One type of extreme conduct was counteracted with extremes of another kind. Marriage was treated so freely that practically any sort of an arrangement would pass. On one hand, men and women lived together as married couples without any thought of lawful wedlock, while another group condemned all sexual intercourse as degrading and unclean. These two attitudes both followed the logical Hellenistic dualism that taught that body and soul are separate from, and contrary to, each other.[13] As long as Paul was in Corinth the sheer strength of his person and spirit kept the Christian community together. But by the time Paul wrote the epistle called I Corinthians[14] some four years had passed since he had been with them. The frivolity and sexual license of Corinth had taken their toll on the Christian fellowship.

The problems about which the Corinthians asked advice were peculiar to Corinth and so the answers that Paul gave might appear to be meant for Corinth and Corinth alone. However, the principles that underlie the immediate solutions have a much wider implication, and it is important that we discover how to apply the deeper meaning of Paul's counsel to the life of new converts in any place. By looking at these deeper levels of truth we find enlightenment and guidance from the Spirit rather than control by the law. I shall discuss four of these basic principles.

12. See Joseph Holzner, *St. Paul the Apostle: His Life and Times,* William J. Doheny, CSC, trans. and rev. (Vatican City: Private distribution, 1978), p. 304.

13. Ibid., p. 312.

14. A helpful review of the chronology of the Corinthian correspondence is found in Donald Guthrie, *New Testament Introduction, The Pauline Epistles* (London: Tyndale Press, 1968), pp. 46-62.

### *Converts Should Not Set Unrealistic Standards for Themselves (I Cor. 7:36-38)*

As might be expected, problems concerning marriage were many in a place such as Corinth, and it is no longer possible for us to decide the exact details of some of the issues raised. The Corinthians knew of Paul's personal preference for being unmarried and he reminded them of this conviction in his letter (I Cor. 7:7, 28, 32-34, 40). This obviously influenced many, especially those who not only had a loyalty to Paul but also were deeply offended by the depravity of marriage practices in Corinth.

This led to one of the delicate pieces of counsel that Paul offers to couples who wanted to marry but felt it would be an unchristian thing to do. The exact situation to which Paul refers in this passage (I Cor. 7:36-38) has been a subject of much debate. The free rendering of Today's English Version leaves no question that here is an engaged couple who have decided that the sexual act of marriage is wrong. "The girl" (I Cor. 7:36) is certainly a sensible way to translate the word *parthenon* ("virgin") as we look at it from a practical point of view. This seems much closer to the original meaning than the alternative idea that the passage refers to a father who must exercise his legal rights over his "virgin daughter."[15] It is hard to conceive of Paul wanting anyone to think that it was a sin for a father to give his daughter in marriage.[16] Rather, we are dealing here with one of two possibilities or, perhaps, both. It may be that an engaged couple had decided not to marry, or that a man and woman had married and then made vows of celibacy, to live in what might be called a spiritual marriage. This would have followed closely Paul's own preference, and would also reflect one of the extreme attitudes taken toward marriage in Corinth at the time.

However, the problem created was a very human one. The resolve, however sincere, not to have sexual intercourse was still subject to natural desire. As a result the man in this case came to feel that he was no longer acting properly toward the woman. Paul's counsel was that "if his passions are too strong and he feels that they ought to marry, then they should get married, as he wants to" (I Cor. 7:36). Paul said clearly, "There is no sin in this." To renounce the physical side of marriage may seem to be a fine spiritual act, but unless one has the special gift of continence (I Cor. 7:7), harm can

15. This is the view of C. K. Barrett, who also quotes Werner Georg Kümmel in support. See possible interpretations in *Harper's New Testament Commentaries* (New York: Harper and Row, 1968), vol. 7, pp. 183-184.

16. The traditional interpretation is assumed by A. T. Robertson and Alfred Plummer. The idea of "sin" is explained this way: "In Corinth there was danger that a girl who was old enough to marry and anxious to marry, might go disastrously astray if marriage was refused." *The International Critical Commentary* (Edinburgh: T. & T. Clark, 1911), vol. 46, p. 159. For the argument contra, see James Moffatt, *New Testament Commentary* (London: Hodder and Stoughton, 1938), vol. 7, p. 99.

follow. For in addition to the impossible resolve these couples have made to each other physically, there is the sense of guilt they will have to bear if they break what they felt was a promise to God.[17] Paul did not compromise his own ideals. Quite honestly, he felt that marriage is something that hinders a person from serving God with a single mind. But although this was his personal opinion (I Cor. 7:10), he never advocated a marriage that was no marriage. Insisting on such a relationship causes "havoc within the Christian community," says Richard N. Longenecker. For if the ascetic parties insist upon this style of relationship as an obligation for others, they fail to respect the rights of others and do not accept fellow Christians in love.[18]

The important point, however, goes beyond the issue of marriage. Christians who are new in the faith often find themselves involved in a struggle with practices from the traditional environment that do not conform to the new standard. We recall that conversion is a turning that requires subsequent stages of growth and strengthening. Good and justifiable standards may certainly be expected of recent converts, but when they attempt to live up to an impossibly high ideal, their failure will result in a demoralization of spirit and, often, heavy guilt. Paul is saying that the new life is something that is learned. It does not come as a finished experience. I would have insisted that Ishaku destroy the *buru,* but Pastor Jonah said, "Have patience." When missionaries press for unrealistic laws of Christian behavior that do not allow for the massive influence the traditional life still has, failure and discouragement will often come to the new Christian. Paul was not going to press for an issue that he could see would lead to disruption. In his conclusion he is faithful to himself, but completely fair to others. "So the man who marries does well, but the one who doesn't marry does even better" (I Cor. 7:38).

If we missionaries are tempted to criticize Paul for showing his personal bias here, we should remember how many times converts in mission churches have been told by the missionary to do this or that, to act in this way or that way because "it is the Christian thing to do," thus leaving no room for individual choice or personal reflection. God is much more patient, more tolerant of those who "turn to him from false idols" than we usually allow. When Paul spoke of sanctification to the Thessalonian, for example (I Thess. 4:3), he did so in terms of abstaining from immorality. Of course, we know that sanctification means much more than this. Holiness as Paul understood it would require a "cleansed" mind, soul, and body given wholly to God. But here, where people were so recently converted and were just beginning to learn how to live in order to please God, men had to learn to live with their own wives "in a holy and honorable way, not with a lustful

17. Richard N. Longenecker, *Paul, Apostle of Liberty* (Grand Rapids: Baker, 1976), p. 239.
18. Ibid.

desire, like the heathen who do not know God" (I Thess. 4:4-5). "Your sanctification: that you abstain from immorality" (4:3, RSV). To paraphrase Paul, "Be faithful in what you already know; take the new life one step at a time; don't attempt what you are unable, as yet, to perform, and the Lord Jesus will help you to do even more."

### *The Christian Witness Will Ultimately Prevail (I Cor. 7:12-16)*

Paul had great faith in the power of the gospel and Christian witness. He believed that God would honor the person who confesses Jesus as Lord. A test of this would come in the case of a married couple where one is a Christian and the other is not; serious problems would be bound to arise. When marriage was regarded so loosely and morals were purely relative, the Christian partners would be caught in situations that would be completely against Christian standards. There was a widespread notion that Christians should separate from their non-Christian partners chiefly on the grounds that a relationship between partners in this kind of mixed marriage would be unclean. This belief grew out of a sincere desire to keep the Christian witness pure. But Paul saw that this was going too far. His advice is clear: Unless the unbelieving partner decides to leave the Christian partner, there should be no change in the relationship. This is charitable and respects the vows of marriage.

However, something more profound is involved. There is a strong conviction that good can come only if the marriage is kept intact. "The unbelieving husband is made acceptable to God by being united to his wife, and the unbelieving wife is made acceptable to God by being united to her Christian husband" (I Cor. 7:14). Paul certainly did not mean that there is an automatic salvation for the other partner when one of the two becomes a Christian. And yet it is a very fortunate thing for an unbelieving person to be married to a true and faithful believing spouse. Paul had confidence in the power of the gospel as it affects those closest to believers. As R. C. H. Lenski says,

> A certain sanctity is conferred on the unbelieving spouse, unbelieving though this spouse is, when by the marriage tie he is joined to a believing spouse who is one of God's saints. The unbelieving spouse is party to a Christian marriage . . . and thus more is given [to the unbelieving spouse] than his unbelief deserves.[20]

19. Carl von Weizsacker, *The Apostolic Age of the Christian Church,* John Miller, trans. (New York: G. P. Putnam's Sons, 1895), vol. 2, p. 377.

20. *Interpretation of I and II Corinthians* (Columbus, OH: Wartburg, 1946), p. 292.

Connected to this is the conviction that faithfulness in earthly relationships will prove that Christ in the believer is stronger than the powers of the world and that the dominating influence of God's grace will ultimately draw the children to Christ. There is no magic in this. It is not that sanctification will be transmitted physically to the unbeliever through the marriage relationship. But it is a scriptural principle that the blessings that come from fellowship with God are not limited to the immediate recipients but are intended also for others (Gen. 15:18; 17:7). The covenant with Abram carried a great promise of hope for those outside the family of the patriarch. God told Abram, "Through you I will bless all the nations" (Gen. 12:3; cf. Gal. 3:8). With Abram, Yahweh began a new chapter in the history of man. Abram was Yahweh's instrument for the redemption of the world. The Abrahamic covenant was foundational for the salvation of the Gentiles and Paul saw the theme as analagous to the mixed marriage.[21] This is the reason for his optimism when one out of a family turns to Christ. God's grace extended to one of the partners will have its saving effect on the non-Christian partner. Paul was always optimistic about the power of the gospel.

A striking situation developed in the city of Jos, Nigeria, between 1973 and 1975. It concerned a well-to-do merchant named Hamidu who was a nominal Muslim and had a lot of political influence in the area. Hamidu had three wives. For a Muslim, he allowed them considerable freedom. They were popular in their own circles, always well dressed, and seemed to share equally the wealth of their husband. Hannatu was the middle wife, which meant that she had the least desirable position among the wives. She would not have had the authority of the eldest wife, and probably not the same attention as the third wife who, as a younger woman, would be treated in a special way by her husband. Hannatu began to attend a large church that had a very active women's fellowship. This, by itself, caused some tension between Hannatu and Hamidu, but it was not unusual for such a thing to happen in a plural marriage, especially in the cities. That Hamidu was ostensibly a Muslim further complicated Hannatu's frequent attendance at church. And then Hannatu, after some time, accepted Christ and gave an open witness to her faith.

Immediately, Hamidu demanded that Hannatu stop attending the services and forbade her to speak to people about being a Christian. When Hannatu refused, Hamidu threatened to take away all her personal goods. Still she would not recant in any way. She continued to fulfill all her obligations and tried to work with the other wives. After four months of unhappiness she decided it would be best for her husband, if he preferred, that she leave him. She said later that she was guided by God to take this step as a way to

21. See Richard R. De Ridder, *Discipling the Nations* (1971; reprint ed. Grand Rapids: Baker, 1979), p. 23.

neutralize the tension in the entire household. Hamidu gave her the freedom to go, but sent her away with nothing of her own. Almost miraculously, six months after Hannatu had returned to her own home, the third wife also became a Christian. Through the intervention of this younger woman, Hannatu was invited to return to Hamidu, and she decided to. Now his attitude began to change. He became tolerant of his Christian wives, and began to show them kindnesses, even allowing other Christian women to visit them in their home. Where this may lead as far as Hamidu is concerned we cannot tell, but there is evidence of the work of God's Spirit, and there is the faithfulness of the Christian presence around him.

Polygamy is, obviously, not an ideal form of marriage. But the lack of morality in marriages among the Corinthians in Paul's day was appalling; in most cases it was probably worse than polygamy. And yet the power of God in the life of the Christian partner in even these circumstances, Paul believed, would have its effect for good. Hannatu had carefully worked out the way in which she believed her life would have the greatest influence to bring salvation to that home. The congruence of polygamy and Christian witness may sound strange to Christians in the West, but can we not sense that Hannatu's story shows how God honors those who truly seek to follow him? Paul trusted in God to instruct new believers in whatever context they found themselves, and he had complete confidence in the overcoming power of Christian witness. Of course, this principle applies to much more than marriage. Such optimism, stemming from a total trust in God's grace, should condition our approach to the many problems of encounter that arise between the authority of the old way and the new lordship of Christ.

### *The Body of Christ Is Real (I Cor. 7:10–11)*

Paul's convictions about divorce where both partners are Christian is presented in a very straightforward way. He gives what he feels is the word of the Lord and not his own opinion. The injunction is that "a wife must not leave her husband . . . and a husband must not divorce his wife" (I Cor. 7:10-11). Here Paul is answering questions that had arisen as a result of the abuse of marriages and the many forms of illicit relationships that would have been found in Corinth. A full discussion of this attitude of Paul would require us to take into account a number of factors that we are not able to deal with here. Apparently Paul's insistence on the absolute indissolubility of marriage cannot be based entirely on Jesus' words. In both Mark and Luke Jesus seems to forbid divorce on any grounds, just as Paul does, but Matthew introduces the exceptive clause where Jesus says, "Whoever divorces his wife, except for *unchastity,* and marries another, commits adultery" (Matt. 19:9, RSV; italics added). The term used for this exception is *porneia.* Since the word *porneia* could refer to a variety of things,[22] there can be no justification for saying that adultery is the exclusive ground for divorce. Adrian Hastings observes that "the decisive question is not how radical was Jesus' condemnation of divorce, but how that condemnation is to be interpreted in the face of complexities and ambiguities of individual human situations."[23] Once we relate Jesus' or Paul's words to the precise situation at Corinth, we will better understand the position that Paul took. But first it will be helpful to review briefly how this injunction has been interpreted through the history of the church.

In the first centuries the church held that marriage is indissoluble, an opinion most clearly articulated by Augustine. But in the fourth century divorce and remarriage were being admitted in the Eastern church, and later also in the West, especially in England. However, after the Gregorian reform of the eleventh century the position once again became very strict, and this interpretation continued through the Middle Ages. Generally speaking, the leaders of the Reformation rejected the stand of indissolubility on the basis of Matthew 19:9, and a few Catholic theologians, notably Cajetan, agreed with the reformers. John Calvin was quite sure that Paul did not differ with Jesus when he did not permit divorce under any circumstance.[24] Divorce is a widely discussed issue in the Roman Catholic Church today, and there are those who would accept the possibility of a total breakdown of marriage among the baptized so that a second marriage is possible.[25] There has always been a shifting view of divorce and remarriage in the Western church. Many sensitive Christians still feel that divorce is forbidden for all Christians by the words of Paul and allowed only in very special cases by Jesus. Yet it is well known that a hard-and-fast stand against all divorce among Christians is harder to maintain today than ever before.

The debate over the centuries provides an illustration of the struggle the church has had in order to speak with relevance to a specific people, in a specific time and place. In order to defend the absolute indissolubility of marriage as stated so clearly by Paul, we have to fall back not on the words of Jesus, but on the nature of Christian marriage. Even if we do not take a strictly sacramental view of marriage, we are still to see it as the most precious symbol we have of the union of Christ with his church. Paul taught

22. The literature concerning this Matthaean clause is massive. This verse has been accepted by both Eastern Christians and many Protestants as justifying divorce on the ground of adultery. Most exegetes consider Mark's text as the original saying, which would correspond to Paul's teaching. See Adrian Hastings, *Christian Marriage in Africa* (London: SPCK, 1973), pp. 81-82.

23. Ibid.

24. *Calvin's Commentaries,* David W. and Thomas F. Torrance, eds., J. W. Fraser, trans. (Grand Rapids: Eerdmans, 1960), vol. 9, p. 145.

25. Refer to Hastings, *Christian Marriage in Africa,* pp. 82-87, for a summary on the church's attitudes toward divorce.

that the Christian belongs to his Lord in a way analogous to that in which a wife belongs to her husband (Rom. 7:1-6; II Cor. 11:2-3).

In responding to questions asked by the leaders of the church in Corinth, Paul gave answers that had special application to the broken situation there. Problems relating to marriage affected both liberal and conservative groups in the church. In fact, there was a group for almost every interest or foible. James Moffatt even saw a "feminist party" that claimed to have freedom to desert or divorce their husbands, so causing the problem that the Christians faced.[26] In Paul's day, the Judaistic schools of Hillel and Shammai did not agree on the issue of divorce, although both allowed divorce. Then Paul prohibited divorce, regardless of the circumstance. But why did he say that his words were also those of the Lord (I Cor. 7:10) and yet take a position that is stricter than that of the Master? The reason is that in Corinth, morals and marriage were regarded with shocking laxity. Therefore, Paul was determined not to give any cause for allowing the situation to continue among Christians. The issue of the sanctity of marriage had to be settled, for the important reason that nowhere is the reality of the body of Christ more perfectly understood, or more easily distorted, than in the marriage relationship. The relationship of Christian partners is not to be tampered with. It is real. In marriage, Christians must stay together as a symbol of the body of Christ that cannot be broken. It is impossible to separate the members of Christ from each other. If this fact is not respected and demonstrated within the vows of marriage, how will it ever be understood in relationships outside of this most intimate union between Christians? Let converts understand that the body of Christ cannot be regarded lightly. Let them know that each believer is joined to every other believer through the inseparable union of them all in Christ, the Head.

### *Some Ethical Issues Are Absolute, Others Are Not*

One of the regrets of my earlier days of missionary work was the lack of clarity about what was really important and what was secondary. Things that should have been treated as matters of purely personal preference were often made the subject of hard-and-fast rules. It is very easy for a missionary from America or England to make an issue out of something that should never be an issue at all. I recall the way in which it was insisted that schoolboys remove their hats whenever they came into the school building or stood before a teacher. Yet in some parts of Africa it is considered good manners to wear a hat at all times, even in church. If it seems silly to make this a misdemeanor for Christians, many other issues that were scarcely

26. *New Testament Commentary,* vol. 7, p. 78.

more serious were raised. Some churches said the betel nut must not be chewed because it allegedly contains a narcotic, yet the sharing of a betel nut between friends is a traditional symbol of hospitality and fraternity. Most churches insisted that Christians should never drink beer, even though the rule was very hard to enforce and caused a lot of hypocrisy. However, other churches taught temperance and self-control rather than abstinence. One church demanded that all artifacts of the "pagan" life be destroyed, while another group made a distinction between art as such and art that was obviously used in "pagan" rituals. At one point there was a long discussion about a certain word that contained the Arabic name for God.[27] One group of elders banned the use of the word by its flock, while the rest said it was merely an explicative and should not be taken as profanity. There was one topic that seemed equally important to all; this was the question of seasonal rites. Should Christians attend dances that were organized around the traditional values? Could they be permitted to honor the ancestors by a libation or "feed" them by leaving food at their shrines? A problem about which there was less consensus was the whole question of baptism for Christian polygamists. Should only the women in such a marriage be baptized? Or should the husband also be baptized? Or should all be refused? The ethical decisions covered a great variety of issues; some matters were obviously peripheral, but others involved decisions so normative to right Christian living that they needed to be taken seriously by all.

Paul did not confuse less important issues with others that were really important. In the former he expected each Christian to make up his own mind. Paul would not get involved in such secondary matters. We have already shown that decisions about food, even food offered to idols, and many other superficial things were left to the individual. But on questions of right morals Paul did not allow a subjective approach. When it came to the sanctity of the body and basic morality there was no compromise. As F. F. Bruce says, "While food was ethically and spiritually a matter of indifference, sexual relations were not: They had profound and lasting effects on those involved."[28] Paul wrote a letter to the Corinthians that has been lost. In it he commanded the Corinthian Christians not to "associate with immoral people" (I Cor. 5:9). In fact, what he meant was that Christians should break off all relationships with anyone who called himself a "brother" but who was immoral, greedy, a slanderer, a drunkard, a thief, or worshiped idols (I Cor. 5:11). Paul stated categorically that such behavior is wrong, and there is to be no compromise with it. If tolerated, this kind of conduct could corrupt the whole fellowship.[29]

27. *Wallahi.*

28. *Paul, Apostle of the Heart Set Free* (Grand Rapids: Eerdmans, 1978), p. 261; compare D. S. Bailey, *Sexual Relationship in Christian Thought* (New York: Harper, 1959), p. 10.

29. Bruce, *Paul,* p. 262.

The convert needs to have guidance that distinguishes consistently between those issues that involve important decisions applicable to all and the lesser things that should be left to each one. Eric Wahlstrom feels that the way in which issues should be judged, and treated accordingly, is in the light of three things: The gospel and what it means, the Holy Spirit and what he will say concerning a particular issue, and the fellowship and how it is affected.[30] If it is a peripheral issue, then let there be peace when the convert decides what he shall do. The unity of the believers will not be adversely affected. Even if it is a matter of greater importance, love among the brethren and for the brethren should be able to allow for some differences. But that which is of serious consequence to the fellowship and is equally wrong for all must be resolutely excluded. Even those decisions made by the individual must be made within the context of the community.[31]

There are areas in which Christian living must be absolutely uncompromising and there are areas in which compromise becomes a duty, but "one area in which compromise on matters which are not matters of principle always becomes a duty is in the area of Christian fellowship."[32]

## Practical Obligations of the New Life

### *Social Responsibilities*

Being a citizen of two worlds, so to speak, means the convert has duties to both. There are certain things that are required of him as a member of the world into which he was born, and there is a second set of obligations arising from his membership within the new community of believers. Paul did not give the impression that Christians are going to change the world. These early Christians were living in the expectation of the imminent return of Jesus Christ. This may well explain, in part, why Paul did not treat in any great depth certain ethical issues that we today would regard as foundational. We obviously look at things in a manner different from the way Paul saw things. His expectation of his converts was that they should live carefully and consistently, but there was little reason to "waste time on trying to change social institutions when you are sure this world will soon pass away."[33] The guidance Paul gave had as its rationale the belief that Christians

30. *The New Life in Christ* (Philadelphia: Muhlenberg, 1950), p. 193.

31. Victor P. Furnish emphasizes the communal dimension in deciding right and wrong. "Moral action . . . is always a matter of choosing and doing what is good for the brother and what will uphold the whole community of brethren." *Theology and Ethics in Paul* (Nashville: Abingdon, 1968), p. 233.

32. Barclay, *Turning to God,* p. 68.

33. C. T. Craig, *The Beginning of Christianity* (Nashville: Abingdon-Cokesbury, 1943), p. 307.

ought to live the new life consistently and with discipline. There is no rigid code; no one can predict, or determine in advance, how the Christian should respond in every detail, because the way is new. But one thing is clear: nothing the convert does lies outside the responsibility he has at all times to show himself to be a Christian. Paul's ethics are fittingly summed up in the words, "Everything you do or say, then, should be done in the name of the Lord Jesus, as you give thanks through him to God the Father" (Col. 3:17). "Paul was so convinced of the reality of the new life and of God's active presence in the Christians that he did not find it difficult to believe that each one was capable of spontaneously doing what God willed him to do."[34] The Christian's obligations to society are based on the principle of association with, yet separation from, the world. This principle touches not only secular society but also the church and the home.

*Secular society*

The convert is never asked to leave the world of his birth and withdraw as an ascetic now that he has become a Christian. Nevertheless, Paul recognized that the faith was purchased at an extremely high price, and makes high demands. Therefore, there must be a sharp line of demarcation between those who are Christians and those who are not (II Cor. 6:17). Paul warned the converts not to enter into relationships that would tend to have paganizing effects. "Do not try to work together as equals with unbelievers," he said, "for it cannot be done" (II Cor. 6:14).[35] On the other hand, it was necessary that believers live at peace with the public and local administrators, and be blameless as citizens. This was not only because they would need to ensure their rights as citizens, but also because a cooperative, peaceful lifestyle witnessed to the spiritual character of their faith and kept the idea of a heavenly citizenship before the Christian.[36] So Paul wrote, "Be wise in the way you act toward those who are not believers, making good use of every opportunity you have" (Col. 4:5-6). A group of Christians living at Thessalonica had decided that, because the return of Christ was imminent, they could live independently, even carelessly, as far as secular society was concerned. Paul wrote to put this right, instructing them: "Make it your aim to live a quiet life, to mind your own business, and to earn your own living, just as we told you before" (I Thess. 4:11). The intent of this advice was to gain the respect of those who were not believers and to ensure the economic self-sufficiency of the believer (cf. Phil. 4:5; Titus 3:2).

Clearly, the convert should take great care not to be entangled again in the dark things from which he has been delivered, but this was not done by

34. Wahlstrom, *The New Life in Christ,* p. 199.
35. See also I Corinthians 5:9-10; Ephesians 5:11.
36. Weizsacker, *The Apostolic Age,* p. 373.

living in a ghetto or by removing oneself from society. The ungodly world needs to see what the transforming gospel can do—for it is in such a world of corrupted, sinful people that "you must shine among them like stars lighting up the sky" (Phil. 2:15). The principle of separation *and* association is not a contradiction, as it may seem; in reality these concepts are inseparable and show the essential character of Christianity. "Jesus separated his disciples from the Jewish school and at the same time directed them to fulfill the public duties of religion."[37] The directions given by Paul were not intended to reform the world. Paul's point of departure was the quality of the converted life in an unconverted world that was soon to come to an end. The struggle, as Paul saw it, was that individual Christians keep themselves from vices and yet live actively and carefully in the world, "as you offer them the message of life" (Phil. 2:16).

*The home*

Robert E. Speer writes of the very special place that the home had in the formation of the early church. It is around the uniqueness of the family unit, he says, that the church is best understood. "It was because Christianity first of all built the church in the house that it produced the Christian home, the richest and most fruitful institution ever known." Paul taught that fundamentally a Christian home is a church in the house.[38] The behavior of a Christian family and the openness of one Christian family to another reveal to us what primitive Christianity was really like. Hospitality was a virtue little known among the Gentiles, and the sorry state of marriage had taken its toll on family life. If the church, which was almost exclusively identified with the home, was to be a sound and enduring fellowship, the home itself must be a solid base for Christian nurture.

The "household tables" of Colossians and Ephesians provide us with a summary of what Paul expected in the Christian home. Colossians 3:17 is an introduction to the entire section: "Everything you do or say, then, should be done in the name of the Lord Jesus" (cf. 3:23; Eph. 5:21). For the Jews, at least, these tables do not appear to say anything new,[39] and Wahlstrom feels that these admonitions might have been taken from any secular moralist[40]—but for one thing: all the duties are to be carried out, and all relationships regulated, as "in the Lord." The duties of family members to each other are transformed from matters of custom and respect into a demonstration of the all-encompassing power of Christian love. Beginning right in the home, the

37. Ibid.

38. Robert E. Speer, *When Christianity Was New* (New York: Revell, 1939), p. 33.

39. Jewish teaching about the home is included in Howard Tillman Kuist, *The Pedagogy of St. Paul* (New York: Doran, 1925), pp. 32ff.

40. *The New Life in Christ*, p. 201.

convert is to experience what it means to be "in Christ." Converts need to learn how Christian family members should act; for this reason, among others, much activity for early Christians took place in the various homes. Therefore it was important that Christians should keep the home as a place of witness where wives and husbands, as well as parents and children, love and obey each other.

The sanctity of the home is the strength of the church. The home and family were the center, constituted the working unit of Christianity, and became its evangelizing force. Because the message of the gospel is the perfect expression of love through Christ, this truth must first be practiced in the crucible of family relationships. "The worst of all schisms in the Church," says Speer, "is any rupture in the church in the house."[41]

*The church leaders*

The leaders of the new churches were in a difficult situation. There was a lot of caring that had to be done. Because of the incredible diversity within the congregations, a wide range of problems arose. Most of these leaders had to oversee the church in their spare time. Since the church will be the topic of the following chapter, I note here simply that Paul expected the individual converts to support their leaders in every way. Usually such leaders were the first to become Christians in the community. The earliest record we have of Paul's instructions to the converts concerning these leaders is found in I Thessalonians 5:12-13: "We beg you, our brothers, to pay proper respect to those who work among you, who guide and instruct you in the Christian life. Treat them with the greatest respect and love because of the work they do." In the case of leaders such as Stephanus, Fortunatus, and Achaicus, even more than love and respect is expected for them. In writing to the Corinthians, Paul notes that the Stephanus' family were, indeed, the first Christians in Achaia and that they had given themselves to the service of God's people.

The converts, then, were to be under the authority of such people, literally, "subject to them" (***upotassesthe***) and to any others who work and serve with them. There was also a system of financial support for leaders, and Paul insisted that all converts cooperate in providing them with whatever help was needed. Certain elders were even to be considered for double pay, "especially those who work hard at preaching and teaching" (I Tim. 5:17). Paul carefully laid the responsibility for the church's economy upon the converts themselves (I Cor. 16:2), and no one was allowed to excuse himself. Even the poorest of converts shared in financial responsibility. In the following chapters we shall be concerned with the need to train young Christians in stewardship and in disciplined giving.

41. *When Christianity Was New,* p. 18.

### *Political Responsibilities*

The history of the expansion of the Christian movement is filled with encounters between the kingdom that John the Baptist and Jesus preached and the kingdoms of the world. Nothing could be more relevant to mission in our own day than a recognition of these fierce tensions. In many areas of the world, churches are facing the hostility of governments, much as the church did in those years immediately following Paul's ministry. Nationalism in various forms, dictatorships, repressive regimes, Marxist-communist governments, and even systems that seem open to Christianity are bringing pressures and persecution on what are often minority Christian groups. Whatever attitude a government takes toward the church, how the Christian is to respond in each case has been a struggle in which each generation has had to engage. Tracing out what this means for mission today is a bigger assignment than this study can undertake. But it is very important to see the political implications of the stand that Paul took and taught his converts. This does not mean that we have a firm outline for our attitudes and actions in all cases, particularly with regard to the present. But Paul did not leave his converts without guidance, and his basic principles still provide a reliable guide for what our approach ought to be.

#### *Paul, the Jews, and the state*

We need to understand that the context from which Paul wrote reflected both the Roman and the Jewish worlds of his day. The narrative of the Book of Acts as well as Paul's letters reflect the hard reality of living under the colonialist regime of Rome. Paul does not look for confrontation with the civil authorities, but the situations in which he must take his stand arise as a matter of course. When conflict arises he does not sidestep the issues. He deals with them in firmness, never leaving his converts without instruction as to who they are and what their conduct ought to be. The lordship of Jesus and the power of the state present a dilemma for the convert. So Paul teaches in clear-cut ways what Christian behavior ought to be, and by his own life provides a model for his converts to follow.

As a Roman citizen Paul had an obvious fascination with Rome.[42] Not only did he see it as a great center of government, but also he recognized a special leading from God for a ministry in that city. "I must also see Rome" (Acts 19:21) was a resolve he made while in Ephesus, and when he wrote to the Romans he regretted openly that he had been delayed a number of times in making his journey there (Rom. 1:13).[43] It was rare for Roman authorities to cause problems for Paul. Most of Paul's opposition, including outright

42. Acts 16:37; 19:21; 22:25; 23:11.
43. See also Acts 23:11; 28:14, 16; Romans 1:10.

persecution, came from his fellow Jews. At Philippi he was accused of anti-Roman activity (Acts 16:21), and at Ephesus he was blamed for defaming the established religion (Acts 19:26). These incidents were not primarily initiated by the Jews; but in all other places where Paul became involved with the authorities it was due to the hostilities of his own people. This was true in Pisidia (Acts 13:50; 14:2, 19) and later in Thessalonica (Acts 17:5-7). The Jews were also involved in the opposition at Ephesus (Acts 19:33). In contrast to this, G. B. Caird observes, "Paul was received by Roman officials with polite and friendly interest and he seemed to have the knack of making friends."[44]

Acts provides us with several vignettes that illustrate Paul's attitudes toward governing authorities in various situations, and each encounter teaches something of importance as we see the interaction of the gospel with secular powers.

Paul recognized the privileges of being a Roman citizen and fully expected those rights to be extended to him (Acts 16:35-40). In Philippi Paul refused to be released from jail without a proper hearing and official sanction, including a personal apology from the Roman officials. Only then did Paul and Silas agree to leave the city, but not before they visited Lydia and encouraged the converts.

In Acts 22:22-29, when the commander was about to have him whipped, Paul informed the man of his citizenship with the reminder that to be bound and whipped without a fair trial was illegal. This turn of events frightened the Roman officer. In another instance, Paul closed his argument before Festus by claiming his right of appeal to the emperor, and his request was granted immediately (Acts 25:10-12).

Paul made no apology for the gospel even when it appeared to run counter to the interest of the state, and actually provoked a riot. At Thessalonica he was accused of "teaching another king," and his friend Jason was charged with housing an agitator (Acts 17:5-9). At Ephesus Paul was accused of opposing the state goddess, Artemis, which led to riot; but there is no record that Paul intervened (Acts 19:23-41).

However, Paul did not deliberately agitate, and did not deliberately show disrespect to the authorities, even when he was treated badly. For example, in Acts 23:1-5, the head of the Jewish religious council, Ananias, ordered Paul be hit on the mouth. Paul answered with strong words, calling Ananias a "white-washed wall"; but when he discovered that he had been addressing the high priest he took his words back, quoting the scriptural injunction, "You must not speak evil of the ruler of your people."

The Jewish communities made up about ten percent of the population in

44. *The Apostolic Age* (London: Gerald Duckworth, 1955), p. 460.

the cities. They were far from an easy minority for Rome to govern. Israel saw herself as "a kingdom of priests and a holy nation" (Exod. 19:6, RSV); her destiny was to reveal God's sovereignty before the world. So she had to maintain her identity at all costs. Recognized everywhere by their Sabbath observances, by their exclusivism, and by their insistence on special privileges, Jews projected an image that led Tacitus to say, "The Jewish way of life is absurd and repugnant." Much, if not most, of the trouble the early church found itself in may be seen as a natural result of the well-known antipathy that Rome already had toward the Jews. For the most part, Roman authorities were reluctant to have anything to do with legal matters involving Jews. The scene at Corinth bears this out. When the Jews dragged Paul into the court, Gallio, the governor, declared that he was not interested in the case. Because he saw it as a Jewish religious matter he paid no attention (Acts 18:14-16). Claudius, who had been reared with Agrippa and knew as much about the history of the Jews as any emperor, said, "If they [the Jews] do not follow my orders I shall use every means to prosecute them who bring in a pestilence which is scattered all over the world."[45]

So we find that although the most massive movement to Christ was from among the Gentiles, the church as a whole suffered because of its Jewish heritage. However, as we have seen, Paul was able to see the good as well as the bad side of Roman authority. Actually, Paul had very little to say about the more demonic aspects of government. One passage refers to "heathen judges" (I Cor. 6:1), which puts secular officials, it would seem, at a very low level. But he did not mean to say that Christians will not receive fair treatment. Rather, Paul's concern is that Christians ought to take care of their own affairs.[46] When he wrote his second letter to the Thessalonians it was still very early in his ministry. In it he made reference to the "Mysterious Wickedness" that was "already at work" (II Thess. 2:7). This is probably a reference to Caligula and his diabolical influence on the entire Roman world. But the real Wicked One is yet to come and is worse by far than Caligula, because he will "go in and sit down in God's Temple and claim to be God" (II Thess. 2:4). So Paul did not see even rule by Caligula as the worst possible situation. It may be that he saw Rome in a somewhat nobler aspect if, in fact, it was to Rome that he referred as that which was holding back evil and guarding the peace (II Thess. 2:6-7).[47] Paul did recognize Rome to be the authority that God had instituted; the power that was keeping things, for the time being, at least, from total chaos.

45. Hans Conzelmann, *History of Primitive Christianity,* J. E. Steely, trans. (Nashville: Abingdon, 1973), p. 129.

46. Wahlstrom, *The New Life in Christ,* p. 269.

47. See Caird's discussion, *The Apostolic Age,* pp. 173ff.

*The convert and the state*

It is not claimed that we can settle all problems that confront Christians as they live in today's world by summarizing Paul's injunctions to Christians of his day. We find the churches of our time caught in ideological struggles that are even more complex than those Paul knew. Yet Paul did have some very specific things to say to young Christians about their responsibilities to the state, and how they should live as citizens. Jesus' own statement was, "Pay to the Emperor what belongs to the Emperor, and pay to God what belongs to God" (Mark 12:17). The state is a reality. It functions for purposes of which God approves. This axiom of Jesus was taken up by Paul when he said, "Everyone must obey state authorities" (Rom. 13:1). The political power has been instituted by God for keeping order. The state is a necessary factor in this "old world" in order to regulate society and, as such, it should be respected. There is no talk of revolution here, whether intellectual or actual.

So we may say that the first level of loyalty for a Christian is that he fulfill all his duties as a subject of the state. This involves responsibilities that are spelled out in some detail, since civil authority derives its source and sanction from God himself.

Paul taught that resistance to, or rebellion against, civil authority is wrong and against the convert's best interest. "Whoever opposes the existing authority opposes what God has ordered; and anyone who does so will bring judgment on himself. . . . you must obey the authorities . . . as a matter of conscience" (Rom. 13:2, 5; cf. Titus 3:1).

The four specifications of civil obedience are payment of tribute, payment of taxes, respect, and honor to all who deserve it. "Pay, then, what you owe them; pay them your personal and property taxes, and show respect and honor for them all" (Rom. 13:7).

There is also a second level of loyalty to the state that is revealed later as Paul writes in the pastoral Epistles. Here Christians are asked to pray for all people, including kings and those who are in authority (I Tim. 2:1-2). Supplications of this kind follow the Jewish tradition that the welfare and the peace of the state are centered around the well-being of the ruler. Because the state is a God-appointed agency to administer justice, then let Christians work to make the state as good as it can possibly be.

Some converts may have felt that because they had given themselves over to a new lordship this would release them from obedience to the secular authorities. After all, if, as some maintained, a Christian should be free to leave a "pagan" husband or wife (I Cor. 7:10ff.) or if a slave might disobey or desert his "pagan" master (I Cor. 7:21; Col. 3:22ff.), might not the Christians rise up in rebellion against the heathen oppressor as the Jewish zealots had long advocated? No, said Paul; on the contrary, the convert is to serve God by taking his place in the orderly community. It is not primarily a question of obedience to the state, but of obedience to God. It is for his own conscience's sake that the Christian must obey the authorities (Rom. 13:5). Paul would admit the tension. Paul's own activity did bring him into conflict with civil authority. But the point at which this tension becomes such that the Christian must actively resist instituted authority cannot be determined once and for all.

> The principle of obedience laid down here by Paul cannot be used to determine what is right and what is wrong any more than the words, "Render unto Caesar the things which are Caesar's and unto God the things which are God's," tell us what belongs to Caesar and what belongs to God.[48]

Paul's teaching about the Christian's responsibility to the state does not tell everything. There are many factors in the present-day struggle of Christians with demonic authoritarian systems that call for careful reflection before any kind of action is taken. But as a basic principle, Paul's teaching contained in Romans 13 is identical to that laid down by Jesus. Both recognize the legitimacy of the state, or that government is of divine origin, but leave open the question of its application. At what point the state ceases to be the servant of God or at what point the Christian must "obey God rather than men" cannot be determined directly from these passages. The very fact that Paul says "for conscience sake" reminds us again that each person has a responsibility to work out in each particular case how these principles will apply. But the call for respect and honor vis-à-vis the state is not to be disregarded. It is from this basis that all right conduct begins.

## The State and the Christian Faith

Although Paul does not use the kingdom language of Jesus, it is clear that it is possible for the convert to be subject to the political state because the state is of an order different from the kingdom that Jesus has established. There is no question about where ultimate loyalty lies for the Christian, or where Paul would stand in the event of a choice between his secular citizenship and his loyalty to Christ. "We . . . are citizens of heaven, and we eagerly wait for our Savior, the Lord Jesus Christ, to come from heaven" (Phil. 3:20).[49] It is in the light of mastery by this highest loyalty that the problems relating to conflict with the state come into better perspective. The reference to "citizenship in heaven" does not remove the convert from

48. Wahlstrom, *The New Life in Christ,* p. 274.
49. See also Galatians 4:26; Ephesians 1:4; Colossians 3:1; II Timothy 4:8.

this world. There is no simple way to opt out of facing the struggle that the fact of the two kingdoms presents. But one's relationship with the secular world and the state is defined by faith. Faith gives the Christian a unique identity as being one who is in the world but not of the world. God is over all. He is the ruler and sustainer of creation, the judge of both history and the institutions of society. Wahlstrom observes that

> in the civil or "secular" life God's rule is "hidden"; He works behind the scenes, as it were, and uses men to accomplish his purposes. This is the realm of the law which God has, indeed, ordained and incorporated into the very structure of the universe.[50]

On the other hand, it is through the gospel that God reveals his word directly to men, revealing his forgiveness and grace. Let the convert see God supremely in the Word, but let him also see God's provision for his life in the world. Obedience, the essence of the new life, involves both the acceptance of the gospel and the willingness to accept God's providence as expressed in the ordinances of society.

50. *The New Life in Christ,* p. 274.

*Part Four*

# The Church

## *A Witnessing Community*

# 7

# Foundations for the New Community

In the life of a missionary, especially one who works in a place where the gospel has only recently come, there is nothing more wonderful than to sit among a group of worshipers that through faith has been joined together into a living church. The idea of a church was so different from anything previously known among the Hausa-speaking people of northern Nigeria that it seemed no word existed in their language that would adequately express what was meant. So the early missionaries decided to introduce the word *ekklēsia,* and it is now a common expression. Perhaps it would have been better not to use a foreign term, but nevertheless it was obvious that when people came to worship together under Christ's lordship something new and quite different was taking place. I have vivid memories of reaching some village or other after miles of walking or driving, and watching as the church was called together. Usually the "bell" was a long piece of rusty iron that the leader would strike vigorously with a heavy bolt or a hammer. One by one or in small groups the believers came and took their places on the mud benches in the unpretentious "house of prayer." The most vivid impression was of a gathering of people; not just any people, but a people who were joined by a common loyalty to the Lord called Jesus who had in a real way brought them together.

These village churches could boast of little of what we would normally think of as organization. But by uniting heads of families, learning new forms of worship, and forming new loyalties, they were, it would seem, rather similar to the churches Paul established in his day.

## The Mission Church

The term *mission church* has been used in so many ways and over such a long period of time that when we use the phrase we are not always sure what we are talking about. In fact, certain ideas commonly associated with the phrase are distinctly contrary to the way in which I propose to use the term. For example, there is a certain stereotype of the mission church that is based on finance. A church is begun by using outside funds and continues to receive subsidies. Such churches may have been organized for many years, but since there is continuing financial dependency, they are regarded as mission churches.

Another common concept relates the mission church to its geographical location. Mission is something that happens "out there," far away from the home church or the sending church. The term *overseas churches* becomes synonymous with mission churches. The idea of mission belongs exclusively to what happens across the ocean or on another continent. How long the church has existed is not so much the point as that it is far away from us.

A third use of the term *mission church* refers to an extension of a local church. A church is started as an offspring of a congregation and is managed in such a way as to ensure the continuing control and the stamp of the parent body. Reference to a daughter church often carries the implicit meaning that it is regarded as a dependent church or as a mission church.

For the purposes of this study, a church is not a mission church because it is dependent, or far away, or a by-product. By the phrase *mission church* I refer to a community that has been brought together recently by its acceptance of the gospel, in an area and among a people where the gospel was not known before. Mission churches are distinguished from what are often called the older churches, simply because they are in the first or second generation of existence. But the term also indicates that the church is planted in a situation where there is little or no precedent for Christianity, and where the Christian life for these people is being established, as it were, from the start.

## The Church in Scripture: Old Testament

The word *church* has taken on meanings in our day that were not known to Paul and, when we look carefully at New Testament teaching, we can see these meanings were probably never intended. The word *ekklēsia* itself occurs only twice in Jesus' teachings (Matt. 16:18; 18:17). What Jesus actually meant by the term is somewhat obscure.[1] It was certainly not a highly organized, politically powerful institution possessing massive estates

1. "He may have meant a special fellowship or company represented by his followers, which he saw as the remnant in Israel, the true people of God." See K. L. Schmidt in *Theological Dictionary of The New Testament,* Gerhard Kittel, ed., G. W. Bromiley, trans. (Grand Rapids: Eerdmans, 1966), vol. 3, p. 530.

or pretentious buildings. Any such ideas would have been completely foreign to the disciples who listened to him. From the beginning Paul adopted the term *ekklēsia* for the church, even though that word was used far and wide in the secular Greek of the time. From the fifth century B.C. it had come to refer to an assembly of citizens that met regularly to decide on various matters affecting social welfare within a city.[2]

The Old Testament word *qāhāl* had come to have a distinctly religious meaning, first with reference to a religious gathering or "solemn assembly," and later to indicate the people themselves, for example, "the people of Jehovah."[3] The Septuagint translates *qāhāl* by the term *ekklēsia* in nearly every case. This is always so when the reference is to Israel as a whole, that is, the people of God, as they are assembled before Jehovah.[4] It is a people, as a nation and as individuals who live in community, that becomes the vehicle through which God's purpose is revealed. The words *family* or *families* are the common expressions used when referring to Abraham's place in history. Time and again, Paul selects this theme of a people in fellowship as his motif for describing the church. "Abraham is the spiritual father of us all; as the Scripture says, 'I have made you father of many nations'" (Rom. 4:16-17). He stresses that it is not the people who by birth are descended from Abraham who are important, but it is the people who are of faith. "For we are the people he called, not only from among the Jews but also from among the Gentiles." Quoting that poignant saga of the prophet Hosea, he says, "The people who were not mine I will call 'My People.' The nation that I did not love I will call 'My Beloved.' And in the very place where they were told, 'You are not my people,' there they will be called the sons of the living God" (Rom. 9:24-26). Borrowing from Ezekiel, Paul calls the young Christians at Ephesus out from associations with paganism, with the reminder that God is their Father, so that they have now become members of a different family. "I will make my home with my people and live among them; I will be their God, and they shall be my people. . . . I will be your father, and you shall be my sons and daughters" (II Cor. 6:16, 18). Some of these durable Hebrew images always underlay Paul's understanding of the church.

Yet Paul's teaching was new and radical, which is why we are justified in

2. Robert Banks, *Paul's Idea of Community: The Early House Churches in the Historical Setting* (Grand Rapids: Eerdmans, 1980), p. 34; See also G. E. Ladd, *A Theology of the New Testament* (Grand Rapids: Eerdmans, 1974), p. 537.

3. The Septuagint also translates *qāhāl* as *sunagōgē* ("synagogue") twenty times. For a discussion, see Colin Brown, *"Ekklēsia,"* in *Dictionary of New Testament Theology* (Grand Rapids: Zondervan, 1975), vol. 1, p. 291.

4. When Israel ceased to count as a nation politically, the term *ekklēsia* came more and more to denote faithful Israel as a believing and worshiping church. See H. F. Rall, *According to Paul* (New York: Charles Scribner's Sons, 1945), p. 152.

speaking of Pauline theology of the church.[5] The very local and ethnic association of terms such as "chosen," "called," and "people of God" were transformed by Paul to describe a new kind of community. Thus it came about that the early Christians chose the word *ekklēsia,* rather than "synagogue," as the name for their community.[6] The term *ekklēsia* in Paul's day denoted faithful Israel, the believing and worshiping people of God.

## Paul's Convictions about the Church

### *The Church Is People*

The church, therefore, is not a newly established institution; indeed, it is not an institution at all. It is a people, God's people,[7] assembled, worshiping, and pledged in loyalty to Jesus Christ. It is vital for us to grasp this meaning for a mission understanding of the church. Paul speaks most often of the church as a particular local gathering of Christians,[8] or an actual assembling together of believers as they meet for worship (I Cor. 11:18; 14:19, 23). Often it applies to the small house churches, the regular meeting places for a little group of followers (Rom. 16:5; I Cor. 16:19). It is always a gathering together; a meeting for worship and the expression of community life under Christ's lordship. The true expression of church always centers on the corporateness of people who, while they individually are in Christ, express that new life by belonging to others. We may say, therefore, that the special quality of Paul's churches was fellowship, and that the special function of the church was witnessing.

*A people for fellowship*

The people who are God's belong to one another in such a way that special metaphors are required to describe this togetherness. Paul's favorite way of expressing what the church means is to see it as a body. We shall give special attention to this. But he also sees himself as a "master builder" directing an enterprise in which all members are included as together they

5. Paul recognized the church to be the real heir of the promise; a theology of the church is centered on three significant factors in Jewish history: Abraham, Moses, and the temple. See the discussion by Lucien Cerfaux in *The Church in the Theology of St. Paul* (New York: Herder and Herder, 1959), pp. 7-9.

6. The term *synagogue* is never used to signify a Christian gathering in the New Testament, with the exception of the Epistle of James. Even there it is used alongside the term *ekklēsia.* Banks, *Paul's Idea of Community,* p. 35.

7. See the full discussion on the "Church as God's People" by Herman N. Ridderbos, *Paul, an Outline of His Theology,* J. R. DeWitt, trans. (Grand Rapids: Eerdmans, 1975), pp. 328-361.

8. Romans 16:1; I Corinthians 1:2; Colossians 4:16; I Thessalonians 1:1.

construct a building.[9] When Paul describes the building as a "temple," he is emphasizing a special relationship, which finds its roots in the Old Testament, between the church and God.[10] A further set of metaphors that comes from the agricultural world is used by Paul to describe certain qualities and privileges of the new community. There is reference to both "grafting" and "planting" (Rom. 11:17-24; I Cor. 3:9; Col. 2:7). The church is also pictured as the bride of Christ (II Cor. 11:2; Eph. 5:25-27). Another term that is often overlooked is that of "household" or "family." Although Paul rarely uses the actual word *household* (*oikeios*), related expressions are so frequent that the comparison of the Christian community with a family cannot be overlooked. In his earliest letters, Paul insists that God is the head of the family (I Thess. 1:1; 3:11; II Thess. 1:1-2; 2:16). There is "adoption as sons" into the family (Gal. 4:4-5, RSV). The members, taken together, considering their intimate and permanent relationship, are considered a "household of faith," and "of God" (Gal. 6:10; Eph. 2:19).

The leading idea in each of these metaphors has to do with relationships. These people are joined to one another by ties of love, redemption, and service. No individual can function without another; each person is, as it were, a stone that is joined and interlocked with others on each side. Growth, even survival itself, depends upon the surrounding environment and nourishment provided by the life of others. Can anything better express the relationships in a church than the ties indicated by terms such as "bride" or "family"? The mission church is made up of people who are in fellowship. These individual converts who have been turned around in their own lives and are now headed in the direction of Christ so often find themselves struggling against the tide of earthly family and cultural traditions. There is tremendous significance therefore in discovering that fellowship was the capstone of the early Pentecostal church. "They spent their time in learning from the apostles, taking part in the fellowship, and sharing in the fellowship meals and the prayers" (Acts 2:42). Paul's churches were centers of sharing, linking the believers with each other even as they are linked with God through Christ (I Cor. 1:9).

This fellowship exists because the Holy Spirit has been given to each and every Christian. Through this Spirit the earliest believers were led to share their possessions. The most natural way to express that everyone in the entire group of believers had become one in mind and heart was to treat even one's own belongings as the property of all the others (Acts 4:32). While the community of possessions was the outward symbol of an inner community of thought and purpose, both were the product of the Holy

9. Romans 15:20; I Corinthians 3:10-14; Galatians 2:18.

10. See Banks for the distinctions and references to Old Testament metaphors. *Paul's Idea of Community,* pp. 52, 53.

Spirit. Paul openly thanked the Philippians for their fellowship in the gospel (Phil. 1:5, RV) and characterized that church as a group that had true fellowship in the Spirit (Phil. 2:1). The fellowship of the Christians at Corinth reached far beyond their own borders through the offering they had collected for the church at Jerusalem (II Cor. 8:4, KJV). God, said Paul, had called the Christians to have fellowship with his Son Jesus Christ as Lord (I Cor. 1:9). This theme of fellowship, of intimate and mutual trust, of sharing and belonging both to God and to one another, is the essence of what it means to be a church.

I vividly remember a favorite saying of Claude Ries, a Bible scholar and a teacher at Houghton College. "This is just what fellowship is, 'two fellows in the same ship.'" The meaning is obvious. People joined together by Christ have a common point of departure and a common terminus. Meanwhile, whatever they experience of calm or storm, of sickness, joy, work, even the temptation to turn back, will be shared in some way by all. This is the church: persons who belong to each other and who support, serve, admonish, teach, and love each other without reservation or selfishness.

My family and I began missionary life in 1956 by living among people who had known nothing of the church thirty years before. The first converts were baptized in 1933, but it was not until 1954 that eighteen Christians in one large village were judged to be strong enough as a community to organize a local church. This was, however, the result of many years of faithful witnessing on the part of missionaries and early African believers. That small group of Africans finally understood that they must be the people who would step out from the structured traditional life. They knew that resentment from the majority would be intense. Decisions about how to live as Christians—as a very tiny group in the midst of misunderstanding and open persecution—demanded mutual love and many long meetings. There were questions about loyalty to fertility festivals, about ancestor rituals, and about divided marriages. Without trust and endless patience with each other, the enormous decision to become a church would have been impossible. There were, indeed, sharp divisions and angry feelings, but also much prayer and waiting on God. Without openness to the Spirit they would not have been ready for the tedious gatherings that often continued far into the night.

On one occasion an elder opened his Bible and read the account of Jesus washing the disciples' feet. His appeal, as he responded to the impact of the story, was that the church is a fellowship. Jesus, he said, gave his example so that the Christians would never forget that we must love one another, submit to one another, and always, as he put it, "eat from the same dish." And so, right in the meeting, to the indignation of some, this humble man brought in a gourd full of water and, with towel in hand, washed the feet of all who were present. As he knelt before each person, he said, "I wash your because you are my brother." That night would never be forgotten. These believers learned that the fellowship that means belonging to each other lies at the very heart of the gospel. Lest they forget their community in Christ, this group of Christians kept the ritual of footwashing for a number of years. It was practiced periodically, first among the elders and then later by all the Christians.

Paul's statements about the reality of Christian community are some of the most profound in the writings of the New Testament. While no one is more realistic than Paul about the frailties of humankind and the flawed nature of human relationships, nevertheless he continually sets before young churches a vision of what their life together ought to be. Nothing is more important for new converts who have been called out from their traditional groups and relationships than to be surrounded by the care, and supported by the sense of identity, that the Christian group "is able to provide." Fellowship among the people of God has to be planned and promoted as one of the highest priorities in mission work.

*A witnessing people*

The conviction of Harry R. Boer's book, *Pentecost and Mission,* is that it was Pentecost rather than the Great Commission that provided the primary impetus to witness in the early church. There is no thought that the Great Commission is anything less than the final mandate given by Jesus to his disciples, and it remains as a foundation stone of all true missionary labor. But it would have proved impossible for the disciples to have responded to the Great Commission if they had not obeyed Jesus' command to wait in Jerusalem for the coming of the Holy Spirit (Luke 24:49).[11] Pentecost, then, became the means by which the discipling was to be accomplished. Pentecost made witnessing the norm for the church, the natural quality of its life and the very reason for its existence. The Great Commission was given to the church as a command and as a law. Pentecost transformed this law from an external mandate into an "organic part of her being, an essential expression of her life."[12] It is one thing to have a command, says Boer, but a command can be obeyed or disobeyed. Law had both objective and subjective force, as we see, for example, in the law given by God that mankind should multiply and fill the earth. There is an inward force about such a law that "carries within itself its own effectuation." There is an instinctive response to what God has commanded. In this sense the command to procreate is a law of the being.[13] Similarly, Pentecost brings an inner dynamic

11. Boer's thesis: "The Great Commission . . . derives its meaning and powers wholly and exclusively from the Pentecost event." *Pentecost and Missions* (Grand Rapids: Eerdmans, 1961), pp. 118-134.

12. Ibid., p. 120.

13. Ibid., p. 121.

as the normal and expected evidence of new life. It does not need the prodding or the pushing of an apostle to bring about a response from the church. Because it is a law of her being, the church spontaneously shares her faith with others.

> The obedience of the church to the law of her being was a natural obedience, unreflective, spontaneous. It was the response of a healthy organism to the law of its life. . . . So spontaneous was the response of the church to the Spirit-effected law that informs her life that the need of consciously obeying the command of Christ was not felt.[14]

Roland Allen also saw that it is the Holy Spirit, given to the church, who really empowers it for witnessing. The "obligation depends not upon the letter, but upon the Spirit of Christ, not upon what He orders, (Matt. 28:19) but upon what He is."[15] Therefore this command that Christ gave the early church and that must be recognized by every mission church is not to be obeyed in any legalistic way; rather, obedience provides a clear sign that these people of God have been given the Spirit of Christ. It is expected of a church that she witness, in much the same way as it is expected that humankind will be fruitful and multiply. Procreation results from the law of nature within and does not depend on a command from God, even though in the beginning the command was given.

In reviewing Paul's letters one is impressed that the direct references to witnessing are few. Surely there was no question in his mind but that the new fellowship was by nature a witnessing fellowship. It is simply taken for granted. From Rome, he speaks in an almost casual way about the fact that his imprisonment gave "most of the brothers more confidence in the Lord, so that they grew bolder all the time to preach the message fearlessly" (Phil. 1:14). In one of his earliest letters he writes that the news of the Thessalonians' faith in God had "gone everywhere" (I Thess. 1:8). It is an axiom of the church that it must share its faith.[16] The apostolic writers, Paul among them, did not seem to feel the necessity of urging upon their converts their duty to make disciples of all nations.[17] We find it is simply the general rule that all Christians were spreading the gospel, with the result that "the churches were made stronger in the faith and grew in numbers every day" (Acts 16:5).

14. Ibid., p. 128.

15. *The Ministry of the Spirit:* Selected writings of Roland Allen, David M. Paton, ed. (London: World Dominion Press, 1960), pp. 22-43.

16. Witnessing is a norm of the church, fundamental to its life. See Philippians 1:4-5; Colossians 1:6; I Thessalonians 1:8; II Thessalonians 3:1.

17. This is also the observation of Roland Allen in *Spontaneous Expansion of the Church and the Causes which Hinder It* (London: World Dominion Press, 1927), p. 8.

The term *spontaneous expansion* was popularized by Allen more than fifty years ago to describe what he called the "unexhorted and unorganized activities of individual members of the church explaining to others the gospel which they have found for themselves."[18] This kind of witnessing cannot be contrived, which is precisely the reason it conveys the freshest, most dynamic appeal possible. This telling of the Good News springs not from what the convert has been taught but from what he has experienced of Christ. Explained Allen, "[by spontaneous expansion] I mean the expansion which follows the irresistible attraction of the Christian church for men who see its ordered life and are drawn to it by desire to discover the secret of a life which they instinctively desire to share."[19]

This irrepressible witnessing of the church is recorded, for example, by the short, dynamic statements about what took place in Ephesus. Here we have a picture of the life of a church as it developed during one of Paul's longest stays in a single place. Usually he moved quickly from place to place. In Ephesus, however, he continued his ministry, uninterrupted, over a period of two years. The narrative of the church's witness is summarized in a surprisingly casual way, emphasizing that there was no undue attention given to what was accepted everywhere as the norm for Christians. Believers shared their faith as matter of course. From the hall of Tyrannus where Paul was teaching, new Christians went out, charged with the power of the new life, to tell of what they had experienced and to share the simple facts of the Good News. The record is phenomenal. We are told that, in this way, "all the people who lived in the province of Asia, both Jews and Gentiles, heard the word of the Lord" (Acts 19:10). Luke was a good historian: even if this cannot be literally true, it is still a clear and amazing testimony to the witnessing character of the church.

Such qualities of the church—fellowship and witness—are two sides of the same coin. They complement and enhance each other. The church that is in true fellowship in the Spirit is a witnessing church. The church that bears witness and thus sees the fruit of the sharing of its own life is always richer in its fellowship. How clearly we see these two principles operating together in the early chapters of Acts. The waiting and praying in the upper room led directly to the power of Pentecost (Acts 1-2). After the healing of the lame man and the warning of the council not to speak or teach in the name of Jesus (Acts 4:18), the believers gathered together in the fellowship of prayer. This in turn was followed by a visitation of God's power and filling by the Spirit, so they "began to proclaim God's message with boldness" (Acts 4:31). When the company turned to finding solutions for internal tensions and the right people were appointed to minister to the needs of

18. Ibid., p. 20.
19. Ibid.

the group, the result was that "the word of God continued to spread" and "the number of disciples in Jerusalem grew larger and larger, and a great number of priests accepted the faith" (Acts 6:1-7). It was during worship together at Antioch that the Holy Spirit spoke to the church and Barnabas and Saul were set aside for the work of outreach, thus marking the beginning of Paul's career. It is surely significant that it was during such a period of deep fellowship together that the call and the commissioning of these two men took place (Acts 13:1-3).

This kind of interaction between fellowship and witness is also evident in the author's own experience in planning for evangelism in northern Nigeria. It was found that the one thing that drew together the various mission societies and denominations was evangelism. Through meetings called to plan and pray about carrying out the evangelistic program and through conferences and study groups, the meaning of the oneness of the Body and our understanding of each other grew and deepened. During the years when the New Life for All evangelistic effort was having its greatest effect among the peoples of Nigeria (1964-1968), the joy of sharing and worshiping was at its height.

On one occasion a week was set aside for training evangelists, pastors, and lay people in the art of witnessing to their faith. Each local church sent its representative to the central gathering, for what turned out to be a remarkable week. The spirit of fellowship was felt everywhere. There was absolutely no tension over things such as food and lodging, leaders, or program details. A deep sense of oneness united the different groups as they ate together and shared in various ways. Delegates, speaking different languages and representing different local churches, enjoyed each other as though they were one family. Songs were composed and sung. Spontaneous testimonies about God's blessing and guidance enlivened the services throughout the week. All were concentrating on the purpose of the conference, which was to discover the most effective tools for witness and to seek the friendship and the encouragement of others before beginning the new adventure. No other conference ever did so much for the entire church as did this one week of intense fellowship centered on the sharing of the gospel with others. As God's people truly serve each other they also will be thrust out to witness. At the same time they will enjoy that fellowship that upbuilds and strengthens the church.

### *The Church Is a Body*

We have already noted the variety of metaphors Paul uses to describe the church. At one place he sees the church as a building; in another the church is like a bride.[20] But by far the most characteristic figure used by Paul is to see the church as a body (Rom. 12:4-5; I Cor. 10:17; 12:27). And it is just this metaphor that holds the greatest significance for mission. Chosen from the familiar biological realm, this powerful image obviously includes a number of things basic to our understanding of the church. As a body the church must function properly, it must have mobility, and it must be an instrument available for use. The body does not fulfill its function if the care of the body becomes an end in itself.

The function of the body, the church, as a serving agency depends on two relationships that Paul is careful to emphasize. First there is the relationship of all members to the head, who is Christ (Rom. 12:5; I Cor. 12:27). This living organic entity can fulfill its purpose only if all the parts work harmoniously together. Every member, whether "joint or sinew," must contribute to the life and the functioning of the body to its full potential (Eph. 4:16). There is a unified life that no individual by himself or herself can fully express (I Cor. 12:13-14).[21] "We are all joined to each other as different parts of one body" (Rom. 12:5; cf. Eph. 3:6). Paul is against the individualism and the pride, for example, that characterized the Corinthians. In writing to them, he shows how dependent each one is on the life of the whole and is under obligation to contribute to that life. "All of you are Christ's body, and each one is a part of it" (I Cor. 12:27).

Secondly there is the relationship of all the members of the body to the Head. It is this distinction that sets the church apart from all other human institutions. While the body is the sum total of all its members, it is not merely the sum of the individuals who have each been separately joined together by faith in God. It is a special body because it is qualified as the body that is "in union with Christ" (Rom. 12:5). The right of Christ to rule—the headship of Christ, so typical of Paul's theology—is powerfully taught by the metaphor of the body. The history of interpretation as to what Paul intends when he speaks of Christ as the "head" is long and tedious.[22] But certainly in every reference to the headship of Christ over the body, the emphasis lies on his authority and rulership over the church. We may also affirm that Paul's intention in speaking of the body with Christ as its head is to denote the unity of all members in and with Christ. The idea of the headship of Christ over the body borrows from complex Jewish imagery rather than from Greek philosophy.[23] For example, in the frequent references

20. An extended discussion of the church as a "building" and as a "bride" is found in David Watson, *I Believe in the Church* (Grand Rapids: Eerdmans, 1978), pp. 115-139.

21. John A. Mackay says, "A body achieves its true glory when it gives itself up, even loses physical life for that which is more than body." *God's Order* (New York: Macmillan, 1953), p. 134.

22. For a summary, see Ridderbos, *Paul,* pp. 376-387.

23. Ibid., p. 385.

to this concept in Ephesians (1:22; 4:4, 12, 15, 25; 5:23, 30), we find not simply a diluted idea that Christ is somehow the holiest part of the church; rather, "he is identified as the indispensible ruler who dominated, as the life that quickens, as the Lord who protects, as the will who directs, as the leader that nourishes."[24]

*The body as the people of God*

We have spoken at length of the fact that Paul understands the church to be God's new people. That emphasis needs to be taken up once more as we look more closely at what the idea of the body implies. The concept of the church as the body of Christ means that a new people have been brought together under Christ's headship. There is a close connection here between the body of Christ and the people of God that reaches back to Abraham, Isaac, and Jacob, who were figures of the head in the Old Testament corporate community.[25] The phrase *body of Christ* expresses the true oneness of those who are the people of God through Christ, and who, in fact, are also of the seed of Abraham (Gal. 3:16, 27-29). The basic thought is that the church as the people of God centers its life in Christ. Nevertheless, there is also included here rich meaning for the individual members of this incorporated body. The body includes both the head and the individual members, and Paul lays great stress on the latter, human aspect.

The Corinthian church had a lot of difficulty with this human side of the body; a fact that led Paul to teach openly and practically about what it means for members of the body to relate to one another as they should (see I Cor. 12:12-30). It is here, in the realm of everyday relationships between one member and another, that the meaning of the body is best learned. It is in the movements of the body, and in the health of its parts, that the head is best honored.

Each member of the body is given a ministry to other members. And it is precisely in the diversity of ministries and the differences of function of one member in relation to another that the wholeness and the unity of the body are best revealed. "God put every different part in the body just as he wanted it to be" (I Cor. 12:18). God, therefore, has designed things so that every person is involved with his or her special function (I Cor. 12:14-20), with the result that each member has to depend on others and at the same time has to minister to others.

The link between members of the community is so close that what affects one necessarily affects all. There is an intense sharing in the body.

24. Markus Barth, *The Broken Wall* (Chicago: Judson, 1959), p. 116.

25. See Romans 4:1; 9:7; and Moses, I Corinthians 10:2.

> He does not say that the experiences of individuals within the community both pleasurable and sorrowful *should* be shared by all the others who belong to it. He says instead that they *are* so shared whether others consciously experience them or not. The "body" has a common nerve.[26]

"If one part of the body suffers, all the other parts suffer with it; if one part is praised, all the other parts share its happiness" (I Cor. 12:26). There is hardly any way to express more strongly the interdependence of the whole community.

Now because this is a body that is composed of humans, not angels, we have to consider that the facts of life of any growing organism will apply also to the church. The body is reaching for maturity and struggles to grow in a world that is often antagonistic to its redeemed members.

*The body is holy but not perfect*

Because this is a body of people, there is no reason to believe that every sin will quickly cease, or that the members are going to be anything but flesh-and-blood people. One of the most unfair expectations applied to mission churches is that these new believers will somehow live an idealistic and unreal life in which wrongs are easily discerned and all sins are quickly corrected. A missionary who imagines that the new churches are going to be free from all the imperfections found in the older churches (from which the missionary has usually been sent) is doomed to frustration and disappointment. Paul did not have perfect churches. And he was straightforward and honest as he pointed to the flaws in the fellowship. The troubles can be variously attributed to doctrinal, social, or organizational inadequacies, as well as to moral lapses and sheer ignorance. There was an alarming failure to comprehend Christian doctrine, as his epistles reveal. His authority was disputed by irresponsible teachers (as well as by some of the faithful); some of them—Hymenaeus, Alexander, and Philetus (I Tim. 1:20; II Tim. 2:17)—have been immortalized as men whose influence Paul could regard only as "gangrenous." Robert E. Speer, discussing the early church, observed,

> Paul deplores the presence in the church of many "unruly men, vain teachers, and deceivers who overthrow whole houses, teaching things which they ought not for filthy lucre's sake" (Tit. 1:10, 11). He supported himself by manual work to escape any such suspicion as hung about the names of other Christian teachers (Acts 20:33). False teachers divided the little groups he had gathered (Gal. 4:17; Acts 20:30).[27]

26. Banks, *Paul's Idea of Community,* p. 64.
27. *When Christianity Was New* (New York: Revell, 1939), p. 83.

He wrote to Timothy with profound regret that "everyone in the province of Asia, including Phygelus and Hermogenes, ha[d] deserted [him]" (II Tim. 1:15). Religious impostors filled him with anxiety and grief (II Tim. 3:1-9, 13). The moral looseness in Corinth was appalling (I Cor. 5:1). In addition, bitter factionalism had set in, and some who found the profession of Christianity to be financially profitable were literally poisoning the church (I Tim. 6:3-10).

The sad reporting could go on. The church was, and still is, an imperfect body. But the beautiful part is that, time and again, Paul called those Christians saints, even though we know full well that many in every place were living below (and some far below) the standards expected of those who have come under the authority of the Head. John Bright brings his study of the kingdom of God to an appropriate conclusion by addressing the dilemma of the New Testament church. It is a church, he says, that is in the desperate grip of a world of time moving toward eternity. We have to believe in the victory of the kingdom and the ultimate perfection of the church, even though it is a state "which as yet no human eye can see."[28] Bright continues, "It is a fearful struggle. A struggle that beggars the vocabulary. There are portents in Heaven, torment and tribulation on earth as evil hurls itself at the kingdom of the saints."[29]

This is a struggle that is bound to take place. The war of the flesh against the Spirit is as devastating to the wholeness of the church as are the powers of evil real and devastating in the natural world. We must face this fact and admit it. The church is not perfect, but it is still his church, and is the best example of what God expects his kingdom to be. Missionaries have been shocked at the sins of their brothers and sisters in this or that place around the world, but a little reflection would have forced them to see that the sending church is really no better. Any substandard Christian living is not to be praised or encouraged. It is not God's will, nor is it what is taught in the Bible, but it is the situation we face as long as we are on this side of the end of the age.

When I first went to Africa I, too, found it easy to be judgmental and felt I had quite a bit of personal holiness. Many pages could be taken up not only with the details of the way in which the notions of my own "perfectness" were shown to be exaggerated, but also of how I was helped to an understanding of the stress placed on those who turn to Christ from other religions.

One of my students, Nuhu, already a pastor, was so troubled by his wife's mental disability that he turned to animistic rituals of exorcism when doctors at the mission hospital said they could not help her. Nuhu felt that his wife's

28. *The Kingdom of God* (Nashville: Abingdon, 1953), p. 239.
29. Ibid., p. 241.

schizophrenic behavior was of demonic origin. Unfortunately, though we missionaries and the church pastors had a lot to say about the Holy Spirit, we still had no way of dealing with this kind of problem. One of the subjects in our teaching should have concerned the power of God's Spirit over "the spirits"—but we had never developed this, nor had we any understanding of exorcism. Nuhu could not accept that there was really no help for his wife. So the traditional ritual was carried out in a dark hut. His wife sat covered with a blanket. A fire was lit and two traditional priests, chanting formulas and waving banana leaves, walked around her. It was sad to realize that here was a pastor whose desperation had brought him to trust again in "those weak and pitiful ruling spirits" (Gal. 4:9).

Is this really the church? Yes, it is: not, indeed, a perfect church, but one that is loved by and will one day be perfectly ruled by the Christ who died for it.

Paul does not condemn or even pronounce judgment (except in extreme cases).[30] Ephesians is a key epistle in regard to his teaching concerning the need to allow the church to face its own shortcomings and profit by them. It is in this way, says Paul, that "we shall become mature people, reaching to the very height of Christ's full stature" (Eph. 4:13). For while Jesus Christ is the "perfect man," the body of Christ is not yet finished.[31]

Here we need to be reminded of the open-set view of conversion that was dealt with in chapter 4.[32] There must be steady movement toward the Center. The right to fellowship in the church will be based on this continued movement toward the Center rather than conformity to a rigid standard of outward perfection.

Therefore, we must regard imperfection and holiness as two aspects of the mission church. Understanding this will help us greatly in forming right attitudes, especially when the maturing process seems to be moving very slowly. Young Christians, even though inexperienced in the new life, and with much to learn of Christian doctrine, are holy because they belong to God through Christ. It is neither personal virtue nor sinless behavior that merits them the right to be called Christians, even saints, but the fact that they have surrendered themselves to the call of Christ in an act of saving faith. But this fact of belonging is not a superficial, external affair. The saints are those who are being sanctified. The church is holy because it belongs to God; it is the seat of transforming spiritual power and as a human fellowship it is, itself, being transformed. Or to put it another way, the "holy are being made holy."

30. For example, see I Corinthians 5:1-5.
31. See Barth, *The Broken Wall*, p. 116.
32. Pp. 113-114.

*The body is a living organism*

Describing the church as a body emphasizes also that we are not talking about an inadequate, paralyzed entity. The mission church can all too easily become self-centered and institutional, struggling to maintain its own life and leaning on others to support its outreach, provide its education, and underwrite its budget. But what Paul had in mind when he spoke of the body is essentially adequacy of function. This body is a living organism. Each separate part, each joint, fits together to ensure the working of the whole as it should, so that it builds itself up in love (Eph. 4:16). It was only after the resurrection of Christ that the true meaning of the body of Christ became clear.

There is no way in which Paul could have spoken of the body of Christ except in the light of resurrection. Chalmer Faw, speaking of the early church as the community of the resurrection, says, "The risen Lord moved in their midst not as a disembodied spirit, a phantom, but as a real person from whom they received their instruction, their commission, and power."[33] The meaning of the body of Christ as Paul develops it is even richer in content, because of the resurrection, than what is meant when Jesus speaks of his own body being broken on the cross.

We know it is a living body because it is a body that grows. This is the day of exciting research into the growth of churches. The church-growth movement is well known. It is expected that any church should give constant testimony to its inner life by reproduction and growth. Nothing was more characteristic of the apostolic church than startling, steady growth.

Reports of growth in and around Jerusalem after Pentecost stand out like cryptic news releases in the Book of Acts. The disciples began to sell their property and distribute their money according to need, meeting together to eat and to praise God. The result was that "every day the Lord added to their group those who were being saved" (Acts 2:47). Opposition was followed by blessing and further growth after the healing of the lame man (Acts 3). Peter and John were still preaching when the temple guards and the Sadducees arrested them and put them in jail. But we read that "many who heard the message believed; and the number of men grew to about five thousand" (Acts 4:4). After the crisis of Ananias and Sapphira the church surged forward again with dynamic life. Miracles and wonders of many kinds were done through the apostles, and the result was that "more and more people were added to the group—a crowd of men and women believed in the Lord" (Acts 5:14). The persecution worsened, and the apostles were put back in jail. But after their stunning deliverance by an angel, they went right back to preaching, and rejoiced that God had considered them worthy to

33. *When the Way Is New* (Elgin, IL: Brethren, 1974), p. 14.

suffer. Indeed, rejoicing and spiritual growth characterized the everyday experience of this church both in homes and in the temple (Acts 5:42).

So the body of Christ grows. Christ does not grow, but the members of the body and the body as a whole grow, according to biblical teaching. There is growth by maturation as well as by numerical increase, for "we must grow up in every way to Christ, who is the head" (Eph. 4:15).[34] Under Christ's control "the whole body is nourished . . . and it grows as God wants it to grow" (Col. 2:19). In Ephesians, the phrase "growth of the body of Christ" implies both the deepening in knowledge, love, and obedience, and the growth in numbers. Such growth is always the work of God. Using a different analogy, Paul says it is God who makes the plant grow (I Cor. 3:6).

Secondly, it is a living body because it feels. When we speak of the church as a living body that has feeling, we are speaking of those needs that touch the emotions, the physical body, and the mind. People who live in Christ and are constantly in touch with others who are their brothers and sisters in Christ have a debt, or duty, to one another. This duty is not only to seek to compassionately understand the hurts and the pains of this body of Christ, but also to minister to one another. Those who have needs must seek help from the church and encourage the church's ministry on their behalf. It does not matter where in the world we are when we study the mission church; we will, in every place, find the hurting and the needy. People need to find help and love not only in relation to the intellect, in "proving the doctrine," but also for the physical, social, and economic problems that cause them pain and devastating insecurity.

The fact that the body of Christ has experienced schisms of various kinds is still another reminder of our failure to minister to the deep feelings of people. Many so-called independent churches in various parts of the world are growing faster than the historic churches ever have. The independency movement on the African continent is well known, and even superficial research leads one to the conviction that Christians have not had their needs met in the typical mission-church Christianity and so turn to one of the many "fringe" groups to get help. Often these indigenous or schismatic churches have minimal Christian teaching and give almost no place to the Scriptures, but the truth that they proclaim is that the physical, psychological, and spiritual needs cannot be separated. To claim the love of Christ and fail to minister to the deep needs of people is a truncated, if not a false, gospel.

The whole emphasis on spiritual gifts supports the church's obligation to serve. The church affirms by the preaching of the whole gospel that there is no need of man that Christ cannot meet. But from its beginnings in any place, the new community of the resurrection must practice this truth in an everyday, personal, active love for God, so that his power is released into

34. Compare Ephesians 2:21.

every part of life. The chains of tradition, the old habits of trust, and the patterns of power of the past can be broken only as the body expresses its new life and seeks for ways that answer the new deep feelings being generated. We need to see how Paul allowed God to use him for healing in Ephesus. The local books of magic were burned only after his own demonstration of miracles, including exorcism (Acts 19:11-20). We also need to see how he insists on a collection for the poor saints in Jerusalem at every stop along the way. There are real needs that must be met and ministered to because flesh-and-blood people, who make up the body of Christ, are living in a real world. It is not simply theory that "if one part of the body suffers, all the other parts suffer with it; if one part is praised, all the other parts share its happiness" (I Cor. 12:26). It bears repeating that this is one of the most incisive statements Paul ever made concerning the body.

## The Oneness of the Church

### *The Problem of Disunity*

Nothing has been more devastating to the teaching that the church is the body of Christ than its division into denominations, including Catholic, Orthodox, and Protestant communities. Moreover, groups of this or that persuasion are splitting even further into more or less exclusive, eclectic "churches" of every imaginable variety. The history of conferences and councils and the countless hours and the reams of paper that have gone into discussions about church unity are a fact of history. The subject of one church has bred both boredom and hostility. Yet the multiplicity of churches and the contentions between conciliary and nonconciliary bodies continue. At one point, thirteen different mission agencies maintained headquarters in a single African city where the author lived. These represented ten distinct autonomous and separate African churches, not including the Roman Catholic. This was only part of the complexity of the situation. There were many independent churches, both large and small, not accounted for in church councils or known in ecumenical gatherings. The fragmented state of the church is so well known and has for so long been a complicating factor of church planting among non-Christians throughout the world's cultures that it is now taken for granted.

This divisiveness within the church has affected our ability to communicate the wholeness of the gospel. It has resulted in a desire to perpetuate around the world the differences, even foibles, of the Western churches; it has fostered suspicions and negative attitudes among groups and between leaders of these groups, and has crippled the fellowship and the love that ought to bind Christians together and motivate them to evangelize as a single body. There is a strength and a virility in the natural diversity of the body, and this we must note, but if we are to take seriously the church as Paul taught it and propagated it, then the true oneness of the church under Christ is the only model we have. In Corinth, where his greatest problems arose with regard to partisan groups and personality cults, Paul appealed to the divided body to be "completely united, with only one thought and one purpose." It was unthinkable that "Christ has been divided into groups!" (I Cor. 1:10-13).

The unity of the church, the fact that all Christians are members of the body of Christ, is not something that becomes a reality by planning or by theorizing. Allen did some of his finest writing on the subject of unity for the mission church. He not only felt the fragmentation of the churches in India, but also saw the tendency for the Anglican church in his day to treat these young churches as incomplete units and to subordinate them to the parent body in England.

The Fellowship of the Churches of Christ in Nigeria was formed in 1954. This is a federation of seven autonomous churches that developed from the work of the Sudan United Mission and the Church of the Brethren. Many missionaries and Africans alike had hoped in the early days of deliberation on union that the result would be an organically united church. But, just after World War II, when the discussions were taking place, the missionary profile was very high and African church leadership was not strong. Wilber C. Harr analyzed the tenor of those early negotiations with deep insight as he lamented the movement that finally led away from the formation of one church to the federation.

> The missionary argument was that the original concept [one church] was premature. Let operations work through the cooperative community first and then organic unity will follow. They [missionaries] were saying, in essence, let the church be divided first, then allow it to get together instead of encouraging it to stay together. Some missionaries bluntly [said] that they did not trust the African church to guide its own destiny. What they were actually saying, I believe, was that the church would stray from the moorings initiated by the missionary.[35]

### *Paul's Basis for Unity*

Allen's conviction about the oneness of the church touched upon the attitude of local churches to each other, and that of churches in the various provinces to the sending church at Antioch and, ultimately, to the mother church at Jerusalem. The same bond that united individual groups to each other in one place united churches everywhere one to another.

35. "The Christian Mission Since 1938: Africa South of the Sahara," in *Frontiers of the Christian World Mission Since 1938,* Wilber C. Harr, ed. (New York: Harper, 1962), p. 111.

> In his [Paul's] view, the unity of the church was not something to be created, but something which already existed and was to be maintained. . . . There could be no such thing as two churches in the same place, both holding the Head, yet not in communion with one another. There could be no such thing as a Christian baptized into Christ Jesus not in communion with all other members of the body of which Christ is the Head. If a member was united to the head, he was united to all other members.[36]

The simple fact is that there is one Head and one body. Any rationale to the contrary, any appeal to history, and all attempts to justify sectarianism will have to answer to the truth that Christ is one—he is not divided. The mystery of the unity of the church was made known to Paul through revelation (Eph. 3:3); "Gentiles have a part with the Jews in God's blessings; they are members of the same body and share in the promise that God made through Christ Jesus" (Eph. 3:6; cf. Gal. 3:28-29). Nothing can be more Pauline than the miracle of grace that makes, of many peoples, one body and one spirit (Eph. 4:4). This is the gospel. It is the new way. "It does not matter at all whether or not one is circumcised; what does matter is *being a new creature"* (Gal. 6:15; italics added).

For Paul there could be only one church because there is only one Christ (Gal. 3:27).[37] The Lord's Supper became a symbol of this unity: "Because there is one loaf of bread, all of us, though many, are one body, for we all share the same loaf" (I Cor. 10:17). G. B. Caird believes that it is from this context that Paul derived one of his favorite pictures of the church's unity: "as the body is one . . . so it is Christ" (I Cor. 12:12, RSV; cf. Rom. 12:5; Col. 1:18).

> Those who participated in the sacrament without regard for the one fellowship which it both symbolized and sustained, were eating and drinking to their own condemnation, not discerning the Lord's body. Those who lived by the gospel belonged to an indissoluble fellowship.[38]

Tracing the concept even further back, one finds there could be only one church because there was only one Israel. As we have seen, the Jewish nation had forfeited this title, which had been passed on to Christ and through him to the church (Gal. 6:16). All of the promises of the Old Testament that were meant for Israel became the possession of those who are Abraham's by faith rather than by descent (Gal. 3:6-14). In this way, Gentile Christianity became firmly rooted in the "soil of the scriptures."[39]

36. Roland Allen, *Missionary Methods: St. Paul's or Ours?* (1912; reprint ed. London: World Dominion Press, 1960), p. 138.
37. See also Romans 5:15; 12:5; I Corinthians 12:12; Ephesians 4:5; I Timothy 2:5-6.
38. *The Apostolic Age* (London: Gerald Duckworth, 1955), p. 133.
39. Ibid.

### *Implications of Unity for Mission Churches*

To Paul, then, belongs the credit that he was the first to teach this unity openly, and to think through the practical consequences of "one church." Nothing in the communal life of the church dared obscure absolute unity of all Christians in Christ. Paul's famous confrontation with Peter, for example (Gal. 2:11-14), provided ample proof that he could refuse even to contemplate the possibility that there should be two communions within one church.

The practical side of this unity was something that Paul worked at tirelessly. The powers working against a unified church were real and very serious because of the Gentile-Jewish problem, as well as the profound differences between peoples and places. There was also the prestige of the church at Jerusalem, and the obvious feeling by many there that Jerusalem should set the standards for all churches. Paul was determined that unity should not be understood as implying that the Jerusalem church be held in such regard that all new Christians would come under the authority of Jerusalem. As Allen contended, all churches, regardless of where they originated or how long they existed, are equal and complete churches and are regarded as complete parts of a still-incomplete whole. It would follow that the "new additions would at once be recognized as members of the Spirit-bearing body, equally enjoying the inspiration of the Spirit with the older members."[40] Because the church is one and made up of many parts, as the body has many parts, there must be freedom for the churches to pursue their own life and form their own special character. This certainly led the way to affirm the diversity in Paul's churches, and this diversity must be recognized.

Practically speaking, Allen cited four principles that he felt guided Paul, especially in regard to the parent church in Jerusalem. He saw each church as a complete church, so that all churches must respect each other and, indeed, belong to each other.

1. Paul refused to transplant the law and the customs of the church in Judea into the four provinces. He let the church express its own life wherever it was.
2. Paul refused to set up any central administrative authority from which the whole church was to receive directions. Rather, each church was entrusted with the responsibility for its own life.
3. Paul declined to establish a priori tests of orthodoxy. Laws were not prescribed. It was not stated precisely what a church must think or do in every case.

40. *Missionary Methods,* p. 131.

4. Paul refused to allow the universal application of precedents. What was right for one place may not be appropriate for another. Much less could uniformity of thought or action for all be demanded.[41]

Obviously it would have been easier to ignore Jerusalem and to concentrate on the building up of his own churches, but this Paul did not do. The Jerusalem church was very different from his Gentile churches; but Jersusalem was the mother church, and the offering he collected from mainly Gentile congregations proved to both the givers and the recipients that they were ultimately one community. Interdependence, rather than independence, would be the term to describe the Pauline view of the churches' relationship. Paul's solution to the Jew-Gentile problem was not that "Gentiles should live like Jews, not that Jews should live like Gentiles, but that both ways of life should be transcended in the greater unity of Christ.[42] (See Gal. 3:28; 6:15.)

This brings us to a point that is just as Pauline as is his insistence on unity. The differences in the community of Christ must be recognized and utilized in such a way that the body maintains its integrity as one body, but is strengthened, enriched, and mobilized by the differences, often radical, that characterize this body.

## Differences among the Churches

While the highest aim of the church is that it be one, even as the Master prayed, it would be irresponsible, even detrimental, to ignore the fact of diversity. The nurture of young churches in the world's cultures must seek to reconcile the radical ethnic, social, and economic differences among peoples on the broad level. At the more intimate level of the local gatherings of Christians and in the many house churches arises the diversity of personalities and gifts. This body is one but it has deep-seated natural differences, prejudices that are often long-standing, and great complexity in levels of understanding.

### *The Dilemma of Diversity*

The difficulties that Paul faced, if the church was to be truly one, were, humanly speaking, insurmountable. That these diverse groups of people could be brought together into one church was a miracle that never failed to amaze even Paul. The "building" would never stand but for Christ who holds it together (Eph. 2:21); it is only through Christ that a Jew and a

41. Ibid., pp. 131-138.
42. Caird, *The Apostolic Age,* p. 135.

Gentile "are able to come in the one Spirit into the presence of the Father" (Eph. 2:18). What this means often escapes us. Among the Jews alone were both the Jerusalem conservatives and the Hellenized liberals. Politically, there were the leftists who worked with the Roman state and those on the right who were adamant against Rome. There were both Greek-speaking and Aramaic-speaking Jews. The Gentiles represented all kinds of social and economic classes, among them the trade groups (silversmiths, tentmakers, weavers, and artisans); the proselytes of Judaism; the colonialists, both oppressors and oppressed; producers; consumers; Stoics and Epicurians; and so on.

Joseph A. Grassi, in *The Secret of Paul the Apostle,* speaks of the "diamond of diversity," by which he refers to the valuable asset that differences can be in the Christian fellowship. In addition to the obvious differences among the people to whom Paul ministered, Grassi sees some of the tendencies within Paul's churches as "far out" when compared with the more general standards of orthodoxy.[43] There were the extreme loyalists to the Torah, converts from among the Pharisees, keeping all the traditional Jewish practices. They scarcely would be recognized as distinct from their fellow Jews but for their secret house meetings and quite privately-held belief in Jesus as the Messiah (Acts 2). In contrast were Christians, mostly Gentiles, who were emotionally involved in seeking gifts, wanted the pleasure of the ecstatic experiences such as speaking in tongues above all others, and caused disorder and confusion in the worship meetings (I Cor. 14:22-23). Some at Thessalonica were radical enthusiasts about the imminent return of the Lord. They had quit their work and were, in fact, becoming a general nuisance to the community, on the pretense of waiting for the second coming (I Thess. 4:9-12). The Gnostic-oriented Christians saw Christ in a rather different way. Their view of Christ was much more metaphysical. Their view of the resurrection was somewhat watered down (I Cor. 15:12), for since they did not think very highly of the physical body, they saw little need for an immortal body.[44]

The situation for Paul was as complex as anything we can imagine. His generosity in dealing with this diversity (which seems to give the lie to his teaching on unity) is nothing short of phenomenal. Not only does he allow for the differences, but also he actually looks for ways to use them positively in order to enhance the dignity of the body and accelerate its growth. At every level, whether ethnic, social, economic, or linguistic, these differences have to be turned into a positive creative force for building the church. This

43. *The Secret of Paul the Apostle* (Maryknoll, NY: Orbis Books, 1978), pp. 143-147.

44. For a controversial study of Christian Gnosticism in the early churches, see Walter Schmithals, *Paul and the Gnostics,* J. E. Seely, trans. (Nashville: Abingdon, 1972). Also see Ralph P. Martin, *Reconciliation: A Study of Paul's Theology* (Atlanta: John Knox, 1981), pp. 20-24.

Paul sought to do, and this he accomplished with amazing success. Diversity, like spontaneity, is allowed and even encouraged, but it is never allowed to destroy the oneness of the body. Diversity for Paul was regarded as a glorious expression of a free and sovereign God. Faw emphasizes the dynamic of diversity:

> In the creative diversity of such a church there was proof that this was not the product of some dictatorial human mind or will seeking to superimpose itself upon a society and demand conformity. It was proof that here were persons created in the image of God to be free but not rebellious, creative but not chaotic, spontaneous but not undisciplined. This meant that under God in Christ members in the church could give and take rebuke, could engage in free and sometimes sharp debate precisely because they were bound together in a community which was not of their own making but was the gift of God. They could agree to differ and yet stay together until they should discover the will of God through their differences.[45]

We must look more closely at ways in which diversity becomes a blessing rather than a burden in missions. This diversity operates on two levels. First, each differing culture offers its many people groups[46] to the church as the pattern for evangelizing and planting churches among those who understand each other. Second, once a local community of believers has been established, the various gifts and strengths among the members must be recognized and developed.

### *Church Planting and Diversity*

It would not be difficult to show that Paul had an immediate as well as an ultimate goal in planting churches as he did. His purpose was to preach Christ and to lay foundations by whatever means and methods were appropriate. The differences of the various cultural and linguistic groups were turned into opportunities rather than allowed to become barriers to mission. There is ample evidence for the widespread house-church style of worship, beginning at Jerusalem and going right through the provinces of Asia and Europe. People worshiped with those with whom they associated naturally, and who were close to them both socially and economically. Paul was very careful not to stifle the proliferation of house churches, but he opposed pride or sectarian ideas that would prove divisive (I Cor. 3:3-4). The

45. *When the Way Is New,* p. 76.

46. A people group has been defined as "a significantly large sociological grouping of individuals who perceive themselves to have a common affinity for one another, because of their shared language, religion, ethnicity, residence, occupation, etc." *That Everyone May Hear,* Edward R. Dayton, ed. (Monrovia, CA: MARCC, 1979), pp. 25-26.

freedom and spontaneity of each group provided the spark for its witness and evangelism. Forcing people together, even in worship, when they are not ready for it, or tying all to one monolithic structure, whether of organization or doctrine, is not what Paul meant by unity. This would have been an "attempt to trap the Holy Spirit of God in straight jackets of human origin, and in the end would have meant the strangulation of the very unity it was expected to promote."[47]

Those who work in church planting among the cultures of the world know that coming to Christ and experiencing his love among others happens most often when people are able to share with their fellows in the most immediate and most meaningful way. Donald A. McGavran saw this and initiated a new approach to church planting that centers on people, people who share common roots and histories. The key phrase in *Bridges of God* was, "Peoples become Christians faster when the least change of race or color is involved."[48] This was further amplified by McGavran in *Understanding Church Growth,* where he said, "Men like to become Christians without crossing racial, linguistic, or class barriers."[49] This is far too brief a summation of a principle that utilizes diversity for evangelism, for the literature is now comprehensive and church growth has developed into a worldwide movement.

The unity of the church—the fact that in Christ all people are brought together—is not denigrated or contradicted by the homogeneous way in which people most frequently become Christian. Paul recognized from his own conversion how difficult, if not impossible, it would be for the pluralistic Gentile world to enter the fellowship of the Christian church through the narrow door of Judaism as it was practiced at Jerusalem. Paul could see that it was natural for people to come to Christ together with their own kind. It is not to say this is the ideal, for the gospel unites all races and all peoples into one body. But to utilize the differences for discipling, that is, bringing people to Christ in response to the Great Commission, is in harmony with Paul's approach. This is not to endorse a church that is based on distinctions of class or to imply that Christians should develop habits of exclusiveness that would obviously destroy the unity of the body.

Recognition of ethnic distinctions is a phenomenological principle. By this we do not idealize or legalize the notion so that we say people *must* be responsive in the familiar group setting. We simply describe what happens. It is interesting that some mission boards, particularly those of major denominations, are no longer sending evangelistic missionaries overseas. These mission boards claim that indigenous Christians can best communicate

47. Faw, *When the Way Is New,* p. 75.
48. (New York: Friendship Press, 1955), p. 23.
49. Revised edition (Grand Rapids: Eerdmans, 1980), p. 223.

and effectively plant churches among their own people. This is a flawed assumption, but nevertheless it reflects the validity of cultural ethnicity in the spreading of the gospel, a point that very often these same churches deny.

In my own years of missionary work, I have seen the blessing and the advantage of being sensitive to planning evangelism among people who share their lives in common. Language, world view, the myths of the people, customs and culture, ethnocentrism of all kinds are shared and can be accepted as the soil in which the gospel is to be sown. The communication of the gospel and the awakening of the desire of people for the gospel is the paramount concern. Organization of the wider church so that the greatest degree of freedom is given to local and district churches, allowing people to live intimately and meaningfully together in the Lord, is being sensitive to diversity. On the other hand, when diversity rules the church and a sense of responsibility to promote the spirit of unity is lost, great harm can result. I have seen ruthless demands for independence, and even schism, based on issues that are carnal and selfish and that cannot be justified as part of the discipling process. One church broke from another along tribal lines after feuding, anger, bitterness, and even riot. This is not tolerable in the body of Christ. A straightforward recognition of differences is called for, and should characterize different churches which can then meet to plan and pray and which are committed to one Lord, one faith, one baptism (Eph. 4:5).

The principle of evangelizing among people who share the most meaningful areas of their lives together has come to be known as the "homogeneous-unit principle." This principle concerns the method of effective evangelization. It is a tool to bring people to Christ and does not speak of the final shape of the church. Obviously, the gospel pulls down barriers. It is not the gospel if it raises them (Eph. 2). C. Peter Wagner carefully lines up the church-growth movement behind Paul's own approach when he says, "[The homogeneous-unit principle] should not be interpretated as expounding the ideal way that Christians should relate to one another, but the way in which unbelievers become followers of Jesus Christ and responsible members of His church."[50] Further, the fact that people most easily come to Christ in groups that are congenial does not describe the shape of the church. The perfecting of the church cannot be conceived of as segmenting people into classes and ethnic units. Therefore, by beginning with a homogeneous group, we do not arrive at a picture of what the church is meant to be in the final sense. It must, in maturing, move toward a heterogeneous, scriptural ideal,[51] which is truly a oneness in Christ, and which includes all differences, even while superseding them.[52]

50. *Church Growth and the Whole Gospel* (San Francisco: Harper and Row, 1981), p. 168.

51. Nowhere is this better expressed in Pauline thought than in Galatians 3:26-29 and Ephesians 2:13-22.

52. In this light, Wagner has recently stated, "The homogeneous unit principle should be

The mission church, planted and growing in a plurality of cultures, does not need encouragement to diversify. It must recognize the diversity that already exists and utilize it for good, while at the same time it must work energetically toward oneness with all other churches that are made up of people who might never have known or loved each other, apart from the reconciling work of Christ.

### *Church Nurture and Diversity*

The other level where diversity must become a tool and not a weapon, so to speak, is at the local level. Here brothers and sisters in Christ, while they are likely members of the same language group and in the same culture, will differ from each other in potential gifts, in personalities, and in ministries. Once it is assumed that all Christians must serve the body, it is imperative that Paul's teachings about the many functions within the body be released among the members. "For the body itself is not made up of only one part, but of many parts. . . . All of you are Christ's body, and each one is a part in it" (I Cor. 12:14, 27). The local church, from the outset of its covenant to be a community in the Lord, must study and pray concerning the function of each member.

Paul is candid about this. In describing the unity of the body in his letter to the Ephesians, he gives graphic detail as to how the body is joined together and how it functions. When the healthy, growing body is "under his [Christ's] control all the different parts of the body fit together, and the whole body is held together by every joint with which it is provided" (Eph. 4:16). It may escape the casual reader that Paul here describes in surprising detail how the church functions. In addition to the most important point—that each member is related to the Head—two additional points are made. Each member is in its place fulfilling its function, and each member is rightly related by joints to other members. Here the tension, the seeming contradiction between unity and diversity is resolved.

This single passage has been helpfully applied to the growing church by Derek Prince. The terms *joints* and *ligaments* become the keys to our understanding of the analogy. In a figurative sense, joints are interpersonal relationships, those places and occasions where members "touch and fit one another." Ligaments, however, hold joints in place and bind the members of the body together in love. Prince extends the metaphor to include the muscles, which make the body move. This term denotes the activities or the ministries of the body. It is here where diversity, tension, even contradiction have their greatest benefit.

---

regarded as a *penultimate* spiritual dynamic. The *ultimate* is that believers are all one in the body of Christ, and the more this is manifested in a tangible way, the better." *Church Growth and the Whole Gospel,* p. 168.

> Oddly enough, muscles in the body work against each other. In other words, some muscles bend my arm while others extend it. So it is in the body of Christ. The activities of the body work in tension, some binding and some extending as the body moves. For years I missed this point completely. I wanted to be with a group of people who thought, believed, preached, and dressed like me. If I had succeeded, I would have constructed a paralysed body of Christ incapable of moving at all.[53]

Let all muscles be put to work and the body will be healthy and will function as one body. There are various gifts, which I have already discussed. These must all be at work, both the more spectacular and the lesser gifts. People who love each other and who are under the headship of Christ will be "tension-producing" people. Prince cited "the outgoing versus the reflective, the impulsive versus the cautious, the inspirational versus the analytical, the mystical-prophetic versus the practical-administrative."[54] Without this diversity, the body will become paralyzed.

These counterbalancing tensions need to be recognized and turned into strengths for growing and maturity. Mission churches that have little or no history of their own, no precedents and no tradition to fall back on, too easily allow the clerical few, including the missionary, to think for them and do all their planning for them. The trained ministers, especially the expatriate professionals, overlook the multiplied possibilities for exciting ministry among "ordinary," untrained lay people even while they make every effort to train and indoctrinate. The diversity of ministry gifts is there, but the gifts go undiscerned and unawakened. It takes great love for people and true faith in the Holy Spirit to encourage the pulling and pushing that sometimes happens when people who are redeemed are also expected to exercise the spirit of ministry (*diakonia*).

This diversity is not along with unity, as though these are two equal values that, "like the lion and the lamb[,] should lie down together."[55] Unity has its true meaning in and through diversity, which, as Faw points out, is a precious gift to the spiritual dynamism of the church:

> Diversity, like spontaneity, was not only allowed to exist, but was regarded as a glorious expression of a free and sovereign God. Therefore, diversities of viewpoint and expression held together by a solid commitment to one Lord, one faith, and one baptism were actually evidences of this higher unity of the Spirit. . . . It was proof that here were persons created in the image of God to be free but not rebellious, creative but not chaotic, spontaneous but not

53. Derek Prince, "Unity and Growth in the Body of Christ," *New Covenant,* January 1976, p. 11.

54. Ibid.

55. Faw, *When the Way Is New,* p. 75.

> undisciplined . . . they could agree to differ yet stay together until they should discover the will of God through their differences.[56]

## The Contextuality of the Church

The dynamic life of Paul's churches is revealed in his theology. There is the consistent core of the gospel, which is found in each church wherever it may be. Nothing of the essence of Christian truth is ever omitted, regardless of the place or the people. But the way in which this core of truth is applied and enlarged upon in teaching is developed specifically for each place. This new life must be appropriate and authentic for each believing community. In systematizing Paul's doctrine for the church universal, theologians have failed to see these contextual presuppositions of Paul. It is this aspect that is part of the reason his churches survived under immense pressure, grew in each place, and multiplied among the unevangelized. Christianity was vibrant and alive because each local church found its own expression of the Christian life while at the same time it was joined in faith and truth to all other congregations that were also under Christ's lordship.

### *The House Churches*

The churches from Palestine to Rome bore very little resemblance to our modern stereotype of the church. I have already referred to the fact that these were house churches[57] in almost every case. These churches were always addressed as being in a very specific place, whether it be Rome, Corinth, Thessalonica, or Galatia. The most important feature of the church was the multitude of small units, each of which met together, working out its new life in sharing blessings and working through problems. It is error to think even of Paul's urban churches as large single congregations. They were, on the contrary, gatherings of God's people who shared similar lives, people who related naturally to each other, and who corporately were, in very fact, expressions of the diversity of the people of God. This is the key to the contextual quality of Paul's churches. Paul S. Minear has seen this intensely local quality of the apostolic church in a remarkable way. In commenting on Romans, he says,

> It is my view that in their study, many scholars have chosen wrong options, followed wrong roads and have, as a consequence, rendered Paul's meaning

56. Ibid., p. 76.

57. For discussions on house churches, see Banks, *Paul's Idea of Community,* pp. 33-42; and Speer, *When Christianity Was New,* pp. 9-33.

> less accessible than it should be. They visualize a single Christian community where Jewish Christians worshipped side by side with Gentile Christians. On the arrival of Phoebe [with Paul's letter—Rom. 16:1, 2] both factions would listen simultaneously to the letter being read at a single assembly. Virtually no evidence exists in the letter itself, however, to support this picture of a single congregation. On the contrary, Chapter 16 distinguishes at least five or six different house churches. There were many scattered house churches in greater Rome, many of which were isolated either by distance, by ethnic background, or by hostility.[58]

It would seem that the church did meet at times in large groups. In I Corinthians Paul speaks of an occasion when "the whole church meets together" (I Cor. 14:23). It is implied by this that at other times the Christians in Corinth met in smaller units. In the concluding section of Romans, Paul greets Gaius whom he describes as "my host Gaius, in whose house the church meets" (Rom. 16:23).[59] Gaius was probably one of the more eminent men in the city and doubtless would have had ample space in his house for large gatherings. Paul's comments in the last chapter of Romans would leave the impression that there were about sixteen various Christian groups in this capital city of the empire.

The important point that underlies this is that Paul's churches were meeting the special needs of natural groupings of people and were communicating the gospel in relevant forms and in language that was suitable to each group and place. These churches of Paul's were not foreign or strange. They fitted each locale in temperament and expression. They were flexible, open fellowships, differing in style and form, yet committed to basic teaching and features of worship that identified them all as one.

### *Churches Are Shaped by Context*

Allen brought mission thinking a long way in returning us to Paul's idea of the church. As I mentioned before, he saw each new church, each new group of Christians who met together, as equal and complete parts of the still-incomplete whole.[60] The insight here that has figured so heavily in mission thinking today is that the churches born out of a mission agency are not tied to, nor are they emanations of, the parent mission body. In other words, the churches of Paul did not "join" the church in Jerusalem and

58. *The Obedience of Faith: A Study in Romans,* Studies in Biblical Theology, no. 19, second series (Naperville, IL: Alec Allenson, 1971), pp. 9, 27.

59. In the Greek Old Testament this expression consistently refers to an assembly of all Israel (e.g., Exod. 12:6; Num. 8:9), so it is likely the totality of Christians in Corinth is in view here.

60. See *Missionary Methods,* p. 131.

thereby receive their right to be called a church; rather, they were independent and totally viable bodies. All these true churches, of which Jerusalem was one, together reveal the growing total body that is also the church. Refer to Figure 3 for a diagram that shows how Allen's convictions about Paul's churches might be pictured.

**Figure 3**
***Paul's View of Unity***

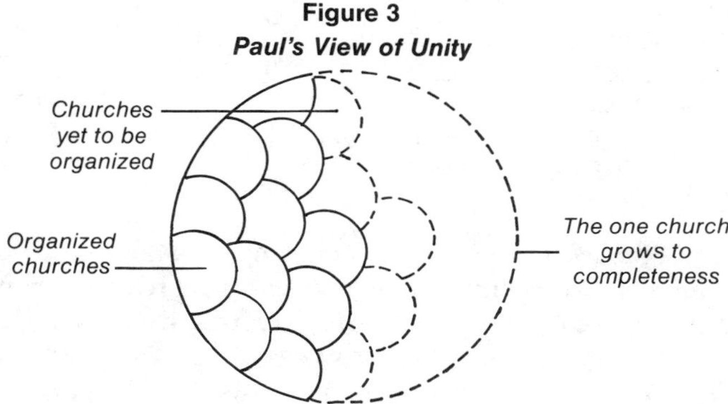


While Allen's concern for the autonomy and the equality of new churches is as important in our day as it was in his, the point needs to be pressed even further. When we speak of authentic or contextual churches, we are saying that churches among a given people must have features that are unique to the particular locale where the church is planted. With all of Paul's churches, there was an acceptance of the oneness of all believers centering on absolute loyalty to the incarnate Word, Christ. All adhere to the basic Christian teaching (*didachē*), those irreducible components of Christian truth that do not change from place to place. As time went on, and the written gospels as well as Paul's letters were made available to the churches, a further basis for unity was equally binding on all. But differences in the way truth was expressed, variations in emphasis, style of communication, worship patterns, and ways in which ethical issues were faced all became theological issues that began to particularize the gospel. That is, these differences began to reflect the distinctiveness of the people in each particular place. What is more, the visible church—its forms, its symbols, and its style, including the confessional as well as the physical aspects of style—will possess the qualities that enable it to be the church of Jesus Christ in its own situation.

This is an important refinement of Allen's understanding of Paul. The emphasis on culturally authentic churches was always the underlying assumption of Allen's work, though he did not express it in the cross-cultural

Figure 4*

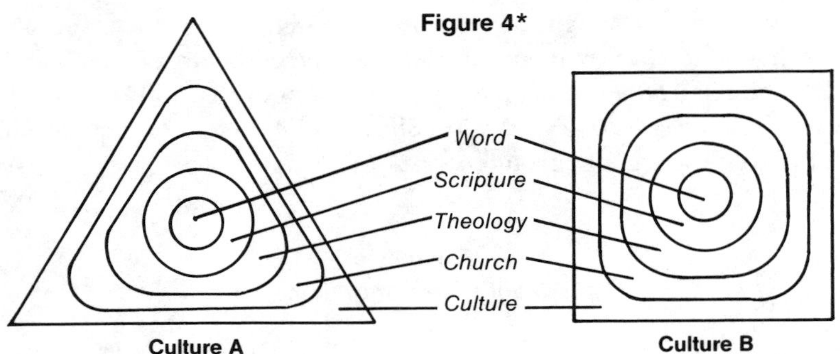


*Adapted from Stephen C. Knapp, "Contextualization and Its Implications for U.S. Evangelical Churches and Missions" (paper delivered at the Institute of Mennonite Studies, Elkhart, IN), diagram 2, p. 23.

way. Paul's churches provide the model for anyone who seeks to know the true meaning of indigeneity. Culturally relevant churches are appropriate and understandable to the receptor; familiar forms that possess, adapt, and infill with Christian meanings. In the words of Stephen C. Knapp, "Every church if it is to be truly *the* church in a particular place and time must take on, to some extent, the shape of its surrounding milieu."[61]

Therefore, churches can be called truly authentic, truly indigenous, when this local dynamic of the church's life is realized. It is not enough to say that a church is indigenous because it is self-supporting, self-governing, and self-propagating. This can even be a misleading idea. A church may claim all of these ideals yet not be contextual, while it is hard to conceive of a fully contextual church that is not at the same time autonomous in these three areas. The diagram of Paul's churches as conceived by Allen needs to be modified as Knapp has done, to show the shape that each church will take in a given culture. (Refer to Figure 4).

61. "Contextualization and Its Implications for U.S. Evangelical Churches and Missions." Paper delivered at the Institute of Mennonite Studies, Elkhart, IN, 1976, p. 23.

# 8

# Growth and Care of the Community

## *Leadership and Worship*

Having looked at some of the foundational dimensions of the mission church, we can now be more specific. How do the people of God who are one yet many, scattered throughout the world's cultures yet gathered together in Christ, govern their life and witness from day to day? How can spontaneity in the Spirit be maintained once administrative responsibilities grow, and how can a consistent standard of conduct be assured within such a variety of situations? We want to consider Paul's response in four areas where the mission church has to work out its life. In Paul's day, as in every mission enterprise since his time, four factors have either contributed to or hindered growth. These are leadership, worship, discipline, and finance.

### Leadership

We have already seen that what set Paul's churches apart from many of those found in the modern missionary era was their willingness and ability to manage their own affairs right from the start. The congregations that Paul organized were self-governing, it appears, within a matter of weeks or at most months after the gospel was first brought to them. At the end of each stay, Paul left behind not dependent groups of worshipers or unorganized "chapels," but a line of fully self-governing congregations. What this says concerning his views and practice in regard to leadership is extremely important.

#### *Paul's Own Background*

Paul had an incredible ability to attract key people who in turn had the capacity for leadership. Paul never refers to anyone as his disciple, and he probably would have objected to any such a designation had it been used. However, it is Luke, his very close friend, who reports that in Damascus Paul's disciples lowered him from the wall to allow him to escape his enemies (Acts 9:25). This is startling. He had been a convert for only a matter of days and already had his loyal group of trainees. Some scholars are so disturbed by the idea of Paul having disciples so soon after his conversion that they have chosen a weak textual variant in which the phrase *his disciples* becomes simply "the disciples." They would say it is unlikely that in so short a time a group had already gathered around him with such loyalties.

Yet Paul showed consistently that he could attract around him gifted and committed people, and draw from them qualities of true leadership. We can assume that Paul's own development as a leader began immediately at his conversion. His Damascus ministry (Acts 9:20-25) was followed by further activity in Jerusalem and Tarsus (Acts 9:26-30). The importance of his years in Arabia is difficult to assess (Gal. 1:17), though this period, Paul's "hidden years," was crucial to his own development as a leader.[1]

For all his natural gifts and his impressive background, it would appear that Paul did go through an apprenticeship. There was evidently a succession of experiences—whether in Damascus, Arabia, Jerusalem, Tarsus, or Antioch—that formed what we might call his training period. Barnabas recognized his leadership qualities and brought him from Tarsus to help in the preaching and teaching ministry at Antioch (Acts 11:25-26). It is fair to say that Paul came to apostolic maturity in an apprenticeship under the encouragement of Barnabas. With his tutelage, Paul taught large numbers of new converts in Antioch (Acts 11:26). Paul's training continued during the first missionary journey, since Luke made it clear that it was Barnabas who was initially sent out as the head of that first missionary team (Acts 13).

The transition from Barnabas' to Paul's leadership during the first missionary journey is striking. After Saul's confrontation with Elymas, the magician at Paphos (Acts 13:8-12), there is a shift in Luke's account. Paul becomes more prominent than Barnabas, and with one exception Paul is thereafter always named first. It was Paul who preached the sermon at Antioch (Pisidia) that resulted in many followers and converts (Acts 13:43). It is apparent that by the time Paul returned to Syria with Barnabas, his apprenticeship had ended.

### *The Need for Early Selection and Training*

During this early period, a naturally gifted man, Paul, was selected by an astute and committed leader, Barnabas. Mission churches desperately need

1. Refer to Arthur F. Glasser, "The Apostle Paul and the Missionary Task," in *Crucial Dimensions in World Evangelization,* Arthur F. Glasser et al., eds. (Pasadena, CA: William Carey Library, 1976), p. 25.

the foresight and trust that leadership selection demands. One of the most destructive habits of missionaries has been to assume, sometimes for years, that no converts, or at most very few, are able to assume leadership. Taking the initiative which Barnabas did with the controversial new Christian, Saul of Tarsus, not only produced the greatest of leaders but also set a pattern that Paul himself followed in his own ministry.

The reluctance to think in terms of potential leaders among national Christians is illustrated by a remark made to me in 1962 by a missionary who had been in Nigeria for forty years. He said, "How can I really believe in the idea that these people can lead the church? I have known them since they were children, and I know too much about their pagan history. The leaders will have to come in the next generation." How shortsighted and demeaning such an attitude is! The church where that missionary worked suffered in many ways—economically, educationally, and in discipleship. Much of the lack of growth and the internal tension that characterized that church can be traced to the resistance of missionaries to give over their positions to those who appeared to them to be backward and untutored.

By contrast, one of the first missionaries of another mission[2] will always be remembered for his insistence that leaders should be recognized very early. Training and responsibility should be given them, and the missionary must step aside at an early stage to allow for their development. Daddy Bristow, as he was affectionately called, is remembered for the gifted leadership that at least three of his "Timothys" have given over the years, both to the church and as Christians in government positions. Bitrus for sixteen years was the secretary of the Church of Christ in Nigeria; Barnabas is a highly respected leader in education, in state government, and in Bible translation; and Yusuhu is a secondary-school administrator, a church leader, and a government officer. The spirit of urgency in leadership selection and training has always been a characteristic of this mission agency, and over the years this practice has resulted in both depth and creativity in the church that has been planted. Leadership must be fostered and nurtured. Converts will not develop the qualities necessary for leadership, when missionaries are reluctant to trust young Christians and refuse to invest time and energy in leadership development.

Leaders for the church must come from among the natural and trusted leaders the people themselves put forward. Obviously, no one can lead who does not have the support of his or her own people. It not only seems artificial, but also may be counterproductive, therefore, for the expatriate missionary to arbitrarily select and arrange for the development of leaders. Nevertheless, at the outset this may be the only way leadership will emerge. What is basic is the missionary's attitude. Will he hold tightly to the authority

2. Sudan United Mission (British branch).

and the status that his position as outsider often carries, or will he consciously and sincerely seek out those gifted people who can learn the art of leadership? Will care be taken by the missionary that he does not hold to authority or be found grasping for power for a single hour, as soon as capable, committed, indigenous people can be given these responsibilities? It was extremely important to Paul that the churches be fully equipped to carry on their own lives.

### *Paul's Practice: Training* in *Ministry*

Whether or not Paul consciously set up an apprenticeship program, this is, in fact, what happened. It is accurate to say that Paul did not train anyone *for* ministry. The training he did was training *in* ministry. For those in the early apostolic teams, this meant apprenticeship under Paul. For the others who resided permanently in one place, this meant learning by doing. Elders, for example, were not elected after they had graduated from a prescribed course. Paul believed that Christians can best learn while serving, and this principle governed his practice.

#### *Early selection*

Matriculation into Paul's "course" took place at baptism, with appointment to ministry following almost immediately, even while people still were engaged, as it were, in the first courses of study. New converts not only were to be instructed but were to teach as well, beginning with the first days after their conversion (Rom. 15:14; Phil. 1:5; Col. 3:16).

This urgency to develop leaders and the trust placed in leaders are incredible by general standards of practice today. When Paul and Barnabas retraced their journey on the first missionary venture, "in each church they appointed elders" (Acts 14:23). When Paul first wrote to the Thessalonians, there was already a recognized and active group of leaders (I Thess. 5:12-13). Obviously, there was little time for any of those first leaders to be trained to carry out their ministry before they were appointed to office. This does not mean to say that there is special virtue in untrained leaders, but what is important is Paul's insistence on immediate care for local congregations by those who are indigenous to that congregation.

Paul's priority was to find authentic resident leadership rather than postponing the appointment of elders while he, or one of the apostolic team, continued to govern, teach, and control. But he did not abandon these newly-appointed leaders. He returned again and again to "strengthen" these brothers as they held the flock together (Acts 14:21-22; 15:32-35).[3] He

3. See also Acts 15:4; 16:5; 18:23; 20:2.

affirmed them and encouraged them in their continuing ministry in the churches. Most of their teaching and training would have come after they had assumed their positions of ministry.

*Qualifications*

It was not of the highest importance in Paul's selection of leaders that they be doctrinally perfect or reputable Bible teachers, much less profound theologians. There was no way that these early Christians, especially those from Gentile communities, could have had an extensive background in Christian knowledge. Roland Allen observes that Paul must have been satisfied with

> a more or less meager acquaintance with the Septuagint . . . and with a knowledge of the brief outline of Christian doctrine set forth in the epistles of Thessalonians and some instruction in the meaning and method of administration of the two sacraments of baptism and the Lord's Supper.[4]

However, the training while *in* ministry did require certain moral standards as a first priority. The important characteristics were a converted life, a commitment to the redeemed community, and personal morality. These, therefore, were willing people, gifted people, and people who had been sanctioned by their fellow Christians. They were to be persons who had accepted the lordship of Christ and who sought to live by this standard. Paul was not inclined to set up regulations by which elders were to be judged. God alone knows the heart. The church probably will not always be right in leadership selection. Even Paul did not have a perfect record. Ultimately to try to judge the spiritual condition of a person, or to seek guarantees that he will not fail, is not man's responsibility. Morality of life and confession of the basic doctrine were what Paul had to work with. Missionaries have too often rationalized that because indigenous leaders must be exemplary almost to the point of perfection, they cannot be given responsibility too soon. But the missionary, also a flesh-and-blood person, is often blind to his or her own imperfections and yet continues in the significant role of leadership. Months become years and a syndrome of dependency on the foreigner develops, making change very difficult.

*Autonomy*

Paul of course was almost constantly on the move. His objective in each place was to appoint elders who would soon become familiar with all the facets of the ministry. In this way, they did not develop a dependency on

4. *Missionary Methods: St. Paul's or Ours?* (1912; reprint ed. London: World Dominion Press, 1960), p. 101.

Paul. When he went away, the churches remained. The practice of training while in ministry becomes even more obvious when we look at Paul's mobile team. The New Testament calls our attention to more than thirty persons who ministered in various ways under the tutelage of Paul. Nine of these were women.[5] Paul refers to these faithful people in a variety of ways: as brother, apostle, minister, servant, pastor, worker, fellow worker, fellow soldier, and fellow prisoner. Some of these were directly under Paul's authority as a teacher, while others were outside of his tutelage. Yet Paul trusted all of them with responsibility, fully and from the earliest moment.

At times, not surprisingly, this trust brought difficulties. It is possible that Timothy was not completely effective in his initial ministry at Corinth, so Paul wrote to him when he came to Ephesus, giving loving guidance and pushing him on to maturity. Others, such as Demas, who loved the world (II Tim. 4:10), disappointed Paul.

Yet Paul does not regret these experiences. He would rather see failure on the part of a few than try to manage everything himself. Not only would this have been impossible, but also without his boldness the amazing success that the majority of these new Christian leaders showed would never have resulted. He constantly encouraged and gave personal guidance to the appointed elders. He sent off his companions, young converts that they were, to minister without supervision in faraway places. They would no sooner join him than they left him again to prepare the way in a new place, or to follow up on some previous work, or perhaps just to be present in a place where Paul could not go.

### *Benefits of Early Leadership Training*

Much could be written at this point about the methodology of leadership development. The question of what an effective leader of a young church is, and how that leader is to be discovered and encouraged, is one of the most important areas of current mission study. We see five reasons why Paul had no second thoughts about an early, autonomous leadership for the churches. Each reason is, individually, a factor that will benefit the new fellowship and will foster development in a number of important areas.

#### *Initiative*

Developing leaders at the early stage of a mission church fosters initiative. This means the burden for the total church—its growth, the quality of its witness, and the administration of its life—is not seen as the responsibility of an outsider but is accepted by the church itself. Paul left no question in the

5. Francis Badcock lists thirty-five associates in Ephesus alone. *The Pauline Epistles* (London: Macmillan, 1937).

minds of local Christians, wherever he went, as to who was in charge. By insisting that authority lies with the Christians themselves and by appointing elders,[6] Paul made the message of independence and responsibility understood. The church in each place belonged to the local people. They, not the apostle or the apostle's helper, had the care of all in their charge. In this way new Christians took action by responding to their own needs and felt the excitement of responsibility. Churches and congregations that Western missionaries tend to oversee and dominate are the very churches that tend to take little initiative for their own affairs. They are consequently judged as not being "ready" or as being uncreative and dependent. Dependent and uncreative they may be; however, the fault lies not with the people but with the missionary who "cares for and feeds" them, and who, by his domination, gives no signal that God desires to call out, direct, and inspire his own people. Allen deplored the control of ministry by missionaries.

> Where a superior order consists almost wholly of foreigners, the result is often deplorable. Catechists, teachers, deacons, and priests are wholly independent of the one authority which they really understand—native public opinion; solely dependent on the one authority which they seldom can understand, the foreign missionary.[7]

### *Equality*

Developing leaders at the early stage of a mission church teaches equality. The young Christians must understand that this body, the church, has many members and that all have gifts and opportunities for service (Rom. 12:5; I Cor. 12:18). It has already been shown that it is all too easy for the gifts of ministry to be overlooked when the missionary or a few powerful leaders dominate the church. Recognition of the worth of each Christian and the potential of each to serve is basic to the development of the ministry. In fact, some will be apostles, some prophets, and others teachers. The areas of need for special leadership and the office required will become apparent to the body. These developments are natural and good for the church. The gifts for various kinds of leadership should be sought as early as possible by the members themselves, so that the various ministries arise from within the fellowship.

All Christians, regardless of social rank or educational qualifications, must see each other as equal in Christ. The recognition of offices of special leadership is not forced by an outsider or managed arbitrarily by a few.[8]

6. Though this appointment was not made on his own, but in consultation with the Christian group. See Allen, *Missionary Methods,* p. 99.

7. Ibid., p. 101.

8. Ibid., p. 100.

From the beginning, the church must learn that not only is it the responsibility of all members of the body to regulate the life of the body, but also that all have a function, whether large or small, and all are equally regarded by God and by each other.

*Independence*

Developing leaders at the early stage of a mission church encourages independence. Jerusalem did not control Paul's churches. The same Spirit who was given to the Jews was given also to the Gentiles. Peter saw this and witnessed to it at the Jerusalem Council (Acts 15:8). Independence for each church and interdependence are in harmony with the gospel of freedom and can be discovered early, or can be frustrated and denied to the church's experience. Says Harry R. Boer,

> If we transmit to others the life of the Spirit, we must not hinder them in fully expressing the freedom and joy of life: If we are eager to see them gather knowledge in the Spirit, we should also be eager to see them express the knowledge they have gathered. If we exert ourselves to give them the Spirit of holiness and life, we should be eager to give them the Spirit of liberty through which that life comes to expression.[9]

The facts of mission history show all too clearly and painfully that Christians are not trusted with responsibility. We have the same worthy end in mind as did Paul, that of autonomy and independence for the churches, but Paul "achieved immediately what we hope to achieve after an extended period of time."

> Where we begin with independence, we shall end with independence, and this independence will express itself in the framework of the communion of the saints which is a holy interdependence. But when we begin with dependence, we shall end independence and as we have indeed so often ended.[10]

*Spiritual growth*

Developing leaders at an early stage promoted spiritual growth. Maturity is what Paul wanted most for his churches. When new Christians develop a sense of dependence on the Lord who redeemed them, rather than on human persons or institutions, and when Christians are given the right to be free in the unfettered Spirit of God, then we will begin to see the growth Paul hoped for. The problem with the Corinthian church was that it had become a prisoner to human ideas about what the church is. The members

9. *Pentecost and Missions* (Grand Rapids: Eerdmans, 1961), p. 222.
10. Ibid., p. 223.

had become so selfish and ingrown that Paul could not address them as people who had the Spirit (I Cor. 3:1). Little wonder there was no growth. They had to be fed as babies, with milk rather than with solid food (I Cor. 3:2). They lacked maturity. Paul expected the churches to find their own solutions and to work out their own problems. Certainly they would make errors in judgment. But they would grow by doing, not by imitating or by pleading ignorance or inexperience.

God's people, however recent they are in the faith, must understand for themselves the reasons for things and exercise their own intelligence. In turn, they will become more sure in their own faith and will be able to help those who are less courageous or less experienced. In this way those who have noticeable gifts for special leadership will emerge while all grow in the faith. Paul taught that spiritual growth is stimulated when the members of the church accept their responsibility to minister to each other. It is by urging the church into Christian service and building up the body of Christ that Paul believes Christians will become more mature, "no longer . . . children, carried by the waves and blown about by every shifting wind," for "we must grow up in every way to Christ, who is the head" (Eph. 4:14-15).

The church cannot be indigenous if it does not develop spiritually. An indigenous church is a self-functioning church, the interacting and interdependent parts working together as a body. Growth enables function and the function in turn promotes growth (Eph. 4:16).

*Contextual Christianity*

Developing leaders at an early stage emphasizes contextual Christianity.[11] The greatest gift a missionary or a mission agency can give to a young church is the right to think out and act out the Christian life for itself. Alan R. Tippett raises the issue of self-image as the first mark of a truly indigenous church.[12] This is a church that sees itself as "mediating the work, the mind, the word, and the ministry of Christ in its own environment. Does the church see itself as the body of Christ in a particular place?" All we have said in the previous chapter concerning the contextual church—that expressions of life and worship radiate from the very center of being—takes hold here. Those who are Christians in the local situation are the persons best suited to know what the shape of the church shall be in that place. If no emphasis is placed on early thinking by leaders from within the indigenous

11. An ideal book that gives the rationale and various methodologies for leadership training in various churches is Kenneth Mulholland's *Adventures in Training the Ministry* (Phillipsburg, NJ: Presbyterian and Reformed, 1976).

12. The five additional traits of an indigenous church are its self-functioning, self-determining capacity, self-supporting nature, self-propagating fervor, and devotion to self-giving. *Verdict Theology in Mission Theory*, revised edition (Pasadena, CA: William Carey Library, 1973), pp. 155-158.

Christian group, forms can develop that are alien and irrelevant because they have been instituted by a foreigner. It is almost impossible to change things once the pattern is set. Tippett regretfully cites the church in China as an example of a church that never was established on contextual principles. "We shall probably never be able to measure the extent to which this threw the populace into the arms of Communism, but if the archival data were open to us, I believe we would find this a major factor."[13]

As the church worldwide considers modern China, it would be incredible if we were to repeat the failures of the past. It is the people there in that place, the Chinese Christians who have suffered and endured so much, who will now determine the course for the future. Paul would have insisted that those Chinese Christians develop a contextual Christianity from the very beginning.

## Worship

At no time is the church more keenly aware of what it means to be a redeemed community, or better able to express the meaning of membership in Christ's body, than when it is at worship. The significance of worship for the mission church may be compared with that of breath for the body. All the body's activities, the thinking process as well as physical movement, depend on the inflow of oxygen. Each limb and organ, literally every part, functions only as respiration continues. When Christians worship, they are making the most open statement possible about God: that he is God and that he is truly worthy of the praise being ascribed to him.[14] For their corporate worship, God's people need to set aside the special times and conceive the appropriate forms by which they can render to God the honor he deserves.

Worship is always the central focus of the life of Christians together. It is at worship that leaders are most visible. Theology is taught through preaching and singing. The community of believers is joined with Christ through the sacraments. The variety of gifts is shared, and the invitation to discipleship is made.

During our years in Africa, we saw how the very essence of the Christian life is expressed in worship conducted in meaningful ways. In Ibadan, for example, the whole spectrum of different forms of worship can be experienced without ever leaving the city. At one extreme are those congregations that have first copied, then exaggerated, Western forms. Highly

13. Ibid., p. 153.

14. See Ralph P. Martin's discussion on the term *worship. Worship in the Early Church*, revised edition (Grand Rapids: Eerdmans, 1975), pp. 11-12.

ritualistic, with every possible vestment and formality, worship is an expression of an entirely new subculture. There is very little of such sophistication and rigidity found in any part of the traditional culture. On the other hand, worship in one of the many independent churches is intensely emotional, informal, seemingly unorganized in both content and structure. Most of the churches fall somewhere between these two contrasting expressions, but in each church one is always aware of the special differences.

### *Worship in Paul's Churches*

In a way, rather like witnessing, worship in Pauline churches was something that was going on constantly, even though comparatively little was actually written about it. Yet a considerable amount of indirect material helps to shed light on the subject. Paul uses the word *worship* (*latreia*), only twice; once (as Herman N. Ridderbos points out) "as a denotation of the Old Testament worship of God (Rom. 9:4), and once of the life of the New Testament believers (Rom. 12:2). He does not apply it to the 'meeting,' but to the daily walk of the church."[15] Yet the meetings of the church were very important, and what happened when the body met was of foundational significance for the life and the growth of Christians.

*The spirit of the gathered community*

Paul does not describe worship gatherings in his epistles, except for the teaching that he gives in I Corinthians 14. Luke's accounts of what took place when Christians met together are almost as infrequent. He evidently did not consider detailed descriptions of worship gatherings to be of special importance; however, in three places we do have brief, candid pictures, which provide us with a summary of the spiritual components of early Christian worship.

*Acts 14:27* Paul and Barnabas have just completed that notable first missionary journey in Galatia. They have retraced their steps, strengthening the believers and encouraging them to remain true to the faith. Now they have returned to their home church, Antioch, to give the report. The narrative reads, "When they arrived in Antioch, they gathered the people of the church together and told them about all that God had done with them and how he had opened the way for the Gentiles to believe." At first this may seem to convey very little, but closer study reveals that three elements are present. The congregation is gathered for the purpose of hearing what God has done in other places, and how he has used two of their own number in the ministry. The leading features are witnessing, sharing, and fellowship.

15. *Paul, an Outline of His Theology*, J. R. DeWitt, trans. (Grand Rapids: Eerdmans, 1975), p. 481.

*Acts 15:30–33* The scene at Antioch is now changed. The controversy over the admission of Gentiles into the church has been discussed at Jerusalem. The decision would be important to Antiochian Christians, since they had inaugurated the mission and there were many Gentiles among the Christians in Antioch itself. The whole group of believers gathered and once the letter had been read, "they were filled with joy by the message of encouragement." Two of the local prophets, Judas and Silas, spoke a long time, "giving them courage and strength." The picture again is one of sharing, with the added dimension of joy, and a strong feeling of concern for one another.[16]

*Acts 20:7–12* Paul is now on the last leg of his third journey and returns to that memorable place, Troas, where first he had received the vision to preach in Macedonia. He is spending a week here after having crossed the Aegean Sea from Philippi. The gathering is on a Saturday evening, first for the fellowship meal, and then to hear Paul speak. It is a long meeting that actually lasts until sunrise. One can only imagine what Paul's sermon must have covered. He would have reported on all that had happened since the last meeting, and no doubt would have reviewed the truths of the faith and encouraged the Christians at Troas. It is an interesting account, including the incident of the accident suffered by Eutychus and his healing by Paul. Leading features are the fellowship of eating together (possibly followed by the Lord's Supper), the exposition of the word, and a heightened sense of love and concern for one another.

In summary, the spirit that prevailed in the early churches is demonstrated by the sharing of and rejoicing in the Word, by mutual concern and love for the fellowship (expressed in various ways), and by flexibility and freedom as to forms, all in a context of ascribing glory to God through Christ. But these gatherings did not just happen without precedents. The first Christians in Jerusalem, for example, could not have conceived of the church outside of the framework of the ancient Jewish tradition. So in each place where Paul planted churches, the worship had both rich elements of the Jewish faith and distinctive new components that set their communities apart from all others.

### *Continuity with Jewish forms*

The fact that Christian gatherings did have continuity with synagogue and even temple worship shows how worship, wherever it takes place in the world, will have similar features everywhere. Even the Gentiles, who had little or no precedent for worship, accepted forms that were of Jewish

16. Martin notes that "nothing is more characteristic of the Apostle's [Paul's] sacramental teaching as a whole than his use of the term 'fellowship' (koinonia)." *Worship,* p. 122.

origin. At the same time, the inclusion of Gentiles in the Christian worship brought some new and fresh practices that set early Christian worship apart from the services conducted in the synagogue. "Christian worship as a distinctive, indigenous thing arose from a fusion, in the crucible of Christian experience, of the synagogue and the Upper Room."[17]

Jewish historians give a reasonably reliable picture of what synagogue worship was like, even though we do not have the picture in detail. Ralph P. Martin sums up the three main elements of synagogue worship as praise, prayer, and instruction.[18] Fasting, a common Jewish practice, was also carried over into the church. All of these major elements of worship were important to the early church and took on a new and deeper meaning.

References to the worship of Christians that bears resemblance to that of the Jews are scattered throughout Paul's epistles. These are important because they show what was foremost in his thinking when he was instructing the young churches. When writing to Timothy, he speaks of prayer with upraised hands and mentions three kinds of prayers: "supplications," "intercessions," and "thanksgivings" (I Tim. 2:1, 8). Worship was expected to be an orderly exercise. He instructs Timothy to know "how we should conduct ourselves in God's household, which is the church of the living God" (I Tim. 3:15). Again, Paul's advice to the Corinthian church is that "everything must be done in a proper and orderly way" (I Cor. 14:40).

There is an emphasis too on teaching, which was always important in Jewish worship. Teachers were set aside from the very earliest at Antioch (Acts 13:1), and Paul seems to have spent considerable time in each place as a teacher (Acts 15:35; II Thess. 2:15). His instructions to Timothy frequently refer to the need for (the provision of) corporate teaching (I Tim. 4:6, 11, 16; 6:2).

### *New elements and new meanings*

The new covenant that Jesus instituted in the upper room means that no form of worship can ever be the same again. In addition to changes in the old forms, new and distinctly Christian practices appear. Probably the most striking new feature is exhortation and proclamation as an aspect of teaching. There is an urgency and a depth of emotion added to what had become pedantic and formal. The term for "exhortation" (*noutheteō*) was rarely used in the Old Testament.[19] It now describes the care and the discipline needed by Christians in order to live in an unfriendly world. The word *taught* is synonymous with "admonish" (RSV). Paul reminded the Ephesian

17. W. D. Maxwell, *An Outline of Christian Worship* (Oxford: At the University Press, 1945), p. 5, quoted by Martin in *Worship,* pp. 26-27.

18. See *Worship,* pp. 24-27; and Ridderbos's discussion on worship in *Paul,* pp. 480-486.

19. Only in wisdom literature.

elders that "with many tears, day and night, I taught every one of you" (Acts 20:31). We can assume that it was at large meetings that Paul taught "with all possible wisdom," and in which he warned and taught the Colossians "in order to bring each one into God's presence as a mature individual in union with Christ" (Col. 1:28). He also asked the Colossians themselves to "teach and admonish one another" (Col. 3:16, RSV), and told the Romans that it was their responsibility to "instruct one another" (Rom. 15:14, RSV). He stresses that all exhortation is to be "in the Lord" and "by the Lord" (Phil. 4:2; I Thess. 4:1; II Thess. 3:12).[20]

A second new element was preaching of the Word. The church was begun by preaching and its very existence depended on continued preaching (I Cor. 15:1-2; Col. 2:7; I Tim. 6:14). Paul expected that his own epistles would be read aloud in the church assembly (Col. 4:16; I Thess. 5:27).[21]

A most notable addition, and one that was a mark of the church wherever it met, was the singing of psalms, hymns, and spiritual songs. Paul mentioned this joyful aspect of worship frequently (Eph. 5:19; Col. 3:16).[22] The whole idea of "melody in the heart" suggests that the psalms must have been brought to worship as testimonies of joy, whether by the whole congregation or by individuals. Singing was a mark of Christian worship from the inception of the church. How else could the excitement of Pentecost, the joy of thousands of changed lives from every strata of society, be released, if not by song? There had always been singing in temple and synagogue worship. Many of the Psalms were intended for singing, and antiphonal choirs were well known in Judaism,[23] but the old psalms are now sung with understanding. It may well be that some of the poetic references that Paul makes to Jesus Christ in his epistles are, in fact, well-known New Testament hymns (Phil. 2:6-11; Col. 1:15-20; I Tim. 3:16).[24]

It is difficult to distinguish between psalms, hymns, and spiritual songs. Psalms were connected with the Old Testament, hymns with the Christian community and those who may have carried them from place to place. Sacred or spiritual songs were those songs taught spontaneously by the Spirit and sung perhaps by the entire congregation, groups, or individuals. The overall impression is that such music affirmed both an identity with God's people everywhere and a spontaneity and freedom. This is extremely important for our concept of indigenous worship, for music is universally the way in which God's people express themselves in the Spirit.

The worship also included the beginning of Christian affirmation or the

20. See also I Corinthians 4:14; I Thessalonians 5:11, 12, 14.

21. The word used is *anaginōskō,* which is the technical term for the cultic reading aloud of the Old Testament in the synagogue (see Luke 4:16; Acts 13:15; 15:21; II Cor. 3:14-15). See also Ridderbos, *Paul,* p. 483.

22. See the helpful treatment on these classifications by Martin in *Worship,* pp. 37-52.

23. Ibid., p. 40.

24. Ibid., pp. 48-52.

recital of simple creeds, of which Romans 10:9 is probably the best illustration. "If you confess that Jesus is Lord and believe that God raised him from death, you will be saved." Other traces of early creeds are found in I Corinthians 8:6, Ephesians 4:5-6, and Philippians 2:6-11.

The most foundational change in worship was the remembrance of the Lord's death through the Eucharist (I Cor. 11:23). How frequently the Supper was observed cannot be concluded from what Paul writes. The church, however, apparently observed the Eucharist in close connection with a fellowship meal (Acts 2:42; 20:7; I Cor. 10:25-26). Considering the intimacy of worship and the fact that the believers usually met in small groups, the eating of the fellowship meal, in association with the Eucharist, probably became quite a regular practice.[25]

The public expression of spiritual gifts would have been something new in the meetings. The variety of the *charismata* made the worship experiences something radically different from anything the Jews had known before. What would a Jerusalem conservative have thought when attending worship at Corinth, for example? Here "one person has a hymn, another a teaching, another a revelation from God, another a message in strange tongues, and still another the explanation of what is said" (I Cor. 14:26). As we have seen, Paul expected that the different gifts would be used for the common good as the Spirit directed (Rom. 12:6; I Cor. 12:4-7). It would seem that while both elements of Judaism and these new features were commonly present in early Christian worship, there was no set pattern that all congregations followed. The specific forms, the times and place depended on local situations. Worship meant the presence of God in the midst of his people and the people's response, in a variety of ways, to this divine presence.

### *The Nature of Christian Worship*

When the church gathers together, God is in the midst. Recognizing this holy presence and responding as God desires is the way each new group of Christians grasps the meaning of its new life. Worship services are also opportunities to instruct, to empower, and to confront needs, all in the spirit of giving praise to the Lord. Worship, by the very fact of gathering together the members, is meant to give support and spiritual help to the whole body. It is to create an atmosphere in which the casual attender or the stranger can be led to immediate receptivity and be drawn into the fellowship.

The worshipers themselves are to be edified and helped by each other. This quality of mutual up-building stands out above all others. All that takes

25. Ridderbos, *Paul,* p. 484.

es under this test. Is the body being strengthened? Are the weak ɔorted and the strong sharing their strength? Everything—whether r a teaching message—must be of help to the church (I Cor. ıul was distressed by the tendency to individualism. He was against anyone who made a show or who got help only for himself at the expense of others. This tendency seemed to arise most frequently in connection with speaking in tongues. Therefore, Paul called for caution, because strange or unknown tongues minister only to one or two, "but the one who proclaims God's message helps the whole church" (I Cor. 14:4). This does not mean that the gift of tongues is to be excluded but that the whole body must profit by it, or it would be better not permitted. It is the principle of up-building that controls worship. When a form or a practice does not function for the good of all, it is out of place. The expression of gifts must be organized in such a way that the entire gathering is edified. Gifts that contribute the most to the entire community are the ones to be preferred. Paul ranks the value of prophecy, therefore, higher than the value of tongues, because it is better suited for edification.[26]

For Paul, worship was not an ecstatic, esoteric exercise that is unconnected to real life. Relevant worship is fashioned from life and prepares for life. For as J. G. Davies states, "Forms of worship can only be made relevant by those who fashion them from their situation in the world."[27] Those who attend worship come from various levels of society and from various religious backgrounds. The strong Christian ought to give way to the weaker. No one is to pressure another into accepting a style or form of worship that will be hurtful to others. Each one is to be accepted for who he is and what his particular background has made him. He is to be understood and helped on those terms. So the argument of Paul, especially in I Corinthians, keeps coming back to the use of gifts. There is no reason, but for the good of the whole (I Cor. 14:12), why a Christian should seek to excel in spiritual gifts. The leaders must plan every part of the worship gathering so that it embraces and lifts up all.[28]

But worship is also a communication to the "outsider." Just as the building up of all the members is one dimension of worship, a second, equally important dimension is the need to give a clear message to those who come in off the street, so to speak. If the ordinary person who has no background in what Christians do and say in church were to tell how he felt about some of our services, it would be an incredible report. This is also painfully true of the majority of overseas mission churches.

One man who entered an Anglican church in the Nigerian town of

26. O. H. Schmidt, *St. Paul Shows Us How* (Saint Louis: Concordia, 1950), pp. 45-46.
27. *Worship and Mission* (New York: Association Press, 1967), p. 148.
28. Romans 14:9; 15:2; Ephesians 4:12, 16; I Thessalonians 5:11.

Bukuru said afterward, "Is this a group of people who are already in heaven?" I asked him why he should say this. He replied, "There was a lot of language used which I think will be spoken in heaven, but which I have never heard here on earth." In another case, one of the respected old men of the Sura tribe finally went to Sunday morning worship. He said he was not able to control his disappointment during the singing of the hymns. When I asked him why, he replied, "My people who knew our music well and who are some of our best performers were in the service. But as I saw them singing, they were very unhappy. There was nothing in their words which sounded anything like us. I don't know why, but they seemed like strangers to me." I recalled that two of the hymns that morning were word-for-word translations of "When Morning Gilds the Skies" and "Bringing in the Sheaves." A quick study of many older hymns, dear to those who have been brought up in the churches of Europe and America, will reveal anachronisms and clichés that no longer speak to the unchurched.

Paul had a term for visitors and casual attenders. The word *idiōtēs*[29] is usually translated as "outsider" or "unlearned." However, Today's English Version translates this word as "ordinary person," which comes closer to the point. If someone whose heart and mind are right and really wants to understand and accept the Christian way is in the service, how important it is that he is reached and touched by the worship service itself. For worship has an evangelistic function. In the synagogue it was customary for those who had not yet learned the forms and the customs of Jewish worship to be segregated from the others. Paul insisted that both the ordinary person and the unbeliever (I Cor. 14:24) who happen to attend worship must understand all that takes place. Every component of the worship must be readily grasped by everyone.[30]

To illustrate his point, Paul referred to the gift of tongues, which tended to cause disorder and lack of communication in Corinthian worship. It is easy to see how one of the untutored, ordinary people might leave in confusion. Paul's ideal was that when the "outsider" slips in from the street, "he will be convinced of his sin by what he hears. He will be judged by all he hears, his secret thoughts will be brought into the open, and he will bow down and worship God, confessing, 'Truly God is here among you!'" (I Cor. 14:24-25).

How carefully balanced, then, must be the nature and the form of Christian worship. It includes both a building up of the members themselves and a reaching out to those who are not yet in the fellowship. This latter function applies to all aspects of worship. In I Corinthians 14, Paul is concerned with communication. Language, symbols, forms, and attitudes must

29. See I Corinthians 14:16, 23, 24.
30. Davies, *Worship and Mission*, p. 149.

never shut out the unbeliever. Rather, when the unbeliever is touched by the power of the fellowship, this will best bring praise to God, so fulfilling the highest aim of worship. It becomes clear why truly indigenous forms and effective verbal communication are so important in mission-church worship.

### *Worship As Mission*

Worship is not meant to be an ingrown, self-enhancing cultic act done by, and on behalf of, a select group. Worship is a celebration of what God did in Christ. What he did is best summed up by the incarnation. By the incarnation, says Dietrich Bonhoeffer, "God makes himself known as he who wishes to exist not for Himself, but for us. Hence those who worship God in Christ do not do so just for their own sakes but for God *and other people.*"[31] Worship is a celebration of God's mission through Christ who came to serve. Worship, therefore, never ends with the lives of the worshipers but ends in mission. Mission and worship are rarely joined in theology, yet it is the product of mission that any group of believers will worship together. When the redeemed community meets for worship it is in mission. To understand this could work a revolutionary change for the weak, hesitant, often untrained new churches that think only of themselves and their immediate internal interests as they worship.

Mission is, in essence, what God himself is. Mission is not a fabricated doctrine of the church.

> Mission is no more a department or a derivation of the church than are the concepts of grace, and mercy and forgiveness. Mission is central to theology because it springs out of the character of God. It is not the consequence of a command, but the outgoing expression of divine love.[32]

In the same way, worship, rightly conceived, is not an act that begins with man and is afterward directed to God, but results from the fact that God has done something for man. Mission is the proof that God has already taken the first step, and that redeemed people have been changed because of God's initiative. Therefore, worship cannot be separated from mission, for in worship Christians are participating in truth, in what Christ has done and is continuing to do.[33]

31. *Ethics,* Eberhard Bethge, ed., N. H. Smith, trans. (New York: Macmillan, 1955), p. 297. Italics added.

32. Davies, *Worship and Mission,* p. 31, quoting D. Webster, "Should an Image of Mission Go?," *Prism Pamphlets,* no. 15, n.d., p. 4.

33. See F. W. Young, *Worship in Scripture and Tradition,* World Council of Churches, Commission on Faith and Order, M. H. Shepherd, Jr., ed. (New York: Oxford University Press, n.d.), p. 90.

The New Testament churches kept alive the saving acts of Christ by continued interaction with the outside world. Worship was a time when God's Spirit moved freely among Christians, calling them to serve. It was while the Christians were at prayer at Antioch that the Spirit broke in upon them and said, "'Set apart for me Barnabas and Saul, to do the work to which I have called them.' [The church members] fasted and prayed, placed their hands on them, and sent them off" (Acts 13:2-3).

What a difference it would make if new Christians were to see the mission of God in every aspect of worship! This would mean the believing community would become a vibrant center for outreach and ministry. It is not enough that the occasional sermon or hymn reminds believers that God wants to reach those outside his grace. Mission must become the very essence of worship.

By worship that is mission, the sacraments become symbols of God's intention for the world, as much as they are symbols of what he has done for the church. Take, for example, the Lord's Supper. In my experience, this most sacred, intimate act of worship has failed to teach or motivate young Christians in the way Christ intended. Instead of opening the hearts of worshipers to the unredeemed around them, the Lord's Supper has become a cultic observance that reinforces, or even hardens, the self-awareness of a group of select people in a society. What is worse, among Christians whose lives have been saturated with animism, the Lord's Supper can easily be used to meet personal needs by taking the place of former symbols that represented magical powers. What goes on in the mind of the worshiper may be very different from that which the words of the institution, or the teaching of the sacrament, intends.

One missionary who worked in Upper Volta[34] explained that when people there first became Christians, he allowed several years to pass before he planned a regular celebration of the Lord's Supper. While this may seem strange, he was reacting to distortion that the Lord's Supper caused. He had observed that it was primarily an occasion for demonstrating divisions and making judgments among Christians, since, for example, polygamists and those who drank beer were always excluded. Until a more scriptural basis could be taught, it seemed unwise to continue in a faulty and even destructive practice.

It is not uncommon that the withholding of the Lord's Supper becomes a way to exercise discipline over Christians for various sins. What, therefore, should be an intensely spiritual act, one that brings the worshiper into a participation with Christ in all that he did, becomes a hindrance to unity and service—a veritable withdrawal from the world outside. This is precisely

34. Brian Woodford, working with Worldwide Evangelization Crusade.

the opposite of what the sacrament intends! The work of Christ as reconciliation is the summation of the gospel and is at the heart of mission. Mission is the "actualization of this [reconciliation] on a world-wide scale."[35] The Lord's Supper, celebrated in the church, is a sign of the flesh given "for the life of the world" (John 6:51, RSV) and of the "blood . . . poured out for many for the forgiveness of sins" (Matt. 26:28, RSV). The Christian who partakes of the emblems of the Lord's death remembers before any other meaning the God who reconciles and who "through Christ changed us from enemies into his friends and *gave us* the task of making others his friends also. Our message is that God was making all mankind his friends through Christ. . . . and he has given *us* the message which tells how he makes them his friends" (II Cor. 5:18-19; italics added).[36]

Far from being an ingrown, magical ritual, which the Eucharist can so easily become, it is meant to be an act that reaches out, declaring Christ as the Savior of the world. Paul taught the Corinthians that "every time you eat this bread and drink from this cup you proclaim the Lord's death until he comes" (I Cor. 11:26). Says Davies,

> Thus Eucharist and mission have the same content and intent as the first fruits of the Kingdom, the church is to reveal the actualization of reconciliation and to declare it to all men by participating in the mission of God. It is a community of reconciliation not of alienation and its proclamation is one of reconciliation. . . . We give thanks, not because we have been reconciled but because Christ has given Himself for the life of the world whereof we are witnesses.[37]

In the same way, baptism also teaches mission. The emphasis must be that baptism is the sign that the newly recreated person is now enabled to participate in Christ's death for the world and in the newness of life that God intends for all. Paul does not consider baptism to be an external condition for entering the fellowship of Christ. It is rather evidence of one's willingness "to be numbered with those who are sent out to be a suffering body in the world showing forth the Lord's death till He comes."[38]

### *Worship in Context*

The churches of Paul did have a certain uniformity about them. They were not free to pursue every whim without responsibility. We have seen

35. Davies, *Worship and Mission,* p. 101.

36. See also Romans 5:10; 11:15; Colossians 1:19, 22.

37. *Worship and Mission,* p. 101.

38. Oscar Cullmann, *Baptism in the New Testament* (London: SCM, 1950), pp. 15ff. Compare Rudolf Schnakenburg, *Baptism in the Thought of Paul,* G. R. Beasley-Murray, trans. (New York: Herder and Herder, 1964), p. 157.

that worship had a basic content. There is always the need for mission churches to show a seriousness about worship. Perhaps it is this seriousness that made Paul send Timothy to Corinth so that he could "remind you of the principles which I follow in the new life in union with Christ Jesus and which I teach in all the churches everywhere" (I Cor. 4:17). It was that the climate of worship should allow for everything to be done in a proper and orderly way (I Cor. 14:40), and that everywhere the purpose of worship be realized, that the body be edified and helped (I Cor. 14:5). Apart from these central considerations there is an openness among the various churches to worship in the way best suited to each place.

Thus the place of worship was flexible: in homes as well as in synagogues (Acts 13:14-43; 14:1-3; 17:1-4), at the riverside (Acts 16:13-14), or if need be, right at the center of the city (Acts 17:17). Paul did not want to stereotype the place of meeting, but always wanted people to meet where they could best be reached and in an environment that was congenial. His concern was also the appropriate use of forms that would best convey the message and guarantee freedom. Spontaneity was expected. Opportunity was given for "free words," whether impromptu prayer, prophecies, exhortations, speaking in tongues, or interpretations. With this transparent, honest moving of the Spirit, worship must have been a remarkable experience of joy. Martin notes that "no fruit of the Spirit was more characteristic of the early church than the possession and display of joy in the Lord."[39] (See Gal. 5:22; Phil. 4:4.)

*Freedom to innovate*

Worship that is in context will, in the first place, guarantee the freedom to innovate. Freedom is the essence of the gospel itself, and leads to creativity in the Spirit. No worship pattern that does not fit Ephesus or Philippi is allowed to be exported from Jerusalem. Paul did not expect any such imitating, nor did he foster it. In Africa we have wondered many times if self-expression in worship might not more readily be achieved out of doors. Sitting in rows to worship may be what is accepted as correct by most orthodox churches, but who is to say that this is the only "Christian" form? J. H. Nkeita once commented, "So long as we continue to worship in pews we can have no place for dancing as a means of worship."[40] Obviously, the prior question, already settled with a negative response by most mission groups, is, "Should Africans dance in worship?" Freedom to innovate will say, "Yes, dance, but dance to the glory of the Lord Christ."

39. *Worship,* p. 39.

40. "The Contribution of African Culture to Christian Worship," *International Review of Missions,* vol. 47, 1958, p. 269.

*Expression of theological concepts*

Worship in context will, secondly, express the theological concepts held by the people. This very important mark of indigenous worship will depend on how much "thinking through" the faith has been done by the new Christians. Prayer should show patterns of address and content arising from the everyday needs and habits of the people. There is evidence that certain quite local creeds were beginning to develop by the time Paul wrote his pastoral epistles. He quotes one of these "faithful" or "true" sayings in II Timothy 2:11-13. A confession of faith that Paul speaks of as the "secret of our religion" stands out in I Timothy 3:16; there is a doxology in I Timothy 1:17; and the various hymns are referred to in several places (Eph. 5:14; Phil. 2:6-11; Col. 1:15-20). It is sad that mission churches that have used Western theological concepts and liturgies often object to change simply because they have been using the foreign form for so long that truly indigenous concepts and texts would be unfamiliar. What we Westerners have given to churches many places in the world is Christianity "in the mild form."[41] G. C. Oosthuizen has not overstated this when, calling for creative theology, he says, "Our liturgy in many respects is very poor indeed when compared with the heathen cult."[42]

*Demonstration of universal and local aspects of worship*

Worship in context will, in the third place, show both the universal and local aspects of worship. As I have mentioned, Paul expected continuity among the churches. The mission church is a part of the kingdom of God wherever it is in the world and it must have those qualities that identify it readily as the church. The sacraments are faithfully observed and the proclamation of the Word is central. Without these elements, practiced in a way that builds up, the orthodoxy of the worshiping group is in question.

*Use of best forms from culture*

In the fourth place, worship in context is worship that utilizes the best forms available from the culture or creates appropriate forms where none exist. Nothing is needed more in the newly-formed Christian congregations than to allow the Spirit to teach and lead in worship. Even where there is conviction on the part of the missionary that worship must be "indigenous," it is too often the missionary who makes the decision about which forms are acceptable and which are not.[43] In a sort of cultural paternalism the mis-

41. Isaac Delano, *One Church for Nigeria* (London: U.S.C.L. Lutterworth Press, 1945), p. 16.

42. *Theological Discussions and Confessional Developments in the Churches of Asia and Africa* (Franeke: T. Wever, 1955), p. 418.

43. John V. Taylor speaks of these judgments by missionaries as risky and unacceptable. "The hesitancy of many Africans to share our [the Westerners'] enthusiasm for indigenization

sionary is tempted to pick and choose the elements of culture that can be adopted to worship. But the "outsider" can never fully apprehend the meaning of local symbols and forms. Drums in Africa were ruled out of worship for many years on the false premise that all drumming is tainted with the demonic. One African pastor said, "We know the difference. Some drum beats belong in church and some must never be sounded before the Lord. But," he continued, "the missionary could not tell the difference, so we were not allowed to take our 'souls' to church. The beat of the drum reveals who we are." It is the church in each place, the redeemed people of the Lord, who by the guidance of the Holy Spirit must take up the task of filling cultural forms with Christian substance.

The independent churches represent one of the fastest-growing movements on the African continent. The literature about "separatist" churches is impressive. Denominational churches and mission-related churches are finally taking note of a phenomenon that has been building for more than fifty years. It is in worship perhaps more than in any other area where these "nonmission" churches have the most to teach us. In many cases the independent churches give us a model for worship that is close to the taproot of the African soul. Though often inadequate, the worship is both contextual and honest, revealing an unsophisticated rebellion against a Christianity that has been handed over from the West.

The pastor of a Methodist church in the town of Jalingo, Nigeria, planned a harvest festival that would include all the active Christian groups in the area. When the time came the church building was decorated brightly and everyone was to bring a harvest gift. The African National Church was one of the independent churches invited. Members of this church presented their own number in typical fashion. Lines of singing dancers, swaying and shaking castanets, headed the procession, while drummers beat out chants and psalms. Others prostrated themselves, shouting in rhythm. Then all joined in a large circle and opened Bibles, even though some could not read. They listened attentively to the Scripture passage, then joined in singing an original song, after which the Lord's Prayer was recited with loud voices.

While all this was going on I thought of the formal and very predictable way the church would have normally conducted this harvest service. As a missionary, I wondered if the "pure" tradition could allow such activities, yet I felt rebuked that this group had been cut off from our fellowship. I also was brought to consider whether in fact our ideas of what an indigenous church should be had not been held over the views of the African. Our customary forms often fall short of meeting real needs because the channels of communication between man and God are distorted with so much that is foreign.

---

stems from the unspoken question 'Do they know what they are asking for?'" *The Primal Vision* (Philadelphia: Fortress, 1963), p. 24.

# 9

# Growth and Care of the Community

## *Discipline and Finance*

### Discipline and Christian Witness

As Paul was making his farewell to the Ephesian elders he warned them: "Keep watch over yourselves and over all the flock which the Holy Spirit has placed in your care." This was no cheap injunction, and has never been an easy task. The church is not to be allowed to drift into worldliness. It cannot be the church if her ethics, morality, and lifestyle are indistinguishable from those of the unredeemed, whether they are pagan Gentiles or religious Jews. Christians cannot become enmeshed in the world without bringing abuse upon the name of Christ (II Tim. 2:4) and exposing the whole church to shame (I Cor. 5:1). The lesson the church must learn is that she is Christ's body, virtually Christ's presence in the world. Christ's holy life, standards of righteousness, and code of behavior are now summed up in the church. The elders therefore were given the solemn responsibility of discipline.[1]

Discipline has to do with the upholding of Christ-like standards at all levels in the church. Any action taken against offending members beyond counseling and admonishment may be considered discipline. We are dealing with a subject that has brought no small amount of controversy in mission practice. Disciplinary action, carefully and prayerfully carried out in love, can bring the offender back into the fellowship and be the means of remarkable spiritual growth. This is the intention of discipline. On the other hand, unfairly harsh action taken against a person and carried out in a judgmental, hypocritical spirit can cause much harm.

1. General references dealing with discipline are I Corinthians 5:5; II Corinthians 2:6-7; Galatians 6:1; II Thessalonians 3:6, 14-15; I Timothy 1:20; 5:19-20; Titus 3:10.

In an unredeemed world, the need for modeling what it means to be a Christian is always important for the new church, and the integrity of the whole community depends on the quality of life of each member. Paul said, "Be shepherds of the church of God, which he made his own through the death of his Son" (Acts 20:28). The tremendous price paid for the creation of the church shows how invaluable is her honor, and with what care she must be administered.

### *Two Case Studies*

#### *Jauro: Alienation*

For years the mission had been supervising the sale of school supplies and books in one of the larger villages of Gongala State, Nigeria. The missionaries felt it was time to put responsibility for the bookstore into the hands of the church. The church elders accepted the decision even though they had not asked for the change. It was difficult to find a person who would be able to manage the small store. There were only primary schools in the area, and the job required someone who could handle ordering and bookkeeping, as well as sales and general supervision. After an extended search, one of the bright young men who had been away to high school was selected. His name was Jauro. He was a close relative of the chief of the village.

Things went along well for a time, until after six months it was suggested by the missionary in charge that an audit be done. Jauro resisted at first but later brought in his balance sheet and the sales records. As it turned out, there was a serious shortfall of cash, and investigations began. At first there was only suspicion, but later the elders were called together to review charges of theft.

When the meeting was convened, three of the five elders seemed eager to proceed with the accusations, while the other two were silent and appeared disinterested. Jauro was questioned in detail by the missionary and the pastor. He was not able to satisfy his questioners at every point, and the elders themselves became increasingly divided on the matter of guilt. At last Jauro was asked, pointedly, "Did you steal the money or didn't you?" Jauro replied in an oblique manner: "If you say I did, then I did." The elders would not accept this as an answer; yet, in light of the accusations and the spirit of the inquest, it was a reasonable response.

For lack of evidence to the contrary and because of Jauro's uncooperative spirit, it was decided that he was guilty. Then, led by the missionary, the elders asked Jauro to stand in the Sunday worship service and make his confession. Following the confession, he was to return the stolen money in full—about sixteen dollars. Unless he did this, he was told, there would be no way for him to be reinstated in the job or to receive communion. Jauro agreed to take his stand in church, though with considerable reluctance.

At the following Sunday service the pastor announced that Jauro had something to say. Jauro did not come forward but stood where he was near the back of the church and said,

> It was the decision of the elders that I stole from the bookshop. Because I could not prove otherwise I admitted to the theft. They then told me that I should witness before you all that I did this, so I am doing what they said. I do not want to show disrespect to my elders.

This was all he said and there was no further word on the matter.

Jauro did not make any progress in his Christian life after that regrettable Sunday morning. He did not return to his job at the bookstore and rarely attended church. Before long he moved away from the village of his birth and married outside of the church. He had been one of the most promising young Christian leaders. However, the way in which discipline was carried out was at least one factor in his being lost to the fellowship of Christians.

*Esta: Reconciliation*

Attitudes toward sexual relations before marriage differ considerably from one group to another in Africa. It is not uncommon for the traditional practices to be quite unlike what accepted Christian standards would be. For example, among most of the tribal communities it is not considered morally wrong to become pregnant before marriage, especially if the father of the child is the intended husband. However, it is extremely important to the tribe that the rules that apply in that kind of a situation be kept. The unwed mother understands that the child becomes property of her father. He, the father of the unwed mother, rears the child and has full rights over the child until he or she is married.

Esta was a sixteen-year-old girl who lived in one of the villages of the Jos Plateau. Her parents were animists and, except for one brother, the rest of her immediate family were Muslims. Esta, a recent Christian, was attending a class for inquirers and was soon to be baptized. Then it was discovered that Esta had become pregnant. This meant the elders were to review all that happened. There had been little teaching on the sanctity of marriage or on biblical principles relating to the meaning of the marriage relationship.

In an unusual move for a group of African elders, one of the leading Christian women, Saratu, was invited to the inquiry to give the woman's point of view. It was revealed that the father of the child was a local boy who made no profession of the Christian faith. This presented a problem, in addition to the evident fact that the baby would become the property of a non-Christian.

It is impossible to recount all the details of the way in which Esta's case was handled. In summary, she was put under the spiritual care of Saratu. Esta and Saratu were to meet together twice a week for prayer and a short Bible reading. Saratu was asked to report to the elders as to how faithful Esta was in coming to meet her. The senior elder was asked to visit the young man who was the father, to speak to him about his spiritual life, and to invite him to attend services regularly. Meanwhile Esta was to continue to attend the catechism classes, though it was felt her baptism should be delayed until after the child was born.

That first elders' meeting was not hurried. The deliberations were prayerfully and patiently conducted so that Esta felt she was being treated as a member of the community rather than an offender. She came to see that Christians will often have a standard that is different from the customary habits, and made it clear that many young people were expecting the church to teach what that standard should be.

The result was that Saratu became a sister in the Lord to Esta and kept her close to the fellowship of other sympathetic women. After nearly two years, the young father became a Christian and he and Esta were married in the church. The church took it as a sign of God's blessing when Esta's father, still outside of the church, gave the baby back to Esta and her husband and relinquished all his rights. Both Esta and her husband are faithful Christians today.

## *Discipline and Paul's View of Sin*

### *The pervasiveness of sin*

We cannot come to terms with the way Paul handled problems of discipline unless we understand something of his teaching on sin and evil in the world. It is a complicated picture. There is a veritable battleground of unseen forces that constantly test the individual Christian and the whole church.[2] Briefly, he knows that God originally made both man and the world good (I Cor. 10:26; 11:7), but when sin gained the advantage, the relationship God had intended was spoiled. How this happened Paul does not explain in any detail, but man is constantly being tempted by powers outside himself (II Cor. 11:3; I Thess. 3:5; II Thess. 2:9). Sin within the person is a manifestation of the much broader battle being waged against God's authority by the powers of evil. These are powers that are intelligent, bent on subterfuge and the defeat of the Christians (II Cor. 2:11; Eph. 6:12; II Thess. 2:9). Paul himself is not spared this agony of testing (II Cor. 12:7). There is

2. See Ephesians 6:12; Galatians 4:9; I Corinthians 2:8. Christ triumphs over these powers; see Colossians 2:8-15; Ephesians 3:10.

no question about the ultimate overthrow of these forces (Eph. 1:20-22) but, in the interim, "the church has to live in the arena where contesting parties still engage one another even if the final issue is not still in the balance."[3] (See Col. 2:14-15.)

Yet, while we wait for the final decimation of the whole evil system (Col. 2:15), Christians are very much in the path of direct assault. Paul's picture of sin is primarily that of an outside force that knows exactly how and where to attack. It is as though sin were an almost separate entity from the person when Paul distinguishes between the "I" and the "sin that lives in me" (Rom. 7:17). Nonetheless, sin has an inward quality about it, making it part of the person. "All are infected," says Ralph P. Martin, "by a universal disease that attacked them, and all human beings in Paul's view have given a permanent lodging to the invading demon and succumbed to its approach."[4] Adam set the course for the fall (Rom. 5:12ff.; I Cor. 15:21ff.). No culture or family of peoples can claim exception.

> The upshot is that sin is a universal master, a demonic despot carrying off humanity as a prisoner of war (Rom. 7:23) and asserting proprietary rights over God's creatures. The term "sinners by nature" . . . is misleading . . . if it obscures the emphasis Paul makes on man as a willing victim, attacked and overcome by an alien power and now in bitter bondage. . . .[5]

*The flesh*

A term closely associated with Paul's teaching on sin cannot be overlooked. This is the idea of the "flesh," *sarx,* as Paul calls it. The word *flesh* refers in some cases to the living tissue of the body (Rom. 2:28; I Cor. 15:39; II Cor. 12:7) or to the whole body itself (I Cor. 5:3; 6:16-17; Col. 2:5). But there is a more subtle application that comes very close in meaning to the powers that tempt and control the whole person. This further extension of *sarx,* explains G. E. Ladd, "reaches beyond man in his bodily life to include other factors that are inseparable elements to human existence."[6] For example, "confidence in the flesh" (Phil. 3:3ff., RSV), does not refer to the physical body, but to a dependence on the whole complex of the outward realm of the world in which a person lives.[7]

*Sarx* is a product of family, tribe, and culture. Everyone is subject to the pull of his tradition, which appears to be energized by powers that lie outside of Christ. Everyone is guided by the world view and the value system

3. Ralph P. Martin, *Reconciliation: A Study of Paul's Theology* (Atlanta: John Knox, 1981), p. 57.
4. Ibid., p. 58.
5. Ibid., pp. 58-59.
6. See *A Theology of the New Testament* (Grand Rapids: Eerdmans, 1974), p. 467.
7. Ibid.

·h he is born. For Paul this would include his rearing as a child, the ...ics and the morals he learned as a Jew, his ancestry, and the whole range of customs that he held to be important (II Cor. 11:18; Gal. 6:12-14). There is no person who, having become a Christian, does not find that the flesh is a powerful influence. Even in areas where the natural world does not corrupt, this "base of existence" is unable to provide the resources needed to attain to righteousness.[8] When Paul speaks of "living in the flesh,"[9] he may not be speaking of an intrinsically evil situation; but he is saying that existence on the natural level puts one under the command of forces that can lead one away from Christ and cause spiritual downfall.[10]

*The old life and the new*

"Powers," therefore, that would send the Christian off course, causing lapses back into the "old life," arise from dark spiritual forces that maybe are both within and without the person. Being "in Christ" does not do away with the reality of the evil. The Christian is painfully aware of the struggle between the flesh and the Spirit. The conflict between the two forces actually prevents one from doing what he wants to do (Gal. 5:17). It is part of the Christian's early discipline to learn that the Holy Spirit must have dominance (Gal. 5:16-26), and what is required if this is to take place.

The Christian, therefore, is a target for the destructive aspects of the culture into which he is born. The problem arises from within the individual life; for example, the awareness of unmet needs, or natural desires, or the quest for an acceptable basis for trust. The practices and the beliefs of traditional culture that have developed over generations do give a modicum of stability and relief. Rituals, formulas, or specialists in various services are often immediately available. Turning to the indigenous system for "salvation" is as natural as breathing, before Jesus enters as the new Lord. After conversion, these claims on the life remain powerful and temptations are strong. Paul did not hide his regret that people who have "died with Christ and are set free from the ruling spirits of the universe" should afterward live as though they belonged to this world (Col. 2:20).

### *Discipline As Paul Practiced It*

*Pastoral care*

All too often Paul is characterized as a fierce legalist, a sort of vigilante for the faith who would excommunicate on any provocation. A well-known

8. Ibid., p. 468.

9. For example, Romans 7:5; 8:4, 12-13; II Corinthians 10:2; Galatians 2:20; Philippians 1:22.

10. "The flesh is anything that is placed in rivalry to Christ; to trust in the flesh is to place

missionary handbook produced just after the Second World War carefully outlines the steps that are to be taken by church leaders in matters of discipline. It shows how easily a Westerner can use the Bible in a quite rigid and subjective manner while attempting to solve sensitive cultural problems. By bringing all the New Testament references concerning discipline into a kind of universal mandate, A. R. Hay lays down six steps that he feels must be taken if the procedure is going to be "scriptural."[11] The fifth step reads,

> If bringing the case before the church does not lead to repentance, the believer who then persists in sin and rebellion is to be "delivered unto Satan for the destruction of the flesh that the Spirit may be saved in the day of the Lord Jesus."[12]

These strong words that Hay quotes were originally written in connection with a very special case that arose in Corinth. It is risky to say that we understand fully what Paul meant by the phrase "hand over to Satan" (I Cor. 5:5; I Tim. 1:20).[13] The Christian who lapses into unchristian behavior requires patience, much teaching, and genuine caring and love. The discipline of the Christian church must be the work of those who have a truly pastoral heart. It is this that needs to be emphasized as characterizing Paul's approach. Harshness, unwise use of authority, or unfeeling judgment are always out of place. The church is a spiritual fellowship, and teaching aided by the Holy Spirit and given to the whole fellowship is constantly needed. Humble dependence on the Holy Spirit is never more crucial than when a member has offended and the matter is being investigated. Paul writes more provocatively about how to deal with offenders in I Corinthians than in any other epistle. As Roland Allen observes,

> It is a striking characterization of the epistle that the writer never forgets that his duty is to point out the right course of action rather than to lay commands upon the church . . . again and again he expressed the firm convictions that the church praises the will of God and will surrender itself to the guidance of the Spirit.[14]

---

confidence outside of Christ. . . . Sarx is like a demonic force that seeks to intrude into the place of Christ." Martin, *Reconciliation,* pp. 59-60.

11. *The New Testament Order for Church and Missionary* (Buenos Aires: New Testament Missionary Union SEMCA, 1947). In Hay's use of Scripture there is almost no mention of the variety of cultures into which the Word must be planted. Hay uses the Bible in a rigid way, overriding the truth that the Spirit is still teaching his church today.

12. Ibid., p. 344.

13. Ibid., p. 345.

14. *Missionary Methods: St. Paul's or Ours?* (1912; reprint ed. London: World Dominion Press, 1960), pp. 114-115.

Rules that have been drawn up and must be enforced cannot be what Paul had in mind even when he had to recommend stern measures. Certainly, when individuals broke all bounds and were guilty of flagrant offenses, he did not hesitate to take action. But both the purpose and the process of discipline show the caution with which this function must be carried out.

*The purpose of discipline*

The purpose of discipline, therefore, is to bring both restoration of the errant person and healing to the entire fellowship. It is just as important to focus on the group as it is on the individual. The tendency to judge the individual alone violates the principle of the oneness of the body of Christ. The defection of anyone is a corporate failure. It is obvious that something was tragically wrong with the church at Corinth, so that the flagrant offense of one member became a symptom of the church's sin. "How then can you be proud?" says Paul. "On the contrary, you should be filled with sadness" (I Cor. 5:2). The church that has a conscience about the standards of the Christian life and that has built strong bonds of love and has been faithful in teaching will be less likely to have members who backslide.

Discipline, carefully administered, is a means of teaching the individual and the group what the standards of the Christian life are. The redemptive purpose of discipline must be kept sacred. The reinstatement of the offender and subsequent growth in grace, forgiveness, and love are the rationale for discipline. Teaching and restoration are motives for Paul's strongest words of discipline (I Cor. 5:5; I Tim. 1:20). Repentance of course underlies the restoration, but this is the work of God's Spirit. Any notion that stern measures, in and of themselves, enforced on an errant person, will bring about spiritual repentance is wrong. The sin of one should cause grief and humble repentance on the part of all. Such an attitude teaches the meaning of the body of Christ and shows the individual how far-reaching the offense can be in its effects.

*The process of discipline*

Paul recognized that the Master had given the church the authority to bind and to loose (Matt. 18:18). The emphasis Paul gave is that the whole church shall be involved, and that nothing should be done simply by reference to a law.

Unquestionably, when the ethics and the morality of the church are offended, then the whole church should take action. So often minor offenses are treated severely, and sins of shocking magnitude seem to paralyze the church. In the special case in Corinth (I Cor. 5:1-5), it was Paul himself who took action because the church had failed. But Paul wanted to avoid this kind of action as the nonresident missionary. Even here, while his words were strong, he did not tell the church what penalty to mete out, nor did he directly call on the offender to repent.

> He wrote to accuse the church of its failure to realize its duty in the matter. In a case of this kind, according to his view, the church, as a church, had a duty to perform, a duty to the offender and a duty to itself. . . . Therefore he wanted to see if the church would do its duty before he interfered himself.[15]

Discipline, therefore, must be an act of the majority, not simply a judgment passed by a few elders to which the rest of the body may not agree or show concern. It is unlikely that any discipline will result in repentance and restoration unless the common conscience of the church is really injured by the offense. That conscience needs to be sensitized, so that when the action is taken corporately the purpose of discipline is clear to both the church and the offender. Because it is the entire church that is affected, the church deals with the individual within the context of the church fellowship and in that context only. Allen observed that when one leader or a few individuals are quick to judge offenders and the fellowship is ignored in the process, then in place of redemption we find fragmentation and defeat.

> We exercise discipline and leave the church undisciplined. He disciplined the church, not individuals. He left the church and it stood, tottering on its feet but still standing; we leave the church without any power of standing at all.[16]

Discipline is not by law but through the teaching of God's Spirit. Manmade laws destroy the basis of the Christian life. The notion that certain offenses deserve excommunication while others are less serious and call for this or that lesser penalty would be anathema to Paul. Even in cases of fornication he resists what would have been the easy way for a Jew. He does not quote laws and punishments (I Thess. 4:1-8). There is no series of codes or penalties. Even knowing that the Corinthians have been taught, he does not wave a list of consequences before them. He would rather see people surrender themselves to the Holy Spirit, recognizing that he is given to them that they may be holy. It follows, then, that uncleanness carries with it the rejection of the Holy Spirit and incurs the wrath of God.

Paul reluctantly advised discipline, but he certainly did pursue various means of setting things right. As a mission pastor, he did not rely on just one way of confronting wrong in the church, as so often happens today. To correct the sad situation at Corinth, Paul wrote several letters, instructing and exhorting; he sent his ambassadors Timothy (I Cor. 16:10) and Titus

15. Ibid., p. 122.
16. Ibid., p. 124.

(II Cor. 12:18); and, of course, Paul visited Corinth himself, at great pain personally (II Cor. 13:1, 3). Always his expectation was that the church should pray, study, and work tirelessly to find solutions to its own problems. Paul did not allow dependence upon himself, as the missionary, in cases of discipline, any more than in any other area.

> Dependence does not train for independence, slavery does not educate men for freedom. Moreover they have the Holy Ghost to strengthen and to guide them. Christians are not only what they are by nature, they are a Spirit-bearing body. It is not a question merely of our faith in them, it is still more a question of faith in the Holy Ghost. We look too much on our converts as they are by nature; St. Paul looked at his converts as they were by grace.[17]

## Finance

### *The Problem*

Nothing comes more quickly to the very nerve of mission than finance. It touches in one way or another almost every aspect of the mission enterprise. Attitudes toward money can bring people close together or can cause contention and mistrust. There is no way to plant and nurture churches without facing the question of money. By far the majority of missionaries come from countries of the West, mainly the United States, where there is affluence and waste. Such missionaries usually work among people who, until recently, were ruled through the long years of colonialism. There are people who have had very little and have longed for a life much closer to the standard modeled by expatriates from the West. Among the underprivileged are the churches, communities of believers that also have desperate needs. The governments of developing countries look on all sides for solutions to their pressing economic problems and so turn to the older, rich nations of the world for help. In much the same way the mission church looks to its obvious benefactors, the missionaries and the mission boards, for relief from what is often a heavy financial burden.

It is beyond the scope of my study to illustrate the various types of involvement by expatriate agencies in the financing of mission churches. The approaches that denominational and interdenominational boards have taken to their churches overseas present a wide diversity of models. Involvement in the support of mission churches ranges from very strict rules aiming at total self-support (in which no unnecessary foreign monies are given to the church) to high levels of aid for such overseas churches. It would be

17. Ibid., p. 125.

claimed even by those who provide massive subsidies for a wide variety of mission-church "projects" that this is not meant to create dependence in the church, but simply to provide it with the facilities for its growth and ministry in response to our Lord's command. Usually those boards that provide any portion of the budget of mission churches would hold that eventual self-support is the ideal. The funds given are seen as an interim arrangement, or are for special ministries that lie outside the ability of the church to initiate or maintain.

What makes the subject of finance so important is that it touches on nearly every area of the life of the church, and is an underlying cause of church and mission tensions. Allen observed many years ago that

> it is of comparatively small importance how the missionary is maintained: it is of comparatively small importance how the finances of the church are organized. What is of supreme importance is how these arrangements, whatever they may be, affect the minds of the people, and so promote or hinder the spread of the gospel.[18]

The importance of finance in relation to the success of the gospel is what Allen feels was in Paul's mind. It was not so much the particular plan, right or wrong, or whether Paul had anything personal at stake; the concern was the planting, nurture, and growth of the churches. "It is regrettable," says Melvin L. Hodges, "that the use of money by the missionary has often weakened the church rather than strengthened it."[19] Such a statement proves true not only in external areas such as those where buildings and salaries are concerned, but also in the more subtle area of attitude and spirit. Missionary life is, paradoxically, quite secular, and a devastating sense of materialism can be learned quickly by the church. This negates the spiritual basis of God's work and the loving trust the missionary and the national must have for each other.

> We load our missionaries with secular business, negotiations with contractors, the superintendence of works, the management of a considerable establishment to which is often added anxiety about the supply of funds for providing and maintaining the establishment. In this way their attention is detracted from their proper spiritual work, their energy and power dissipated, and their first contact with the people whom they desire to evangelize is connected with contracts and other purely secular concerns.[20]

18. Ibid., p. 49.
19. *The Indigenous Church and the Missionary: A Sequel to "The Indigenous Church"* (Pasadena, CA: William Carey Library, 1978), p. 67.
20. Allen, *Missionary Methods,* p. 53.

These words were written more than seventy years ago, yet they describe the trap into which missionaries still find themselves drawn. Much more of the actual physical work and management is done by nationals today than before, but the underlying problem, regrettably, has not changed that much. Spreading the Word is perceived as a materialistic enterprise, a business project, so to speak, and thus it becomes secularized. The real purpose is misrepresented. The spiritual is diffused because the external manifestation of mission purpose does not correspond to the real and inward intention. "If then," Allen says, "the material form really does not express the true spirit, we cannot be surprised if they [the churches] are hindered."[21] The supreme question that should regulate the financial planning of the mission and church is, therefore, How will the church best be able to fulfill its task of proclaiming the gospel, and what plan will best nurture the spiritual quality of the mission endeavor? We must look carefully at Paul's ministry to discover his controlling principles. He insisted on what we could call self-support, and he also expected Christians to share.

### *The Principle of Self-support*

The churches were obviously responsible for their own life as far as finances were concerned. There was no mission board and no home constituency. The whole mission venture of Paul was prompted by the Holy Spirit and began in Antioch. Yet there is not even the slightest indication that the Antioch church, much less the Jerusalem church, which was not only poor but also was not in sympathy with the Pauline mission, accepted full financial responsibility for Paul's mission. The basis of self-support as Paul taught it was fundamental to the very life of the new churches. Systematic and sacrificial giving was essential to their own spiritual life, vital to their early growth in ministry to each other and to the maintenance of their witness in a hostile world.

In appealing to the Corinthians for the offering that he was taking to Jerusalem, Paul in a few words states an important principle. "I am not trying to relieve others by putting a burden on you" (II Cor. 8:13). The principle here is that no church ought to be burdened because some other church is not carrying its own weight. Each congregation is to be self-sufficient. Any gift that was shared between churches, and with Paul, was out of their own generosity, beyond caring for local expenses.

The responsibility to give in order to maintain a local program and its leadership is written in what some scholars believe to be Paul's earliest letter. The Galatians were to remember that "the man who is being taught the Christian message should share all the good things he has with his

21. See Allen's discussion, ibid., pp. 54ff.

teacher" (Gal. 6:6). In his letter to the Ephesians there seemed to be a need for very basic teaching on stewardship. "Start working," Paul said, "in order to earn an honest living . . . and to be able to help the poor" (Eph. 4:28). Later, as the church began to develop more organizational structure, Paul instructed Timothy in terms that leave the impression that some church leaders caused a heavy financial burden, probably because they had to give up their secular jobs. "The elders who do good work as leaders should be considered worthy of receiving double pay, especially those who work at preaching and teaching" (I Tim. 5:17).[22]

The church had the benefit of the model of Paul, who sought no financial aid for himself but took his place as any ordinary person, finding ways to support himself. This was one thing that set Paul apart from the professional public preachers who were such a nuisance in his day. Lecturers and spell-binding orators, expecting support from their listeners, wandered from town to town. There was also a large class of people that wandered about as mystery-mongers, exhibiting their own shows and collecting money from those who attended. Paul refused to be classed with such people. To receive money would have hindered him in his work. He had the right to collect money, as did those evangelists and prophets; and since he was an apostle, he could claim even more right than they. "But," wrote Paul, "we haven't made use of this right. Instead, we have endured everything in order not to put any obstacle in the way of the Good News about Christ" (I Cor. 9:12). Always, it is the honor of the gospel that is foremost when he insisted on self-support.

In setting an example at Thessalonica, Paul says that he adopted the role of a "nurse." To have asked for support from these infant Christians would have been a denial of his nurturing spirit. He recalls how, because of his love for the Good News and his concern for his converts, he supported himself: "We worked day and night so that we would not be any trouble to you" (I Thess. 2:8-9).[23] In that touching scene with the Ephesian elders, knowing he would not be seeing them again, Paul closes his general admonitions by calling attention to his own example and commending it to church leaders.

> I have not wanted anyone's silver or gold or clothing. You yourselves know that I have worked with these hands of mine to provide everything that my companions and I have needed. I have shown you in all things that by working hard in this way we must help the weak, remembering the words that the Lord Jesus himself said, "there is more happiness in giving than in receiving." [Acts 20:33-35]

22. F. D. Gealy, *The Interpreter's Bible: The First and Second Epistle to Timothy and the Epistle to Titus* (New York: Abingdon, 1954), vol. 11, p. 441.

23. See also II Thessalonians 3:7-8.

Books and articles recommending self-support as the ideal for mission churches are numerous.[24] The definition of an indigenous church is still very much connected with the three-self principle.[25] We have already observed that to be indigenous not only is to be self-governing, self-propagating, and self-financing, but also is to be culturally authentic. It is a church that Alan R. Tippett describes as "mediating the work, the mind, the word, and the ministry of Christ in its own environment."[26] The self-sufficient nature of Paul's churches was one of the most visible results of his ministry, but these churches were also contextual churches, as I have emphasized; thus their ability to finance their own life must be seen as a consistent component within this larger reality. Paul surely would not have allowed an insistence on self-support if he had initiated foreign programs or built structures that afterward the mission churches would be expected to maintain. There is no other way to understand Paul's churches except as self-supporting, but the principle of self-support is not given as a mandate quite unrelated to other factors. Rather it is a natural emphasis resulting from the contextual integrity of the churches.

Three men in mission history have had a great impact on the modern missionary movement, especially in this area of understanding what the indigenous church ought to be. These were Rufus Anderson, Henry Venn, and John L. Nevius. All of them were associated with the later years of the nineteenth century, and all three drew heavily on Paul's example for their convictions about self-support.

Rufus Anderson, the American, was a firm proponent of the three-self ideals for mission churches. Considering Paul's own ministry,[27] he wrote,

> Had not the apostolic idea of self-governing, self-supporting and self-propagating churches dropped out of the Christian mind soon after the age of the apostle, not to be fully regained until modern times [1875], how very different had been the history of Christendom and of the world.[28]

Anderson's conviction was that churches should be independent so they could be free to move in further evangelism and mission without being

24. Refer to older works such as John L. Nevius, *Methods of Mission Work* (New York: Foreign Mission Library, 1895), or William Knight, *Memoir of Rev. Henry Venn* (London: Longmans, Green, 1880); and more recently, Melvin L. Hodges, *The Indigenous Church,* revised edition (Springfield, MO: Gospel Publishing House, 1976).

25. Self-financing, self-administering, and self-propagating.

26. *Verdict Theology in Mission Theory,* revised edition (Pasadena, CA: William Carey Library, 1973), p. 155.

27. For a summary of Anderson's influence, see R. Pierce Beaver, *To Advance the Gospel* (Grand Rapids: Eerdmans, 1967). Dr. N. G. Clark, successor to Anderson, said, "The world owes to Dr. Anderson the reviving of the true method of missionary effort as illustrated most fully in the Acts of the Apostles by the Apostle Paul," p. 38.

28. Ibid., p. 15.

limited by, or accountable to, supporting agencies. He did not see churches as ends in themselves, but as the means for the further extension of mission. While he did not rule out completely financial aid from the mission, this aid was to be given with great discretion, and was always to be taken as short-term help. A church should be self-propagating. This is the real measurement of its life as a church. It was Anderson's conviction that "a church which is self-governing and self-supporting will also be self-propagating."[29]

A contemporary of Anderson was Henry Venn, secretary of the Church Missionary Society. Venn was equally important in applying self-support principles in the widespread mission fields of the Anglican church for many years up to the time of his death in 1872. His principle was to teach a church from the beginning to care for its own life. Like Anderson, he felt that any funds that might be granted to a "native" church must be given with a strict understanding that this was to be temporary help only. Any funds given were given with the goal that churches reproduce themselves, and that support would be diminished in successive years until the "native church agency be wholly supported by the native church fund."[30] Venn believed in the power of the Word to generate life, and that growth is natural. The church is weakened and frustrated by the constant presence of the missionary who gathers power around his person and becomes the center for a flow of gratuities and salaries. Allen would have been greatly influenced by Venn and Anderson. His strong appeal for financial independence for mission churches carried the additional insight that, whether such independence is scripturally right or wrong, missionaries do not want to relinquish the power of the purse strings. In his opinion, the missionary would actually fear financial independence.

> We think it quite impossible that a native church should be able to exist without the paternal care of an English overseer. If it were financially independent it might be tempted to dispense with his services, and then, we are persuaded it would at once fall into every error of doctrine and practice.[31]

How unlike Paul. He founded churches with the conviction that the church must think through its own faith based on the Word that he taught. Since Paul did not tie the churches to himself for any long period, he modeled by his ministry that mission is the real reason for being a follower of Christ. The church that is granted freedom to develop its own life and is taught to bear the burdens of others will best be able to bear the burden for its own life (Gal. 6:2, 5).

29. Ibid., p. 31.

30. See William Knight, *The Missionary Secretariat of Henry Venn* (London: Longmans, Green, 1895), p. 329.

31. *Missionary Methods,* p. 60.

### *The Principle of Sharing*

Having seen how widely Paul's insistence on self-support has been understood, one wonders why his equally clear teaching on giving to others is so easily (or perhaps conveniently) overlooked. When we teach mission churches that they must take responsibility for all their expenses, we must not be understood to imply that Christians should not respond to the needs of others, or that churches should not share God's blessings among themselves. To speak of self-support does not always mean that home churches and home boards should never help mission churches with their financial burdens.

The incarnation of our Lord is the foundation upon which Paul made his appeal for sharing our resources to help fellow Christians. This was beautifully expressed when Paul asked for offerings to be carried back to Jerusalem. "You know the grace of our Lord Jesus Christ; rich as he was, he made himself poor for your sake, in order to make you rich by his poverty" (II Cor. 8:9). The offering for the church at Jerusalem is, in itself, convincing evidence that sharing between churches is a Christian obligation. Granted, it is almost unheard of that newly planted mission churches should send offerings to the parent church.[32] But the principle of sharing is heightened by this striking biblical example. The church at Jerusalem was poor. It had little to give and, beyond that, was not even in wholehearted sympathy with the Gentile mission. Sharing comes out of a heart of love and is in proportion to the ability to share (II Cor. 8:12). The fundamental lesson of sharing outside the home church and giving liberally, as new Christians, to those who are culturally different and geographically distant is an unforgettable lesson. Here is a simple case of predominately Gentile churches sharing with needy Jews because they are now brothers and sisters in Christ. Paul's appeal was not based on a written agreement with the home board or on a quota system levied on local churches. The appeal is for the self-giving spirit modeled by the incarnate Jesus.

Sharing is, therefore, an expression of grace. This grace was first received by the believers in Jerusalem, and flowed out from them into the Gentile world through the gates of Pentecost (Rom. 15:26-27). That grace produced such an amazing response among the Gentiles that even the impoverished Christians in Macedonia were moved to extreme generosity (II Cor. 8:2). Paul makes his appeal to the "grace of our Lord Jesus Christ" as the spiritual basis for all Christian sharing. As the needy Christians in Jerusalem received the "service of love" (II Cor. 8:7) their prayers would be lifted up to God in praise for this proof of Gentile obedience to the gospel, and for those to whom they were now connected through the bonds of grace.

32. The Jerusalem offering is mentioned frequently. See Romans 15:25-27; I Corinthians 16:1-3; II Corinthians 8:7-9; 9:6-12.

Paul also expected churches to help him personally when the need became obvious. This was not simply because they were to respect that he was Paul the apostle. Giving was expected because it is an enriching, blessing-filled experience for the giver. So he wrote tenderly to the Philippians:

> It was very good of you to help me in my troubles. You Philippians know very well that when I left Macedonia in the early days of preaching the Good News, you were the only church to help me; you were the only ones who shared my profits and losses. More than once when I needed help in Thessalonica, you sent it to me. It is not that I just want to receive gifts; rather, I want to see profit added to your account. Here, then, is my receipt for everything you have given me—and it has been more than enough! [4:14-18a]

There is no way to discount the high value Paul attached to the gifts sent to him. They were sent in obedience to the Spirit, and sent to further the cause of Christ in Rome. They were carefully used and accounted for, and were regarded as "a sweet-smelling offering to God" (Phil. 4:18). Of course, they were sent to Paul, a responsible and mature leader. He was someone the donor could trust fully even before audits and receipts! The giving and receiving of gifts for the Lord's work must have this element of trust and careful accountability. Glad giving and careful, joyful receiving work for the coming of God's kingdom. We are workers together with God (II Cor. 5:1).

When writing to the Corinthians, Paul was candid about the obligation to share. Apparently the Christians there were much better off than in most places. He did say that he would not want one church to pay the expenses of another (II Cor. 8:13), but he expected the Corinthian church, nevertheless, to give over and above her own expenses. Appealing for the Jerusalem fund, he wrote, "Since you have plenty at this time, it is only fair that you should help those who are in need. Then, when you are in need and they have plenty, they will help you" (II Cor. 8:14). The responsibility to help the weaker and the needy when one is blessed with goods could not be more clearly stated.

The debate on support to overseas churches was taken up in 1960 in *The Indigenous Church*. In this book, an American missionary to Japan gave an account of how responsible, prayerful, and highly disciplined support by the Japanese Baptist church worked in positive ways for church growth. The emphasis was on the kind of giving that sees material goods as God's, not man's; that money given is the property of neither the church that gives it nor the church that receives it.

> If we serve God then money is a servant or tool to be used to bring in God's Kingdom if we are workers together with God. Once the offerings are

made, this is neither Japanese money nor American money. It is holy money for God to use where He directs His servants to use it.[33]

I remember the embarrassment and the flush of resentment felt when, at an annual church meeting, the leaders accused the mission of having little or no interest in evangelism and church planting. After all, it was for evangelism that we had come, or at least so we thought. My own responsibility was that of an ordained pastor, and the remembrance of countless hours of tiring work in evangelism of all kinds flashed through my mind. When I asked how an allegation of that kind could be justified, I was told,

> As a mission, you have spent thousands of dollars in building hospitals and schools but you do not put your money with the church. You are constantly saying, "Build your own church and pay all your own salaries." We say that where you put your money is where your heart is, and so, without any doubt, evangelism is your lowest priority.

It was a difficult accusation to counter. We American missionaries had a luxurious standard of living compared with that of the people around us, and in the eyes of our African brethren we were always able to find funds for the things we really wanted. We had been talking about self-support for evangelism, church building, and the like, but at the same time had been putting what appeared to be massive funds into various supporting services and into our own comforts! Paul did not have to deal with this incongruity.

The contradiction created when mission agencies select and finance massive social-action projects while saying to the church, "support yourself," is one part of the problem. Beyond that, the traditional emphasis on the indigenous church seems, in practice, to have been primarily the call for self-support. When the concept of the indigenous church becomes a matter of who is paying the salaries of church leaders, for church buildings, or the costs of program administration, then the word *indigenous* is unfortunate and inadequate. "Used in the narrow sense it stresses dependence on mission rather than the important spiritual factors of faith in God [and on the] Holy Spirit working through His chosen instruments."[34]

I have experienced the agony of refusing funds that were requested by the church. Feeling the resentment or even anger of the church over such refusals, missionaries usually find ways to support the work here and there so that relationships can be kept intact and they can go on with their work. Often the mission and the church are caught up in a bartering exercise. This

33. Edwin B. Dozier, "One Method of Missionary Use of Funds for Evangelization in Japan," in *The Indigenous Church* (Chicago: Moody, 1960), p. 87.

34. John Ritchie, *Indigenous Church Principles in Theory and Practice* (New York: Revell, 1966), p. 24.

can happen when the mission, which is perceived as having the money, refuses exaggerated demands. Then, however, agreements are worked out to smaller requests; or else the large amounts are finally granted with strings attached, thus creating a situation that will further complicate relationships and damage trust.

Many of our home congregations that now are largely self-supporting are the product of a long history of people who gave in sacrificial ways to get things started for that congregation, but who never were a part of that particular local church.

> The seminaries, Bible Schools, colleges, publishing houses, social reform societies and many other organizations which feed and foster the life of home congregations carry on their activities largely through the support of legacies, foundations, endowments, lands and other properties given by generations of Christians and carefully administered by scrupulous capable men under whose care they have increased in value.[35]

When we look at the young churches, infant churches, many of them, we are considering a situation very different from what obtains in the sending churches. These mission churches usually have no long heritage of committed people and yet often are expected to provide a level of funding equivalent to that of our established churches, even though they are still a minority and, in many cases, are living for Christ in a hostile environment.

Of course, self-support cannot be taught or expected of a young church if there is no spiritual basis for it. If the fellowship has not been trained in responsible ministry to one another, and knows little or nothing about the personal and the corporate disciplines of the Holy Spirit that I described earlier, there can never be a self-supporting church, much less a truly indigenous church. Missionaries who have created a sense of dependence by their presence, and who represent wealth and have shown little accountability in living standards, will be hard put to insist on self-support for their mission churches.

If Paul were among us today there is no question but that he would expect new churches to provide the financial basis for their own lives. I have already shown that financial independence is consistent with everything else that he taught about centering totally on the Spirit of God to lead and direct his people. I have also shown that Paul rejoiced when Christians shared with each other. When he himself was the recipient of a gift given in the name of the fellowship it was an ecstatic experience for him personally.[36] Many missionaries today are becoming more like Paul as he "worked with

35. Ibid., p. 84.
36. See, for example, Philippians 4:14-20.

his hands" to provide the basis of his own support.[37] One inconsistency in much of the teaching given about self-support is that it has come from missionaries who appear to have no inclination to adopt Paul's equally binding principle of "living as one of you," not taking anything for themselves. It will be consistent with Paul's own model when the worker for Christ can demonstrate before a new Christian church that he is prepared to live on the salaries that are available within his adopted country and adapt to lifestyles that are consistent with the economy of the people among whom he witnesses. When this is done we will be much closer to the scriptural model of Paul. It produces distorted results to insist on one feature of Paul's practice while ignoring another. The missionary must work carefully at minimizing the differences in economics and lifestyle between himself and the churches he serves. There are times when absolute self-support is the right path to follow. There are, however, other situations when funds from the parent mission agency and sending churches should be given with commitment and obvious love. This takes mature and mutual trust on the part of both the giver and the recipient. Money can hurt and cripple, but it can also build and bless. The perception on the part of the church to know when not to receive is as important as it is for the mission to know when to give and when to withhold.

37. For a description of self-support models in mission, see J. Christy Wilson, *Today's Tentmakers* (Wheaton, IL: Tyndale, 1979).

*Part Five*

# The Missionary

# 10

# The Missionary's Credentials and Ministry

We turn, finally, to the missionary himself. Any adequate understanding of the work that Paul did has to take into account the person that he was. Our focus, therefore, will be upon the role of the missionary as a person as he or she works among the churches. We will look at Paul the man, as he works out his approach to ministry, as he trains his coworkers, and as he faces his own personal struggles.

## The Missionary in Today's World

Effective mission work today makes many of the same demands upon the individual missionary as it did in Paul's day. There are still vast areas of the world, encompassing massive blocs of people, that remain unevangelized. Careful studies are being done year by year to locate these unreached peoples. Data are being gathered to help us discern those fields where the harvest is promising.[1] On the other hand, where once there were fledgling congregations now we find mature churches, capable of sustaining their own life and quite independent of the missionary presence. Western countries no longer have a monopoly on the cross-cultural mission enterprise. One of the most remarkable yet little-noticed developments in mission has been the formation of mission agencies by churches in the developing nations of the so-called Third World. In a recent study by Lawrence E. Keyes, "The New Age of Missions," we have solid data that indicate that by 1980 no less than 368 Third-World missionary agencies were vitally involved in

1. The most useful study is the annual series entitled *Unreached Peoples,* C. Peter Wagner and Edward R. Dayton, eds. (Elgin, IL: David C. Cook). This is published each year since 1979 as a joint project of the Strategy Working Group of the Lausanne Committee for World Evangelization and the MARC ministry of World Vision International.

cross-cultural ministry, primarily in evangelism. These agencies are directed by non-Western people, employ non-Western workers, and receive the majority of their funds from Third-World sources.[2] In other places, where Western missionaries have been working for years, national churches have matured to the level where they administer their own life. Trained pastors and dedicated lay people carry the total responsibility.

Looking at the complex world of today, we are forced to ask: What is the continuing role of the missionary? First, there is always a need to nurture and perfect those congregations that have been brought into existence. This demands a ministry that is fundamentally one of teaching and training. But there is also a continuing call for the evangelism of the world's peoples in response to Christ's command. This obligation is and always has been of the highest priority. To abandon the search for new fields or to say that overseas churches are to take up the task of evangelism by themselves is irresponsible. The twofold task of discipling (evangelism) and perfecting[3] has always been the mandate of mission and remains so today.

Where there is a strong national church, what is crucial is the ability of the missionary to work side by side with indigenous leaders in the training of others. Today's missionaries must assume the role of advisers rather than chief decisionmakers. They are to be the encouraging supporters of nationals who hold the posts once held by missionaries. They are to be culturally sensitive partners, flexible participants, effective producers, and positive promoters of the visions that the church espouses. This means missionaries will reflect the spirit of the servant rather than of the master. They will have a willingness to defer to colleagues in Christ who probably will see many things differently but who, at the same time, will welcome the counsel of a Christian partner from another culture, if that counsel is sensitively offered. We shall see that Paul provides us with a model for this perfecting role of the missionary.

If the work of supporting the already-established churches were found to be the only thing cross-cultural missionaries are supposed to do, the church might well relax and say that its missionary responsibility is being quite properly taken care of. Recent statistics produced by Ralph Winter of the

2. Lawrence E. Keyes, "The New Age of Missions: A Study of Third World Missionary Societies," unpublished dissertation, Fuller Theological Seminary (Pasadena, CA: School of World Mission, 1981). This lists twenty-two agencies in Africa, fourteen in Asia, sixteen in Latin America, six in Oceania, p. 79.

3. "Perfecting," distinguished from "discipling," includes what Donald A. McGavran calls "post-baptismal care." *Understanding Church Growth* (Grand Rapids: Eerdmans, 1970), p. 325. "Discipling" is generally the call to accept Christ as Lord, including baptism. Alan R. Tippett speaks of a "period of Decision" (discipling) and a "period of Incorporation," followed by maturation. *Verdict Theology in Mission Theory,* revised edition (Pasadena, CA: William Carey Library, 1973), pp. 123ff.

United States Center for World Mission show that no less than 91 percent of the missionaries from North America are working in various kinds of supportive roles in areas of the world where the church has already been established. Only 9 percent are attempting to reach those among whom there is no, or only minimal, Christian witness.[4] This fact alone highlights the need for a fresh and careful study of Paul's absolute loyalty to the call to preach the gospel "where Christ has not been named." In a world where, by any count, all Christians of whatever persuasion and of every variety account for but one-third of the population, we find ourselves as challenged to frontier mission thinking today as ever in the past. While our planning and approach must be guided by every piece of up-to-date data available to us, clearly the day of mission evangelism is by no means over.

Major blocs of the world population include the Chinese, who are approaching one-fourth of the world's people (903 million), the Muslims of Africa and Asia (800 million), Hindu peoples (575 million), other Asians (459 million), and many tribal societies (275 million). Among these major blocs it has been estimated that there are nearly 17 thousand identifiable people groups[5] who have no opportunity of hearing the gospel, since among them there is no culturally relevant church. Certainly Paul faithfully nurtured the churches that became established, but first and foremost he saw himself sent by God to the unevangelized people groups of the Gentile world.

## Paul's Personal Qualities As a Missionary

Let us take another look at this amazing man and try to bring together some of the significant features of his personality and history. Here is the most effective cross-cultural missionary the church has ever seen. What can we learn from this man that may apply to the servant role of the missionary who lives and witnesses among peoples of the world today?

### *Paul Was Called*

That God called Paul is like a steady light, keeping him fixed on the purpose of his conversion and providing throughout his writings the vindication of his authority. The call, which was first confirmed by Ananias, became ever clearer as Paul moved out on his missionary journeys. "Called

4. *The World in Missionary Perspective,* a study available from the United States Center for World Mission, 1605 E. Elizabeth St., Pasadena, CA 91104.

5. People groups are discussed at length in "The People Group Approach to World Evangelization" by C. Peter Wagner and Edward R. Dayton in *Unreached Peoples* (1981), pp. 19-35.

to be an apostle" is his special way of introducing himself (Rom. 1:1; I Cor. 1:1); his claim to apostleship was grounded on his call. Any missionary needs this sustaining confidence and driving conviction about his ministry. It is true that Paul had that unique and unforgettable experience when God's claims were solemnly laid on him. But the important thing is the fact of his call to the work of an apostle, not the manner of its discovery. "God was in Christ reconciling the world to himself. . . . *So we* are ambassadors for Christ, God making his appeal through us" (II Cor. 5:19-20, RSV; italics added). Even though he was set aside from his mother's womb to be a witness among the Gentiles (Gal. 1:15-16), yet only gradually did he come to a clear understanding of the work that God had for him to do (Acts 13:46; 18:6; 22:18-21; 26:12-18).

Paul's was a special calling: the call to be an apostle. The New Testament picture of an apostle is not one of office but of function. This involved the obligation to bring the message of life to people who had never heard. Paul, therefore, was careful not to build on another man's foundation (Rom. 15:20). His ambition was to be the first to arrive in a given place with the gospel of Christ (II Cor. 10:14-16) and this was a vision he never surrendered (Rom. 15:20). If Paul were among us today he would say that his calling to be an apostle would cease only when there were no more frontiers of unbelief to cross.

### *Paul Was Trained*

With all of his natural gifts and the charisma of his presence, Paul was also theologically prepared for his calling as an apostle. It was the superb background that he had as a Jew both in Tarsus and in Jerusalem under Gamaliel (Acts 22:3; Gal. 1:14) that stood him so well in his rigorous encounters with his own people. His conversion, as I have previously pointed out, turned all his past training in a new direction. Conversion, as Louis Berkhof points out, channeled all his past training into an effective ministry.

> His gifts and talents, his education, and the favorable circumstances in which he moved from his earliest years would never have qualified him to be a preacher of the Gospel of Jesus Christ if he had not experienced this inward change of heart. His light would have been darkness, his wisdom folly, his talents instruments of Satan, his guidance deception.[6]

Following his conversion, this highly trained and dynamic person went into seclusion and a period of apprenticeship. First was his quite mysterious stay in Arabia (Gal. 1:17), followed by the preliminary ministries at Tarsus and Antioch (Acts 11:25-26).

6. *Paul the Missionary* (Grand Rapids: Eerdmans-Sevensma, n.d.), p. 2.

What the stay in Arabia must have meant for Paul can be pieced together from the evidence and is more than conjecture. His conversion was a total reorientation. His intellectual life would have been thrown into confusion. He had been called to preach to the Gentiles but this would mean a reordering of his traditional theological priorities and a radical attitudinal shift. Arabia was contextually appropriate for this new thinking.

> How suitable the place for further instruction regarding the relation of the old to the new dispensation. . . . It was in the birth place of the old covenant that he pondered on its transient character. It was in the place where Moses spoke to God as a man with his friend, where Elijah heard the voice of God as he stood in the cave, that Paul now sought a new revelation.[7]

Paul rethought the whole question of the place of the law and came to see that the dispensation of promise had indeed replaced it. The question of circumcision seemed fully settled in his mind by the time he set out on the first missionary journey. He learned this, it would seem, during his early period at Tarsus and later at Antioch. There he encountered Greeks whose lives were changed by the power of the gospel, yet they were not circumcised. Here was a practical illustration of the insights he had received in Arabia. "He saw even clearer that old barriers had been broken down, that all the shadows had fled and that in Christ Jesus there was neither Jew nor Gentile but a new creature."[8]

To live and witness in cultures radically different from one's own is a test not only of commitment, but also of knowledge and openness. It takes only a little reflection to see that Paul had to be emotionally and mentally changed to face his apostolic task. And it was out of this process that the outlines of his doctrine began to emerge. Some theologians would call the result Paulinism. Paul did speak of the end product as "the gospel I preach" (Gal. 1:11). He said he "did not receive it from any man, nor did anyone teach it to me: (Gal. 1:12). He spoke confidently to the Ephesians of "my understanding of the secret of Christ" (Eph. 3:4). He invested years to allow his mind, soul, and spirit to become saturated with the implications of the new way and the meaning of the new truth—the universal plan of salvation. Joseph Holzner spoke of this rethinking as "the transmutation of his religious consciousness."

> Not that he had a Gospel essentially different from that of the other apostles . . . but he preached that Gospel with a greater insistence, with a more powerful persuasion, with a rhetorical force unlike any other, and he imprinted

7. Ibid., p. 19.
8. Ibid., p. 20.

on that Gospel his own distinct personality and carried it far out into the Hellenistic world.[9]

### *Paul Had Cross-cultural Gifts*

"The gift of missionary," says C. Peter Wagner, "is the special ability that God gives to some members of the Body of Christ to minister whatever other spiritual gifts they have in a second culture."[10] Anyone who has spent time living in another culture knows that there are various levels of ease of adaptation. Some people are never really able to accept the feeling of foreignness and the differences that are forced upon them. Such people tend to be frustrated at almost every turn and do not try to understand, much less utilize, the habits and the values of the indigenous people. Many missionaries who have been judged as failures would have been helped considerably by being trained in cross-cultural dynamics before they left for missionary service. Even so, it is not easy for this group to adapt. There are those, however, who do make the transition to another culture with relative ease; who not only accept the new culture but also appropriate it into their own living and find much satisfaction in identifying with it. Such persons often have a natural feeling for languages and are able to see things through a world view that is not their own.

One reason that mission work has frequently produced churches that not only look like churches at home, but also are run the same way as the home church, is the lack of cross-cultural gifts on the part of the missionaries. The indigenous people were a puzzle to culture-bound missionaries. They did not feel at home with all this foreignness and easily assumed that the church could not grow in such an environment. The natural thing, therefore, was to set up their own norms for what they felt was Christian. There seemed to be no need to look for ideas and symbols available in the new culture that could express truth in a contextual way. The result was that many things were introduced that were alien to the people but provided the missionary with a sense of security and well-being.

Paul was remarkably free from the bonds of Judaism, being able to readily adapt to and accept concepts and behavior patterns that were decidedly un-Jewish. True, he had an ideal upbringing, for while he was a strict Jew he was at the same time a Roman citizen and understood the cosmopolitan make-up of the Roman world. Tarsus, his hometown, was not only a crossroads for many ethnic groups but also a center for Greek learning.

9. *St. Paul the Apostle: His Life and Times,* William J. Doheny, CSC, trans. and rev. (Vatican City: Private distribution, 1978), p. 78.

10. *Your Spiritual Gifts Can Help Your Church Grow* (Glendale, CA: Regal, 1979), pp. 204, 263.

Surely all these providential circumstances began to make sense to him once he knew he was called to minister to the Gentile world. His call and then the years in preparation sharpened his cross-cultural senses and gave his whole life a new perspective. His many references to his ministry to the Gentiles are each a tacit statement of his ability to relate to the non-Jew. God used him and his gifts in a revolutionary way (Acts 14:27). The response he found confirmed to him that working outside of Judaism was indeed his ministry (Rom. 11:13) and that this ability to minister was nothing less than a grace given by God himself (Rom. 15:15-16).

The Judaizers tried to discount this gift, but after they followed him into Galatia Paul could say that at last "they saw that God had given me the task of preaching the gospel to the Gentiles, just as he had given Peter the task of preaching the gospel to the Jews" (Gal. 2:7). It is no wonder that Paul had little patience with Peter when he began to disassociate himself from the Gentiles at Antioch (Gal. 2:11-14). Peter had received a special vision in which God challenged his culture-bound personality and convictions. And even though this powerful lesson was followed by a divinely arranged visit to Cornelius the Gentile at his house, it was still very difficult for Peter to make the transition. Peter did not have the cross-cultural gift that Paul had.

### *Paul Had an Openness to Other Religions*

It would be a distortion to say of Paul that he allowed Judaism or the many varieties of Gentile paganism to erode his gospel. He was irrevocably committed to keeping the gospel pure and centered on Christ. Those who tried to weaken or change the teaching were dealt with severely (Gal. 1:8-9; 5:10). But the revolutionary thing about Paul was the way he learned from each particular group of people, which made it possible for him to address them through a basic understanding of their own frame of reference. He was an observer and a learner. He met people where they were religiously. He used the literature of the Greek poets in explaining Christian truth. He effectively used what appear to be Stoic expressions in his early confessional statements (Rom. 11:36; I Cor. 8:6; Eph. 4:6). References to the dark forces of evil and the powers that antagonize Christians were made using terms well known to the Gnostic system (Rom. 8:38-39; II Cor. 4:4). Paul used analogies from the Corinthian games in a way that would have been quite foreign to any Jewish teacher (I Cor. 9:23-27; Phil. 3:14; II Tim. 4:7). Adolf Deissmann comments on the openness of Paul:

> Unlike the small-minded dogmatic zealots, he did not hold that the heathen world was God-forsaken "Is He the God of the Jews only? Is He not also of the Gentiles? Yes of the Gentiles also" (Rom. 3:29). He finds amongst the heathen the unwritten law of conscience (Rom. 2:14). He attributes moral sense to

> them (I Cor. 5:1) and he read upon the altars of heathenism a dedicatory inscription which he interpreted as a longing cry after the One God (Acts 17:23).[11]

From my own experience, I recall that in my early years as a missionary I could not see that I needed to learn anything from animism or Islam. There was a finality about "my" religion that blurred my perception of any truth in "their" religion. I was preoccupied with the conviction that *"my* faith must become *their* faith." While this is the basic motivation in evangelism, it meant I was not open to *their* truth, and consequently little real understanding ever occurred between us. I was rushing in with my answers to their system; my answers raised in their minds many questions different from the ones I sought to answer.

The ability to study and in some measure understand a religion different from one's own is a fundamental prerequisite to communicating Christ. We cannot assume that as a religion Christianity has nothing to learn from other religions, or that non-Christians have nothing to teach a Christian. Hendrik Kraemer was always very careful to separate Christianity as an institutional system from Christianity as the life renewed by Christ. As an institution Christianity is imperfect, as are all other religions. Like others it is mixed with error and evil. When Kraemer said that Christianity is absolute, he did not mean that as a concrete historical phenomenon Christianity alone is true while all other religions are false. It is revelation, including Christ himself, that sets Christianity apart from all others, and in this sense only can we speak of Christianity as absolute. What is absolute about Christianity is therefore not of our own doing. "It is not a matter of clinging to Christianity but of clinging to Jesus Christ to whom Christianity is attached by indissoluable ties."[12]

### *Paul Was Innovative and Resourceful*

Paul was tirelessly creative and a disciplined steward of time. It is hard to imagine a circumstance that Paul did not utilize in some way to preach the Word of life. His worst discouragements came from factionalism in the churches and from that radical wing among the Jews that was determined to force Judaism on the Gentiles. The optimism, the steady hope, and the amazing resourcefulness of Paul's ministry stand out. He always seemed to be working under the pressure of limited time, making good use of every opportunity (Eph. 5:16). In his own words, "the night is nearly over, the day

11. *Paul,* W. E. Wilson, trans. (New York: Doran, 1926), p. 78.
12. Hendrik Kraemer, *Why Christianity of All the Religions?* (Philadelphia: Westminster, 1962), p. 116.

is almost here. Let us stop doing the things that belong to the dark, and let us take up weapons for fighting in the light" (Rom. 13:12). He was an example of his own words to the Corinthians to "keep busy always in your work for the Lord" (I Cor. 15:58). See him as he warns and teaches "with all possible wisdom . . . in order to bring each one into God's presence. . . . To get this done I toil and struggle, using the mighty strength which Christ supplies and which is at work in me" (Col. 1:28-29).

Paul could see God at work in everything; even adverse circumstances became the means of evangelizing. What else but the joy of witnessing would cause Paul and Silas to sing in prison at midnight (Acts 16:25)? While he was waiting for Silas and Timothy at Athens he was not idle. He used this opportunity to argue with the Jews in the synagogue and in the public square with whatever people happened to come by (Acts 17:16-17). He capitalized on very ordinary incidents to get a hearing. On one occasion he actually provoked dissension between Pharisees and Sadducees in order to make his point (Acts 23:6). He used the ordeal of the storm at sea and an impending shipwreck to give hope in the name of God (Acts 27:25). On the island of Malta, even though he was destitute and tired, Paul looked immediately for an opportunity to minister. He healed the father of Publius, the chief of the island, with the result that the island people crowded to Paul for healing (Acts 28:7-9). When he wrote from Rome it was obvious that he saw his imprisonment as something that really helped in the progress of the gospel (Phil. 1:12) and, ultimately, he saw his death as an offering for the glory of God (Phil. 2:17). The practical way in which he worked out the principle of "all things to all men" testifies to the flexibility that kept his mind always open, his convictions relevant, and his methods appropriate.

## The Missionary As a Teacher and Preacher

The proclaimer of truth must also be the teacher of truth. The ministries of preaching and teaching have always been distinguished one from the other, right from the time of the apostles and the spread of the church following Pentecost. Paul's public preaching is carefully summarized by Luke in a number of places in Acts, but Paul the teacher is more difficult to assess. We know from the record that he engaged extensively in teaching and also trained his colleagues to teach. Writing to Timothy, Paul refers to himself as both a teacher and a preacher. It would seem that here we have the dimensions of the apostleship: "To tell about it, I was appointed a preacher, apostle, and teacher" (II Tim. 1:11, *Beck*). I did not see my ministry to be that of a teacher until I began to serve the church in Africa. Previously it was preaching that I had felt was my special calling. But the situation of the church in Africa called for an additional teaching dimension to my ministry that I had not recognized before. The Spirit of God had been adding to the church daily. During the decade of the sixties the increase was so dramatic[13] that Christian nurture, adequate teaching, and the development of leadership became a major problem. Some have a special gift for preaching, others for teaching. But the model Paul gives is that the apostle must be ready to do both. Preaching and teaching combined in his case into a single powerful ministry. By preaching we mean the calling of people to accept Jesus Christ as Lord, while it is through teaching that they are shown what that gospel means as a body of truth and as a way of life.

### *The Teacher*

Among the changes that have shaped the role of the missionary in the last decade has been the growing need for the teaching ministry. People movements and rapid church growth can be conserved only if there is adequate teaching. Paul has not been fully appreciated for the teacher that he was. When his effectiveness as a teacher is recognized we can better understand why his converts were baptized so quickly and why he generated so many warm friends around him, many of whom were also good teachers. He taught everywhere (I Cor. 4:17) and he taught carefully (II Thess. 2:15).[14]

#### *Paul's aims as a teacher*

Paul's aim was that the new church should be brought to maturity, with each member becoming a well-rounded, Spirit-controlled Christian. It is as lives are Christ-centered that they become whole, so Paul's focus is always on Christ.[15] His aim was to see Christians develop into complete persons[16] having the same qualities that create a personal attractiveness and enhance the whole fellowship (Phil. 1:11; 4:8-9; Col. 3:12-14). Such Christ-centered living, Paul taught, will have its effect on the whole personality, its values and attitudes. By careful teaching and by the model of his own life, Paul kept pressing the church to understand this basic truth. His aim was maturity, completeness in the knowledge of Jesus Christ and what that means for the daily life (Eph. 4:13-15). He could say with confidence to the Ephesian elders, "You know that I did not hold back anything that would be of help to you as I preached and taught you in public and in your homes" (Acts 20:20). When it was impossible for Paul to instruct personally, his colleagues, equally committed to the teaching ministry, represented him. So he sent

13. From 1962 to 1968 the average annual net growth was 23 percent.

14. Howard Tillman Kuist, *The Pedagogy of St. Paul* (New York: Doran, 1925), pp. 136-137.

15. Romans 6:11; 13:14; Galatians 4:19-20; Colossians 1:27-28.

16. Galatians 2:20; 4:19; Colossians 1:27-28.

Timothy to Corinth where teaching was desperately needed. "Timothy," Paul said, "will remind you of the principles which I follow in the new life in Christ Jesus and which I teach in all the churches everywhere" (I Cor. 4:17).

Paul's aim was to bring the whole of life into balance. His teaching assumed a supreme loyalty to the person of Jesus, and from that Center life would be renewed and changed in every area. To be under this new lordship Paul saw as the way to be truly free. In his teaching Paul aimed for expression in life, not simply in belief. The teaching must have impact on behavior, so that Paul did not hesitate to insist on practical implications for everyday life. Howard Tillman Kuist of Princeton Theological Seminary carefully reviewed Paul's writings from the vantage point of his teaching skills.[17] He showed that Paul's teaching touched the emotional life: peace, love, affection, sympathy, compassion, kindness, and sincerity are some of the common expressions that characterize the growing Christian.[18] In addition, Paul did not forget the need for health and a strong physical body and insisted on discipline that would make the body a fit residence for the Spirit (Rom. 6:6, 12-13; I Cor. 6:13-20; I Thess. 5:23). The teacher actually healed people's bodies on several occasions (Acts 14:8-10; 16:16-18; 20:7-12; 28:7-9), and it should never be forgotten that one of Paul's closest companions was the beloved physician Luke. Again, the Christian is to be taught that the will must be energized. Paul's teachings were aimed at moving men to action,[19] and at the same time he sought to instill a firmness of will that would stand in the face of heresies and persecution. He cautioned Timothy: "Watch yourself and watch your teaching. Keep on doing these things, because, if you do, you will save both yourself and those who hear you" (I Tim. 4:16). Finally, Paul aimed also for a renewed mind. New ideals, changed attitudes, and a transformed outlook on the world are the ultimate proof of sound teaching. "Those who live as the Spirit tells them to, have their *minds* controlled by what the Spirit wants" (Rom. 8:5; italics added). Simply stated, "Your hearts and minds must be taught faithfully. They must be taught of Christ in such a way that from the reality of his presence the whole person is moved to change and maturity."[20] Paul's teaching aim is illustrated by Kuist (see Figure 5).[21]

17. See *The Pedagogy of St. Paul.*

18. Romans 5:5; Ephesians 3:17; Philippians 1:18; 2:1; 4:7; Colossians 3:11-12, 15; I Timothy 1:5.

19. I Corinthians 12:6; Ephesians 6:6-7; Philippians 2:12-13.

20. On "minds," see Romans 12:2-3; I Corinthians 2:16; Philippians 2:2, 5; Colossians 3:1-2; II Timothy 1:7.

21. See Kuist's discussion on maturity (*teleos*) in *The Pedagogy of St. Paul,* p. 65.

Figure 5

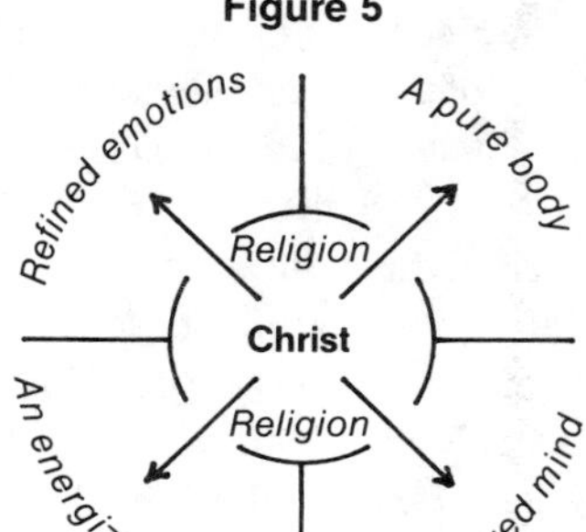


*The content of the teaching*

Paul's teaching cannot easily be separated from his preaching, and it is somewhat artificial to try to do this. Paul was a missionary in places where there had been no previous knowledge of the gospel, and was also the teaching pastor to those new congregations that needed to be built up in the faith and that sought answers for the many problems that arose. He was a teacher of basic truth. The content of his teaching (as well as his preaching) always was determined by two factors: how Christians must believe, and how they must act. First-generation Christians were faced with real dangers of three kinds.[22]

There was the danger of relapse or backsliding. For the Jews this meant easy slippage back into the law, which would deny their dependence on the work of God's grace. For the Jew and the Gentile alike there were the dangers of relapsing into a popular gnosticism or astrology. The "elemental spirits" (RSV) were a part of the old world view and Paul met the temptation head-on (Rom. 8:39; Gal. 4:3; Col. 2:20).

There was the danger of syncretism. The tendency to mix Jesus and what he taught with current religions was the usual way of handling any new religion. Exclusiveness in religion was something that the ancient world, with the exception of the Jews, could not understand.[23] To commit one's life to one Lord and to abandon all other lords was a new concept in the Gentile world (Col. 1:15-20).

There was the danger of perversion of the faith. For example, Paul struggled against those who thought that a religion of grace would allow for sinning without a bad conscience. Some had perverted the good news of grace to mean that if we sin, we are doing ourselves a favor, because the

22. From William Barclay, "A Comparison of Paul's Missionary Preaching and Preaching to the Church," in *Apostolic History and the Gospel,* Ward W. Gasque and Ralph P. Martin, eds. (Grand Rapids: Eerdmans, 1970), pp. 170-172.

23. Ibid., p. 171.

effect of sin is to produce more and more grace. This kind of distortion of the gospel is the background of Romans 6.

Paul constantly brought the believers back to the essentials of the faith through the letters he wrote. There is no way to understand the ethical and moral implications of the gospel unless the fundamentals of Christian truth are learned and learned well (Gal. 1:6-7; Col. 2:6-7). The new Christian finds himself in a life that is complicated by multiple choices, divided loyalties, and conflicting values. The teaching needs to be basic. It must drive home the fundamental facts of Jesus' life and teachings and what these mean for all Christians as the gospel crosses boundaries of culture.

An example of truth of first importance is summarized in Paul's First Epistle to the Thessalonians, one of his earliest letters, perhaps the first. Paul puts in writing what were obviously the main points of his teaching while he was with them. Here is a clear and coherent outline of his missionary teaching.[24]

1. There is one living and true God (1:9).
2. Idolatry is sinful and must be forsaken (1:9).
3. The wrath of God is ready to be revealed against the heathen for their impurity (4:6) and against the Jews for their rejection of Christ and opposition to the gospel (2:15-16).
4. The judgment will come suddenly and unexpectedly (5:2-3).
5. Jesus the Son of God (1:10), given over to death (5:10) and raised from the dead (4:14), is the Savior from the wrath of God (1:10).
6. The kingdom of Jesus is now set up and all men are invited to enter it (2:12).[25]
7. Those who believe and turn to God are now expecting the coming of the Savior who will return from heaven to receive them (1:10; 4:15-17).
8. Meanwhile their lives must be pure (4:1-8), useful (4:11-12), and watchful (5:4-5).
9. To that end, God has given his Holy Spirit (4:8; 5:19).

The missionary must be the teacher in today's world. Since the church has grown so rapidly in many areas, the discovery and training of leaders stands out as a primary task. As the church in Africa has matured over the

24. It is difficult to distinguish between preaching and teaching. Functionally, preaching is aimed at unbelievers and presses for decision, while teaching is the truth that is taught to believers. See Roland Allen, *Missionary Methods: St. Paul's or Ours?* (1912; reprint ed. London: World Dominion Press, 1960), p. 68.

25. Points 5 and 6 are the only elements in the list that C. H. Dodd cites as essential to the kerygma. This fact illustrates how much Paul taught beyond the basic facts of the apostolic preaching. See *The Apostolic Preaching* (New York: Harper, 1936), pp. 21-23.

last twenty-five years one of the remarkable changes has been to see the missionary move into the classroom to concentrate on teaching nationals who then take up the preaching task. Of course, the missionary preaches often, but in many parts of the world teaching is more fundamental to the missionary task than ever before.

### *The Preacher*

As a preacher Paul's hallmark was his ability to communicate dynamically and to press for a decision. The results of his preaching give irrefutable witness to its effectiveness. He referred to his preaching frequently and left no doubt that it is through preaching that people are turned to God or may be turned away from God (I Cor. 1:18-21). References to preaching occur fifty-three times in his epistles. Paul ranked the call to preaching at almost the same level as his apostleship (I Tim. 2:7; II Tim. 1:11). And doubtless the history of mission has been built on the preaching of God's word. Paul's exhortation to Timothy was simple and direct: "Preach the word" (II Tim. 4:2). The missionary still calls men and women to a decision and God is still pleased that by the "folly" of preaching people should be saved.

#### *Characteristics of Paul's preaching*

Communication as a preacher is something that Paul understood readily. When he spoke to the Greeks in Athens he never mentioned the Jewish Scriptures. "He knew it would be futile to talk about a history which no one knew and to quote from a book which no one had read and the authority of which no one would accept."[26] Instead he began from the terms of the local form of worship and quoted from the Greek poets (Acts 17:28). Apparently, as a Jew he was very much at home with the audience at Antioch of Pisidia, where he used the Old Testament as "an arsenal of proof texts to prove his case."[27] His audience at Antioch was instantly in touch with Jewish history and the Scriptures (Acts 13:16-41). This natural capacity to be in touch with the moment at hand was Paul's secret. His method and the content always go hand in hand. Lystra provides a classic example of a third kind of audience for which the preacher had to adjust his message (Acts 14:15-17). In Lystra, says William Barclay, Paul was "out in the wilds."[28] It is unlikely that anyone there would have known much about Jewish law or history. Lystra was also well away from Athenian culture, so there was no point in quoting Greek poets. The healing of the cripple had electrified the crowd; Barnabas and Paul were taken for gods and then Paul preached. What he did

26. Barclay, "A Comparison of Preaching," p. 166.
27. Ibid., p. 165.
28. Ibid., p. 166.

was to start straight from nature, "from the sun and the wind, the rain and the growing things."[29] It was a sermon that was captivating in its effect (Acts 14:18).

In short, Paul's preaching was receptor-oriented. Charles H. Kraft makes this a first principle if the preaching is going to have meaning and power.

> A receptor oriented communicator . . . is careful to bend every effort to meet his receptors where they are. He will choose topics that relate directly to the felt needs of the receptors. He will choose methods of presentation that are appealing to them, he will use language that is maximally intelligible to them.[30]

To be open to and guided by the context is very important in receptor-oriented preaching. The first characteristic that Roland Allen notes about Paul's approach is what he quaintly calls "conciliatoriness and sympathy with the condition of the hearers." He notes Paul's "readiness to recognize all that is good in them and in their doctrine, sympathy with their difficulties and care to make the way for them as plain and simple as possible."[31] Allen then calls attention to Paul's courage, that is, an awareness and open acknowledgment of difficulties that cannot be avoided, coupled with a commitment to speak the truth.

> There is no attempt to keep the door open by partial statements, no concealment of the real issue and all that it involved, no timid fear of giving offense, no suggestion of possible compromise, no attempt to make things really difficult appear easy.[32]

The third characteristic is simple respect. This is respect at a deep level. Paul does not condemn his hearers for their own religious views but builds on the assumption that they are religious people, conscious of spiritual realities and spiritual needs. He approaches this spiritual awareness with a message that is profoundly suitable, yet, fourthly, with an "unhesitating confidence in the truth of his message and in its power to meet and satisfy the spiritual needs of men."[33]

29. Charles H. Kraft, *Communicating the Gospel God's Way* (Pasadena, CA: William Carey Library, n.d.). Originally published as volume 12, number 14 of the *Ashland Theological Bulletin,* spring 1979, p. 7.

30. Ibid.

31. *Missionary Methods,* pp. 63-64.

32. Ibid., p. 64.

33. Ibid.

*The content of the preaching*

The temptation here would be to analyze in detail how Paul modeled what missionary preaching is, but this has been done by others, notably C. H. Dodd and Barclay.[34] Certain basic principles, however, must be taken into account.

Paul's preaching shows a remarkable ability to keep in place the central truths of the gospel (kerygma) while the more secondary features of the message are suited to the context. The essence of Paul's gospel concerns equally the cross and the empty tomb. The emphasis on the death of Christ that appears throughout the epistles assumes that a considerable amount of preaching and teaching on the life of Jesus has already taken place. Most of what Paul writes about Jesus appeals to facts that Christians have already been given about him. The actual proof of Jesus' messiahship would have been in the fulfillment of Old Testament prophecy by the events of his life.

Except for the resurrection, no theme is more prominent than Jesus' death. References to the cross are abundant in Paul's letters. Jesus' death must have been eloquently preached. To the Galatians he wrote, "Who put a spell on you? Before your very eyes you had a clear description of the death of Jesus Christ on the cross!" (Gal. 3:1). Speaking of the so-called foolish message that he preached, Paul said he did not indulge in miracles or wisdom, because "we proclaim the crucified Christ" (I Cor. 1:23).[35]

Paul's preaching in the synagogues and also to some extent before Gentile audiences reveals six features that I see as essential to missionary preaching.

There is an appeal to history, to the past, bringing the hearers' minds into focus and thereby gaining their interest. Paul's theme is that God has already been at work in history. This note of a familiar past prepares the way for what will follow. But it is of first importance to Paul to gain the approval of his hearers.[36]

Following this are the basic facts of the message, the story of Jesus simply and objectively told. It is a story of a divine life and death, of the man who lived on this earth and was in touch with all the pain common to man. These concrete facts bring men and women into a new situation requiring a definite response.[37]

The coming of Jesus brings an amazing offer to people: the promise of a salvation that includes forgiveness and freedom. These precious gifts are found nowhere except through Christ.[38]

34. Dodd, *The Apostolic Preaching;* Barclay, "A Comparison of Preaching."

35. Other references are I Corinthians 2:2; 5:3; Galatians 3:13; 5:11; 6:14; Ephesians 2:16; Philippians 2:8; Colossians 1:20; I Thessalonians 2:15.

36. Acts 13:16-23; 17:26-28.

37. Acts 14:16; 17:30.

38. Acts 13:23, 32, 38-39.

Yet it is a matter of record that the Jews rejected this offer and ordered Jesus' death; so he was crucified and buried. Let everyone be warned by this act of rejection.

The good news is that his rejection and death were turned into victory through the resurrection, which not only had been foretold in the Scriptures, but also has the evidence of the apostles who witnessed it.[39]

The final word is a call to repentance and a grave warning. The invitation to salvation may be refused, but to refuse carries great danger, since the resurrection has given Jesus the right of final judgment. If the offer of salvation is rejected, man is bringing judgment and destruction upon himself.[40]

In summary we may say that Paul's missionary preaching, regardless of the cultural situation, models for us three dimensions of appeal. Paul says first, Consider the past. The hearer's own religion is put before him and this represents a major part of the appeal. Paul thus calls attention to the one true God who has always been revealing his goodness to men. Next, consider the present. Here is a new set of facts. They center on Jesus, sent by God into the hearer's own history. The messenger (Paul) stands before them in present time as the bearer of good news. Third, consider your future. You who hear must make a response. This Jesus is alive and will someday judge the way a person chooses in light of the resurrection message.[41]

These dimensions of the message are filled out with appropriate symbols, language, and references to things that are familiar, but it is always the Good News presented in the historical frame of reference with a spiritual message and with an imperative purpose. In this way Paul always places his hearers right in the stream of an ongoing salvation history.

## Paul's Convictions about the Missionary Role

The way in which the missionary works depends very much on the state of the church where he goes (if indeed, there is a church) and how that church relates to the world around it. In many places that were formerly frontier stations we now find strong churches that have developed their own administration and leadership. The missionary ministry is one of training, edifying, and nurturing. While opportunities for primary evangelism remain the responsibility of the whole church worldwide, such new ventures should be undertaken alongside of an indigenous church wherever possible.

39. Acts 13:31, 34-37.
40. Acts 13:34-37, 40-41; 17:31.
41. I credit my teaching assistant, Brian D. Woodford, for the insights of this paragraph.

The current development and coming to maturity of once-weak and untrained churches means an important shift in the missionary's role.[42]

Paul primarily planted churches but he also took seriously the need for the nurturing (watering) of these churches. Both are valid missionary functions, and both are equally important and illustrate how the missionary fits into the life of the mission church today. We want to look at the ways Paul worked out his own relationship with the churches he founded, how he provided for a support ministry through his associates, how he viewed himself as a person, and how he conducted himself under stress. While today's mission is much different from Paul's in many ways, the principles that motivated and guided him are still urgently applicable.

### *Paul Granted Freedom to the Churches*

This principle of giving the churches the right to determine their own life has already been touched upon. Admittedly, the style of Paul's work as the itinerating evangelist made it much easier for him to encourage the churches to take responsibility for their own life from the beginning. He did not set up a headquarters for a mission agency, live on a mission station, build buildings of any kind, or draw up ten-year plans that would lock him into a place. It would be much easier for the modern missionary to encourage self-development if the faults of recent history were not so obvious. In most cases we must first hand over physical property and reconstitute administrative policies that have been mission-fashioned and mission-dominated for many years. With Paul, authority for the day-to-day progress of the church was given to the churches themselves, immediately. As he moved from one place to another he insisted that Christians pledge their loyalties to local leaders. "I beg you, my brothers, to follow the leadership of such people as these [Stephanus], and of anyone else who works and serves with them" (I Cor. 16:15-16).[43]

Paul exercised careful restraint, resisting the temptation to give in to his feelings and put things right without first honoring the system that he had established. When there was serious tension between himself and the church at Corinth he held back from making a personal visit to try to settle the problem. He was candid about the reason for this. "We are not trying to dictate to you what you must believe; we know that you stand firm in the faith. Instead, we are working with you for your own happiness" (II Cor. 1:24). Paul's commitment to the right and the freedom of the churches to settle their own problems and his promise to support them is illustrated in

42. See Melvin L. Hodges, *The Indigenous Church and the Missionary: A Sequel to "The Indigenous Church"* (Pasadena, CA: William Carey Library, 1978).

43. See also I Thessalonians 5:12-13.

the way in which he was able to put the Corinthian case behind him. He recognized the judgment of the Christians at Corinth. "When you forgive someone for what he has done," he wrote, "I forgive him too" (II Cor. 2:10). And that, for him, was the end of the matter.

Control by missionaries, even where churches have been planted for many years, is still a problem that we must face honestly and objectively. Where the mission is no longer in direct control, still the power to decide and administer may remain in the hands of missionaries. This may come through funding of various kinds, gifts with strings attached, or through other means, such as selecting certain indigenous leaders who are "captive" to the missionary. In 1978 I heard a home executive of a mission board say in public that further financial aid to a certain church in Africa should be suspended until the male-dominated church there shows it is serious about the place of women in the church structure! An even more deceptive form of using power is the pressure of Western culture on the church through forms and administrative systems that are alien.

Every case of mission-church relationship will be different, but in our day the principle of freedom for the churches has urgent and universal application. Paul expected the elders to rule. He, the missionary, declined to exercise this right, although as an apostle he might have claimed it. "He scarcely ever lays down the law" says Allen, "preferring doubt and strife to an enforced obedience to a rule."[44] This indirect relationship was not abandonment. It was creative trust, which resulted in strong churches. This gave Paul the freedom to press on in evangelism, which, after all, was his first and highest calling (Rom. 15:20; I Cor. 1:17; 3:10).

### *Paul Made Use of His Friends*

Paul always worked with friends and kept his associates close to him. It was a rare occasion to find Paul alone and this would be when he had temporarily left a companion or was waiting for one to join him. Paul seems to have been a gregarious person by nature. He used his friends in a variety of ways to advance the cause of Christ. While his first companion, Barnabas, was at least his equal in authority, his other associates were subordinate to him. Some were closer than others and the impression is given of a certain ranking through function. These were team members, partners, and companions.

It would be impossible for Paul to think of a missionary working alone. It takes little imagination to see Paul and his friends praying, studying, planning, traveling, always together. The impact on the people was of a unit, of people witnessing together. He reminded his churches of this when he wrote to

44. *Missionary Methods,* p. 112.

them. The gospel was always a joint effort. It was the Good News that he brought (I Thess. 1:5). It was God who gave them courage to tell the Good News (I Thess. 2:2).

The list of those who helped Paul in such a variety of ways is a long one.[45] He obviously held these friends in high regard. No one was unimportant to him and "he was fond of coining expressive names full of personal feeling for these helpers."[46] He called a number of people, such as Timothy, Tychicus, Titus, Silvanus, Aquila and Priscilla, Urbanus, Epaphroditus, Euodia, Syntyche, Aristarchus, and others (I Cor. 3:9; Phil. 2:25; 4:2-3), "fellow workers." Or, aware of the spiritual battle, he called them "fellow soldiers" (Phil. 2:25; Philem. 2). Using a rougher metaphor, he spoke of them as "yokefellows" (Phil. 4:3, RSV), as he saw the gospel ministry as a matter of obedience and hard work (I Cor. 9:9-10; I Tim. 5:17-18). Aristarchus, with whom he was imprisoned, Paul called a "fellow captive" (Col. 4:10), a term he also used of Epaphras (Col. 4:12), Andronicus, and Junias (Rom. 16:7). Women were noticeably singled out as he recognized his friends. Phoebe was remembered as a "good friend" (Rom. 16:2) and the mother of his friend Rufus, he said, "has always treated me like a son" (Rom. 16:13). Paul honored his friends for the way they stood by him in his ministry. Donald A. McGavran takes note of these friends and the wider communities of people that they represent. Through them Paul came to know "scores of communities in which the Gospel would be heartily welcomed."[47] It is through these firm friends in the gospel that the work spreads out.

> Paul is simply the greatest among a host of witnesses, all moving within the bond of relationship to bring their kinsmen to the Christian faith . . . without the people movement we have Paul of the silent years, with it we have Paul the great missionary.[48]

The most important new method in Paul's mission was the way in which his associates joined both Paul and each other to form mobile missionary teams. This approach to mission work began of course at Antioch when the Holy Spirit directed the church there to "set apart for me Barnabas and Saul, to do the work to which I have called them" (Acts 13:2). References to these teams can be discovered all through the Book of Acts. Paul needed his associates and he used them in ways that best fitted their gifts. Of seven missionary teams, all except one were teams organized and supervised by Paul.[49]

45. For example, see Romans 16:2-3, 22; Philippians 2:19, 22; 4:3; Colossians 4:7-8, 17; II Timothy 4:11; Titus 3:13; Philemon 22.

46. Deissmann, *Paul,* p. 240.

47. *Bridges of God* (New York: Friendship Press, 1955), p. 28.

48. Ibid., p. 30.

49. The team of Barnabas and Mark is the exception. See the article by Edward F. Murphy,

This method gave a corporate and visible picture of the church in action. The group can better invite people to join it as a microchurch. The converts then will be joining not Paul but a community (Acts 17:4).

Paul needed companionship. This was a need for him personally, but he also felt that converts should understand from the beginning how much they mean to each other. His affection for his friends taught a basic principle of the new life and what people mean to one another in Christ (Col. 4:7, 9).

The whole group gave a balanced picture of what the gospel is. Paul's main gift was preaching, but this alone could distort the pastoral and the caring aspects of the church. When Paul was unable to continue his preaching, as in Thessalonica, Silas and Timothy stayed on and were able to consolidate work that otherwise might have been lost.[50]

Paul's traveling team served as a training school for those who joined him in the work. Just as Paul had been an apprentice under Barnabas, so those who joined Paul received the same kind of in-service training. He drew the best out of Titus and Timothy, helping them to see their strengths and weaknesses while in service, with Paul's firm support (I Cor. 16:10-11).

So, with his friends, Paul demonstrated the value of the team approach to mission. Together they demonstrated the church to be a caring and witnessing community. Here was a training school, a miniature church, as well as a mutual support group, committed to the leader Paul and to the church that "sent them off."

### *Paul Practiced Firmness Based on Truth*

All that has been said on the subject of Paul's flexibility and sensitivity to the context does not mean that he did not take a position on issues or that he was ambiguous about the truth. As a missionary, he distinguished between the secondary problems that could be settled locally and the matters that were fundamental, concerning the character of the church and how her members should live. Paul's firmness, which he revealed consistently, was shown toward issues of the first magnitude, the resolution of which would be binding on all churches. His rebuke to Peter was necessary because of his teaching about the church as one body. The stern attitude that Paul took toward the Judaizers throughout the entire Book of Galatians or the way in which he refused to have his apostleship demeaned (II Cor. 10-12) are examples of his judgment on error in the church, and would apply everywhere. There was no compromising once he was convinced he was on the

---

"The Missionary Society is an Apostolic Team," *Missiology,* vol. 4, no. 1 (January 1976), pp. 103-118, in which Murphy identifies eleven teams in the Book of Acts.

50. See Joseph A. Grassi, *A World to Win* (New York: Maryknoll, 1965), pp. 74-76.

side of truth. These qualities stand out in the way he dealt with difficult issues.

*Paul dealt with problems firmly and openly*

There is no hedging or double-dealing where the truth is at stake. His arguments are directed at the whole body and are always based on teaching that the church already has. On the issue of fornication among the Christians at Thessalonica (I Thess. 4:1-8) he reminds his readers of his personal teaching while he was with them. He suggests that there should be a difference between the conduct of the Christian and that of the Gentiles who do not know God. But his final word is that the Lord will avenge these misdeeds. Reference has been made to the various problems at Corinth. On the matter of divisions and party spirit, the Corinthians are reminded of the foundation of the church, which is the message of the crucified Christ (I Cor. 2:1ff.; 3:11). Paul appeals often to the authentic apostolic tradition that they knew and builds his arguments on this. His teaching was received directly from the Lord (I Cor. 11:23) and the advice he gave was not his but the Lord's own command (I Cor. 7:10; 14:37). When the cross-cultural missionary is convinced that the issues at stake are basic, unchanging, and universal truths, there is no course to take but a solid stand. This can mean pain, even alienation, for the missionary, as it did for Paul, but for the sake of the gospel there is no other way. But the matter at hand must be an essential one and not a peripheral matter in which authoritarian answers may easily lead into a form of legalism, defeating the right of the Holy Spirit to move his church.

*Paul did not rely on just one method*

Paul shows us how to be resourceful while exercising patience. His strong actions were not taken on impulse, nor did he insist on one approach. He was ready to move in several different ways to find a solution. The Corinthian dilemma is again an example of the variety of ways in which he approached a situation—aiming always for a solution and not giving up until the solution came. When the trouble got to a point where his letter did no good, he made a quick trip from Ephesus across the Aegean Sea (II Cor. 2:1). The hope, of course, was that by seeing him personally, the Christians would also see their error. But instead, the church rebuffed him and he remembered that attempt as his "painful visit." Back at Ephesus he wrote another letter, which became a vigorous, almost bitter, self-defense (II Cor. 2:4; 7:8).[51] This time Paul sent his friend Titus as a mediator. For the moment the missionary stepped aside, admitted his inability to handle the problem, and gave it to someone who was respected by both Paul and the

51. The letter itself is generally assumed to be contained in II Corinthians 10-13.

church. Titus was able to resolve the issue amicably and Paul could respond afterward with the "thankful letter" (II Cor. 7:6ff.), which opened the way for a peaceful third visit (II Cor. 12:14; 13:2).[52]

The missionary must be very sure all factors have been carefully examined, and that he is on the side of truth. It is too easy to be drawn into factions or be short-sighted when working among people who are not of one's own culture. When there has been openness in seeking the right solution, the missionary needs to follow the example of Paul and hold on faithfully, looking for more than one approach until a satisfactory conclusion can be reached.

### *Paul Had to Face Criticism*

Paul did not attempt to cover up his humanness. He felt things very deeply. He was hurt by unfaithful friends and could become indignant over attacks made on him and his gospel. He could not separate himself from his apostolic mission. These two things—his person and the apostolate—were identical in Paul's mind. "The integrity of his apostolic commission and the truth of his Gospel were inseparable," notes Calvin J. Roetzel.[53] Paul found it hard to take taunts and defamation because he felt the dignity of the gospel was at stake. An attack on himself, Paul felt, was an attack on Christ. Words of self-defense were flung at his detractors in what was possibly his earliest letter. In almost threatening language he said to the Judaistic troublemakers in the Galatian churches, "Let no one give me any more trouble, because the scars I have on my body show that I am a slave of Jesus" (Gal. 6:17).

In sections of II Corinthians (chaps. 10-13) we find some of the harshest words that Paul ever wrote and that reveal a hurt and discouraged missionary. While obviously his personal feelings were involved, the principal purpose in writing was to end these attacks, silence his opponents, and defend the apostolate.

> The chief weapon employed by his enemies was the argument that his sufferings, persecutions, and even his scars deprived him of apostolic dignity. Paul snatched this weapon from their hands and used his sufferings as the great proof and glorification of his apostolic work.[54]

Looking carefully at the text, it is remarkable that much of the basis for the attack against Paul concerns mundane things having to do with his physical appearance or his personality. Paul responds as a totally believable

52. See Calvin J. Roetzel, *The Letters of Paul: Conversations in Context* (Atlanta: John Knox, 1975).

53. Ibid., p. 55.

54. Holzner, *St. Paul the Apostle,* p. 334.

human being. The charges were serious and because he was absent they must have seemed all the more damaging. From Paul's response we can discover eight different points of attack.[55]

He was accused of being a poor, amateurish speaker (II Cor. 11:6). Because he spent most of his time preaching, this criticism would have hurt him.

He was represented as a deceiver (II Cor. 11:7-11). His willingness to earn his own living was misunderstood and then used against him. Nothing destroys fellowship as does animosity that centers on finance.

His apostleship was challenged and even ridiculed (II Cor. 11:12-13; 12:11-12). This seems to have been the point on which Paul was most vulnerable. He seems never to have satisfactorily convinced his opponents that he had the rank of those "other apostles." His detractors were suspicious of his credentials.

His illness was taken to be a weakness (II Cor. 12:7-9). He had to explain his problem. His enemies perhaps implied that God's power was not with him, or that such a weakling did not qualify to be an apostle.

He was accused of taking advantage of other people (II Cor. 12:16-18). His motives were misrepresented. He was characterized as a slick pragmatist who trapped people with his lies.

He was labeled as hypocritical and inconsistent (II Cor. 10:1, 10). He is portrayed as unable to stand up to people face to face but as having excessive courage and unjustified boldness with people who responded to him from afar.

He was pictured as worldly and foolish (II Cor. 10:2; 11:6). This was what he would never want to be as an apostle. How distorted things had become!

He had to prepare for a court case against him (II Cor. 13:1). The situation had deteriorated so much that it seemed only a public hearing could straighten things out. Could anything have been more painful, more devastating to the missionary's spirit?

Paul was human, of course. There were qualities about him that some would not have appreciated. For one who was convinced of the importance of the gospel rather than his own reputation, he seems overly sensitive about personal slanders. But it is the authentic human response that endears Paul to us. Neither physically nor emotionally was he without his flaws and foibles.

The missionary who works under criticism, being misunderstood or even defamed, can take direction and comfort from Paul, so long as truth and love

55. Helpful insights into the relational problems of Paul are found in Ernest Dobschutz, *Christian Life in the Primitive Church,* G. Brammer and W. D. Morrison, trans. (London: William Norgate, 1909), pp. 76ff.

have been allowed to govern the missionary's motives. The author once arrived at a mission station to find a missionary and his wife who had packed their bags and were in the process of arranging transport for a final journey home. They were discouraged to the point of failure. Most of what had happened had to do with unfair criticism that had been leveled against them by the leaders of the African church. Broken in spirit and feeling weak physically, they had decided to return home. After urging them to give the situation a little time, I called in others to listen to their story, and finally African leaders were asked to join in the discussion. As the story unfolded it became clear that there was blame on both sides. In their demoralized mental state it had been easy for the missionaries to say and do wrong things. This had caused alienation, which further compounded their loneliness. But with the help of friends, and much patience and prayer, the situation was resolved and reconciliation took place.

In that critical situation I have just discussed, Paul's confrontation with his critics at Corinth was one of the Scriptures we studied. Understanding Paul's anguish, his anger, and yet his deep love for the Christians at Corinth ministered in a redemptive way to the couple concerned. Seeing Paul's authentic response enabled those modern missionaries to face their own problems without feelings of guilt. There is scarcely a cross-cultural apostle in our day who will not have these difficult experiences to some degree. When such times come we can thank Paul for the honest, persistent way in which he dealt with his own difficulties and kept his love for the church intact.

## Strategy in Paul's Ministry

### *Did Paul Have a Strategy?*

Our question is: Did Paul consciously develop and plan for reaching the great masses and varieties of people in the Roman world, or was the situation of the day so perfectly suited for the spread of the gospel that it extended and took root naturally? Louis Berkhof feels that the main cause for the success of Christianity is to be found in its intrinsic excellence and in its remarkable relevance to the situation at the time of the Roman Empire.

> The Christian religion is a religion adapted to all nations and races and classes; it changes the entire life of a man, elevating the women, ameliorating the condition of the poor, and binding hearts together in holy love.[56]

56. *Paul the Missionary,* p. 23.

Certainly the very power of the gospel itself took over the lives of people as no religion had before. Supporting the life-altering message was the witness of Old Testament prophecies, the unity and the order of the Roman Empire, and the spread of the Greek language in the time of Christ. The greatest days of the Roman Empire had passed and a sense of uncertainty increased the attractiveness of the gospel.[57]

However, Berkhof goes on to show that the seed was also wisely distributed. It was not without planning or attention to detail that the churches in Asia and Europe were born. It takes nothing away from the work of God's Spirit to say that Paul developed a definite missionary style. The term *strategy* has been borrowed from the vocabulary of war. Strategy has to do with the conception of a plan before the campaign and its modification as the war progresses. The parallel is obvious, for the apostle was himself contending in a battle, not with flesh and blood, but against "the wicked spiritual forces in the heavenly world, the rulers, authorities, and cosmic powers of this dark age" (Eph. 6:10). Evangelism for him was spiritual warfare.

Some would prefer to say that evangelization is so much the work of God and his Spirit that to speak of strategy lays too much emphasis on the human component. All that we have been studying indeed shows that the entire life and work of Paul were the expression of God's power. But does this mean Paul worked without goals, plans, and a deliberate style? Berkhof asks, "Did he simply cast himself on the turbulent waves, the surging sea of humanity to have them bear him whither they would: to a sandy reef, to a rock bound place, or to a fertile land of promise?"[58] We would have to say no. This is not what it means to be directed by the Spirit.

More than once Paul's plans did not coincide with the divine plan of God (Acts 16:7; Rom. 15:22). But such conflicts only serve to show that his own designs were adaptable to the higher mind of the Spirit. It does not mean that he did no planning—where he would visit, how he would make his first contacts, or how he would communicate in a given place. To all these things Paul gave careful attention, but God had the final say. Berkhof feels it is more accurate to speak of a strategic element in Paul's ministry, because his work was not always of his own choosing. This sensitive combination of the human and the divine could be described as the miracle of mission.

### *General Features of Paul's Missionary Strategy*

Paul was first and foremost a planter of churches. Both in the sowing of the seed and in the nurture of the churches Paul involved a great number of people with him, and he modeled for them how the work of church planting

57. Ibid.
58. Ibid., p. 26.

was to be carried out. There are at least six general characteristics of his ministry.

*Paul's ministry was fraternal in spirit*

As we have seen, Paul's friends were precious to him and wherever people believed on the Lord Jesus Christ he cultivated their friendship. Of course Paul was working in a world where the racial distinctions were not so radical as they are today, but we note that all Christians, regardless of their place of origin, were his *brothers*.[59] This is how he addressed them, not as "the natives" or as "converts."[60] To speak of someone as a brother was common among the Jews (Acts 22:1; 23:5, RSV; Rom. 9:3, RSV), but Paul had no second thoughts about using such a special, intimate term even when he addressed Gentile believers. From the start, when he planned to revisit the Christians in Galatia, he said, "Let us go back and visit *our brothers* in every town where we preached the word of the Lord, and let us find out how they are getting along" (Acts 15:36; italics added). In the epistles to the Thessalonians alone, there are twenty-eight references to "brothers."[61] Some of the Thessalonians' conduct was such that we might not have wanted to think of them as brothers, but this was not so with Paul. This reflects the deep concern, the sense of responsibility and love Paul had for all those who share the Spirit of Christ regardless of their origin or background.

*The note of authority and domination was not present*

This is a characteristic of Paul that Allen emphasized again and again.[62] The missionary life becomes too easily a "power trip." Nothing is more tempting than to assume power among those who seem to be powerless. This is not to say that indigenous religion has absolutely no answers for meeting crucial needs, but the word of truth is even more "quick and powerful"; it has power to change all of life, and it is in the hand and the mouth of the messenger. To resist the tendency to become an authoritative, dominating person in many mission situations is something we have to work at constantly.

Paul's ministry on his journeys involved a combination of telling the Good News for the first time and visiting the believers in each place. His aim was to confirm, encourage, and strengthen the fellowship (Acts 15:36, 41; 16:5). It was not to rebuke or to show his authority or to have his personal way. It is unfair to Paul to picture him as a stern man who had no feeling for the deep needs of people. The Corinthians admitted that he was humble when he was with them (II Cor. 10:1). He was careful not to give "commands,"

59. See Acts 16:40; 17:6, 10; 18:18; 21:7; 28:14-15.
60. Robert E. Speer, *Missionary Principles and Practice* (New York: Revell, 1902), pp. 267ff.
61. Grassi, *A World to Win*, p. 159.
62. *Missionary Methods*, pp. 111-125.

and when he was not sure, he admitted it (II Cor. 8:8). He "urge[d]" (Eph. 4:1), "appealed" (Rom. 12:1), "beg[ged]" (II Cor. 2:8; 4:16), and had expectations (II Cor. 6:1). He saw himself and his team as those who nurture and strengthen the saints (Acts 20:18-19; 22; Col. 2:1-2; 4:8).

*There was no needless haste*

Paul's plans could be changed. He had the advantage of not being tied to an institution, a mission station, or a family. But it is his flexibility, his readiness to make changes as the mission developed that is so characteristic of Paul. It seems he was always traveling from one place to another, but the willingness to take the time needed at any one place is also very much part of Paul's method. Robert E. Speer notes that "when the tour developed beyond its original purpose and became not a revisitation but an opening up of new fields Paul did not hurry."[63] He could shift his plans to remain in Philippi when he originally had wanted to go to Bithynia (Acts 16:6-10). He had time to stay at Lydia's house for a few days (Acts 16:15). He stayed eighteen months in Corinth because he saw the great awakening of the church to the Word (Acts 18:11). It is possible that his friendship with Aquila and Priscilla developed into a team relationship there and he needed time for this (Acts 18:18). He planned a detour to visit Jerusalem on his way to Antioch (Acts 18:22). In Ephesus Paul's stay was unusual, as after a successful three months of teaching in the synagogue he remained, teaching and evangelizing the province of Asia (Acts 19:8-10), for two years.

If anything is needed in modern mission, it is a willingness to be flexible, to have the gift of time to take opportunities to cultivate friendships. It takes time to know the people and to learn the culture well. It takes time to do the extra things that build bonds of love and respect between the missionary and the people. Rushing about with everything settled and sealed—efficiency without warmth, motivated by goals rather than people—this too easily can become the style of the missionary.

*Paul made first contacts in the synagogue*

In 1955, McGavran showed how very strategic the synagogues became for Paul as the natural center for the teaching of the Good News. Here were "Jews of the Hebrew race, Jews of the Greek race and a fringe of unbelieving but uncircumcised Greeks."[64] Richard R. De Ridder takes note of the diverse kinds of people who attended the synagogue. There were those who wanted to know more about "this strange people [the Jews] and their singularly different faith."[65] Some of the Gentiles who attended the synagogues rejected

63. *Missionary Principles,* p. 268.
64. *Bridges for God,* p. 32.
65. *Discipling the Nations* (1971; reprint ed. Grand Rapids: Baker, 1979), p. 88.

the faith of the Jews, while others were true believers of Jewish ideas and customs. They were "the partly informed and the partly persuaded among whom were the open-minded and the willing-hearted."[66] It is very likely that this group of persons provided the fertile soil for the sowing of the gospel.

What this highlights is that Paul had, as his overriding purpose, the communication of the gospel to those who were most ready to receive it, and he was committed to finding the means and the method that would turn their inquiry into saving faith. In the synagogues he could ground his message in the Jewish tradition and Scriptures while reaching the borderline Gentile enquirers. Paul never wavered from his apostolic call to the Gentiles. "The intentional missionary labors of the church, headed by Paul, were devoted in large measure deliberately to following responsible people and to expanding existing impulses to Christ in the hearts of peoples."[67]

*Paul went first to the urban centers*

One of the most obvious features of Paul's work was his emphasis on the cities. The narrative of Acts tells of an exciting series of events that took place in some of the most important centers of Paul's day. It was obviously not accidental that places such as Antioch, Corinth, Ephesus, Philippi, and Thessalonica became vital communities of the early church. The risks of evangelizing in the cities were always present. There evil was concentrated and many special-interest groups competed. There was always a close tie-in of vested interest with politics. The people often seemed to be on the brink of some kind of mass hysteria or mob violence. But what was more important to Paul was that in the cities he found the greatest concentration of people. More people could be reached in a shorter period of time in the city than anywhere else. The cities provided the best facilities for mass communication. Here were the libraries and the scholarly communities. Here lived the potential leaders. Here in the city, says Chalmer Faw, "in spite of the tangled nature of urban life the church can make its impact felt and help change the course of society."[68]

Paul chose his cities carefully. They all were places of importance, places where diverse ethnic groups traveled and intermingled. Consider Pisidian Antioch, for example. It was the center of a Roman *regio* (region) and the administrative and military headquarters for an even larger territory. People were constantly on the move. It is not surprising therefore, that the result of Paul's work in that city was that "the word of the Lord spread everywhere in that region" (Acts 13:49). Paul usually chose cities where there were synagogues, for, as we have seen, these provided his most productive first con-

66. F. M. Derwacter, *Preparing the Way for Paul* (New York: Macmillan, 1930), p. 40.
67. De Ridder, *Discipling the Nations,* p. 89.
68. *When the Way Is New* (Elgin, IL: Brethren, 1974), p. 76.

tacts. The cities Paul chose were nearly all great centers of trade. They were on the most important highways connecting east and west.[69]

In the overall history of missions, cities have not been taken very seriously. Urban missions have commonly presented peculiar problems, especially to the Western missionary. We are still neglecting the cities even while they dramatically increase in population. According to Ray Bakke, a recognized authority in urban missions today, 48-49 percent of the world's peoples already live in the cities and the average is expected to reach 65 percent within the next twenty years.[70] It is possible, as Allen says, that our efforts in the city can result in the city becoming "a great prison or a great market." The city "may be a safe in which all the best intellect of the day is shut up, or it may be a mint from which the coin of new thought is put into circulation." Through Paul's ministry the cities became centers of productivity and life that touched people on all sides, "mints from which the new coin of the gospel was spread in every direction."[71]

*Evangelism is always the first priority*

In a day when the demands on the missionary are so many, when there is so much to do in relief of human misery and in educating and empowering the illiterate and the poor, when social justice is calling for study and action, we need to recover the primary purpose of mission. That is, productive evangelism. The telling of the Good News always carries with it the call for decision. The first calling of the apostle is "to open their eyes and turn them from the darkness to the light and from the power of Satan to God" (Acts 26:18). All Paul's strategy, all his prestige and personal power were focused on this one purpose, even though he adapted to the characteristics of each locale and kept himself flexible in order to meet the demands of any new situation.

Paul's work at Ephesus provides us with an example of his commitment to evangelism and of the kind of program that produces results (Acts 19:1-17). When Paul arrived at Ephesus, he found a group of national converts who were ignorant of even the first principles of the Christian life. They had not heard of Jesus' baptism or the Holy Spirit. From this it would seem unreasonable for Paul to hope that the provinces of Asia could be evangelized from the city of Ephesus. But he stayed in this city and began a staged program. Of course the response to his early preaching was an important factor in developing his plan (Acts 19:9). But the program was positively and remarkably effective, with the focus clearly on evangelism.

69. Deissmann, *Paul,* pp. 29-51.

70. David Rambo quotes Ray Bakke in church-growth lectures, 1981, at the School of World Mission, Fuller Theological Seminary.

71. Allen, *Missionary Methods,* p. 17.

1. Paul concentrated on the nominal nucleus with the result that these people were soon rejoicing in a vital experience of Christ (Acts 19:1-7).
2. With the cooperation of the nucleus, now aflame for Christ, the apostle conducted a three-month evangelistic campaign in the Jewish synagogue with the usual results (genuine conversions and bitter opposition) (Acts 19:7-8).
3. Paul did not, at this stage, go elsewhere to conduct further evangelistic campaigns, but hired a local school building and conducted a two-year course in the Scriptures. This was not so much a continuation of evangelism, but specifically instruction for the disciples (Acts 19:9-10).
4. During the course of the two-year instruction, the whole province of Asia, including the provincial capital, was evangelized. "All the people who lived in the Province of Asia, both Jews and Gentiles, heard the word of the Lord." Since Paul was daily and systematically teaching the disciples in Ephesus, it would appear that this work of evangelism was done by the newly-won converts. None of them would have had more than three years of experience and many would have had less.[72]

I have already shown that evangelism by word and life was the highest claim made on each convert in all the churches. There is nothing more compelling than the spontaneous witness of the new Christian. Paul sent these exciting messengers of life out into the regions around Ephesus. They could tell only what they had experienced. More important than a finished doctrine or a logical system was the need to get them moving in spontaneous, dynamic witnessing. So Paul kept inspiring the churches to see that sharing Christ and calling for decisions to accept him are the first order of business for any group of Christians. The church at Thessalonica was an imperfect and immature fellowship when we judge it by the standards that Paul was urging, yet in spite of this, the Thessalonians became an example of spontaneous evangelism. "Not only did the message about the Lord go out from you throughout Macedonia and Greece, but the news about your faith in God has gone everywhere. There is nothing, then, that we need to say" (I Thess. 1:8).

While we recognize the massive social needs of people in our world today, nothing can be allowed to take the place of evangelism. A careful definition of evangelism would not allow the term to describe almost everything that is done in the name of missionary work. Evangelism is the presenting of Christ in a way that will lead people to make decisions to accept

72. See article by Leslie Lyall, "The Task of Missions in a Changing World," *The Churchman*, vol. 73, no. 4 (December 1959), p. 179.

him as Lord and to seek the nurture of the new faith within the company of believers. Paul set this pattern with the first evangelistic journey into Galatia. First came the preaching and the making of disciples, then the bringing of these disciples to a sense of corporateness as members of Christ's body and organizing them into congregations with their own elders (Acts 14:21-23). Paul thereafter expected this new congregation to engage in witness in the same way so that the converts would reproduce themselves. The plan was carried out at Ephesus, as we have seen. While their training continued, believers with a minimum amount of experience were witnessing and, in turn, were establishing centers where the process would be repeated again and again.

What final challenge is there from this faithful man of God? I see it in the situation surrounding his last days. We shall never know the details for sure, but the picture can be painted in broad strokes. The final days of the apostle are intimated in his last letter (II Timothy). It was a time of terrible danger. The persecution of Nero was mounting in fury. The emperor had set fire to Rome (A.D. 64) and then turned the popular anger against the suspected and hated Christians. The government was determined to show its intolerance of what was regarded as a pernicious, subversive group in society. All who were prominent in Christian activities were marked for destruction. The shadows of death were gathering around Paul. At the beginning of the second letter to Timothy there is reference to Timothy's tears (1:4) shed when Paul was separated from him by the soldiers and taken to prison.

How could this man of God be faithful to his apostolic calling in this desperate situation? Review the details of his trial (II Tim. 4:16-17). Paul referred to his "first answer," which I take to be the preliminary hearing. Apparently the situation was so threatening that he was abandoned by all who might have helped him with legal counsel or brotherly support: "No man stood with me." He was then remanded to his cell and took the last opportunity to write what is regarded as his "dying letter."

But he had not been alone at that trial. When the accusations were heaped on him we sense that the solitary figure was not alone. "The Lord stayed with me," he said, "and gave me strength." Was that strength given only to sustain his spirit through those prolonged proceedings in that hostile crowd? No, it was for more than that. Symbolically the world was there at his trial and witnessed his words. There were tiers of seats in the amphitheater that were occupied by representatives from every part of the empire. By declaring the Word to this special gathering, Paul felt he had lifted up the gospel in a final summation to his own generation. "So that I was able to proclaim the full message for all the Gentiles [nations] to hear." Before this universal audience he completed his missionary career. The absolute commitment of mind and body, soul and spirit that was Paul's, his love for the

Lord Jesus and all lost people everywhere, must be the very heart of the church.

The Good News is being heard by more tribes and nations of people today than ever before. We accept that call to serve and witness in our time with optimism and hope. The great apostle to the Gentiles has shown us that in Christ we can prevail. "I have complete confidence in the gospel; it is God's power to save *all* who believe, first the Jews and also the Gentiles" (Rom. 1:16; italics added).

# Bibliography


Albright, W. F. *From the Stone Age to Christianity.* Baltimore: Johns Hopkins, 1940.

Allen, Roland. *The Establishment of the Church in the Mission Field.* London: World Dominion Press, n.d.

———. *The Ministry of the Spirit.* Selected writings of Roland Allen. Edited by David M. Paton. London: World Dominion Press, 1960.

———. *Missionary Methods: St. Paul's or Ours?* Reprint. London: World Dominion Press, 1960.

———. *The Spontaneous Expansion of the Church and the Causes which Hinder It.* London: World Dominion Press, 1927.

Anderson, Gerald H., ed. *The Theology of the Christian Mission.* New York: McGraw-Hill, 1961.

Banks, Robert. *Paul's Idea of Community: The Early House Churches in the Historical Setting.* Grand Rapids: Eerdmans, 1980.

Barclay, William. *The Mind of St. Paul.* New York: Harper and Row, 1975.

———. *Turning to God.* Philadelphia: Westminster, 1964.

Barker, Glenn et al. *The New Testament Speaks.* New York: Harper and Row, 1967.

Barth, Karl. *The Epistle to the Romans.* Translated by E. C. Hoskyne. 6th ed. Oxford: At the University Press, 1933.

Barth, Markus. *The Broken Wall.* Philadelphia: Judson, 1959.

Bavinck, J. H. *The Impact of Christianity on the Non-Christian World.* Grand Rapids: Eerdmans, 1949.

Beaver, R. Pierce. *To Advance the Gospel.* Grand Rapids: Eerdmans, 1967.

Berkhof, Louis. *Paul the Missionary.* Grand Rapids: Eerdmans-Sevensma, n.d.

Boer, Harry R. *Pentecost and Missions.* Grand Rapids: Eerdmans, 1961.

Bonhoeffer, Dietrich. *Ethics.* Edited by Eberhard Bethge. Translated by N. H. Smith. New York: Macmillan, 1955.

Bornkamm, Gunther. *Paul.* Translated by M. G. Stalker. New York: Harper and Row, 1971.

Bright, John. *The Kingdom of God.* Nashville: Abingdon, 1953.

Bromiley, G. W. *Christian Ministry.* Grand Rapids: Eerdmans, 1960.

Brown, Colin, ed. *Dictionary of New Testament Theology.* Grand Rapids: Zondervan, 1980.

Bruce, A. B. *St. Paul's Conception of Christianity.* New York: Charles Scribner's, 1894.

Bruce, F. F. *Paul, Apostle of the Heart Set Free.* Grand Rapids: Eerdmans, 1978.

———. *The Book of the Acts.* New International Commentary on the New Testament. Grand Rapids: Eerdmans, 1954.

Cadbury, H. J. *Beginnings of Christianity.* Edited by F. Jackson and K. Lake. London: Macmillan, 1933.

Caird, G. B. *The Apostolic Age.* London: Gerald Duckworth, 1955.

Cerfaux, Lucien. *The Church in the Theology of St. Paul.* New York: Herder and Herder, 1959.

———. *The Spiritual Journey of St. Paul.* Translated by J. C. Guinness. New York: Sheed and Ward, 1968.

Cone, Orello. *Paul, the Man, the Missionary and the Teacher.* London: Adam and Charles Black, 1898.

Conn, Walter, ed. *Conversion: Perspectives on Personal and Social Transformation.* New York: Alba House, 1978.

Craig, C. T. *The Beginnings of Christianity.* Nashville: Abingdon-Cokesbury, 1943.

Cullmann, Oscar. *Baptism in the New Testament.* London: SCM, 1950.

Davies, J. G. *Worship and Mission.* New York: Association Press, 1967.

Dayton, Edward R., ed. *That Everyone May Hear.* Monrovia, CA: MARCC, 1979.

De Ridder, Richard R. *Discipling the Nations.* Reprint. Grand Rapids: Baker, 1979.

Deissmann, Adolf. *Paul.* Translated by W. E. Wilson. New York: Doran, 1926.

Delano, Isaac. *One Church for Nigeria.* London: Lutterworth Press U.S.C.L., 1945.

Dodd, C. H. *The Apostolic Preaching and its Developments.* New York: Harper, 1936.

Eichhorn, D. M. *Conversion to Judaism: History and Analysis.* New York: Ktav, 1966.

Enslin, M. S. *The Ethics of Paul.* Nashville: Abingdon, 1957.

———. *Reapproaching Paul.* Philadelphia: Westminster, 1972.

Faw, Chalmer. *When the Way Is New.* Elgin, IL: Brethren, 1974.

Fiene, Paul. *St. Paul As a Theologian.* New York: Eaton-Mains, 1908.

Furnish, Victor P. *Theology and Ethics in Paul.* Nashville: Abingdon, 1968.

Gasque, Ward W., and Martin, Ralph P., eds. *Apostolic History and the Gospel.* Grand Rapids: Eerdmans, 1970.

Glasser, Arthur F. et al., eds. *Crucial Dimensions in World Evangelization.* Pasadena, CA: William Carey Library, 1976.

Grassi, Joseph A. *The Secret of Paul the Apostle.* Maryknoll, NY: Orbis Books, 1978.

———. *A World to Win.* New York: Maryknoll, 1965.

Guthrie, Donald. *New Testament Introduction, the Pauline Epistles.* London: Tyndale Press, 1968.

Hahn, Ferdinand. *Mission in the New Testament.* Studies in Biblical Theology, no. 47. London: SCM, 1963.

Harr, Wilber C., ed. *Frontiers of the Christian World Mission Since 1938.* New York: Harper, 1962.

Hastings, Adrian. *Christian Marriage in Africa.* London: SPCK, 1973.

Hay, A. R. *The New Testament Order for Church and Missionary.* Buenos Aires: New Testament Missionary Union SEMCA, 1947.

Hesselgrave, D. J., ed. *New Horizons in World Mission.* Grand Rapids: Baker, 1980.

Hodges, Melvin L. *The Indigenous Church.* Rev. ed. Springfield, MO: Gospel Publishing House, 1976.

———. *The Indigenous Church and the Missionary: A Sequel to "The Indigenous Church."* Pasadena, CA: William Carey Library, 1978.

Holmes, Arthur. *The Mind of St. Paul: A Psychological Study.* New York: Macmillan, 1929.

Holzner, Joseph. *St. Paul the Apostle: His Life and Times.* Translated and revised by William Doheny, CSC. Vatican City: Private distribution, 1978.

Jeremias, Joachim. *Infant Baptism in the First Four Centuries.* Philadelphia: Westminster, 1961.

Keck, Leander. *Paul and His Letters.* Proclamation Commentaries, the New Testament Witnesses for Preaching. Edited by Gerhard Krodel. Philadelphia: Fortress, 1979.

Kepler, Thomas S., ed. *Contemporary Thinking about Paul.* Nashville: Abingdon-Cokesbury, 1950.

Klausner, Joseph. *From Jesus to Paul.* Translated by W. F. Stinespring. New York: Macmillan, 1944.

Knight, William. *The Missionary Secretariat of Henry Venn.* London: Longmans, Green, 1880.

Knowling, R. J. *The Acts of the Apostles, The Expositor's Greek New Testament.* Edited by W. R. Nicoll. London: Hodder and Stoughton, n.d.

Kraemer, Hendrick. *Why Christianity of All the Religions?* Philadelphia: Westminster, 1962.

Kraft, Charles H. *Christianity in Culture.* Maryknoll, NY: Orbis Books, 1979.

Kuist, Howard Tillman. *The Pedagogy of St. Paul.* New York: Doran, 1925.

Küng, Hans. *The Church.* Translated by R. and R. Ockenden. New York: Sheed and Ward, 1968.

Ladd, G. E. *A Theology of the New Testament.* Grand Rapids: Eerdmans, 1974.

Lenski, R. C. H. *The Interpretation of I and II Corinthians.* Columbus, OH: Wartburg, 1946.

———. *St. Paul's Epistle to the Romans.* Columbus, OH: Wartburg, 1945.

Lightfoot, J. B. *The Apostolic Fathers.* London: Macmillan, 1917.

Longenecker, Richard N. *Paul, Apostle of Liberty.* Grand Rapids: Baker, 1976.

McGavran, Donald A. *Bridges of God.* New York: Friendship Press, 1955.

———. *Understanding Church Growth.* Rev. ed. Grand Rapids: Eerdmans, 1980.

Mackay, John A. *God's Order.* New York: Macmillan, 1953.

McKinnon, James. *The Gospel in the Early Church.* New York: Longmans, Green, 1933.

Martin, Ralph P. *Reconciliation: A Study of Paul's Theology.* Atlanta: John Knox, 1981.

———. *Worship in the Early Church.* Rev. ed. Grand Rapids: Eerdmans, 1975.

Moe, Olaf. *The Apostle Paul: His Life and Work.* Translated by L. A. Vigness. Minneapolis: Augsburg, 1950.

Mulholland, Kenneth. *Adventures in Training the Ministry.* Nutley, NJ: Presbyterian and Reformed, 1976.

Münck, Johannes. *Paul and the Salvation of Mankind.* Atlanta: John Knox, 1977.

Neibuhr, H. R. *Christ and Culture.* New York: Harper, 1956.

Nevius, John L. *Methods of Mission Work.* New York: Foreign Missions Library, 1895.

Nyamiti, Charles. *African Theology: Its Nature, Problems, and Methods.* Kampala, Uganda: Gaba Publications, 1971.

———. *The Scope of African Theology.* Kampala, Uganda: Gaba Publications, 1973.

Oosthuizen, G. C. *Theological Discussions and Confessional Developments in the Churches of Asia and Africa.* Franeke: T. Wever, 1955.

Pinnock, C.; and Wells, D., eds. *Toward a Theology for the Future.* Carol Stream, IL: Creation House, 1971.

Rackham, R. B. *The Acts of the Apostles.* 3d ed. London: Methuen, 1906.

Raisin, Jacob S. *Gentile Reactions to Jewish Ideals.* New York: Philosophical Library, 1953.

Rall, H. F. *According to Paul.* New York: Charles Scribner's Sons, 1945.

Ramsey, William. *St. Paul the Traveller and Roman Citizen.* Reprint. Grand Rapids: Baker, 1982.

Richardson, Don. *Peace Child.* Glendale, CA: Regal, 1974.

Ridderbos, Herman N. *Paul, an Outline of His Theology.* Translated by J. R. DeWitt. Grand Rapids: Eerdmans, 1975.

Ritchie, John. *Indigenous Church Principles in Theory and Practice.* New York: Revell, 1966.

Robertson, A. T. *Epochs in the Life of Paul.* New York: Charles Scribner and Sons, 1916.

Robinson, W. Gordon. *The Gospel and the Church in a Pagan World.* London: Independent Press, 1958.

Roetzel, Calvin J. *The Letters of Paul: Conversations in Context.* Atlanta: John Knox, 1975.

Rowley, H. H. *The Faith of Israel.* London: SCM, 1965.

Schmidt, O. H. *St. Paul Shows Us How.* Saint Louis: Concordia, 1950.

Schweitzer, Albert. *The Mysticism of Paul the Apostle.* Translated by William Montgomery. New York: Henry Holt, 1931.

Shedd, W. G. T. *Dogmatic Theology.* Vol. 1. New York: Charles Scribner's Sons, 1888-1894.

Speer, Robert E. *When Christianity Was New.* New York: Revell, 1939.

Stendahl, Krister. *Paul among Jews and Gentiles.* Philadelphia: Fortress, 1976.

Stott, J. R., ed. *Gospel and Culture.* Pasadena, CA: William Carey Library, 1979.

Strong, Augustus H. *Systematic Theology: A Compendium.* London: Pickering and Inglis, 1907.

Taylor, John V. *The Primal Vision.* Philadelphia: Fortress, 1963.

Tippett, Alan R. *Solomon Islands Christianity: A Study in Growth and Obstruction.* Applied Cultural Anthropology series. Reprint. Pasadena, CA: William Carey Library, 1975.

———. *Verdict Theology in Missionary Theory.* Rev. ed. Pasadena, CA: William Carey Library, 1973.

Tracy, David. *Blessed Rage for Order: The New Pluralism in Theology.* Library of Contemporary Theology series. New York: Seabury, 1979.

von Weizsacker, Carl. *The Apostolic Age of the Christian Church.* Translated by John Miller. Vol. 2. New York: G. P. Putnam's Sons, 1895.

Wagner, C. Peter. *Church Growth and the Whole Gospel.* San Francisco: Harper and Row, 1981.

———; and Dayton, Edward R., eds. *Unreached Peoples, 1981.* Elgin, IL: David C. Cook, 1981.

Wagner, C. Peter. *Your Spiritual Gifts Can Help Your Church Grow.* Glendale, CA: Regal, 1979.

Wahlstrom, Eric. *The New Life in Christ.* Philadelphia: Muhlenberg, 1950.

Watson, David. *I Believe in the Church.* Grand Rapids: Eerdmans, 1978.

Weiss, Johannes. *Paul and Jesus.* Translated by H. J. Chaytor. London and New York: Harper, 1909.

Wiley, J. Orton. *Christian Theology.* Vol. 1. Kansas City, MO: Beacon Hill Press, 1940.

Williams, C. S. C. *A Commentary on the Acts of the Apostles.* London: Adam and Charles Black, 1957.

Williams, R. R. *The Acts of the Apostles.* London: SCM, 1912.

Wilson, J. Christy. *Today's Tentmakers.* Wheaton, IL: Tyndale, 1979.

# Index of Authors and Subjects

# Index of Scripture References

**Romans**



**I Corinthians**

**II Corinthians**